Thomas Pyle

A paraphrase on the Acts of the Holy Apostles and upon all the Epistles of the New Testament

Thomas Pyle

A paraphrase on the Acts of the Holy Apostles and upon all the Epistles of the New Testament

ISBN/EAN: 9783337283193

Printed in Europe, USA, Canada, Australia, Japan

Cover: Foto ©Lupo / pixelio.de

More available books at **www.hansebooks.com**

PARAPHRASE
THE
ACTS OF THE HOLY APOSTLES,
AND UPON ALL THE
EPISTLES OF THE NEW TESTAMENT.

BEING

A Complete SUPPLEMENT to DR. CLARKE'S PARAPHRASE on the FOUR GOSPELS.

WITH NOTES, AND A SHORT PREFACE TO EACH EPISTLE;

SHOWING

The Occaſion and Deſign of it; with the ſeveral ARGUMENTS ſet at the Head of each Chapter.

AND

A GENERAL INDEX to all the Principal MATTERS, WORDS, and PHRASES of the NEW TESTAMENT, excepting the REVELATION.

FOR THE USE OF FAMILIES.

IN TWO VOLUMES.

BY THOMAS PYLE, M. A.

MINISTER OF LYN-REGIS IN NORFOLK, AND PREBENDARY OF THE CATHEDRAL CHURCH OF SARUM.

A NEW EDITION.

VOL. II.

LONDON:

PRINTED FOR G. G. & J. ROBINSON, LONDON; W. H. LUNN, CAMBRIDGE; J. COOKE, OXFORD; J. MUNDELL & CO. EDINBURGH; AND THE OTHER PROPRIETORS.

1795.

TO

THE RIGHT REVEREND FATHER IN GOD,

CHARLES, LORD BISHOP OF NORWICH,

AND

CLERK OF THE CLOSET TO HIS MAJESTY.

MY LORD,

NOT only the relation I have the happineſs to bear to you, as my Reverend Dioceſan, but the juſt ſenſe I ever had of that truly religious wiſdom you have exerted as a biſhop of this church; and the difficult and conſtant part you have acted in Parliament, under the moſt critical juncture of affairs, may, I hope, warrant my addreſs of the following papers to you.

Your Lordſhip's great abilities, and known diſpoſition for advancing of whatever tends to good learning, real piety, and the true intereſts of our reformed religion, is what gives heart to any ſincere (though but mean) contributor to ſue for your favourable protection.

My

the *Jewish* law; but to others that knew him better, they represented the apostle as one not immediately commissioned by Christ, as Peter, James, and John, &c. were; but to be an apostle at *second-hand:* thus derogating from the authority of his *commission*, and the certainty of his *doctrine*. This will give the reader the true spirit of the several expressions which tend to vindicate both his *apostleship*, and the sincerity and consistency of St. Paul's behaviour in the controversy handled in this epistle; as of Chap. i. 1, 8, 9, 10, &c. to the end; the whole *second*, and the twelve first verses of the *fifth* chapters, with the 13th and 17th ver. of the *sixth* chapter: in the two latter of which chapters are some *practical* exhortations, designed chiefly against the animosities and great partialities that this dispute had bred and ripened among them.

CHAP. I.

The Title * *the Apostle gives himself, levelled against the suggestions of their False Teachers of the* Judaizing *Faction. He wondereth at their relapse from the true Christian Doctrine of* Mens being justified and saved by the Christian Religion alone, *into the* Jewish *Principle* of the Necessity of the Ceremonial Law: *To cure them of which Prejudice is the main purpose of this Epistle. His Answer to the Insinuations against the Authority of his Commission* †, *and the Sincerity of its Preaching.*

* This Epistle was written in or about the Year of our Lord 58.

† See the Preface.

A. D. 58.

1 PAUL an apostle, not of men, neither by man, but by * Jesus Christ, and God the † Father, who raised him from the dead.

1. I Paul who am a Christian apostle, nor by any favour or authority of *men*, nor receiving my commission by the choice of the other *apostles*, as Matthias did; but having it from the extraor-

traordinary * and expreſs revelation of Jeſus Chriſt A. D. 58.
himſelf, and God the † *Father* who raiſed him from the dead;

* Acts ix. xxii. & xxvi. chap.
† Acts xxii. 14, 15.

2 And all the brethren which are with me, unto the churches of Galatia:

3 Grace *be* to you and peace, from God the Father, and from our Lord Jeſus Chriſt.

2. & 3. Send this epiſtle to the churches of Galatia, wiſhing you all favours and bleſſings from God the Father, and our Lord Jeſus Chriſt; as do alſo the Chriſtian brethren that are with me here at Rome.

4 Who gave himſelf for our ſins, that he might deliver us from this preſent evil world, according to the will of God and our Father:

4. Wiſhing you, I ſay, the bleſſings of Jeſus Chriſt, who, according to the merciful and gracious purpoſe of God, and the predictions of his *prophets*, gave himſelf a ſacrifice for our ſins, to redeem us from the puniſhment and condemnation that is juſtly to fall upon the vicious and obſtinate unbelievers || of the preſent age.

5 To whom be glory for ever and ever. Amen.

5. For which mercy be he praiſed and glorified for ever and ever! Amen.

6 I marvel, that ye are ſo ſoon removed from him that called you into the grace of Chriſt, unto another goſpel.

6. He therefore being the only Saviour by whom we obtain pardon and redemption, I am amazed to hear you ſhould, ſo ſoon after your converſion, be thus changed in your belief of this grand *article*, and be brought to embrace the neceſſity of obſerving the *Jewiſh ceremonies*, as a *Chriſtian* doctrine; whereas there is no ſuch matter. The *Chriſtian* religion is the only ſufficient foundation of your juſtification and happineſs.

B 2 7. There

|| Ver. 4. From this preſent evil *world*, or rather αἰῶνος, the preſent *age*. The ſenſe being the ſame with that of Acts ii. 47. *this untoward generation.*

A. D. 58.

7 Which is not another; but there be some that trouble you, and would pervert the gospel of Christ.

7. There can be no other: nor could you have been persuaded there was, unless by the sly insinuations and false suggestions of designing men; whose art and business is to pervert the *gospel* doctrine, and model your principles to their own private interests and ambitious purposes.

8 But though we, or an angel from heaven, preach *any other gospel* unto you, than that which we have preached unto you, let him be accursed.

8. The better to gain their ends upon you, those *Judaizing* teachers would have you believe, that not only Peter and the other *apostles*, but I myself also do sometimes preach up the *Jewish law*, as absolutely necessary along with the *Christian faith*. So far from it, that I now solemnly pronounce, were any one *apostle*, nay, or (were it possible) should an *angel* from heaven be supposed to preach a thing so contradictory to the doctrine I at first delivered to you, he ought to be rejected and called * *accursed*.

* Ver. 8, 9. Rom. ix. 3. 1 Cor. xvi. 22.

9 As we said before, so say I now again. If any *man* preach any other gospel unto you, ‡ than that ye have received, let him be * accursed.

9. And, to show you I speak it not hastily, but with all deliberation and sincerity, I repeat it again, *Should an apostle, or even an angel, preach any thing so derogatory to, and wide of, the true gospel doctrine, let him be * accursed.*

10 For do I now persuade men, or God? or do I seek to please men? for if I yet pleased men, I should not be the servant of Christ.

10. As to *myself*, should I do it, I know it would gain me the favour of a set of *men*, the *Jewish* zealots; but I hope you have no reason to think the design of my ministry is to curry favour with *men*, but to discharge my duty to *God*, as his faithful *apostle*; which I could never do by that method; and were *that* my principle, I need never to

‡ Ver. 9. *Any other gospel than that ye have received.* παρ' ὁ παρελαβετο, *any thing beside or more than ye have received from the apostle*; viz. any thing as *necessary to salvation*.

to have turned *Christian* *, and suffered so much as I have done for the sake of that profession.

A. D. 58.

* Chap. v. 12. & vi. 12.

11 But I certify you, brethren, that the gospel which was preached of me, is not after man.

12 For I neither received it of man, neither was I taught it, but by the revelation of Jesus Christ.

11. & 12. And as to their disparagement of my apostolical *commission*, or my *doctrine*, because it may not suit with their prejudices or designs; be you fully assured, I received my commission from no *man*, from no other *apostles*, but had both *that* and the doctrine I preached to you, from the immediate revelation of Jesus Christ himself.

13 For ye have heard of my conversation in time past, in the Jews religion, *how* that beyond measure I persecuted the church of God, and wasted it.

13. Nor indeed can you well think such a bigot as I should be converted at all, much less turn an *apostle of his* religion, by any but *extraordinary* means. For you must have heard what a raging *zealot* for the *Jewish* religion I formerly was; and how I persecuted the *Christian* faith with uncommon fury and cruelty.

14 And profited in the Jews religion, above many my equals in mine own nation, being more exceedingly zealous of the traditions of my fathers.

14. I was, you know, noted above any men of my age and standing, for learning in, and zeal for, the *Jewish* traditions and doctrines.

15 But when it pleased God, who separated † me from my mother's womb, and called me by his grace,

16 To reveal his Son in me, that I might preach him among

15. & 16. *My* conversion, therefore, is wholly attributed to a divine and extraordinary favour originally intended to me by God. And, accordingly, when it pleased God thus miraculously to convert and commission me to be a preacher of his gospel to the *Gentile* world, I made

† Ver. 15. *Who separated me from my mother's womb.* See Jerem. i. 5.

A. D. 58. mong the heathen, immediately I conferred not with flesh and blood:

made my application to no *man*, to none of the *apostles* for *their* warrant or instructions how to perform my office.

17 Neither went I up to Jerusalem, to them which *were* apostles before me, but I went into Arabia, and returned again unto Damascus.

17. I addressed myself to none of the apostles at Jerusalem, who were ordained to that office before me; but from Damascus, the place of my conversion, I retired into Arabia, and returned thither again, and preached the gospel, without any order or authority from any of their *college*.

18 Then after three years I went up to Jerusalem, to see Peter, and abide with him fifteen days.

18. Indeed, about three years after my conversion, I went to Jerusalem, where Barnabas brought me to Peter, who readily owned me for his fellow *apostle*, upon the account I give him of the manner and circumstances of my call to that office; and with him I stayed, not to receive any authority from him, but only to converse with him for about fifteen days.

19 But other of the apostles saw I none, save James the Lord's brother.

19. The only person of note I saw, besides Peter, was James *the Just*, our Lord's kinsman, and bishop of Jerusalem. So that I could not be supposed to derive my commission from the *apostolical college*.

20 Now the things which I write unto you, behold, before God, I lie not.

20. (And for the truth of these facts I appeal to God, the Author of truth itself.)

21 Afterwards I came into the regions of Syria and Cilicia.

21. After this short stay at Jerusalem, I went upon the exercise of my office into Syria, and preached at Cæsarea (Acts xxii. 17. 18.), and at Troas in Cilicia (Acts ix. 30. xxii. 3.)

22 And was unknown by face unto the churches of Judea, which were in Christ.

22. All which time, neither the churches of Jerusalem, or of the rest of Judea, they nor their apostolical *ministers*, had ever seen, or had any personal knowledge of me.

23 But they had heard only, That he which persecuted us in times past, now preacheth the faith which once he destroyed.

23. All they knew of me was by accounts they had from abroad, that the great persecutor Paul was turned a preacher of the very gospel he had so persecuted. A. D. 58.

24 And they glorified God in me.

24. For which marvellous conversion in me, they rejoiced, and blessed God.

CHAP. II.

He proceeds further to clear himself of the Imputation of ever having preached up the necessity of Circumcision *and the* Ceremonial Law. *And to vindicate his Apostolical Commission. Proving both these Points * from his next Journey to* Jerusalem, *his Management of Titus, his Reception from the Apostles, his Behaviour there, and at* Antioch, *with Peter, and from the Inconsistency of supposing* He *should preach such a Doctrine.*

* See the Preface.

1 THEN fourteen years after I went up again to Jerusalem with Barnabas, † and took Titus with me also.

1. TO show you still further the falsity of their † suggestions, and the immediate authority of my apostleship, let me remember you, that eleven years after my former journey to *Jerusalem*, which is fourteen years after my first conversion, I went thither † again, and took Barnabas and Titus along with me.

† Chap. i. 8. 18.
Acts xv.

2 And I went up by revelation, and communicated unto them that gospel which I preach among the Gentiles, but privately to them which were

2. I then went by the special appointment of God, and gave the *apostles* that were there a full account of the doctrines ‡ I had been preaching to the *idolatrous* as well as *proselyte Gentiles*, as I received them

‡ Acts. xv. 4. 12.

A. D. 58. were of reputation, lest by any means I should run, or had run in vain.

them from Jesus Christ, and of the success of my ministry among them. I gave this account only to some of the chief *apostles* and governors of that church, and to them too in private, not out of distrust of my doctrine and behaviour, or want of their information; but only to prevent the scandalous reports the *Judaizing* faction might raise upon me, to the disparagement and hindrance of the further success of my ministry: For these *zealots*, even of the *converted Jews*, were not as yet in any temper to hear of *Christianity* being preached to the *idolatrous Gentiles*.

3 But neither Titus, who was with me, being a Greek, was compelled to be circumcised:

3. And in this whole affair I was so consistent with myself, and just to my own principle, that though Titus that went with me was a *Gentile* born, yet at his conversion to *Christianity*, and his ordination to the *ministry*, I never insisted on his being *circumcised*; nor did the *apostles*, to whom I carried him, require any such thing; which, it is plain, both *they* and I should have done, had we thought the observation of the ceremonial *law* necessary to the justification of a converted idolatrous *Gentile*.

4 And that because of false brethren unawares brought in, who came in privily to spy out our liberty, which we have in Christ Jesus, that they might bring us into bondage.

4. I kept Titus *uncircumcised*, and carried him so to the *apostles*, on purpose to show my sentiments were quite opposite to those false *Jewish* zealots that came to *Antioch* *, and insinuated themselves into our assemblies there; with a design to catch at, and oppose the doctrine I preached, and to bring all you *Gentile* Christians to embrace the unnecessary slavery of the *Jewish ceremonies*.

* Acts xv.

5 To whom we gave place by subjection, no not for an hour, that the truth of the gospel might continue with you.

5. For though I am willing to yield to any indifferent thing for the present, in compliance with the weakness and prejudices of men; in hopes the sooner to draw them off from them *; yet, to *these* false zealots, that so furiously insisted upon the absolute necessity of the *Jewish* law, I never yielded an inch, but

but maintained *the Christian religion to be the sufficient and only condition of a Christian's justification and happiness.* A. D. 58.

6 But of these, who seemed to be somewhat, (whatsoever they were maketh no matter to me, God accepteth no man's person), for they who seemed to be *somewhat*, in conference added nothing to me.

6. Thus I behaved myself to those zealots. And as to the disparagement your false teachers are pleased to cast upon *me*, and their setting up Peter *, James, or John, as apostles far greater than *I*; be they as great as they will, their eminency makes *me* neither greater nor less. God, who made us *all* equally his apostles, looks not upon present and external reputation in the church. In the mean time, when I gave those eminent men the account of my doctrine, and proceedings in my ministry with the Gentile Christians; they could find no fault, pretended to correct nothing, nor to instruct me in any point that I did not know as well as themselves.

7 But contrariwise, when they saw that the gospel of the uncircumcision was committed unto me, as the gospel of the circumcision was unto Peter:

7. But, on the contrary, upon the testimonies I gave them of as sufficient a call to preach the gospel to the Gentile world, as Peter in particular, or any of them had to preach it to the Jewish nation, they highly approved of what I had done.

8 (For he that wrought effectually in Peter to the apostleship of the circumcision, the same was mighty in me towards the Gentiles).

8. (And indeed well they might; for God had endowed *me* with as miraculous powers and evidences for the *one*, as he had *them* for the *other*).

9 And when James, Cephas, and John, who seemed to be pillars, perceived the grace that was given unto me,

9. Accordingly those three leading apostles, being fully satisfied both of my *office*, and the method and success of my preaching, did, with great respect, own me and my

* See Ver. 9. and see the Paraphrase on 1 Cor. ix. 20.

A. D. 58. me, they gave to me and Barnabas the right hands of fellowship, that we *should go* unto the heathen, and they unto the circumcision.

my fellow traveller Barnabas for *apostles* as fully commissioned to convert the *Gentiles*, as they were to convert the *Jews*; and concluded, we ought to go on in that ministry, in the same manner as we had begun.

10 Only they *would* that we should remember the * poor the same which I also was forward to do.

10. They prescribed no rules to me at parting; they only requested of me to collect some charities among the converts I made, for the relief of the poor Christians of *Judea* *; a thing I was very ready to do.

* See Acts xix. 21. xxi. 4. 10, 11, 12. &c. 1 Cor. xvi. 2 Cor. viii. & ix.

11 But when Peter was come to Antioch, I withstood him to the face, because he was to be blamed.

11. Thus far Peter and *I* entirely agreed: And so constant and steady was *I* to this doctrine *of the necessity of the ceremonial law, to the Christian converts*, that when *he* would once have dissembled, and flinched from it at *Antioch*, I stood my ground, and freely and boldly upbraided him with his insincerity.

12 For before that certain came from James, he did eat with the Gentiles; but when they were come, he withdrew, and separated himself, fearing them *which were* of the circumcision.

† Acts xv.

12. For before those *Jewish zealots* came to *Antioch* † with a pretended authority from *James* and the apostles at *Jerusalem*, and cried up the necessity of the *Jewish* law; *Peter* was as free and familiar with the *Gentile* Christians (who were *proselytes* to the *Jewish* worship of the *true God*, though not *circumcised*) as I myself was. But when they had spread their notions, and possessed the minds of some people, *he* grew shy, and avoided the conversation of the *uncircumcised Christians*, for fear of disgusting the *Jews*, and these zealots of the *Jewish* converts.

13 And the other Jews dissembled likewise with him, insomuch that Barnabas also was carried away with their dissimulation.

13. And by his example, several other of those converts did the same; and even Barnabas himself began to give in to that way of dissimulation, to the great discouragement of the *Gentile* Christians.

14 But when I saw that they walked not uprightly, according to the truth of the gospel, I said unto Peter, before them all, If thou being a Jew, livest after the manner of Gentiles, and not as do the Jews, why compellest thou the Gentiles to live as do the Jews?

14. Such a prevarication with the main design of the *gospel* religion I could not bear; but demanded of Peter in plain terms, before all the *Judaizers*, how he, that was originally a Jew, but now turned *Christian*, and had forsaken the ceremonial *law* himself, could ever answer it, to encourage the *Gentile* Christians to believe it was obligatory upon *them*, that were never *Jews* at all; directly contrary to his own principle and practice? A.D. 58.

15 We *who are* Jews by nature, and not sinners of the Gentiles,

16 Knowing that a man is not justified by the works of the law, but by the faith of Jesus Christ, even we have believed in Jesus Christ, that we might be justified by the faith of Christ, and not by the works of the law: for by the works of the law shall no flesh be justified.

15. & 16. For surely, said I, if we that were born and brought up in the *Jewish* religion, being now convinced of its insufficiency to justify us, have left it, and embraced the *Christian* religion, as the only sufficient means of pardon and salvation; it must be most absurd for us to imagine that the *Gentiles*, that were never brought up in it at all, should be *now* obliged to it, after their conversion to *Christianity*. It is plain, you countenance this for no real *advantage* to them; for *you* and *we* all own, the *law* can justify no man, now after the revelation of the *gospel*; but the *gospel* alone can fully do it.

17 But if while we seek to be justified by Christ, we ourselves also are found sinners, is therefore Christ the minister of sin? God forbid *.

17. On the other side, do but consider the consequence of this principle: A *Christian* that relies still upon the *Jewish* law for his justification, must allow himself to be still in a state of *guilt* and *sin* (for the *law* leaves us all so). Which is as much as to

A. D. 58. ſay, that Chriſt, our *Redeemer*, has given us a diſpenſation that leaves us but where we were, viz. in an *unpardoned and unjuſtified* condition: which God forbid any *Chriſtian* ſhould hold * !

18 For if I build again the things which I deſtroyed, I make myſelf a tranſgreſſor †.

18. For it is evident beyond exception, if after having taken upon me the *Chriſtian* profeſſion, as the means of this juſtification, I run back again for it to the *Jewiſh* law, I am but where I was, an *unjuſtified ſinner;* and act juſt like a fooliſh man that pulls down his houſe to make it better, and then builds it up again with the very ſame materials, juſt as it was, upon its old foundation †.

19. For I through the law am dead to the law, that I might live unto God.

19. Let others think and act as they will. I know that by the very tenor and deſign of the *Jewiſh* law itſelf, a *Chriſtian* is now as perfectly free from its obligation, as a woman is from her marriage contract at her huſband's death ‡; ſo that even a *Jewiſh* Chriſtian, much more a *Gentile* one, is bound to nothing but the obſervance of the *Chriſtian* religion, as the true ſervice of God.

‡ See Rom. vii. to ver. 7. iii. 21. —vi. 3, 4.

20 I am crucified with Chriſt. Nevertheleſs I live, yet not I, but Chriſt liveth in me: and the life which I now live in the fleſh, I live by the faith of the Son of God, who loved me, and gave himſelf for me.

20. By this new diſpenſation of Chriſt, I am dead to the *ceremonial* law, and the law to *me.* The life I now live is no longer the life of a *Jew*, but the obedience of a *Chriſtian*, to that Saviour and Redeemer, who ſo loved me as to give himſelf for a full ſatisfaction for all my ſins.

21 I do 21. For

* *Is Chriſt the miniſter of ſin?* Or elſe thus with Oecumenius, *If the law be obligatory ſtill, then we Chriſtians are tranſgreſſors, in not adhering to it; and do we think that Chriſt would enjoin us to ſin againſt a divine law? God forbid!* But I chooſe the paraphraſe as the moſt natural ſenſe. Or laſtly, It may be read without an interrogation, thus, *If we be ſinners in ſeeking to be juſtified by Chriſt, then Chriſt, is the miniſter of ſin.*

† *I make myſelf a tranſgreſſor, i. e.* ſays Chryſoſtom, by ſetting up that law which I allow God has aboliſhed.

21 I do not frustrate the grace of God: for if righteousness *come* by the law, then Christ is dead in vain.

21. For my part I shall never countenance a doctrine that frustrates the main and merciful design of the Christian covenant. For it is clear, could the Jewish law have justified and saved us, there had been no need of Christ's death; nay, and if *that* law has any part in our justification, then *his* death was insufficient of itself for it.

A. D. 58

CHAP. III.

The Apostle having absolutely cleared himself *of having ever preached up the Necessity of the Ceremonial* Law *to* Christian *Believers, comes now to argue* directly *against that Principle of the* Jewish Zealots. *His first argument taken from the miraculous Gifts of the Holy Spirit conferred upon Christians. His next, from the Case of Abraham's Justification; proving all true Christians, whether circumcised or not, are accepted and pardoned upon the same* Faith *and from the same* Promise *that justified that eminent* Patriarch; *and not at all from the Observance of the* Jewish *Law. The* Jewish *Zealots object*, To what purpose then was the Law given? *He answers it: Shows the* Law *to have been only preparatory to the* Gospel, *and that all Believers*, Gentile *and* Jewish, *are to be saved by the* Christian *Religion alone.*

1 O FOOLISH Galatians, who hath bewitched you, that you should not obey the truth, before whose eyes Jesus Christ

1. O FOOLISH Galatians, who is it, or by what magical arts have they deluded you from this fundamental article of the Christian faith, viz. *That the gospel religion is sufficient for salvation without*

A. D. 58. Christ * hath been evidently set forth, crucified among you?

without the Mosaical law? You that have had the crucified Jesus represented * to you as the *only Redeemer* of mankind, with as much earnestness and clearness, as if you had seen him hanging on the cross before your eyes?

2 This only would I learn of you, Received ye the Spirit by the works of the law, or by the hearing of faith?

2. Nor have you only *heard* his true doctrine, but had it confirmed to you by such powers and gifts of the Holy Spirit conferred on you, as were never before seen in the church of God. Now let me argue with your Jewish zealots, from these very *endowments*, in the *first* place. Were *they* conferred on you upon any consideration of your observance of the Mosaical law, or as you were Jews? Was it not absolutely on account of your becoming Christian disciples?

3 Are ye so foolish? having begun in the Spirit, are ye now made perfect by the flesh?

3. How weak and foolish a proceeding is this, for men to lay the foundation of their pardon and happiness in the Christian religion, as demonstrated by such evidences of the Holy Spirit, and then run back and build upon the ceremonial law, which they before allowed to be so external and carnal a dispensation, as to be insufficient for it.

4 Have ye suffered so many things in vain; if it be yet in vain.

4. And then, to what purpose have you endured so many persecutions for the sake of your *gospel* profession, if you now lose all its happy privileges, by relinquishing the main articles of it? But I hope you will prevent that by considering better.

5. I say

---

* Ver. 1. *Hath been evidently set forth.* προεγράφη was *before described* and *represented* to you: *Viz.* Before ever these Jewish notions, of the necessity of their *law*, were heard of amongst them.

A. D. 58.

5 He therefore that ministreth to you the Spirit, and worketh miracles among you, doth he it by the works of the law, or by the * hearing of faith?

5. I ſay then, when I wrought ſuch *miracles* for your converſion, and conferred the power of working them upon ſeveral members of your church; did I do it as a Jewiſh teacher, or had the leaſt regard to the *ceremonial* law? No, it was purely as a *goſpel* miniſter, and as *you* were Chriſtian profeſſors. Wherefore, as this *earneſt* and *pledge* of your juſtification was not in the leaſt owing to that *law*, neither can the thing *itſelf* be.

6 Even as Abraham ‡ believed God, and it was accounted to him for righteouſneſs;

7 Know ye therefore, that they which are of faith, the ſame are the children of Abraham.

6. & 7. In the next place, Can any of thoſe who are ſo zealous for the Jewiſh rites, deſire to be juſtified and accepted of God, upon a better foot than Abraham the very father ‡ of the Jewiſh nation was? Now, it is certain the *Chriſtian faith* is that very principle *of believing God's revelation and obeying his will*, that obtained him his juſtification; and whoever he be, whether Jew or Gentile, that ſo believes in God through Chriſt the Meſſiah, is the ſpiritual ſon of Abraham, and has a right to the promiſe made to that great patriarch.

8 And the ſcripture foreſeeing that God would juſtify the heathen through faith, preached before the goſpel

8. For it being the original and gracious deſign of God to ſave the Gentiles, as well as the Jews, by bringing them all, one day, under the *Chriſtian* covenant; you are

* Ver. 5. *The hearing of faith.* The word *hearing* ſignifies either the *doctrine of faith*, i. e. of the *goſpel*, or elſe *obedience* to the *faith*. In this *former* ſenſe, it is the ſame as in *Iſa.* liii. 1. *Lord who hath believed our* report, (Heb. *our hearing*, i. e. the *doctrine heard.*) From whence St. Paul probably took it.

‡ See the ſame argument in Rom. iv.

A. D. 58. goſpel unto Abraham, *ſaying*, In thee ſhall all nations be bleſſed.

are to underſtand that ſpecial bleſſing promiſed to Abraham (Gen. xii. 3.) to be meant of Chriſt, who was to be born of *his* family, *and become the Saviour of* all *nations that would embrace his religion.*

9 So then they which be of faith, are bleſſed with faithful Abraham.

9. As therefore it was faith in God that juſtified Abraham, ſo is it *faith in* Chriſt, and obedience to his religion, that ſaves all *Chriſtians*, and the *ceremonial law* has no hand at all in it.

10 For as many as are of the works of the law, are under the curſe: for it is written, Curſed is every one that continueth not in all things which are written in the book of the law to do them.

10. For indeed, that *law* is of quite a different nature from one that is to juſtify and ſave mankind. It is a moſt *ſevere* diſpenſation, abounding in duties and injunctions, and laying all under guilt that breaks || any one of them; but provides no ſufficient atonement to clear their conſciences of that guilt.

|| See Deut. xxvii. 26. Rom. iii. 20. viii. 3. Heb. x.

11 But that no man is juſtified by the law in the ſight of God, it is evident: for, The juſt ſhall live by faith.

12 And the law is not of faith: but, the man that doth them ſhall live in them.

11. & 12. And accordingly, the prophet Habakkuk aſcribes the juſtification of all good men to *religious faith in* God. Whereas the *ceremonial law* puts it not upon *that principle*, but inſiſts on an exact and rigid obſervance of all its numerous *rites and precepts*; propoſing the promiſed land of Canaan for its reward; but *ſin* and *guilt* was the effect of the tranſgreſſion of any one of them.

13 Chriſt hath redeemed us from the curſe of the law, being made a curſe for us: for it is written, Curſed

13. Now from this ſevere diſpenſation, and from the guilt of our numberleſs violations of its injunctions, has Chriſt our Meſſiah redeemed ‡ us by his death; whereby

‡ *Redeemed us* ἐξηγόρασεν; *Has brought us out*—as from a ſlavery. Or has *delivered* us from it as effectually, as if he had paid down a *price* for us. Compare 2 Tim. ii. 26. 1 Pet. i. 18. 19. with Deut. vii. 8. Exod. vi. 6. Deut.

A. D. 58.

Curſed is every one that hangeth on a tree *:

whereby he ſuffered the curſe, in our ſtead, agreeably to the words of the *law* (Deut. xxii. 23.) which call *hanging on the tree* an * *accurſed death*.

14 That the bleſſing of Abraham might come on the Gentiles through Jeſus Chriſt, that we might receive || the promiſe of the ſpirit through faith.

14. And thus the grand promiſe made to Abraham, of *his ſeed being a bleſſing to all nations*, is fulfilled in Chriſt; and makes it plain, that as his death was the ſole and ſufficient expiation for the ſins of both Gentiles and Jews; ſo it is the embracing of *his religion* alone that procures all Chriſtians theſe gifts and graces promiſed to the church of the Meſſiah; and the *ceremonial law* contributes nothing towards it.

15 Brethren, I ſpeak after the manner of men: though it be but a mans covenant, yet if it be confirmed, no man diſannulleth or addeth thereto.

15. Thus the *Chriſtian* covenant is grounded on Abraham's promiſe. Now common equity, even in human *affairs*, makes it utterly unlawful to any man to cancel or alter a *covenant*, *will*, or *contract*, that is once regularly made, and duly ratiſied. How much leſs ſhould any perſon dare to break or change the ſolemn covenant of God!

16 Now to Abraham and his ſeed were the promiſes made. He ſaith not, and to

16. But now your *Jewiſh zealots*, by preaching up the abſolute neceſſity of the *ceremonial law* to *Chriſtian* people, are evidently guilty

* [Made a curſe—Curſed.] Chriſt was not *accurſed of God*, in the proper ſenſe of that phraſe; but by being crucified, was in the eſteem of the Jews, the ſame *polluted and abominable thing* that, by their law, all perſons were that were hanged as *malefactors*. As Le Clerc well obſerves.

|| [Τὴν ἐπαγγελίαν τοῦ πνεύματος, The promiſe of the Spirit,] *i. e.* Either the ſpiritual bleſſings promiſed to Abraham in general, or elſe the *particular* gifts and endowments of the Holy Spirit on the apoſtles and the primitive church, called emphatically, *the promiſe*, Acts ii. 32. and xiii. 32. and the *promiſe* of the Father, Acts ii. 33. i. 4.

A. D. 58.

seeds, as of many; but as of one, and to thy seed, which is Christ.

guilty of this crime. For it is clear, the promise made to Abraham was meant of one particular *person*, that was to be born of a *particular branch* of his family. Christ was the Saviour promised, of Isaac's line; and it was not every one that should be merely* born of Abraham, but only such as should be members of the church of this Messiah, that were entitled to his blessings; and *all* that were his members, be they Gentiles or Jews, were certainly to enjoy them.

* See the same argument, Rom. ix.

17 And this I say, That the covenant that was confirmed before of God in Christ, the law which was four hundred and thirty years after, cannot disannul, that it should make the promise of none effect.

17. Whereas your *zealots* say, No; the blessing must be by the observation of the *law*. As if a *law* of God could ever be supposed to come, and disannul, and set aside a most solemn and *absolute promise*; a promise of infinite importance made to the pious ancestors of the *very* people to whom that *law* is given (and in him to all the obedient part of mankind) four hundred and thirty years before.

18 For if the inheritance be of the law, it is no more of promise: but God gave it to Abraham by promise.

18. Either, therefore, this great blessing of mens pardon and salvation is wholly founded in the promise to Abraham, or not; if it be (it is most evident from scripture it was) then it is *faith in Christ's religion* alone that is the condition of a *Christian's* justification; and for you to join the *ceremonial* law to it, is to alter the promise and solemn covenant of God.

19 Wherefore then *serveth* the law? It was added because of transgressions, till the seed should come, to whom the promise was made, *and it was* ordained by angels in the hand of a mediator.

19. To this argument I know the *Jewish* zealots will make this objection, *viz.* "If pardon and "salvation were not to be had "by virtue of the Mosaical law, "why then was that law given, "and what was it good for?" I answer, It was given to the *Jewish* people for very wise and good purposes, *viz.* To preserve and fence *them*, who were the church of God, and of whose nation Christ was to be born, from the idolatrous rites and practices of the *heathen*

heathen world, into which they were ſo apt to fall; to A. D. 58.
ſhow them the guilt of their own ſins *, and the puniſhment due to them; and by the figurative nature of its ordinances, to train up that people to the hope and expectation of Chriſt the Meſſiah, the great *Sacrifice* and Saviour of mankind. And you muſt obſerve, this *law* was not, like the promiſe to Abraham, given *abſolutely* and *immediately* from God to all *mankind;* but conveyed, by the miniſtry of *angels*, to Moſes, the mediator between God and that *ſingle* people.

20 Now a mediator is not *a mediator* of one, but God is one.

20. (For a *mediator* ſuppoſes two parties concerned in any affair). It is falſe, therefore, that juſtification cannot be had but by the obſervance of that *law*, whereof Moſes was the *mediator;* when it is plain, God was the only *ſingle* † party that gave the great promiſe *abſolutely* and *immediately* to Abraham; and *he* was juſtified without any *mediator* at all.

21. Is the law then againſt the promiſes of God? God forbid! for if there had been a law given which could have given life, verily righteouſneſs ſhould have been by the law.

21. So that the doctrine of theſe *zealots* ſets the *Moſaic law* quite contrary to, and makes it diſannul the promiſe to Abraham, and the *Chriſtian* religion. For, if the obſervance of the *ceremonial* law could have put men into a ſtate of pardon and redemption, the promiſe to Abraham was needleſs, and the *Chriſtian religion* ſignifies nothing *. Which God forbid any man ſhould imagine!

* See ver. 18.

* [Τῶν παραβάσεων χάριν, Because of the tranſgreſſion.] I have given the *two* moſt natural ſenſes of the expreſſion; which is not exactly agreed upon by learned interpreters. I will only remark, that if it be obſerved that, after the giving of the law of the *ten commandments*, Deut. v. 22. it was ſaid, *And he added no more;* i. e. gave them no other ſtatutes at that *time:* and that after their proneneſs to idolatry, ſhown in the inſtance of the *golden calf*, the whole *ceremonial law* was impoſed upon the Jews; it will render it very probable, That the words *becauſe of tranſgreſſions*, mean, principally to keep them from *idolatrous tranſgreſſions*.

† εἷς ἐστιν.

A. D. 58.

22 But the ſcripture hath concluded all under ſin, that the promiſe by faith of Jeſus Chriſt, might be given to them that believe.

22. But, directly contrary to *their* notion, the ſcriptures of the Old Teſtament repreſent all mankind, Jews and Gentiles, to be in a ſtate of ſin and guilt; and ſet forth Chriſt the Meſſiah promiſed to Abraham, as the only ſufficient Saviour, by whoſe religion their pardon and ſalvation is to be obtained.

23 But before faith came, we were kept under the law, ſhut up unto the faith, which ſhould afterwards be revealed.

23. Now we of the *Jewiſh* nation had the promiſe of this Meſſiah to be born of *our* family; and were accordingly trained up to the view and expectation of him, by being kept ſtrictly under the diſcipline and ceremonies of a *law* that pointed and repreſented to us what he was to do and ſuffer for us, in order to a more perfect and complete diſpenſation.

24 Wherefore the law was our ſchoolmaſter, *to bring us* unto Chriſt, that we might be juſtified by faith.

25 But after that faith is come, we are no longer under a ſchoolmaſter.

24. & 25. Wherefore the *Moſaical* law was intended no further than a ſchoolmaſter is to children, to confine them to certain bounds, to inſtruct and prepare our nation for the higher and more holy inſtitution of Jeſus Chriſt; and now that we are actually under that inſtitution of Chriſt, our confinement is over, and we can have no further occaſion for thoſe mean and lower degrees of inſtruction.

26 For ye are all the children of God by faith in Chriſt Jeſus.

27 For as many of you as have been baptized into Chriſt, have put on Chriſt.

26. & 27. The promiſe to Abraham then, or the *Chriſtian* religion, being the only thing that juſtifies and ſaves you, you muſt remember this bleſſing extends to men of *all* nations indifferently. The Jews and Gentiles are no longer kept ſeparate from each other. Every one that is baptized into Chriſt's profeſſion is *perfectly his*, and has a claim to all the privileges of his church, upon his due obedience to his religion.

A. D. 58.

28 There is neither Jew nor Greek, there is neither bond nor free, there is neither male nor female; for ye are all one in Christ Jesus.

28. This perfect dispensation of his makes no distinction between Jew or Gentile, *circumcised* or *uncircumcised*, *master* or *slave*, *man* ‡ or *woman*; but they have *all* equal privileges upon the same conditions.

29 And if ye *be* Christ's, then are ye Abraham's seed, and heirs according to the promise.

29. And if you Gentile, as well as the *Jewish* converts, be accepted into the *Christian* covenant, you must be acknowledged the true spiritual seed of Abraham as well as *they*; and according to the very tenor and design of the great promise made to that holy patriarch and his posterity, shall inherit the blessing of pardon and salvation

CHAP. IV.

The same Argument continued; by showing the Imperfection of the Jewish, and the Perfection of the Christian Religion; from a Comparison taken from an Heir to an Estate. The Apostle then turns off to Expostulating with them about the Folly of adhering to the Jewish Law; reflects on their false Teachers; and entreats them to continue the same Esteem they formerly had of him as their true Apostle; expressing his tender Regard to their Church. Then he resumes the Argument, illustrating the Difference between the two Dispensations of the Law and Gospel, as figuratively represented by the two Branches of Abraham's Posterity, viz. Of Isaac from Sarah, and of Ismael from Hagar.

 1 & 2. To

‡ Ver. 28. *Male* nor *female*. *Note*, The apostle alludes to the *Jewish* custom in *inheritances* of estates, which descended always by right in the *father*, and never by the *mother's* side. As Selden de Succession: and other learned writers observe out of Maimonides and the *Talmudists*.

A. D. 58.

1 NOW I say, that the heir as long as he is a child, differeth nothing from a servant, though he be lord of all.

2 But is under tutors and governors, until the time appointed of the father.

1. & 2. TO illustrate to you the imperfect nature of the *Mosaical* dispensation, I compared it to a *school*, † wherein children are trained up for higher learning. Let me now further show it you by a comparison taken from a son and *heir* to a man's *estate*. Though you know, an eldest son has, at his father's death, an *immediate* legal right to inheritance, yet while he is a minor, he is no more capable of entering upon, and managing the estate, than a *servant* of the family can do; but is kept under the discipline and allowance of guardians and trustees, till he is of age of inheritance, according to the tenor of his father's last will and testament.

† Cap. iii. 23, 25.

3 Even so we, when we were children, were in bondage under the elements of the world:

3. This is the case of the *Jewish* church and people; they were indeed to inherit the great promise of the Messiah, made to Abraham: but not *immediately* after it was made; but, like *minors*, were first to be kept and educated under the discipline of the figurative and introductory dispensation of the *Mosaical* law, the better to prepare them to receive it.

4 But when the fullness of the time was come, God sent forth his Son, made of a woman, made under the law,

5 To redeem them that were under the law, that we might receive the adoption of sons.

4. & 5. The time that *they* and the *rest* of the world were to come to the full enjoyment of this promise, was, at the appearance of this Christ; whom, at the season foretold by the *prophets*, and when the Divine Wisdom saw mankind most fitted to receive him, God the Father sent into the world, born of a virgin of a *Jewish* family; who himself lived in subjection to the *Jewish* law, and delivered that nation, for ever after, from the burden of its rites and ceremonies; bringing *them* and *all* mankind, to the full age and capacity of inheriting the promise of pardon and salvation.

6. And

A. D. 58.

6 And because ye are sons, God hath sent forth the Spirit of his Son into your hearts, crying, Abba, Father.

6. And accordingly, as *Christian* believers, God has given you *Gentile* converts as well as *Jewish* ones, the complete assurance and pledge ‖ of your being now accepted for his true children, and perfect inheritors of this promised blessing, by the gifts ‖ and graces of his *holy Spirit* conferred on you; so that you may assuredly address and approach him, as to a merciful and gracious Father.

‖ Romans viii. 15, 16.

7 Wherefore thou art no more a servant, but a son; and if a son, then an heir of God through Christ.

7. As to you of the *Jewish* part, your term of *minority* is now out. Wherefore, instead of adhering any longer to the childish and imperfect services of the *law*, consider the dignity and full privilege you are arrived at by the *Christian* covenant. You are now entered, as *sons* at full age, on the inheritance of the promises made to Abraham and your forefathers.

8 Howbeit, then, when ye knew not God, † ye did service unto them which by nature are no gods.

9 But now after that ye have known God, or rather are known of God, how turn ye again to the weak and beggarly elements, whereunto ye desire again to be in bondage?

8. & 9. Thus it is with the *Jewish* converts. But it is yet more foolish and unaccountable, that you *Gentile* Christians, who, from a perfectly false and idolatrous † religion, are now converted to the knowledge, worship and favour of the *true God*, should ever be persuaded to embrace a burdensome dispensation, that you were never at all obliged to; and which, in comparison of that you are now baptized into, is a mean, low, and imperfect

† Ver. 8. [Ye did service to them which by nature are no gods,] i. e. which in *reality* [φύσει] were not gods; were gods in *no sense whatever*. Or else by pointing and reading it thus, ['Εδουλεύσατε τοῖς φύσει μὴ οὖσι, θεοῖς, ye were in bondage to gods that in nature had no being,] or *were not*, had *no divinity* in them: According to St. Paul's language in another place, 1 Cor. viii. 4. [An idol is nothing.] *Images* and demons there might be, but *gods* or *lords* they were not, having neither *supreme* nor *subordinate* power or qualities; mere *fictions*, *vanities*, and *nullities*.

A. D. 58. perfect way of religion; and would reduce you again * to a *bondage*, though not so ill a one as your *heathen* state was.

10 Ye observe days, and months, and times, and years.

11 I am afraid of you, lest I have bestowed upon you labour in vain.

10. & 11. I perceive you are grown zealous observers of the *Jewish Sabbaths*, *new-moons* and *festivals*. If this temper continues on you, I fear my labours of converting you to the *Christian* religion are all lost.

12 Brethren, I beseech you, be as I *am*: for I *am* as ye *are*, ye have not injured me at all.

12. Let me entreat you, dear brethren, to be of *my* sentiment. I was once as zealous a patriot for the *Mosaical* law as any of you can be. And though I am *now* otherwise, yet am willing to condescend and conform to your notions, as far as ever my *Christian* office and profession will permit me. Let no suspicions or resentments between us abate your love toward *me*: for *my* part, I have none against *you*.

13 Ye know how through infirmity of the flesh, I preached the gospel unto you at the first.

14 And my temptation which was in my flesh ye despised not, nor rejected, but received me as an angel of God, *even* as Christ Jesus.

13. & 14. Do not forget what respect you once paid both to my person and *doctrine*, when I first preached to you and made you *Christians*. None of the sufferings and infirmities I laboured under, nor the meanness of my personal appearance, made you then slight me in the least; but ye received me with such respect as if I had been Christ himself, the true Messiah, the great *Angel* of the covenant †.

15 Where 15. You

---

* Turn *again*, and desire *again*: *i. e.* not that the *Galatians* were ever *Jewish* proselytes at all; but that *as* their former *heathen* religion was *beggarly*, weak, und slavish, so by desiring to be *circumcised* they would *again* be reduced to a bondage, though not the *same* they were under before.

† *An angel of God*, ἄγγελον Θεοῦ. The Messenger of God—Emphatically, *the angel of the covenant*.

A. D. 58.

15 Where is then the blessedness you spake of? for I bear you record, that if it had been possible, ye would have plucked out your own eyes, and have given them to me.

15. You then expressed such satisfaction and happiness in me, that I can testify you would have done or suffered almost any thing for my sake. But what blessing was I or my *ministry* to you, if you now leave me, and run to the *Jewish* teachers?

16 Am I therefore become your enemy, because I tell you the truth?

16. Or, what is that has changed your sentiments of me? Is it that I tell you plainly, the *Mosaical law has no hand in your justification and happiness?* If that be it, it is the very *gospel* truth, and I must stand to it.

17 They zealously affect you, but not well: yea, they would exclude you, * that you might affect them.

17. Your false *teachers*, indeed, pretend an extraordinary love and respect for you; they maliciously endeavour to draw you entirely from *me**, and engross all your affections to themselves.

18 But it is good † to be zealously affected always in a good thing, and not only when I am present with you.

18. But pray remember, if ever you had any just reason to esteem me † as a good and true *apostle*, you ought to do so *still* in my absence, as well as when I was preaching among you in person.

19 My little children, of whom I travail in birth again until Christ be formed in you,

19. My dear Christian children! I am in the very pains of a mother in travail, till I have renewed and brought you forth again into better and sounder principles of Christianity.

20 I desire to be present with you now, and to change my voice,

20. I could wish myself with you; and that I had reason to change these complaints into commendations.

---

* Ver. 7. *Exclude you*, i. e. from the *Christian* covenant, unless you be *circumcised*; and thereby make you fond of their principles. Or else, ἡμᾶς, *exclude me*, as some copies read it, and as in the paraphrase.

† To be zealously affected *in a good thing*; or, ἐν καλῳ, toward a good *person*.

A. D. 58. voice, for I stand in doubt of you.

mendations. But indeed at the present, I know not what to think of you.

21 Tell me, ye that desire to be under the law, do ye not hear the law?

22. But let me argue the main *point*, with you again, from the very words of the *Old Testament*, wherein both *law* and *gospel* may be represented. And I hope, you that are so fond of Moses's law, will not refuse to believe his writings.

22 For it is written, that Abraham had two sons, the one by a bond-maid, the other by a free-woman.

22. You read there that Abraham had two sons, from whom the two different branches of his posterity sprung, the one by his bond-maid Hagar, and the other by his proper wife Sarah.

23 But he who was of the bond-woman, was born after the flesh: but he of the free-woman was by promise.

23. Ismael that was born of Hagar (while Abraham was young enough to have children), was by the common course of nature; but Isaac was begotten of Sarah, at an age when they were naturally incapable of procreation. *His* birth was extraordinary, and the pure effect of a divine *promise* appropriated to him and his posterity.

24 Which things are an * allegory; for these and the two covenants, the one from the mount Sinai which gendereth to bondage, which is Agar.

24. You must know then, that this is not only a literal *history*, but may be taken as a figurative representation of the two covenants and religious *dispensations*, viz. The *law* and the *gospel*: And accordingly the prophet Isaiah uses it in the way of *figure* or *allegory*. [Ver. 27.]

25 For this † Agar is mount Sinai in Arabia, and

25. † For Hagar (the mother of the *Ismaelites*) represents the slavish and

* 'Αλληγορȣμένα are *allegorized*, viz. by Isaiah in Ver. 27.

† Τὸ γὰρ Ἄγαρ Σινᾶ ὄρος, &c. This Hagar is *Mount Sinai*. For the construction of this verse, let the critical reader see Dr. Bentley's Epist. to *Joan*, *Mal. Chron.* and the note of Dr. Mills on this place. And for a larger and most excellent explanation of this whole allegory, I refer him to Dr. Jackson, Tom. III. Bock XII. Cap. 10.

A. D. 58.

and anſwereth to Jeruſalem which now is, and is in bondage with her children.

and temporary *diſpenſation* of the *Jewiſh law*, that was given at Mount *Sinai* in the deſert of *Arabia;* and that people of the *Jews*, that were to be kept under the ſevere diſcipline of it.

16 But Jeruſalem which is above, is free, which is the mother of us all †.

26. But Sarah (the mother of Iſaac) denotes the *promiſed ſeed* of Abraham, the *ſpiritual Jeruſalem*, i. e. the *Chriſtian church*, which is truly *ſpiritual* and *free* of all obligation to thoſe troubleſome *ceremonies;* and is not, like the *Jewiſh* religion, confined to one *nation*, but, as an univerſal † mother, receives all, both *Jewiſh* and *Gentile* believers, into her bleſſings and privileges. And you cannot deny the juſtneſs of this repreſentation: For how can you allow that it was of God's mere pleaſure and will, that Sarah, and not Hagar, Iſaac, and not Iſmael, were choſen to be the parents of the *covenanted people*, and of the *promiſed ſeed;* and yet deny, that by the ſame will and pleaſure God cannot and will not chooſe the *Gentile* world to be his *church* in Chriſt?

27 For it is written, Rejoice thou barren that beareſt not; break forth and cry, thou that travaileſt not; for the deſolate hath many more children than ſhe which hath an huſband.

27. Of this church it is you are to underſtand thoſe triumphant words of Iſaiah (Iſai. liv. 1.), wherein he calls upon her (particularly the *Gentile* part of her) *to rejoice in the vaſt number of her members, that ſhould exceed thoſe of the* Jewiſh *people who had been all along the only church and people of God.*

28 Now we, brethren, as Iſaac was, are the children of promiſe.

28. The application then of this allegory is plain, *Chriſtians*, whether *Gentile* or *Jewiſh*, *circumciſed* or not, are the members of this bleſſed covenant intended in the promiſe of Abraham; and are the *ſpiritual* offspring of Iſaac.

29. But

† The *mother* of us all. Μήτηρ, the *metropolis*, ſays Mr. *Dodwel, Diſſert. Cyp.* 5.

A. D. 58.

29 But as then he that was born after the flesh, persecuted him that was *born* after the Spirit, even so it is now.

29. And indeed the *Jews*, by their obstinate behaviour, have carried the resemblance still further. For, as Ismael, who was a mere * *natural son*, did then mock and insult Isaac, that was to be the *inheritor of* Abraham's *promise;* so now the worst and most bitter persecutors of the *Christian* church are the infidel part of the *Jewish* nation, and the zealous adherents to their *ceremonial* law.

30 Nevertheless, what saith the scripture? Cast out the bond-woman and her son: for the son of the bond woman shall not be heir with the son of the free-woman.

30. And God will *complete* the parallel in a just recompence upon them: For *as* Ismael *and his mother were turned out of* Abraham's *family*, so shall these obstinate patriots of the *Jewish* law, who depend upon it for their *justification*, have no share in the blessings of the *Christian* covenant.

31 So then, brethren, we are not children of the bond-woman, but of the free.

31. The sum of the argument is this, then, that every Christian is a member of the *free*, *gracious*, and *spiritual* religion of the *gospel*, as Isaac was the promised seed of Abraham; and consequently, cannot be obliged to the heavy bondage of the *ceremonial* law of Moses.

CHAP.

* Ver. 29. *After the flesh a natural son*, i. e. a son by a *secondary* wife or *concubine*, and begotten without any special and extraordinary concurrence of *Divine Power*, or *promise;* in contradistinction to the case of Isaac.

CHAP V.

The first Verse is an Exhortation from the Discourses of the two foregoing Chapters. Then the Apostle, in more express Terms, declares, He never preached up the Necessity of the Jewish *Law to* Christians; *as their false* Teachers *insinuated he had done. Clears himself of that imputation several Ways. Pronounceth all* Christians *free from the* Jewish Ceremonies; *but exhorts them to avoid all violent Disputes, and uncharitable Censures upon each other, in their Arguments for, and Defence of, that Freedom. Warns them against the several Vices of the* Flesh, *and presses them to the Practice of the* Spiritual *Graces and Virtues of the* Gospel *Religion.*

1 STAND fast therefore in the liberty wherewith Christ hath made us free, and be not ‡ entangled again with the yoke of bondage.

1. IF then the *Christian* religion has thus freed you from all obligation to the burdensome ceremonies of the *Mosaical* law maintain that freedom, and never ‡ submit yourselves to that slavish dispensation. A. D. 58.

2 Behold, I Paul say unto you, that if ye be circumcised, Christ shall profit you nothing.

2. And, for an absolute confutation of that false suggestion of some of your new *teachers* ||, that *I* have given any countenance to the necessity of that *law* upon *Christian* converts: Take notice, I now myself expressly again tell you, That whatever Christian depends upon *circumcision*, and the observance of the *Jewish ceremonies*, for his justification, loses all the benefits of his *Christian* profession.

3. For

‡ *Entangled again.* See chap. iv. 9. the note there.

|| Ὑποκριτὴς ἐςιν ἀλλαχῦ περιτμὴν κηρύσσων ἀλλαχῦ δὲ ὀ. Theodorot in Loc.

A. D. 58.

3 For I testify again * to every man that is circumcised, that he is a debtor to do the whole law.

4 Christ is become of no effect unto you, whosoever of you are justified by the law; ye are fallen from grace.

3. & 4. Nay to show you how much in earnest I am, I repeat it again *; Whatever *Christian* is *circumcised* becomes a perfect *Jew*, and must keep the whole *ceremonial* law: and whoever does that as necessary means of his pardon and salvation, renounces the salvation of the *gospel*, and forfeits all claim to it.

5 For we through the Spirit ‡ wait for the hope of righteousness by faith.

5. For a *Christian's* hope of salvation is founded wholly in his embracing the *Christian* religion; which hope he has fully confirmed to him by the extraordinary gifts and graces of the Holy Spirit ‡ bestowed upon the *Christian* church.

6 For in Jesus Christ neither circumcision availeth any thing, nor uncircumcision, but faith which worketh by love.

6. And in this *gospel dispensation*, *circumcision* or *uncircumcision* signify nothing: The only thing that saves either Jew or Gentile, now, is such a faith in Christ's religion as produces the true love of God and our neighbour.

7 Ye did run well, who did hinder you ||, that you should not obey the truth?

7. When you Galatians were first converted by me, you were in a good way, and went on well; what people are they that stopt || and drew you off from the true *Christian* doctrine?

8 This persuasion *cometh* not of him that calleth you.

8. Be assured, this notion of the necessity of the *Jewish* law to *Christians* comes not from God, the Author of your religion, nor from *me* that first preached it to you.

9. Have

---

* *Again.* See chap. i. 8, 9, 10.

† *We—through the Spirit*——See chap. iii. 2, 5. iv. 6.

‡ *Who did hinder you?* ἀνέκοψε, *justled you out of the way.* It refers to ἐτρέχετε, and seems to me to be a term proper to the *games* wherein the *racers* endeavoured to *justle* and *retard* one another.

A. D. 58.

9 A little leaven leaveneth the whole lump.

9. Have a care of it then. This *one* doctrine like leaven, will sour and spoil all your *Christian* principles; and a few such † *teachers* may soon corrupt your whole church

10 I have confidence in you through the Lord, that you will be none otherwise minded; but he that troubleth you, shall bear *his* judgment, whosoever he be.

10. But, I hope in Christ, what I have said to you will bring you off from it; and that the preachers † of it shall be censured and condemned as they deserve.

11 And I, brethren, if I yet preach circumcision, why do I yet suffer persecution? then is the offence of the cross ceased.

11. How irrational is it for them to suggest that *I* should favour their notions? Were *I* a favourer of that doctrine, how came the Jews to persecute me as they still do. It is plain, would I but give up this *one* principle, *of mens being saved only by the death of a crucified* Jesus (the very principle that gives them so much distaste), they would soon be friends with me.

12 I would they were even ‡ cut off which trouble you.

12. Verily, I have such an aversion to the *teachers* that spread this doctrine, that I would even wish they were expelled ‡ the Christian church, for troubling and perverting you with it.

13. For

---

† Ver. 9, 10. *A little leaven*——and *he that troubleth you. Note,* Some learned men would conjecture, from the two expressions, that it was *one* single *teacher*, or *false apostle*, that gave St. Paul this trouble and opposition. It might be so; yet, I think, the *twelfth verse* renders it very uncertain——There it is, *They which trouble you.*

‡ *Cut off.* The apostle's meaning in this phrase may, perhaps, run higher than bare *excommunication*, according to the conjecture of the judicious Dr. Jackson. Tom. III. p. 182. who supposes him here to wish the same sentence upon those that unreasonably *pressed* circumcision, which was denounced upon such as *omitted* it. Now that was Gen. xvii. 14. *To be cut off or destroyed from among the people.* Which the *Jewish* doctors, and many of our best divines understand of immediate *death*, or at least *shortening of life*, by the *Divine Hand*. See Exod. iv. 24.

A. D. 58.

13 For, brethren, ye have been called unto liberty; only *use* not liberty for an occasion to the flesh, but by love serve one another.

13. For it is evident beyond contradiction, the *Christian* religion has freed all its members from the burden of the *Jewish* law. Only let me advise you that maintain this freedom, not to abuse it into a liberty of uncharitable censures, animosities, or reviling behaviour against such as differ from you; for these are the effects of a carnal and sinful principle. But, on the contrary, be ready to serve them in any kind of good offices.

14 For all the law is fulfilled in one word, *even* in this; Thou shalt love thy neighbour as thyself.

14. Remembering that a just and kind treatment of all mankind is the sum and substance of all the moral laws of the second table.

15 But if ye bite and devour one another, take heed that ye be not consumed one of another.

15. Whereas if your differences and disputes fly out into an outrageous and abusive carriage to each other, it may hazard to end in the ruin of you all, and the discredit and bane of your common profession.

16 *This* I say then, Walk in the Spirit, and ye shall not fulfil the lust of the flesh.

16. To prevent which direful effects, live and converse agreeably to the pure and *spiritual* religion of the *gospel*, and worthy of those extraordinary gifts of the Holy Spirit conferred on your church.

17 For the flesh lusteth against the Spirit, and the Spirit against the flesh: and these are contrary the one to the other; so that ye cannot do the things that ye would.

17. For the corrupt inclinations, of which such vices are the genuine effects, are directly opposite to the temper and *spirit of Christianity;* they are perfectly destructive of each other, and it is impossible you can indulge them both.

18 But if ye be led by the Spirit, ye are not under the law.

18. The religion of Christ is truly *spiritual;* and all its members are under the conduct and influence of the Holy Ghost; which both enables and obliges them to a higher

a higher degree of purity and holineſs than could be expected from a Jew under the *Moſaical* law; and at the same time ſhows them to be in no need of that *law*. A. D. 58.

19 Now the works of the fleſh are manifeſt, which are *theſe*, adultery, fornication, uncleanneſs, laſciviouſneſs,

20 Idolatry, ‡ witchcraft, hatred, variance, emulation, wrath, ſtrife, ſeditions, hereſies.

21 Envyings, murders, drunkenneſs, revellings, and ſuch like: of the which I tell you before, as I have alſo told you in time paſt, that they which do ſuch things, ſhall not inherit the kingdom of God.

19, 20. & 21. And the better to preſerve you from the vices that ſpring from theſe indulged corruptions of human nature, let me point out to you ſome of the chief of them, as adultery, fornication, impurity in *thoughts* or *actions* idolatrous worſhip, with all the unclean practices attending it, ‡ witchcrafts, enmities, quarrels, animoſities, furious anger, ſedition againſt the lawful government, diviſions and ſeparations in the *church* on needleſs occaſions, envyings, murders, drunkenneſs, and night revellings, &c. Which I always told you, and now again particularly warn you, are ſuch enormities, that no practiſer of them can ever be a true *Chriſtian*, or enjoy the happineſs of heaven.

22 But the fruit of the Spirit is love, joy, peace, long ſuffering, gentleneſs, goodneſs, faith,

23 Meekneſs, temperance: againſt ſuch there is no law.

22. & 23. On the contrary, the graces and virtues required of us by the *ſpiritual* religion of the *goſpel*, are ſuch as theſe, viz. *Love* to all mankind, a cheerful and contented mind, peaceableneſs of behaviour, patience under injuries, ſweetneſs of diſpoſition, gentleneſs and beneficence, fidelity to our words, and promiſes, meekneſs and temperance in the uſe of worldly pleaſures. Theſe are agreeable to the Divine Will, and will ſcreen us from all guilt and puniſhment.

24 And they that are Chriſt's, have crucified the fleſh, with the affections and luſts.

24. And every true *Chriſtian* engages by his profeſſion to get ſuch a maſtery over his corrupt and fleſhly inclinations, as to arrive at the habitual practice of all theſe virtues.

‡ Witchcrafts. Φαρμακεία, i. e. The art of poiſoning.

A. D. 58.

25 If we live in the Spirit, let us also walk in the Spirit.

25. Wherefore, if we pretend ourselves members of this pure and spiritual religion of the *gospel*, that is attended with such assistances of the Holy Ghost; it infinitely concerns us to live suitably to its holy dictates and precepts.

26 Let us not be desirous of vain-glory, provoking one another, envying one another.

26. And let me persuade all your contending parties to begin to give an instance of this *Christian* temper, by particularly suppressing that spirit of ambition and vain-glory, that is so apt to make them envy, contemn, and exasperate one another.

CHAP. VI.

He continues his Exhortation to a tender and peaceable Temper. Admonisheth the Spiritual Governors of the Church to endeavour the recovery of such as fall into Errors and Irregularities, by kind and gentle Treatment. Reflects upon the Pride of their false Teachers. *Encourages the* Galatians *to a liberal and* * *impartial Contribution for the Maintainance of their* Ministers: *And to Charity towards all Mankind, especially their Fellow* Christians. *Then sums up the Argument of his whole Epistle, and concludes with his Blessing.*

* See the Preface.

1 BRethren, if a man be overtaken in a fault, ye which are spiritual, restore such an one in the spirit of meekness, considering thyself, lest thou also be tempted.

1. BY the rule of *Christian* charity, then, † it is the indispensible duty of your spiritual and inspired *ministers*, to endeavour, by all gentle and kind methods, to reduce such members as are misled into bad principles or practices, to a just sense of their duty: Remembering that they themselves are not *absolutely* exempted from falling into the like miscarriages.

† Chap. v. 22, 23.

2. Instead

A. D. 58.

2 Bear ye one anothers burdens, and fo fulfil the law of Chrift.

2. Inftead therefore of impofing the drudgery of the *Jewifh* law upon one another; make it your bufinefs fully to obey this noble *Chriftian* law, by bearing with, and relieving the infirmities of each other.

3 For if a man think himfelf to be fomething, when he is nothing, he deceiveth himfelf.

3. For whatever *teacher* exalts and values himfelf, fo as to be above a tender concern for the good and fafety of others, or imperioufly to impofe his own notions upon them, makes himfelf a very little and foolifh perfon.

4 But let every man prove his own work, and then he ‡ fhall have rejoicing in himfelf alone, and not in another.

4. Let none infult the weaknefs of his inferiors, but let every one look into and weigh his *own* actions. In them alone a man can truly ‡ boaft, and not in a mere comparifon of himfelf with other people, or in making them *his* profelytes.

5 For every man fhall bear his own burthen.

5. For it is our *own* behaviour we fhall all be accountable for; let others be of what opinion or what party they will.

6 Let him that is taught in the word, communicate unto him that teacheth, in all good things.

6. And, whereas I find feveral of you very partial in contributing to the maintainance of your *minifters*, by the difference and difputes that prevail amongft you; I now exhort you to be juft and liberal in your collection for them *all*.

7 Be not deceived, God is not mocked: for whatfoever a man foweth, that fhall be alfo reap.

7. Let *none* of them lead you into wrong prejudices againft the *reft*. They may deceive *you*, but God they cannot; who will be fure to reward you in proportion to the prudence and liberality of your diftributions.

D 2 8. He

‡ Ver. 4. Shall have rejoicing. Καύχημα, Glorying or boafting.

7

A.D. 58.

8 For he that soweth to his flesh, shall of the flesh reap corruption: but he that soweth to the spirit, shall of the spirit reap life everlasting.

8. He that lays out his worldly substance to selfish and private purposes only, shall reap the fruits of so worldly and corrupt a principle. But he that spends it agreeably to the charitable spirit of the *gospel*, shall find a full harvest of eternal life and happiness.

9 And let us not be weary in well doing: for in due season we shall reap, if we faint not.

* Luke xiv. 14.

9. Let this encourage us all to be constant and cheerful in acts of bounty and beneficence, which will not fail, in God's due * time, of producing us a plentiful recompence.

10 As we have therefore opportunity, let us do good unto all men, especially unto them who are of the household of faith.

10. As Providence, then, gives us opportunities and abilities, let us extend our charity to all mankind, but especially to our fellow *Christians*, especially to those of them that are under affliction (See v. 12.) and persecution, without partiality and unreasonable distinctions.

11 Ye see how large a letter I have written you † with mine own hand.

11. I have written this letter to you, on this important occasion, with my own † hand. Consider ‡ the contents of it; the sum and substance thereof is this, viz.

12 As

12. Those

---

† [With mine own hand.] His other epistles being mostly written by an *amanuensis*. See Rom. xvi. 26. 1 Cor. xvi. 21. 2 Thes. iii. 17.

‡ Ἴδετε πηλίκοις γράμμασιν. [Ye see how large a letter:] Or rather, [in what words.]

By observing the *five* following verses to be a perfect *recapitulation* of the argument of this whole epistle, I cannot think πηλίκοις denotes either the *largeness* of it, or the bad *hand* in which it was written, (as Theophylact says, but without any proof) but the *matter* and *substance* of it. And that ἴδετε ought to be rendered *imperatively*, the sense being this, viz. [Consider what I have written, the sum whereof is this—] as in the following verses.

A. D 53.

12 As many as desire to make a fair show in the flesh, they constrain you to be circumcised: only lest they should suffer persecution for the cross of Christ.

12. Those zealots that stand up thus for the mere *external* and *carnal* ordinances of the *Jewish* law, would persuade you *Gentile* converts into the necessity of observing them, purely for fear of the *Jews*, and to avoid the persecutions they would otherwise bring on them for their *Christian* t[illegible]ing the *Roman* power against them.

13 For neither they themselves who are circumcised keep the law, but desire to have you circumcised, that they may glory in your flesh.

13. It is not out of any real and religious zeal for the *law* (for they regard *that* as little as other people), but from an itch of vain-glory, to make you *their* proselytes, and save themselves harmless.

14 But God forbid that I should glory save in the cross of our Lord Jesus Christ, by whom the world is crucified unto me, and I unto the world.

14. I on the contrary (notwithstanding their false suggestions) make a perfect conscience of aiming at any credit or favour with any sort of people, but what comes from the sincere discharge of my office, in preaching Jesus Christ as a *crucified Saviour*; by whose religion alone justification and happiness is to be attained. In conformity to whose death all worldly and selfish designs are dead to me, and I to them.

15 For in Christ Jesus neither circumcision availeth any thing, nor uncircumcision, but a new creature.

15. For, as I have abundantly proved to you, it is of no consequence under the *gospel* covenant, whether a man be *circumcised* or not. All that *Christianity* requires is, the reformation of his principles and practices.

16 And as many as walk according to this

16. And therefore all Christians, *Gentile* or *Jewish*, that stick to *this* principle,

A. D. 58. this rule, * peace be on them, and mercy, and upon the Israel of God.

principle, may be fully assured of their pardon and salvation at God's hand, as his true *church* * and people.

17 From henceforth let no man trouble me, for I bear in my body the marks of the Lord Jesus †.

17. Wherefore, for the future, let no more calumnies be raised on me upon this point, nor let me have any further disturbance about it. *Circumcision* is the badge of a *Jew*. But though I be circumcised, I do not look on that as my *Christian* badge. No, my *marks* are the *stripes* and *chains* I have borne for Christ and his religion; the prints whereof remain still upon my body, and are sufficient tokens to whom I belong.

18 Brethren, the grace of our Lord Jesus Christ, *be* with your spirit. Amen.

¶ Unto the Galatians, written from Rome.

18. Brethren the love and favour of our Lord Jesus Christ be with you, and direct your minds. *Amen.*

---

* *And upon the Israel of God.* Καὶ ἐπὶ τὸν Ἰσραὴλ τοῦ Θεοῦ. Peace and mercy be unto them *as the Israel of God.*

† Ver. 17. *The marks of the Lord Jesus. Note*, The *general* sense of this phrase is very clear: And, I think, the *five* foregoing *verses* plainly show the *Jewish circumcision* to be the thing here alluded to. They that would see another conjecture, may consult the author of *The Sac. Classics defended*, Vol. II. pag. 67, 68. Edit. Octav.

A PARA-

A
PARAPHRASE
ON THE
EPISTLE OF ST. PAUL
TO THE
EPHESIANS.

PREFACE.

§ 1. THIS and the two following epiſtles to the Philippians and Colloſſians, were written from the ſame *place*, in the ſame *year*, during St. Paul's impriſonment at Rome, and upon the ſame *occaſion*. From whence the reader ſees how the ſtrain of their expreſſions come to be ſo much alike, and in a great meaſure the ſame. A. D. 62.

§ 2. One cannot attend to the main drift of theſe three writings, without obſerving what it was that lay neareſt the apoſtle's heart while he indited them; *viz.* The confirmation of theſe *Chriſtians* againſt that doctrine of the abſolute neceſſity of the *ceremonial* law in order to the ſalvation of a *Chriſtian* convert; the effect of that proud conceit the *Jewiſh* zealots had

A. D. 62. of themselves, as the ancient people of God, in derogation to all the rest of mankind, whom they would hardly at all grant to have been designed any share in the blessings of Christ the Messiah; but especially not without their first embracing the *Jewish* religion. A principle that, more or less, runs through, and is attacked in all the apostolical *epistles*.

§ 3. But there is this difference between the manner of St. Paul's management of this point in *these*, and that in his *foregoing* epistles to the Romans, Corinthians, and Galatians. In those letters (especially the two *latter*) he had to do with a people *actually* perverted by those *Jewish* principles; and by the cunning and bigotry of their leaders, wrought up into a contempt of his *person*, and apostolical *authority*. Whereas, in *these* he had nothing to do but to back and encourage a steady and orthodox set of Christians to final constancy and perseverance, against those prejudiced teachers who had spread themselves into almost every church. In the *one*, therefore, his method is all *reasoning* and *argumentative*, while in the *other* he runs in cheerful *encouragements* and loving *congratulations*; and as you see *those* to be full of *expostulations* and *complaint*, so *these* abound and even overflow in expressions of endearment and love: of which expressions, though some may, to a modern reader, seem to be but tautology, they are indeed the effect of an inspired mind, transported with joy, striving to vent its unutterable satisfaction at the happy fruits of its endeavours for the good of mankind and the glory of God.

§ 4. The *Jewish* zealots had so contemptuous a notion of an *uncircumcised* person, especially one not at all *proselyted* to their *Jewish* religion, that they thought the duties flowing from the nearest even of civil and natural relations, too much to be observed toward them. This I take to be the proper key to those lessons of St. Paul concerning the *relative* duties in *these* and his other epistles. By comparing them with 1 Cor. vii. or with his exhortations to *love*, *unity*, &c. which have a plain relation to the furious disputes between the *Jewish* and *Gentile* converts; these very admonitions to husbands, masters, wives, &c. appear to me to have

have been perfectly *occasional*, and levelled at the foregoing principle. Thus the admonitions to *husbands* and *wives*, Ephes. v. and Col. iii. may, by several passages of 1 Cor. vii. be understood with reference to such *pairs*, whereof one was a *Heathen*, the other a *Christian*; or perhaps the one a *Gentile* and *uncircumcised* convert, the other a *Jewish* convert; the latter of which, by a *Jewish* prejudice, might think themselves excusable from any further obedience or duty to the former. In like manner, the earnest caution to *children* and *parents* to observe a duty in itself so natural, and which indeed wanted no *gospel revelation* to show it to be a moral duty of the first rank, seems clearly to be understood of *such cases* where one of the *parents* might be of the *former*, and the other of the *latter* of those denominations: and that children should pay an equal reverence to *both*, was the scope of the apostle's exhortation. Then as to *masters* and *servants*, St. Paul is so perfect an interpreter of himself in other places, particularly in 1 Cor. vii. 20, 21, 22. that one cannot but conclude his eye here to have been upon *Christian* masters to *Heathen* slaves, and *Christian* slaves under *Heathen* masters. And thus the obligation to these *relative* duties, so incumbent on a *Christian* toward even *infidel* relations, shows itself much stronger and more engaging upon *Christians* toward one another, by the plain *consequence*, though not the *express design* of the apostle's admonitions. And this observation, which I have not found duly cultivated by any interpreters, I leave to the judicious and careful reader of these epistolary writings. A. D. 62.

§ 5. The rest of these epistles is spent in exhortations to such *Christian* virtues as are the reverse of those unclean and vicious practices these *Gentile Christians* had been formerly most subject to, in their idolatrous and Heathenish condition; as also to prudence, constancy, and patience, under the dangers and oppositions they meet with from their *Jewish* or *Gentile* infidels: all which shall be methodically noted in the contents of each chapter. Concerning this particular *epistle*, see the learned Dr. Mell in his *Prolegom.* § 72, 73, 74, &c.

CHAP.

CHAP. I.

He salutes the Ephesians with the Title of Faithful *Christians, for their steady adherence to the* Christian *Faith, without any regard to the necessity of the* Ceremonial *Law. Blesseth God for calling the* Gentile *World into the Christian Covenant, and bringing them and the Jews together into one Church under Christ the* Messiah. *Declares this to have been the original and gracious Design of God in the* Gospel *Dispensation: and the Gifts and Endowments of the* Holy Spirit *conferred on the* Ephesian *Church, are to them a Pledge and Confirmation of this Truth. His satisfaction in their adherence to it, and his Prayers for their Constancy and Improvement in the Knowledge of this most wise and comprehensive Religion of the* Gospel.

Written A. D. 62.

* Acts ix. Gal. i. 1.

1 PAUL, an apostle of Jesus Christ; by the will of God, to the saints which are at Ephesus, and to the faithful in Christ Jesus:

1. PAUL, called to be a Christian apostle, by the express * will and revelation of God, sendeth this epistle to the church of Ephesus, and to all the *Christians* of the Lesser Asia, those *faithful* Christians that firmly rely upon the *Christian* religion for salvation, without the observation of the *Mosaical ceremonies*.

2 Grace *be* to you, and peace from God our Father, and *from* the Lord Jesus Christ.

2. Wishing you all divine favours and blessings from God the Father, and from our Lord Jesus Christ.

3 Blessed be the God and Father of our Lord Jesus Christ, who hath blessed us with all spiritual blessings in heavenly places in Christ;

3. Expressing my hearty praises to God the Father of our Lord Jesus Christ, for bestowing * on you Gentiles, as well as the Jews, all the privileges of the spiritual religion of the *gospel*, a religion so full of eternal and heavenly blessings.

4 Accord-

4. A mercy

A. D. 62.

4 According as he hath chosen us * in him, before the foundation of the world, that we should be holy, and without blame before him in love:

4. A mercy designed of God toward the *Gentile* world *, even before the world was created, to make *them* also his true church and people, by giving them the means of a pure, peaceable, and holy life, by Jesus Christ the Messiah.

5 Having predestinated us unto the adoption of children, by Jesus Christ, to himself, according to the good pleasure of his will:

5. For as it was by the free bounty and favour of God that the *Jewish* nation should be, for a long time, his peculiar church and people, so is it the same Divine will *now* to bring all the *Gentile* world along with them into this gracious privilege under Christ Jesus, without any farther obligation to the *Jewish* law.

6 To the praise of the glory of his grace, wherein he hath made us accepted in the beloved.

6. Which merciful acceptance of us *all*, through his beloved Son, is that which magnifies and exalts the goodness and bounty of this *gospel* covenant.

7 In whom we have redemption through his blood, the forgiveness of sins; according to the riches of his grace,

7. By the exceeding great blessing of whose death and sufferings for us, both *Gentile* and *Jewish* believers are put into a state of pardon, and capacity of eternal happiness.

8 Wherein he hath abounded toward us in all wisdom † and prudence:

9 Having made known unto us the mystery of his will, according to his good pleasure, which he hath purposed in himself.

8. & 9. A dispensation full of divine wisdom, and that lets us all † into the discovery of the great and wise purpose of God toward mankind;

---

* Ver. 3. & 4. ἡμας, Blessed *us*, chosen *us*. He, in his usual way, makes *himself* as one of the *Gentile* converts, the more to confirm and encourage them to rely upon the *gospel* without the *ceremonial* law.

† *In all wisdom and prudence:* These words may either be referred to *God* or to *Christians* as endowed with them under the gospel. I have expressed both senses.

A. D. 62.

10 That in the dispensation of the fulness of times, he might gather together in one all things in Christ, both which * are in heaven, and which are on earth, even in him:

10. Viz. This special and particular purpose of his gathering people out of all nations, without distinction, into one church under Christ, in this last and great dispensation of the *gospel*, and so committing the whole church of heaven * and earth to his conduct and government.

11 In whom also we have obtained an inheritance, being predestinated according to the purpose of him, who worketh all things after the counsel of his own will:

12 That we should be to the praise of his glory who first trusted in Christ.

11. & 12. To whose religion it was indeed the privilege granted to us of the *Jewish* nation, to have the first call: that as we had been his *ancient* church, we should be the *first* converts that should praise and magnify God under the religion of his Son Jesus Christ, the Messiah promised to us. It being the good pleasure of the Almighty thus to have it.

13 In whom ye also *trusted* after that ye heard the word of truth, the gospel of your salvation: In whom also, after that ye believed, ye were sealed with that holy Spirit of promise.

13. But the blessing of being made the church of *Christ* being not intended to be *confined* to our *nation*, is now come to you *Gentiles* also; who, by your embracing the *gospel* religion, are put into the same capacity of salvation with *us*, and have it confirmed to you by your endowment with those very gifts and graces of the *Holy Spirit*, that were promised to the church of the Messiah.

14. For

---

* *Both which are in heaven, and which are on earth. Heaven and earth* are sometimes a *Jewish* phrase to express the *whole world*. But they seem in these epistles to the *Ephesians* and *Colossians*, with relation to Christ's government, to include the *angels* and *heavenly spirits* along with *mankind*. The phrases of *visible* and *invisible*, in Colos. i. 16. being hardly capable of any other sense; as likewise that of *thrones, principalities, and powers*. See also and compare chap. iii. 15. Col. i. 20. Phil. ii. 9.

A. D. 62.

14 Which is the earnest of our inheritance, until the redemption * of the purchased possession, unto the praise of his glory.

14. For those endowments conferred on your church, are a perfect earnest and *pledge*, that God has now redeemed and purchased you *Gentiles* for his † peculiar † people; and do assure you of the present and *future* * blessings of so noble a privilege; to the honour and praise of this his glorious dispensation.

† See Rom. viii. 23.

15 Wherefore I also, after I heard of your faith in the Lord Jesus, and love unto all the saints,

16 Cease not to give thanks for you, making mention of you in my prayers.

15. & 16. Wherefore, being thus assured of the gracious intent of God toward *you* as well as the *Jewish* nation, I no sooner heard of your steadiness to this *Christian* principle, ever since my first preaching to you, and that universal charity you bear towards all *Christian* brethren, without any partial regard to their being *circumcised* or not; but I blessed God for it, and am ever remembering you in all the prayers I offer up to him.

17 That the God of our Lord Jesus Christ, the Father of glory, may give unto you the Spirit of wisdom and revelation, in the knowledge of him.

17. Beseeching him, the glorious God and Father of our Lord Jesus Christ, to continue and increase upon you the gifts of his spirit, for your still more complete knowledge of Christ's religion, and your final adherence to the true doctrines of it.

18 The eyes of your understanding being enlightened; that ye may know what is the hope of his calling, and what the riches of the glory of his inheritance in the saints.

18. To enlarge your understandings, and give you a just and profound sense of the certainty and glorious advantages of your *Christian* profession.

19. And

* Ver. 14. Until the redemption of the purchased possession, εἰς ἀπολύτρωσιν τῆς περιποιήσεως. So as to make us [Gentiles] a redeemed possession.

A. D. 62.

19 And what is the exceeding greatneſs of his power to us-ward, who believe according to the working of his mighty power.

19. And of that great and Almighty power, by the demonſtrations whereof he at firſt converted you to, and by which he will conſtantly ſupport you in your *Chriſtian* faith; and will at laſt raiſe you up to the final and eternal rewards of it.

20 Which he wrought in Chriſt when he raiſed him from the dead, and ſet him at his own right hand in the heavenly *places*.

20. That Divine Power, I ſay, whereof he gave ſo wonderful and moſt evident an inſtance, in raiſing up Chriſt the head of his church, from the dead, and exalting him to the higheſt degree of majeſty and glory with him in heaven.

21 Far above all principality and power, and might, and dominion, and every name that is named, not only in this world, but alſo in that which is to come;

21. Inveſting him there with a dominion over all creatures, even over all dignities, offices, and powers, both of this and of the future world.

22 And hath put all things under his feet, and gave him to be head over all things to the church.

23 Which is his body, the fulneſs of him that filleth all in all.

22. & 23. Making him the glorious head over the whole church, as his body which is now to be fully perfected and completed by the cleareſt diſcoveries and moſt excellent privileges from him in whom dwelleth all fulneſs * and perfection.

CHAP.

---

* *The fulneſs of him that filleth all in all.* Much the ſame expreſſion with that of John i. 16. *Of his fulneſs have we all received* (fulneſs) and *grace for* (ἀντι, in proportion to his) *grace*. This is the ſenſe, if πληρωμα refers to Chriſt; but if it refers to the *church* (the ſubſtantive laſt mentioned) I have expreſſed that ſenſe alſo.

CHAP. II.

Having ſhown it to have been the original Purpoſe of God to unite the Gentiles to the Church of Chriſt; he declares the Epheſians to be actually Members of it. Gives them ſuch an Account of the Goſpel Privileges and Bleſſings, as exalts it far above, and makes it Independant of the Rites of the Moſaical Law. *He ſhows that Law to be aboliſhed by the Death and Religion of Chriſt, and thereby both Jew and Gentile united into one Church and Society. And all this for their Encouragement to adhere to the* Chriſtian *Faith, without liſtening to the Neceſſity of the* Moſaical *Ceremonies.*

1 AND you *hath he quickened* * who were dead in treſpaſſes and ſins.

1. BE aſſured, therefore, that God who raiſed up* Jeſus Chriſt from the dead, and made him the head of his church, has, by your converſion to Chriſtianity, raiſed * up you *Epheſians* to the hopes of pardon and ſalvation, who were formerly in a ſtate of ſin and death, under your vicious and heatheniſh life. A. D. 62.

2 Wherein in time paſt ye walked according to the courſe of this world, according to the prince of the power of the air, the ſpirit that now worketh in the children of diſobedience.

2. While you lived in the habitual practice of enormities that were common and faſhionable in the *heathen* world; influenced by the temptations of the devil, that powerful and malicious ſpirit, that has his reſidence in the air about us, and ſtill reigns by his influences on the wicked and unconverted *heathens*.

3 Among

3. Of

* I take the conſtruction of this verſe from the 20, 21, &c. verſes of the foregoing chapter, and not from the 19th, as ſome, nor the 5th verſe of this chapter, as other interpreters do. This makes the connection much clearer and leſs interrupted, and is confirmed by the ἐν χερσὶ, in the 5th verſe.

A. D. 62.

3 Among whom also we all had our conversation in times past, in the lusts of our flesh, fulfilling the desires of the flesh, and of the mind, and were by nature the children of wrath, even as others*.

3. Of which number *you* all were before your conversion; indulging your carnal and depraved appetites, and actuated by the dictates and passions of a sensual mind; being, like all other *heathen* people, brought up from your birth to the habits of such vile courses as could not but subject you to the wrath and displeasure of God.

4 But God who is rich in mercy, for his great love wherewith he loved us,

5 Even when we were dead in sins, hath quickened us together with Christ (by grace ye are saved).

4. & 5. But God in abundant mercy and compassion to his sinful creatures, has now, by the death and resurrection of Christ, and by your embracing his religion, recovered you † from this dark and sad estate, and raised you to the hope of pardon and salvation. It is *this religion* that justifies and saves you; the *ceremonial* law has no hand at all in it.

6 And hath raised *us* up together, and hath made *us* sit together in heavenly places in Christ Jesus.

6. For by raising *him* from the dead, God has given you, and all true *Gentile* believers, an assurance of all the noble privileges of his heavenly religion, and of all the blessings of his kingdom.

7 That in the ages to come he might show the exceeding riches of his grace, in his kindness towards us, through Christ Jesus.

7. It being the purpose of God thus to display the wonderful extent of divine love and mercy to all mankind, under the dispensation of Christ the *Messiah*.

8. & 9. And

---

* Ver. 3. *By nature;* Φυσει, either by *customs* and *habits* (of *Kice*); or else *really* and *indeed* children of wrath; as this word is plainly used, Gal. iv. 8. *By nature no gods*, i. e. not gods *at all*.

† Wherewith he loved *us*, hath quickened *us*. See note on chap. i. 3, 4.

A. D. 62.

8 For by grace are ye ſaved, through faith, and that not of yourſelves: *it is* the gift of God:

9 Not of works, leſt any man ſhould boaſt.

8. & 9. And certainly this *goſpel* ſalvation is the fruit of nothing but the pure grace and bounty of God, making our faith in Chriſt's religion the merciful condition of this happineſs. No man has done any thing to deſerve it; it could not be merited by the utmoſt obſervation of the *ceremonial* law, and ſo * the *Jew* could no more pretend to claim it than the vileſt *Gentile*.

10 For we are his workmanſhip, created in Chriſt Jeſus unto good works, which God hath before ordained that we ſhould walk in them.

10. Our regenerate ſtate is wholly owing to what God has done for us in Chriſt, and by his *religion*. By *this* it was his deſign to prepare and enable us to live that life of purity and virtue that will qualify us for life eternal.

11 Wherefore remember that ye *being* in times paſt Gentiles in the fleſh, who are called uncircumciſion by that which is called the circumciſion in the fleſh, made by hands.

12 That at that time ye were without Chriſt, being aliens from the commonwealth of Iſrael, and ſtrangers from the covenants of promiſe, having no hope, and without God in the world.

13 But now in Chriſt Jeſus, ye who ſometimes were afar off, are made nigh by the blood of Chriſt.

11, 12. & 13. Remember then, and ſtand to it; that though you *Gentiles* were formerly quite out of the pale of God's church, without any knowledge of the Meſſiah promiſed to Abraham as the Saviour of all mankind, having little or no proſpect of ſpiritual and future happineſs, eſtranged from the knowledge and worſhip of the true God; in fine, *you* whom the *Jewiſh* people, that boaſted themſelves in their divine laws and privileges, were wont in deriſion, to call *uncircumciſed*, *unclean* and *ſinful*, are now, by Chriſt's religion, taken into covenant with him, and are his peculiar people as much as *they*.

 14. While

* Leſt any man ſhould boaſt, ἵνα μή τις καυχήσηται. So that none can boaſt.

A.D. 62.

14 For he is our peace, who hath made both one, and hath broken down the middle wall of partition between us.

14. While *they* were his enclosed church, you *Gentiles* were kept at a distance; and indeed were no way reconcileable to their ceremonies and worship. But now that Christ by his death hath reconciled us *all* to God, the difference is at an end, and we are *all* united into one church and society.

15 Having abolished in his flesh the enmity, *even* the law of commandments, *contained* in ordinances, for to make in himself, of twain, one new man, so making peace.

16 And that he might reconcile both unto God in one body by the cross, having slain the enmity thereby:

15. & 16. For that part of the *Jewish* law that consisted of such ceremonies as were designed to keep up the distinction between them and all other nations, is now, by the death of Christ upon the cross, abolished and become of no further obligation; whereby he has made the way open for believers of *all* nations to join with them, and make up *one Christian* church under him, the common head and Saviour of us all.

17 And came, and preached peace to you *which were* afar off, and to them that were nigh.

17. And accordingly Christ has appointed his gospel to be preached, as the condition of peace and pardon, as well to the *Gentiles* that were hitherto strangers to his church, as to the *Jews* that had been his ancient people.

18 For through him we both have an access by one Spirit unto the Father.

18. For by the sacrifice of his death, all true believers of every nation are admitted into favour with God the Father and become his true people, all conducted by the same holy Spirit, without any further regard to the *Jewish* law.

19 Now therefore ye are no more strangers and foreigners, but fellow-citizens with the saints, and of the household of God:

19. Wherefore look upon yourselves as no longer excluded from the divine covenant, nor as only in part proselytes to it, because of your not being *circumcised;* but esteem yourselves as *fully* privileged, and as *much* of God's family as *they* can be.

20. Be-

A. D. 62.

20 And are built upon the foundation of the apostles and prophets, Jesus Christ himself being the chief corner-stone.

20. Believe, for certain, you are members of that church of the *Messiah* which is built upon the truth of all the prophecies of the *Old*, and the apostolical doctrines of the *New Testament;* Jesus Christ himself being the head of this body, and as it were the chief corner-stone of this fabric, holding and cementing the two sides of *Jewish* and *Gentile* believers together.

21 In whom all the building fitly framed together, groweth unto an holy temple in the Lord.

21. Under whose divine conduct and influence, all the members of this *Christian* society, like the stones of a material building, are so to unite and increase, as to become the temple and habitation of God.

22 In whom you also are builded together for an habitation of God through the Spirit.

22. You *Gentile* Christians of *Ephesus* being now a part of this glorious fabric as well as the *Jews:* And as God was formerly said to dwell in the *Jewish* tabernacle and temple, by the manifestations of himself there to that people; so may he now, in a much higher and happier sense, be said to *dwell in you,* by the gifts and graces of his holy *Spirit* conferred on you.

CHAP. III.

The same Assurances, viz. *That the Gentiles are received into the Church of Christ, continued. He owns and professeth himself the* Gentile Apostle, *commissioned on purpose to preach the Gospel to them. The calling of the Gentile World, a Doctrine not allowed of by the* Jews, *nor discovered to the* Gentiles *themselves in former Ages, but now clearly revealed to have been always the Purpose of God; and in this respect is styled a* Mystery. *He exhorts them to rejoice in, rather than be discouraged at, his imprisonment and sufferings for this Doctrine. Prays for their confirmation and Progress in the Christian Faith, and blesseth* God *for his extended Mercies to Mankind.*

A. D. 62. 1 FOR this cause, I Paul, the prisoner of Jesus Christ for you Gentiles.

1. FOR preaching this very doctrine, viz. That you *Gentiles* are now received into all the privileges of the Christian church, as well as the *Jews*, am * I Paul, now a prisoner at Rome, prosecuted by the malice of that † people, and to be tried for my life.

2 If ye have heard of the dispensation of the grace f God, which is given me to you ward:

3 How

2. & 3. Nor can you doubt but I am a prisoner for *your* sakes, since ‡ you know my divine commission by an express revelation from

* [I Paul, a prisoner;] i. e. either [am now a prisoner], (as I have ventured to connect it with the 2d and 3d verses); or else [the prisoner], and then most probably all the following verses of this chapter are one continued parenthesis, to the first verse of the 4th chapter, where the apostle resumes his exhortation again in the very same words.

† See Acts xxii. 21, 22. xxvi. 19, 20, 21. xxviii. 17. 20.

‡ If ye have heard; εἴγε ἠκούσατε, Since ye have heard. See Dr. Mill, Prolegom. § 72, 73, &c.

A. D. 62.

3 How that by revelation he made known unto me the myſtery (as I wrote afore in few words,

from God, runs chiefly upon this very thing, to authoriſe me to declare this unthought-of mercy to you; as I briefly explained it to you before, (chap. i. 9, 10).

4 Whereby when ye read ye may underſtand my knowledge in the myſtery of Chriſt),

4. By reading and conſidering whereof, as I there did, and ſhall now give a further account of it; you may clearly underſtand that gracious and ſurpriſing purpoſe of God ſo little expected by the world.

5 Which in other ages was not made known unto the ſons of men, as it is now revealed unto his holy apoſtles and prophets by the Spirit;

6 That the Gentiles ſhould be fellow heirs, and of the ſame body, and partakers of his promiſe in Chriſt by the goſpel:

5. & 6. Viz. That though the *heathen* nations had it not expreſsly declared to *them* in former ages, nor could the *Jews* be brought to apprehend it from the predictions of their prophets; yet it was now clearly revealed and *abſolutely* declared to the inſpired apoſtles of Jeſus Chriſt, that the *Gentiles* ſhould be taken into all the bleſſings of the Chriſtian covenant, and be united to the *Jews* to make up *one church* under the Meſſiah.

7 Whereof I was made a miniſter, according to the gift of the grace of God given unto me, by the effectual working of his power.

7. Of which great and merciful diſpenſation God has made *me* a miniſter, and qualified me for preaching and demonſtrating the truth of it, by the powers of his holy Spirit conferred on me.

8 Unto me, who am leſs than the leaſt of all ſaints, is this grace given, that I ſhould preach among the Gentiles the unſearchable riches of Chriſt.

8. I, who for my former immoderate and furious zeal againſt this very religion, can never ſufficiently humble myſelf, have now the favour to be made an *apoſtle*, to declare this amazing and extenſive love of God by Jeſus Chriſt toward the *Gentile* world.

A. D. 62.

9 And to make all men see what is the fellowship of the mystery, which from the beginning of the world hath been hid in God, who created all things by Jesus Christ.

9. To show both *Jew* and *Gentile* the exceeding great blessings they are now to enjoy, by being united into one church under Christ: a thing that God, who created and governs the world, and all the dispensations of it by *him*, thought not fit so manifestly to reveal to former ages, as he has now done.

10 To the intent that now unto the * principalities and powers in heavenly places, might be known by the church the manifold wisdom of God,

11 According to the eternal purpose which he purposed in Christ Jesus our Lord:

10. & 11. Now that he intends not only to convince the governors and magistrates of this world, who have opposed and persecuted this religion, but to display to all ranks and degrees of creatures, both in heaven * and earth, this manifold wisdom in the wondrous management of his church; so agreeably to the former † dispensations of it; all which were always directed and disposed, but now fully completed by Jesus Christ.

12 In whom we have boldness and access with confidence by the faith of him.

12. Through whose mediation for us, but *Jew* and *Gentile*, that embrace his religion, are accepted of God as his true church and people; and may address to him with full assurance of being rewarded as his true worshippers.

13 Wherefore I desire that ye faint not at my tribulations for you, which is your glory.

13. Wherefore since I am now under persecution for delivering a doctrine so much to the benefit of you *Gentile* Christians: Be not disheartened or affrighted at *my* sufferings;

14 For

---

* To the principalities and powers in heavenly places. See the Note on chap. i. 10.

† [According to the eternal purpose]. Κατὰ πρόθεσιν τῶν αἰώνων; [agreeably to the predisposition of former ages, or dispensations of religion]. Thus the Saviour was promised to Adam, then to Abraham, afterwards typified and represented to the *Jews*, and at last, *fully* and openly *preached* to all the *world*.

ings; but rather rejoice at them, as an argument of the sincerity and truth of this doctrine; and let it raise your hearts and strengthen your resolutions. A. D. 62.

14 For this cause I bow my knees unto the Father of our Lord Jesus Christ.

15 Of whom the whole family in heaven and earth is named;

14. & 15. To which end I humbly and earnestly beg of God the Father, the Supreme Lord and Governor of the whole church in heaven * and earth, uniting both angels and men under his government;

16 That he would grant you according to the riches of his glory, to be strengthened with might, by his Spirit in the inner man:

16. That out of the infinite fulness of divine goodness and mercy, he would confirm your minds by the influence of his Holy Spirit.

17 That Christ may dwell in your hearts by faith; that ye being rooted and grounded in love,

18 May be able to comprehend with all saints what is the breadth and length, and depth and height:

19 And to know the love of Christ, which passeth knowledge, that ye might be filled † with all the fulness of God.

17. 18. & 19. That so, by a due and profound sense of the inexpressible bounty of this dispensation of Christ toward you Gentiles, you and all Christian people may render him all unfeigned returns of love, gratitude and obedience, by an unshaken and firm adherence to his religion; abounding in all the divine † gifts and spiritual graces belonging to it.

20 Now unto him that is able to do exceeding abundantly above all that we ask or think, according to the power that worketh in us,

21 Unto him be glory in the church by Christ Jesus, throughout all ages, world without end. Amen.

20. & 21. To him therefore who has already conferred such spiritual endowments on you, and is both able and willing to encourage your improvement of them, by giving you still more than you can wish or imagine for yourselves, be ascribed, by all succeeding ages of the church, all honour and glory, through Jesus Christ, for evermore. Amen.

* [Family of heaven and earth.] See the Note on chap. i. 10.

† [With all the fulness of God.] See the Note on 2 Cor. viii. 1.

CHAP. IV.

The Apostle having thus given the Gentile *Christians of* Ephesus *all suitable encouragement to continue in. and firmly to rely upon. the* Christian *Faith, without the Observation of the* Jewish *Law; comes now to exhort their whole Church in general to the Practice of such Duties as become their holy Profession, especially that of Unity, Mutual Charity, and Forbearance; adviseth both the* Jewish *and* Gentile *converts to consider themselves as all united into the same Church and Privileges in Christ, without distinction; warning the gifted* Teachers *of both parties to a sober and uniform Improvement of their gifts and offices; by showing them to be all derived from the same Spirit, and intended for the same religious purposes. Then turns his Exhortation to the Gentile Part, showing them their Obligation to renounce all their former* Heathenish *Practices, and live up to the Purity of the* Gospel *Religion. Pointing out to them several of the most notorious Vices to which they had formerly been subject.*

A. D. 62. 1 I Therefore the prisoner * of the Lord, beseech you, that ye walk worthy of the vocation wherewith ye are called,

1. THUS have I that am now a * prisoner for Christ's sake, and particularly for upholding you Gentile Christians to be his true church, without your observance of the *Mosaical ceremonies*, given you full encouragement to maintain that privilege. And let me now by these chains I wear, beseech all parties among you to live worthy the excellency of their holy profession.

2. & 3. Taking

* [I therefore, the prisoner of the Lord:] See Note on chap. iii. ver. 1.

A. D. 62.

2 With all lowliness and meekness, with long-suffering, forbearing one another in love:

3 Endeavouring to keep the unity of the spirit in the bond of peace.

2. & 3. Taking special care to preserve the peace and unity of the church by a gentle, meek, and forbearing behaviour to each other, agreeably to the spirit of the gospel.

4 *There is* one body and one spirit, even as ye are called in one hope of your calling.

5 One Lord, one faith, one baptism.

6 One God and Father of all, who is above all, and through all, and in you all.

4, 5. & 6. Duly considering, that both *Jewish* and *Gentile* believers are now joined together in one Christian *society*, enlightened and endowed with the same *spirit*, and brought into the same common hope of *salvation*; having the same Christ for your Saviour and *Head*, into whose faith you are *all* alike *baptized*; and are become the church and servants of the same God the *Father*, who is equally over you all by his *power*, conducts you all by the same good *Providence*, and dwells in you all by the same *Holy Spirit*.

7 But unto every one of us is given * grace, according to the measure of the gift of Christ.

7. But you ought to remember, That though you all belong to the same Christian *church*, the body of Christ; yet the *gifts* and graces of the *Spirit* may not be distributed to every member or *minister* alike; but to each of them in such measures as Christ knows them best able to improve for the church's benefit. So that none ought to be dissatisfied with his *own*, or to undervalue those of *another*.

8 Wherefore he saith, When he ascended up on high, he led captivity captive, and gave gifts unto men.

8. These spiritual *gifts* to the *Christian* church, and the *variety* of them too, are represented in those prophetic words of the Psalmist (Psal. lxviii. 18.), *Resembling Christ the Messiah in his ascension*

9 (Now

* *Grace* χάρις, either *gifts* and *endowments* for an *office* in the ministry, or the *office* itself.

A. D. 62. *ascension into heaven, after the conquest of sin, Satan, and death, to an earthly* monarch in triumph after victory, *scattering gifts and largesses to his people.*

9 (Now that he ascended, what is it but that he also descended first into the lower parts of the earth?

10 He that descended, is the same also that ascended up far above all heavens, that he might fill all things.)

9. & 10. (But whatever degrees they are given in to any of you, they all come from this triumphant Saviour, the very same Jesus who came down upon earth, died and was buried, to obtain this conquest, and then rose again, and was exalted to the highest degree of heavenly glory and majesty, to become the Lord of the whole church of God, to perfect and complete it, and to guide and model it by such measures as he in wisdom should think fit*.)

11 And he gave some apostles; and some prophets; and some evangelists; and some pastors and teachers;

11. And accordingly he fulfilled that prediction by this *variety** of endowments on the ministers of the Christian church; qualifying some to be apostles, *to declare the doctrines of it first to the world;* others to be prophets, to explain the *passages of the Old Testament, relating to, and confirming that doctrine;* others to be evangelists, to spread it to farther *distant nations, and record it in writing;* and some to be pastors and teachers, *to build men up in the knowledge of it, after they have embraced it* †.

12 For the perfecting of the saints, for the work of the ministry, for the edifying of the body of Christ.

12. Which *variety* of gifts and offices, is so far from being a disadvantage from the excellency of one above another, that it is the very thing intended to knit and compact the Christian members into a more firm and perfect society; to render the discharge of the Christian ministry more orderly and effectual;

---

* I see no connection in these two verses with the foreing and following clauses, but by making them refer to the *variety* of gifts, and their being derived all from Christ. And the connection is best preserved, by including them in a parenthesis.

† See 1 Cor. xii. for the same expressions and argument more at large.

effectual; contributing, in their places and stations, to the better edification of the whole church. A. D. 62.

13 Till we all come in the unity of the faith, and of the knowledge of the Son of God, unto a perfect man, unto the measure of the stature of the fulness of Christ:

13. God so wisely providing, that each member should by this means be trained up to perfect Christianity; and the whole become a complete body under him the common *head* of all.

14 That we henceforth be no more children tossed to and fro, and carried about with every wind of doctrine by the slight of men, and cunning craftiness, whereby they lie in wait to deceive:

14. That, by arriving at this perfection of Christian faith and knowledge, they may be above the influences and stratagems of cunning and deceitful teachers; and not, like children, give ear to every plausible doctrine that is proposed to them.

15 But speaking the truth in love, may grow up into him in all things, which is the head, *even* Christ:

16 From whom the whole body fitly joined together, and compacted by that which every joint supplieth, according to the effectual working in the measure of every part, make the increase of the body, unto the edifying of itself in love.

15. & 16. But that, as the human body is composed of different joints and members, all in their several functions tending to nourish and keep up the whole frame; so, by this variety of spiritual gifts and offices in the church, Christians may grow up into one complete society under Christ their head, unanimously agreeing in the same rule of faith towards God, and conspiring in the same mutual affections to each other.

17 This I say therefore, and testify in the Lord, that ye henceforth walk not as other Gentiles walk in the vanity of their mind,

17. I must again particularly warn you *Gentile* Christians, how much it concerns, and is expected from you, entirely to renounce all the vile practices and idolatrous worship of the *Heathen* world.

18 Having the understanding darkened, being alienated from the

18. Who still remain in that perfect state of ignorance and irreligion which *you* have solemnly forsaken,

A. D. 62. the life of God, through the ignorance that is in them, because of the blindness of their heart:

forsaken, utterly estranged from that virtuous course of life that alone can render men like to God, and happy in his service.

19 Who being past feeling, have given themselves over unto lasciviousness, to work all uncleanness with greediness.

19. And, by impure and unreformed habits, are become so insensible of all goodness, as to commit the worst degrees of uncleanness, not only without all regret and reluctancy, but with the utmost eagerness and delight.

20 But ye have not so learned Christ:

21 * If so be that ye have heard him, and have been taught by him, as the truth is in Jesus:

20. & 21. Remember, that by your * conversion to the Christian religion, you are in quite another state; and obliged by the highest engagements to a direct contrary course of life.

22 That ye put off concerning the former conversation, the old man, which is corrupt according to the deceitful lusts:

23 And be renewed in the spirit of your mind:

24 And that ye put on the new man, which after God is created in righteousness and true holiness.

22, 23. & 24. Namely, to forsake all your old heathenish lusts, and ignorant practices; and to become new and reformed men, by obedience to those holy and righteous laws prescribed in the *gospel*, that will raise you to the imitation of God, and render you his true and happy children.

25 Wherefore putting away lying, speak every man truth with his neighbour: for we are members one of another.

25. Beware then of those vices you have been formerly most subject to, and are most opposite to the *Christian* spirit: for instance, detest that dangerous sin of *lying*, deceiving and over-reaching your neighbours; remembering you are all now members of the same Christian body; so that to deceive another is to injure and abuse *yourselves*.

26. & 27.

---

* If so be ye have heard him—εἴγε αὐτὸν ἠκούσατε. Since you have heard him.

A. D 62.

26 Be ye angry and ſin not: let not the ſun go down upon your wrath.

27 Neither give place to the * devil.

26. & 27. Suppreſs all immoderate anger and reſentment: ſuffer it not to ripen into revenge, reproach, and ſlander; for then you are overcome by that wicked adverſary the *devil* whoſe very *name* ſignifies a *railer* and a *blaſphemer* *.

28 Let him that ſtole, ſteal no more §: but rather let him labour, working with *his* hands the thing which is good, that he may have to give to him that needeth.

28. Whoever has been accuſtomed to *ſteal*, before his converſion, and to eſteem it but a ſmall, or ſcarce any ſin §; muſt now abhor that practice, and by a laborious life in ſome honeſt calling, muſt endeavour not only to ſupply his own wants, but if he can, to have ſomething to ſpare for them that are in abſolute poverty.

29 Let no corrupt communication proceed out of your mouth, but that which is good to the uſe of edifying; that it may miniſter grace unto the hearers.

29. Avoid all manner of ſcurrilous and filthy converſation; and let your words and diſcourſes in company be always ſuch, as may not only be heard by any body with innocence and decency, but, as far as you can, with profit and advantage too; by promoting thoſe virtues that will procure favour and acceptance from God.

30 And grieve not the holy Spirit of God, whereby you are ſealed

30. In fine, do and ſay nothing that maybe inconſiſtent with thoſe bleſſed endowments of the Holy Spirit

---

* Διάβολος, [Devil.] Ver. 27. Neither give place to the devil. *or to the* railer *and* ſlanderer:] And the ſenſe may be, [Give no occaſion to ſlanderers to reproach your holy religion]; as Eraſmus and the French Proteſtant tranſlation render it. See 1 Tim. iii. 6, 7. [give place, τοπον, opportunity. *or* advantage.]

§ As in ſeveral nations it was accounted; and rather countenanced than diſcouraged, by ſome *Grecian* commonwealths; particularly in that of the Lacedemonians, where Plutarch ſays, it was enacted or agreed, [νενόμιστο] κλέπτειν τοὺς ἐλευθέρους παῖδας ὅ, τι τις δύναιτο. [That the free-born youths might ſteal whatever they could.] But of this let the reader ſee Dr. Clarke's Evidences of Natural and Revealed Re-

A. D. 62. ed unto the day of redemption.

Spirit that are conferred on you, or may deprive you of his sacred influences; which are the pledges of your present pardon, and the earnest of your eternal happiness.

31 Let all bitterness, and wrath, and anger, and clamour, and evil-speaking, be put away from you, with all malice.

31. And as he is the Spirit of *peace* and *love*, so let no differences in your religious sentiments and opinions, suffer you to launch out into any expressions of bitterness, rage, and clamorous reproaches, nor to harbour any purposes of malice and revenge.

32 And be ye kind one to another, tender hearted, forgiving one another, even as God for Christ's sake hath forgiven you.

32. But treat one another, even those that injure you, with tenderness, pity and forgiveness; remembering how much a greater debt of guilt and sin God has forgiven us all for the sake of Christ Jesus.

CHAP. V.

The first and second verses conclude the Exhortation to Love and Unanimity in the End of the foregoing Chapter. Then he repeats his caution against their former Heathenish Vices, particularly such as accompanied their Idolatrous Worship. Descends to the Relative *Duties, wherein the* Jewish *Christians, by former Prejudices, were apt to be deficient.* See the Preface to this Epistle, § 4.

1 BE ye therefore followers of God as dear children.

1. SINCE, therefore, you are all, both *Jewish* and *Gentile* converts, become the children and church of God, imitate *him* as your true Father and most perfect example.

2. And

A. D. 62.

2 And walk in love, as Christ also hath loved us, and hath given himself for us, an offering and a sacrifice to God for a sweet smelling savour.

2. And as the death and sacrifice of Christ for our sins was the highest instance of Divine love and mercy to us *all*, and an act most pleasing and acceptable to God; let it be the chief care of all parties among you to resemble this great pattern of love, by charity and unity with each other.

3 But fornication, and all uncleanness, or covetousness, let it not be once named amongst you, as becometh saints.

3. I must again especially warn you *Gentile* Christians from all those extravagant and lustful passions, and unclean practices, that were so common and fashionable in your heathen state; and are still the attendants of idolatrous rites and worship. Let none of them be so much as named or heard of among *Christian* professors.

4 Neither filthiness, nor foolish talking, nor jesting, * which are not convenient: but rather giving of thanks.

4. And be as careful to avoid all that scurrilous, lewd and light way of talking, that is the usual * incentive to such unclean actions. Break it entirely off by accustoming your mouths to continual expressions of praise and thanksgiving to God.

5 For this you know, that no whoremonger, nor unclean person, nor covetous man †, who is an idolater, hath any inheritance in the kingdom of Christ, and of God.

5. For you cannot but know, by the natural design of the *Christian* religion, that no person addicted to such impure affections and practices as † are indulged in *idolatrous* and superstitious worship, can ever be a true member of the church of Christ here, or inherit his kingdom hereafter.

6 Let

6. & 7. Let

---

* [Which are not convenient—] τὰ μὴ ἀνήκοντα, [That are most disagreeable] See Rom. i. 28. where τὰ μὴ καθήκοντα, ought so to be translated.

† [Or covetous man who is an idolater,] ἢ πλεονέκτης ὅς ἐστιν εἰδωλολάτρης, *i. e.* [One that may be called an idolater *for* making his lusts and pleasures his *god; or else* a man of such inordinate desires, as an idolater is and must be.] The former is indeed *good sense*; but the *latter* is plainly most agreeable to the apostle's design.

A. D. 62.

6 Let no man deceive you with vain words: for because of these things cometh the wrath of God upon the children of disobedience.

|| Rom. i. 26, &c.

7 Be not ye therefore partakers with them.

6. & 7. Let no philosophers, therefore, persuade you by any arts of reasoning, that such practices can be any way innocent or allowable. They are the very things for which God gave up the heathens to vile || affections, and ever did, and do still, draw divine vengeance upon them that will not renounce and reform them.

8 For ye were sometimes darkness, but now *are ye* light in the Lord: walk as children of light,

8. In your dark and heathen state, it was indeed no wonder you should be guilty of them; but your *Christian* religion has so clearly instructed and better enlightened you, that you must live in a quite contrary course.

9 (For the fruit of the Spirit *is* in all goodness, and righteousness, and truth)

9. (For the practice of all moral and divine virtues, ought to be the proper effect of your conversion to that pure religion that is attended with such gifts and influences of the Holy Spirit.

10 Proving what is acceptable unto the Lord.

10. These virtues you must study and practise, as things most agreeable to the Divine Will, and by the habitual practice whereof alone you can approve yourselves to God.

11 And have no fellowship with the ‡ unfruitful works of dark-

11. Never therefore be drawn into those dangerous ‡ practices that none but ignorant heathens would commit;

‡ The *unfruitful* works of darkness. Ἀκάρποις here cannot signify merely *unprofitable*, but *mischievous*; in the same manner as τὰ μὴ καθήκοντα, signify most *abominable* things, Rom. i. 28. as I have noted there. And thus ἄκαρπος exactly answers to *inutilis*, which signifies *mischievous*, in the best Latin authors. Thus Cicero, [Potest enim accedere promissum aliquod et conventum, ut id effici sit *inutile*, vel ei cui promissum sit, vel ei qui promiserit. *De Offic. lib. I.*] And again, [Nec promissa igitur servanda sunt ea, quæ sunt iis, quibus promisseris, *inutilia*. Ibid.] The learned reader may see abundant instances of this in the learned Dr. Clarke's Note on Hom. Iliad 2. p. 53.

A. D. 62.

darkneſs, but rather reprove them.

commit; but on the contrary, endeavour to expoſe their indecency, and make them aſhamed of them.

12 For it is a ſhame even to ſpeak of thoſe things which are done of them in ſecret.

12. For certainly it would ſhock the modeſty of a good man, even to mention the abundance and filthy actions committed in the ſecret *myſteries* of *heathen* worſhip.

13 But all things that are reproved, are made manifeſt by the light: for whatſoever doth make manifeſt, is light.

13. But as light is the thing that renders every object clearly viſible to the eye; ſo has the Chriſtian religon demonſtrated the vileneſs and danger of theſe practices to the minds of all that embrace it.

14 Wherefore he ſaith, Awake thou that ſleepeſt, and ariſe from the dead, and Chriſt ſhall give thee light.

14. And accordingly the prophet Iſaiah (Iſa. lx. 1.) has expreſſed the happy condition of the *Gentile* part of the *Chriſtian church*. *Ariſe, ſhine, for thy light is come, and the glory of the Lord is riſen upon thee.* And again, *Awake and ſing ye that dwell in the duſt*, Iſa. xxvi. 19. Signifying *the former dark and ignorant ſtate of the heathen world, and the glorious light and knowledge it ſhould attain to by the religion of Chriſt the Meſſiah; and their great obligation to live ſuitably to the advantages of it.*

15 See then that ye walk circumſpectly, not as fools, but as wiſe,

16 Redeeming the time, becauſe the days are evil.

15. & 16 Conſidering therefore how contrary the religion you have embraced is to that of the reſt of mankind, and what violent oppoſition you are like to meet with; you muſt have a prudential eye to that too, and manage yourſelves not only with *innocency* but *diſcretion;* not expoſing yourſelves to perſecution upon needleſs occaſions; but while you endeavour to convert men, you ought to avoid their fury by all lawful and juſt means.

17 Wherefore be ye not unwiſe, but underſtanding what the will of the Lord is.

17. Remember therefore, that though it be the will of God you ſhould firmly adhere to your Chriſtian principles, and labour to bring others

A. D. 62. others over to them; yet it is none of his will that you should indiscreetly lay yourselves open to their obstinate malice and rage; but only propose the divine truths to them in so prudent a manner, as may best work upon *them*, and secure your own *lives*.

18 And be not drunk with wine, wherein is excess: but be filled with the Spirit:

18. But to proceed concerning the particular vices I was warning you from: To preserve yourselves from the impurities of heathen worship, be sure to shun that excess of *drinking* so usual in their idolatrous festivals; the incentive to all lust and extravagancy. And instead of the beastly custom of filling yourselves with *wine*, endeavour by a habit of temperance and sober conversation, to be full of the gracious gifts and influences of the Holy Spirit.

19 Speaking to yourselves in psalms and hymns, and spiritual songs, singing and making melody in your heart to the Lord;

20 Giving thanks always for all things unto God and the Father, in the name of the Lord Jesus Christ;

|| See 1 Cor. xi. Coloss. iii. 16.

19. & 20. Which will inspire you in your religious || assemblies to praise and bless God in divine psalms and hymns: and, contrary to their extravagant and lewd merriments, will render all your mirth truly spiritual and religious: exalting your minds to grateful and pious expressions of thanksgiving to God the Father, through Jesus Christ, for all his mercies towards you.

21 Submitting yourselves one to another in the fear of God.

21. And these divine influences will conduct you in a regular submission of inferiors to superiors, both in public and private, and in all relative duties to each other.

22 Wives *, submit yourselves unto your own husbands, as unto the Lord.

22. Such as is that, for instance, between *husband* and *wife*, which the *Jewish* zealots are apt to think they may be excused in, where there is a disagreement in *religious* * principles. Whereas, the due

* For the *occasion* and *design* of St. Paul's advice in this and the following relative duties, let the reader see the preface to this epistle, § 4.

due ſubjection of a *wife* to her *huſband* (notwithſtanding any difference in religious opinions between them) is not only the plain will of Chriſt, but is illuſtrated and enforced by the conſtitution of his *church*. A. D. 62.

23 For the huſband is the head of the wife, even as Chriſt is the head of the church: and he is the Saviour of the body.

23. For as Chriſt is the Saviour, head and governor of the whole *church*, as his ſpiritual *body*, ſo is *every huſband* the head and guardian || of his *wiſe*.

|| So in 1 Cor. xi.

24 Therefore as the church is ſubject unto Chriſt, ſo *let* the wives *be* to their own huſbands in every thing.

25. And therefore as the church pays all due ſubjection to Chriſt its *ſpiritual head*, ſo the natural relation of a *wife*, according to the firſt ſolemn inſtitution of marriage, requires a juſt ſubmiſſion and obſervance from her to her *huſband*.

25 Huſbands, love your wives, even as Chriſt alſo loved the church, and gave himſelf for it:

26 That he might ſanctify and cleanſe it with the waſhing of water by the word,

27 That he might preſent it to himſelf a glorious church, not having ſpot or wrinkle, or any ſuch thing: but that it ſhould be holy and without blemiſh.

25. 26. & 27. On the other ſide, this compariſon will as clearly ſhow and highly recommend that *love* and *tenderneſs* that *huſbands* ought to expreſs to their *wives*. For as nothing can be ſo lively and perfect an example of love, care and tenderneſs, as that wherewith Chriſt treats the *church*, his ſpouſe, cleanſing and purifying all its members from the guilt of ſin, by baptiſing them into his holy and pure profeſſion; and by his word and Holy Spirit training them up to ſuch unblemiſhed holineſs of life here upon earth, as will terminate in the perfection of virtue, glory and happineſs in heaven.

28 So ought men to love their wives, as their own bodies: he that loveth his wife, loveth himſelf.

29 For no man ever yet hated his own fleſh;

28. & 29. So does this his tender regard to us, as the dear members of his own ſpiritual body, ſhow every *huſband* to treat his *wiſe* as a ſecond *ſelf*; convincing him by the dictates of *ſelf-love*, to

A. D. 62. flesh; but nourisheth and cherisheth it, even as the Lord the church.

to be kind and gentle towards her, and how unnatural it would be to do otherwise.

30 For we are members of his body, of his flesh, and of his bones.

30. Thus close and dear is the union of Christ with his *church*, and of the *husband* with the *wife*, that they may be respectively considered as head and members of one and the same body.

31 For this cause shall a man leave his father and mother, and shall be joined unto his wife, and they two shall be one flesh.

31. And accordingly you know, when Eve was produced from Adam's rib, and given him for a *wife* (Gen. ii. 22.) it was expressly said, *That the relation between them was nearer and dearer than that of parents and children.*

32 This is a great mystery: but I speak concerning Christ and the church.

32. And thus have I, by this most noble and lively * comparison of Christ and his *church*, illustrated and recommended to you the great duty of *husbands* and *wives*. But indeed my *chief* design was to show you the happy union between Christ and his *church*.

33 Nevertheless, let every one of you in particular, so love his wife, even as himself, and

33. But whether I had made use of this *mystical* way of *illustration* or no, the very original institution of *marriage*, and the plain will of Christ

* [This is a great mystery.] The generality of interpreters understand St. Paul here, as if the marriage of Adam and Eve were intended by the Holy Spirit to represent, and mystically to signify the spiritual union between the Messiah and the *Christian church*. The *Jewish* doctors, indeed, are full of this. But because no other undoubted expressions of scripture are found to demonstrate the thing itself to be *true*, and it not being clear these traditional doctrines of the rabbins were as early as our Saviour's or St. Paul's time, I have therefore expressed it as a *comparison* for *illustration*; and whether the great latitude in which St. Paul uses this word *mystery* will not warrant my so doing, I submit to the judgment of the learned and attentive reader. See Revelat. i. 20. with my Paraph. there.

and the wife *see* that she reverence her husband.

Christ in the gospel religion, is sufficient to convince them of the obligation to love and tenderness on the one part, and to respect and subjection on the other; and that no differences in *religious principles* can excuse either from so evident a moral duty. A. D. 62.

CHAP. VI.

He proceeds in showing the Christian obligation to the other relative Duties of Parents *and* Children, Masters *and* Slaves: *Then encourages them to general Constancy and Resolution against all Temptations and Persecutions for the sake of Christianity: and, by Metaphors taken from the Arts of* Grecian *and* Roman *Soldiery, directs them how to arm themselves against the Assaults of them. Desires their prayers for him, as their* Gentile *Apostle, and concludes with his Blessing.*

1 CHildren, obey your parents in the Lord: for this is right.

1. TO proceed in these relative duties. The same Christian principle that ought to induce *husbands* and *wives* to their reciprocal duties, notwithstanding any differences in religious notions *, obliges all *children* and *young* people to pay all just reverence to their *parents*, and not think themselves exempt from it *to either* * of them upon that account.

2 Honour thy father and thy mother, (which is the first commandment with promise)

3 That

2. & 3. Let them remember, that duty to parents is of so natural and important obligation, that God was pleased in the fifth commandment to his ancient people the Jews,

* See the Pref. to this Epistle, § 4.

A.D. 62.

3 That it may be well with thee, and thou mayest live long on the earth.

Jews to *add the special promise of temporal prosperity and long life in the land of Canaan, for their greater encouragement to it.*

4 And *ye* fathers, * provoke not your children to wrath: but bring them up in the nurture and admonition of the Lord.

4. And let all *Christian* parents be particularly careful to treat their children with such mild and gentle usage as may more easily induce them to believe and embrace the *Christian religion;* and not * prejudice them against it, by their froward and ill example.

5 Servants, be ‡ obedient to them that are your masters according to the flesh, with fear and trembling, in singleness of your heart, as unto Christ:

5. Let such Christians as are *slaves* to heathen *masters,* not think themselves disengaged from their civil obligation by being Christians ‡, but continue to serve them sincerely and industriously, as their *Christian* duty.

6 Not with eye-service, as men pleasers, but as the servants of Christ, doing the will of God from the heart;

7 With good will doing service, as to the Lord, and not to men:

6. & 7. Let them do it sincerely, I say, and not barely in such a manner as to escape their master's observation and punishment; but conscientiously seek their interest, knowing, that in serving them *faithfully,* they serve Jesus Christ their Supreme Lord and Master.

8 Knowing that whatsoever good thing any man doth, the same shall he receive of the Lord, whether he be bond or free.

8. And being fully assured, that Christ will hereafter as impartially and fully reward the diligent services of a *slave,* as the most generous actions of a *freeman.*

---

* [Provoke not your children, but bring them up, &c. Μὴ παροργίζετε—οἷον οἱ πολλοὶ ποιοῦσιν, ἀποκληρονόμους ἐργαζόμενοι, καὶ ἀποκηρύκτους ποιοῦντες. Chrysostom. i. e. Provoke not your children, as many people do, by their ill usage, discouraging them from coming into the Christian church, and from hearkening to the gospel doctrine.

‡ See 1 Cor. vii. 20, 21, 22, 23, 24.

9 And ye maſters, do the ſame things unto them, forbearing threatening; knowing that your Maſter alſo is in heaven; neither is there reſpect of perſons with him.

9. And let all *Chriſtian* maſters, that have any *ſlaves* under them, uſe them with gentleneſs and humanity; forbearing all paſſionate and violent expreſſions toward them; and forgiving their pardonable faults. Remembering *they* themſelves have a heavenly maſter who forgave them infinitely more; and who regards no man's *external* circumſtances, but will reward and puniſh the behaviour of a *maſter* as well as of a *ſlave*.

10 Finally, my brethren, be ſtrong in the Lord, and in the power of his might.

10. And now, to conclude my exhortations to you: Be courageous and reſolute in your profeſſion, making the beſt improvement of the powers that God has given you.

11 Put on the whole * armour of God, that ye may be able to ſtand againſt the wiles of the devil.

11. Your conflict is very great and ſharp. Wherefore, like true ſoldiers, arm yourſelves from head to foot with the * ſpiritual armour wherewith God has furniſhed you, for your defence againſt the ſtratagems and aſſaults of the devil, and wicked men.

12 For we wreſtle not againſt fleſh and blood, but againſt principalities, againſt powers, againſt the rulers of the darkneſs of this world, againſt ſpiritual wickedneſs in high places †.

12. And great need you have ſo to do. For you muſt engage not only with men, with the magiſtrates and rulers of *this* world, but with wicked *ſpirits* too, thoſe malicious *powers*, that have ſo long domineered over the blind and ignorant *heathens*, and have ſtill their habitation in the regions of the air about us.

13 Wherefore take unto you the whole armour of God, that ye may

13. Be ready armed then with the following principles, that will enable you to reſiſt them all, and ſtand

* [Armour of God.] See note on 2 Cor. viii. 1.

† Ver. 12. [Spiritual wickedneſs in high places:] πνεύματα τῆς πονηρίας ἐν τοῖς ἐπουρανίοις. [Againſt the wicked ſpirits in the regions of (*our*) air. 'Επουρανίοις is the ſame with τοῦ σκότους τούτου, *this darkneſs;* the ſame with ζόφου, and ζόφον, *darkneſs*, in St. Peter and St. Jude.

A. D. 62. may be able to withſtand in the evil day, and having done all, to ſtand.

ſtand your ground under the worſt trial and temptation; viz.

14 Stand therefore, having your loins girt about with truth, and having on the breaſt-plate of righteouſneſs.

14. Keep cloſe to the rules and plain precepts of the *goſpel*, the knowledge whereof will ſecure you from all looſe priciples, and like the ſoldiers *girdle*, keep you in a firm and ſteady poſture; and the habitual practice of them be as a breaſt-plate to fence off every mortal wound.

15 And your feet ſhod with the preparation of the goſpel of peace.

15. Be always prepared with a modeſt and peaceable mind toward your adverſaries; which will be a means to prevent and take off the edge of their malice; as the ſoldier's boots preſerves his legs from the roughneſs of the ways, and from the traps and galls that are laid by the enemy to retard his march.

16 Above all, taking the ſhield of faith, wherewith ye ſhall be able to quench all the fiery darts of the wicked.

16. But eſpecially have your thoughts ever poſſeſſed with a firm and ſteady faith in the *promiſes* of the goſpel; that will guard you from the ſecret ſuggeſtions, and open aſſaults of the devil; as the ſhield does the ſoldier from the darts of his enemies.

* 1 Theſ. v. 8.

17 And take the helmet of ſalvation, and the ſword of the Spirit, which is the word of God.

17. Let your hopes * of eternal life and happineſs, be ever ardent and vigorous; which, like a *helmet* on the head, will ſecure you in the main points of your profeſſion. Read and meditate on the word of God in holy ſcripture, the underſtanding whereof will, like the keeneſt *ſword*, enable you not only to reſiſt, but to aſſault your adverſaries.

18 Praying always with all prayer and ſupplication in the Spirit, and watching thereunto with all perſeverance, and ſupplication for all ſaints.

18. And withal be earneſt and conſtant in a courſe of fervent prayer to God for yourſelves and all Chriſtian people.

19. & 20.

A. D. 62.

19 And for me, that utterance may be given unto me, that I may open my mouth boldly to make known the myſtery of the goſpel;

20 For which I am * an ambaſſador in bonds; that therein I may ſpeak boldly, as I ought to ſpeak.

19. & 20. Not forgetting to let *me*, your *Gentile* apoſtle, have a ſhare in thoſe petitions; beſeeching God to enable me with due conſtancy and courage, to maintain this doctrine *of the Gentiles being called into the goſpel covenant*; a doctrine now abſolutely plain and certain, how ſtrange ſoever it ſeem to the *Jewiſh* zealots; and whereof I am now a commiſſioned preacher, and am * impriſoned on that very account.

21 But that ye alſo might know my affairs, *and* how I do, Tychicus, as a beloved brother, and faithful miniſter in the Lord, ſhall make known to you all things.

21. & 22. I ſend Tychicus, my dear Chriſtian brother, and a faithful miniſter of Chriſt, with this letter to you, on purpoſe to acquaint you with my condition, and how it fares with me in my confinement; and to comfort you under your concern at it.

22 Whom I have ſent unto you for the ſame purpoſe, that ye might know our affairs, and that he might comfort your hearts.

23 Peace *be* to the brethren, and love, with faith from God the Father, and the Lord Jeſus Chriſt.

23. May all the Chriſtians in your parts continue ſtedfaſt in the faith, love, and favour of God the Father, and the Lord Jeſus Chriſt.

24 Grace be with all them that love our Lord Jeſus Chriſt.

¶ Written from Rome unto the Epheſians, by Tychicus.

24. His favour and love be upon all ſincere and good Chriſtians. *Amen.*

A PARA-

* [Am an ambaſſador in bonds]. Πρεσβεύω ἐν ἁλύσει. Which ſome render, [I grow old in bonds]; agreeable to Philem. ix. He had indeed been impriſoned in Judea two years, and had now lain two more at Rome, for the ſame cauſe. But I keep to our tranſlation, as more agreeable to the reſt of the expreſſions to the ſame purpoſe in this epiſtle. See note on Philem. ix.

A

PARAPHRASE

ON

THE EPISTLE OF ST. PAUL

TO THE

PHILIPPIANS.

THE PREFACE.

A. D. 62. WHILE St. Paul was a prisoner at Rome, whither he was forced to make his appeal from the inveterate malice of the *Jews*, for his preaching to the *Gentile* world, the *Philippian* church send *Epaphroditus* to visit and salute him in their name; to carry him supplies from them for his support in his confinement; and to give him the comfortable account, how steady and firm their church continued to the Christian faith he had formerly planted amongst them; and especially in that point *of relying upon the gospel religion for salvation, without the observation of the ceremonial law*, which the *Jewish* zealots every where cried up to be of absolute necessity to a *Christian* convert. This epistle is a return of St. Paul's great satisfaction, love and joy at the respects they had shown him, and especially for their

their firm adherence to this *true Christian* doctrine; A. D. 62.
with several fresh exhortations to a resolute, but yet meek and peaceful behaviour in their disputes with those furious adversaries, on whose temper and practices he lets fall some very severe and just reflections. For a further account of the nature of the expressions in which this letter runs, I refer the reader to the preface of the *foregoing* epistle.

CHAP. I.

The Title and Salutation. He expresseth his good Opinion of them for their Kindness and Respect toward him, and especially for their firm Adherence to the true Christian Doctrine; and prays for their final Constancy in it. Acquaints them with the Success his present Sufferings had for the Promotion of the Gospel, even in the Emperor's Court. Intimates a set of contentious Teachers *of the* Judaizing *Party, who levelled their doctrine against* him, *instead of preaching* Jesus Christ *as the common Saviour of Mankind; but mentions* others *that were sincere, and stood by* him *and his Principles. Speaking of his Sufferings and his Constancy under them, he makes himself to be in a strait between the desires of serving Christ by a longer* Life, *and enjoying him in* Death; *but is free to live, and even suffer longer, for the benefit of the Christian Church. Gives them hopes of seeing them again; but whether he should or no, exhorts them to Christian Piety, and Resolution in Suffering after his own Example.*

1 PAUL and Timotheus, the servants of Jesus Christ, to all the saints in Christ

1. & 2. PAUL and Timothy, the servants and ministers of Jesus Christ, with all divine blessings from God the Father and our

A. D. 62. Christ Jesus, which are at Philippi, with the bishops and deacons:

our Lord Jesus Christ, to the bishops and deacons, and the whole Christian church of Philippi.

2 Grace *be* unto you, and peace from God our Father, and from the Lord Jesus Christ.

3 † I thank my God upon every remembrance of you.

4 Always in every prayer of mine for you all, making request with joy,

5 For your fellowship in the gospel, from the first day until now;

3. 4. & 5. Your conversion to the Christian faith, and your steadiness in it, from the very first propagation of it to you, to this day, is matter of such joy and satisfaction to me, that † I am ever blessing God for it, and praying for your further constancy in it, in every petition I put up to him.

6 Being confident of this very thing, that he which hath begun a good work in you, will perform it until the day of Jesus Christ.

6. Being sufficiently satisfied, that God, who has called you Gentiles as well as the Jews, to the profession of the *gospel*, will so assist your endeavours, as to keep you in the faith and practice of it to the great day of Christ's recompence and reward.

7 Even as it is meet for me to think this of you all, because I have you in my heart; in as much as both in my bonds, and in the defence and confirmation of the gospel, ye all are partakers of my grace.

7. Nor can I but thus esteem and pray for *you*, that have thus distinguished your ‡ respects to *me*, in adhering so firmly to the doctrine I preached to you, and suffering for it now along with me, who am a prisoner for the truth and confirmation of it ‖.

8 For

8. And

---

† Ευχαριςῶ, *I* give thanks. Which shows St. Paul to be the *author* of the epistle, though Timothy was joined in the *salutation*.

‡ [Because I have you in my heart.] Δια τὸ ἔχειν με ἐν τῇ καρδίᾳ ὑμᾶς Or, Because you have *me* at heart.

‖ Ver. 7. [Partakers of my grace *or* gift. It is a dubious expression. It may signify, as in the paraphrase, [their being partakers of the honour of his suffering for the gospel;] or their being συγκοινώνοι, *contributors* to the *gift* the Philippians sent him by Epaphroditus, Chap. iv. 18. See Mr. Peirce in Loc.

8 For God is my record, how greatly I long after you all, in the bowels of Jesus Christ.

8. And God can testify, what a hearty degree of Christian love, I, in return, bear toward your whole church. A. D. 64.

9 And this I pray, that your love may abound, yet more and more, in knowledge, and in all judgment.

9. And how earnestly I pray that your love of Christ, and of me his *apostle*, may continually increase, by a more complete and perfect understanding of the great truths of his religion.

10 That ye may approve * things that are excellent, that ye may be sincere, and without offence till the day of Christ.

11 Being filled with the fruits of righteousness, which are by Jesus Christ unto the glory and praise of God.

10. & 11. That by * studying and embracing the most important doctrines, and abounding in the practice of all Christian virtues, you may be found his sincere and true professors at the solemn appearance of Jesus Christ; to the glory and praise of God the Father.

12 But I would ye should understand, brethren, that the things *which happened* unto me, have fallen out rather unto the furtherance of the gospel.

12. But, to give you an account of my present state and condition, according to your desire, know then, that my imprisonment at Rome has been no hindrance, but rather an advantage to the *Christian* cause.

13 So that my bonds in Christ are manifest in all the palace, and in all other *places*.

15. For it is now publicly known in the emperor's court, and through all the city, that I am a prisoner for the Christian faith, and particularly for preaching it to the *Gentile* world.

14. And

* Ver. 10. [That ye may approve the things that are excellent.] εἰς τὸ δοκιμάζειν ὑμᾶς τὰ διαφέροντα, "That ye may "*examine into*, and [proportionably] *approve of*, things, ac-"cording as they *differ* in their *excellency* and *importance*.

A. D. 62.

14 And many of the brethren in the Lord waxing confident by my bonds, are much more bold to ſpeak the word without fear.

14. And my patience and courage under it has raiſed the ſpirits of ſeveral Chriſtians, to profeſs and preach the *ſame* doctrine openly and undauntedly.

15 Some indeed preach Chriſt even of envy and ſtrife, and ſome alſo of good will.

16 The one preach Chriſt of contention, not ſincerely †, ſuppoſing to add affliction to my bonds:

17 But the other of love, knowing that I am ſet for the defence of the goſpel.

15. 16. & 17. There is indeed a ſet of *Jewiſh* * converts, that preach it more out of oppoſition to *me*, than out of love to the goſpel *itſelf*. Their buſineſs is to depreſs my character, and increaſe my ſufferings, (becauſe I will not allow the *ceremonial* law to be neceſſary to a *Chriſtian's* ſalvation.) But, thank God, there are others that ſtand up for me and my principles, being fully ſatisfied what I preach is by *divine* commiſſion, and that I am a ſufferer for the true *goſpel* doctrine.

* See chap. iii. 2, 3, &c.

18 What then? notwithſtanding every way, whether in pretence or in truth, Chriſt is preached; and I therein do rejoice, yea, and will rejoice.

18. And though theſe two parties preach out of very different and contrary deſigns; yet there is this advantage, that they both contribute to make the *Chriſtian* religion in general more known in the world; which is, and always ſhall be a great ſatisfaction to me.

19 For I know that this ſhall turn to my ſalvation through your prayer, and the ſupply of the Spirit of Jeſus Chriſt.

19. And I am aſſured the preſent malice intended againſt *me* will prove ſo ſhort of ſucceeding, that it will rather contribute to my deliverance. For which I queſtion not your prayers, and the Spirit of Chriſt, to aſſiſt me to plead my cauſe ‡.

20. As

† Ver 16. [Not ſincerely], ὐχ ἁγνῶς: [Not without mixture, viz. of *Jewiſh ceremonies* with the *Chriſtian faith*.

‡ [Turn to my ſalvation], εἰς σωτηρίαν: Not to his future *ſalvation, but to his deliverance* at his *trial* at Rome.

A. D. 62.

20 According to my earnest expectation, and my hope, that in nothing I shall be ashamed, but *that* with all boldness, as always, *so* now also Christ shall be magnified in my body, whether *it be* by life or by death.

20. As therefore the only thing I desire is, to demonstrate the power and excellency of Christ's religion, either by living longer to preach it, or by courageously dying for it; I shall not fail, in this juncture, to defend it publicly, as I have always hitherto done.

21 For to me to live *is* Christ, and to die *is* gain.

21. The only difference between life and death, to me is, that by the *one* I shall continue the longer in Christ's service, and by the *other* shall be the sooner rewarded.

22 But if I live in the flesh, this is the fruit of my labour; yet what I shall choose I wot not.

22. It is infinitely worth my pains and sufferings indeed, to continue here still, and do service to his religion; yet is the prospect of my future happiness so ravishing and sweet, that, were it left to my *own* choice, I should hardly know which to determine as best for me.

23 For I am in a strait betwixt two, having a desire to depart, and to be with Christ; which is far better:

24 Nevertheless, to abide in the flesh, *is* more needful for you.

23. & 24. Thus are my desires straitened between the two conditions of longer *life* and present *death*. To die and be with Christ would be much the more immediate benefit to me; but to live longer is better for *you* and the Christian *church*; and I am very free to do it.

25 And having this confidence, I know that I shall abide and continue with you all, for your furtherance and joy of faith:

26 That your rejoicing may be more abundant in Jesus Christ for me, by my coming to you again.

25. & 26. And because it is so, I am fully persuaded God will so order it, and I shall live and see you again, to your still further advancement and comfort in the Christian faith.

27 Only

A. D. 62.

27 Only let your conversation be as it becometh the gospel of Christ: that whether I come and see you, or else be absent, I may hear of your affairs, that ye stand fast in one spirit, with one mind, striving together for the faith of the gospel:

27. But whether I do or not, let me earnestly exhort you to go on in a life agreeable to the gospel religion; that I may hear a comfortable account how vigorously and unanimously you promote the credit and honour of the Christian faith; without partial distinction betwixt *circumcised* and *uncircumcised* converts.

28 And in nothing terrified by your adversaries, which is to them an evident † token of perdition, but to you of salvation, and that of God.

28. And how undauntedly you bear the threats and persecutions of your adversaries, which, while they show *them* to be an obstinate and incurable people, bent upon their own destruction; so will the patient suffering under them become to *you* a means of eternal happiness and salvation.

29 For unto you it is given in the behalf of Christ, not only to believe on him, but also to suffer for his sake;

30 Having the same conflict which ye saw in me, and now hear *to be* in me.

* Acts xiii. 23.

29. & 30. Esteem it, therefore, as a high honour conferred on you, not only to be called into the Christian religion, as well as the *Jews*, but to suffer for it too; undergoing the same trials you saw me, your *apostle*, under, while I was first preaching to you * at Philippi, and that you hear are still upon me here at Rome.

CHAP.

† Ver. 28. [Which is to them an evident token of perdition, *&c.*] *Note*, The word *which* may refer to the *Philippians standing fast*; and *the token of perdition to them* may signify, that their *adversaries* took this *stedfastness* of theirs to be a *token* of their *perdition*; but, says the *apostle*, [look you upon it as a token of your salvation.]

CHAP. II.

He proceeds to exhort their whole Church to Unity, Meekneſs, and Humility, from the great Example of Chriſt ſuffering for us: And to ſteadineſs in Chriſtian Principles and Practices, now in his abſence from them. Hopes to ſend Timothy to them. In the mean while recommends their Meſſenger Epaphroditus, the Bearer of this Letter to them.

A. D. 62.

1 IF *there be* therefore any conſolation in Chriſt, if any comfort of love, if any fellowſhip of the Spirit, if any bowels and mercies:

2 Fulfil ye my joy, that ye be like minded, having the ſame love, *being* of one accord, of one mind.

1. & 2. I Exhorted you (Chap. i. 27.) to unity and peaceableneſs in your Chriſtian profeſſion. And if there be any force in beſeeching you in the name of Chriſt; if you have any ſenſe of the ſweet comforts of mutual *love*; if you have felt any motions of that good Chriſtian *ſpirit* that excites us to love; finally, by all the compaſſions you bear towards *me* your ſuffering *apoſtle*, fail not to practiſe this *great* duty, which will complete all the joy and ſatisfaction I have in you.

3 *Let* nothing *be done* through ſtrife, or vain glory; but in lowlineſs of mind let each eſteem other better than themſelves.

3. Let nothing be ſaid and done amongſt you out of a contentious or ambitious principle; but be all ready to do for and comply with one another, as if they were their ſuperiors.

4 Look not every man on his own things, but every man alſo on the things of others.

4. Let none of you be ſet upon pleaſing his own humour, and minding his private credit or intereſt; but have a juſt regard to the good and edification of all his fellow Chriſtians.

5 Let this mind be in you, which was alſo in Chriſt Jeſus.

5. In this you will imitate no leſs example than that of Jeſus Chriſt, our great Lord and pattern.

A. D. 62.

6 Who being in the form of God *, thought it not robbery to be equal with God:

7 But made himself of no reputation, and took upon him the form of a † servant, and was made in the likeness of men:

8 And being found in fashion as a man, he humbled himself, and became obedient unto death, even the death of the cross.

|| Heb. i. 3 Colos. i. 15

† Luke xxii. 27. John xii. 4—17.

6, 7. & 8. Who though, before his incarnation, he was God, *the Son of God* ||, *the brightness of his Father's glory, and the express image of his person;* and appeared to the patriarchs, and to the *Jewish* church in the form of divine glory and majesty; yet, for the salvation of us sinful men, did not insist * upon appearing in that glory, and to be honoured as God, did not look upon the honour God had given him, as upon a *prize* to be eagerly held fast, and never, upon any account whatever, to be parted with; but divested himself for a while of that majesty; was clothed with human nature, ministering to us as a servant; and so far humbled himself, as not only to live as a mean and ordinary *man*, but to die the ignominious death of the cross, for the expiation of our sins.

9 Wherefore God also hath highly exalted him, and given him a name which is above every name:

9. For which great and wondrous condescension, God has now exalted this very man Christ Jesus the *Messiah*, to the highest degree of divine glory and majesty.

10 That at ‡ the name of Jesus every knee should bow, of *things* in heaven, and *things* on earth, and *things* under the earth;

11 And

10. & 11. Making him the lord and governor of all creatures both in heaven † and earth, the Lord of the *living*, and raiser of the *dead;* and obliging all to worship and adore,

---

* Ver. 6. [Thought it no robbery to be equal with God]; ὀυχ ἁρπαγμὸν ἡγήσατο το εἶναι ἶσα θεῷ. [He did not greedily insist upon showing himself, and being worshipped as God]. Which sense is sufficiently proved by Bishop Bull, Dr. Whitby, and still more fully by Dr. Clarke.

‡ [That at the name of Jesus every knee should bow]. The Greek is, ἐν τῷ ὀνόματι. [In the name of Jesus—every knee should bow]; *i. e.* worship God, agreeable to John xvi. 23, 24. and many like passages.

11 And that every tongue should confess, that Jesus Christ *is* Lord, to the glory of God the Father.

dore, to pray to, and praise God, through him, and in his name, as universal governor and Saviour, to the glory of the supreme Father ‡.

12 Wherefore, my beloved, as ye have always obeyed, not as in my presence only, but now much more in my absence; work out your own salvation with fear and trembling *.

12. Wherefore, dear brethren, being animated by so glorious an example, go on by these and the like virtues, to qualify yourselves for eternal salvation with the utmost diligence and caution. You have hitherto proceeded very well in them, both while I was with you, and since my absence from you*.

13 For it is God which worketh in you, both to will and to do of *his* good pleasure.

13. Nor be ye at all discouraged, at my being so long detained from you. Do your best endeavours, and God will assist you, under all temptations, to act agreeably to his holy will and religion.

† [Of things in heaven, and things on earth, and under the earth]. See the note on Ephes. i. 10. And though καταχθονίων being joined to the other two phrases, may possibly by the *Jewish* idiom, be meant to express only the whole world: Yet in this place I take it to signify the *dead*, in contradistinction to the *living*, agreeably to those other passages of scripture, concerning the government and exaltation of Christ. See Rom. xiv. 9. Rev. i. 18.

‡ Ver. 9. 10. 11. *Note,* If the *bowing the knee*, ver. 10. refers to Christ, then we may render the passage thus, [And hath given him a name, ὄνομα, a character above every (*other*) character, that in that character of Jesus (*the* Saviour) every knee should bow,] and pay him reverence

* Ver. 12. *Note,* I have so paraphrased this verse, that the verb κατεργάζεσθε (work out) may be taken either *imperatively* or *indicatively* (ye do still work out.) So as that this may be understood as *commendation*, not an *exhortation* to the Philippians. Which indeed is very agreeable to the congratulatory style of this epistle. See Werenfel's Desert. Theolog. p. 459—469.

Ibid. [With fear and trembling, *i. e.* with all due carefulness, respect and regard]. So the same phrase is used, Psal. iii. 11. Ephes. vi. 5. 2 Cor. vii. 15.

A. D 62.

14 Do all things without murmurings, and disputings:

15 That ye may be blameless and harmless, the sons of God, without rebuke, in the midst of a crooked and perverse † nation, among whom ye shine|| as lights in the world.

† Acts ii. 40. Matth. xvii. 17. Luke ix. 41. Deut. xxxii. 5. in lxx.

16 Holding forth the word of life, that I may rejoice in the day of Christ, that I have not run in vain, neither laboured in vain.

17 Yea, and if I be offered upon the sacrifice and service of your faith, I joy and rejoice with you all.

18 For the same cause also do ye joy and rejoice with me.

19 But I trust in the Lord Jesus, to send Timotheus shortly unto you, that I also may be of good comfort when I know your state.

20 For I have no man like-minded, who will naturally care for your state.

21 For

14. & 15. Be particularly careful (as I before advised you) to avoid all needless disputes and animosities; and, by an innocent and inoffensive carriage, prove yourselves worthy the character of God's true church and children; and become shining lights, and illustrious examples, to convince and reform the wicked generations of men you live amongst.

16. And that by your perseverance in Christianity, under all opposition, *I*, your *apostle*, may rejoice and triumph in the great day of Christ's appearance, for the happy effects of my labours in your conversion to the *gospel*.

17. & 18. As to myself, if *I* should not only be kept still from you, but die a sacrifice for preaching to you *Gentiles*, I should congratulate myself and you upon spending my life in so good a cause. And *you* ought to rejoice with me too, upon the same account.

19. But be that as it may, I hope in Christ to have an opportunity of sending Timothy shortly to you; and give myself the satisfaction of hearing by him of your happy state and condition.

22. I fix upon *him* as the only person I can find here, that, like myself, is truly ready and willing to serve you, or any other Christian church.

21. For

|| Ver. 15. *Ye shine* φαίνεσθε, or *shine ye*, in the imperative mood.

A. D. 62.

21 For all ſeek their own, not the things which are Jeſus Chriſt's.

21. For the generality of Chriſtians in theſe parts, are more concerned for their own ſafety and private intereſt, than to advance the religion of Chriſt, by taking much pains or running any hazards for it.

22 But ye know the proof of him, that as a ſon with the father, he hath ſerved with me in the goſpel.

22. But Timothy, you know, has always ſtuck cloſe to me, and ſerved me in the *goſpel* concerns with the perfect reſpects of a ſon to a father.

23 Him, therefore, I hope to ſend preſently, ſo ſoon as I ſhall ſee how it will go with me.

24 But I truſt in the Lord I alſo myſelf ſhall come ſhortly.

23. & 24. As ſoon as ever, therefore, I ſee the iſſue of my trial I ſhall ſend him. And I have reaſon to hope I ſhall be cleared, and viſit you ſoon myſelf.

25 Yet I ſuppoſed it neceſſary to ſend you Epaphroditus, my brother and companion in labour, and fellow-ſoldier, but your meſſenger, and he that miniſtred to my wants.

25. In the mean time, I thought it proper with this letter, to ſend you back your worthy meſſenger and miniſter Epaphroditus, who ever ſince his coming to me, with ſupplies from you, hath been my fellow-labourer in *Chriſtanity*, and done me great ſervice.

26 For he longed after you all, and was full of heavineſs, becauſe that ye had heard that he had been ſick.

26. And is very deſirous to ſee you again, and relieve you from the concern he concludes you to be under at his late ſickneſs here.

27 For indeed he was ſick nigh unto death, but God had mercy on him: and not on him only, but on me alſo, leſt I ſhould have ſorrow upon ſorrow.

27. For indeed he has been ſo very ill, as to be at the point of death. And his recovery was not only a great mercy to himſelf, but to *me* in parricular, and has prevented one of the greateſt misfortunes that could have befallen me in my confinement.

28. I pitched

A. D. 62.

28 I ſent him therefore the more † carefully, that when ye ſee him again, ye may rejoice, and that I may be the leſs ſorrowful.

28. I pitched upon him, therefore, for the bearer of this letter, to give myſelf the pleaſure of rejoicing you at the ſight of ſo dear a friend.

29 Receive him therefore in the Lord with all gladneſs, and hold ſuch in reputation.

29. Nor need I much exhort you to receive him with all Chriſtian reſpect, and to ſet a high value upon all ſuch good miniſters of Chriſt as he is.

30 Becauſe for the work of Chriſt he was nigh unto death, not regarding his life to ſupply your lack of ſervice toward me.

30. Who has hazarded his own life in labours and pains for Chriſt's ſake, and in doing that ſervice to me, which you at this diſtance, how willing ſoever you be, were not capable to perform ‡.

CHAP. III.

He encourages them to a cheerful Profeſſion of Chriſtianity; and to a Dependence on the Faith of it *alone, without regard to the* Jewiſh *Law, according to his own Example. Warns them againſt the Principles and Practices of the* Jewiſh *zealots, upon whom he makes very juſt and ſevere Reflections.*

1 FInally, my brethren, rejoice in the Lord. To write the ſame things to you, to me indeed is not grievous, but for you it is ſafe.

2 Be-

1. THE ſum of what I have further to exhort you to, is, a cheerful and joyful profeſſion of Chriſtianity, founded in a true ſenſe of Chriſt's love toward you, and his protection over you. And as I have formerly, by word of mouth,

---

† Ver. 28. [The more carefully; *or* σπουδαιοτέρως, the more ſpeedily;] viz. with this very *epiſtle*. *Vulg.* feſtinantius.

‡ Ver. 30. [To ſupply your lack of ſervice to me—— [*Greek*] To perfect or complete your beneficence to me.]

mouth, warned you againſt the principles of a ſet of men that are its worſt enemies; I think it proper to repeat thoſe cautions again. A. D. 62.

2 Beware of * dogs, beware of evil-workers, beware of the conciſion ‡.

2. I mean the *Jewiſh zealots*, that ſnarling * and malicious people; whoſe buſineſs it is to do miſchief to the true *Chriſtian* faith, and who put all the ſtreſs of religion upon the empty ‡ ceremonies of *circumciſion* and the *Jewiſh law*.

3 For we are the circumciſion, which worſhip God in the ſpirit, and rejoice in Chriſt Jeſus, and have no confidence in the fleſh.

3. It is we *Chriſtians* that are now the true *church* and people of God, by embracing the pure worſhip and ſpiritual religion of the *goſpel*, which it was the deſign and purpoſe of the *law* to lead men to; and placing all our hopes of pardon and ſalvation in that, and not in the external obſervance of the *Moſaical rites*, that are quite out of date.

4 Though I might alſo have confidence in the fleſh. If any other man thinketh that he hath whereof he might truſt in the fleſh, I more.

4. And though we ſhould ſuppoſe the *Jewiſh law* were the main thing yet to be depended on; yet thoſe *zealots* have no manner of reaſon to boaſt themſelves above *me*, who have as many and more *Jewiſh* privileges than moſt of them can pretend to.

5 Circumciſed the eighth day, of the ſtock of Iſrael, of the tribe of Benjamin, an Hebrew

5. For I was a true born Iſraelite, both by father and mother's ſide, of the tribe of Benjamin (a tribe that never revolted to Jeroboam, as

* [Beware of dogs.] So the Jews, by way of contempt, uſed to ſtyle all Heathens; and now, as a juſt return for their contentious and obſtinate oppoſition to the true religion, the apoſtles, St. Paul and St. John, fling it back upon themſelves. See Rev. xxii. 25. Pſal. xx. 16.

‡ [The conciſion:] τὴν κατατομὴν. The ſame natural act as περιτομὴν, *circumciſion*, but now a *mere* and *inſignificant* cutting of the *fleſh*; *circumciſion* as a *religious* ceremony, being *now* quite aboliſhed.

A. D. 62. Hebrew of the Hebrews: as touching the law, a Pharisee.

as the rest did), circumcised the eighth day, and so made a member of the *Jewish* church in exact conformity to the *law;* and was a perfect Jew both by *nation* and *language;* nay, and a Pharisee too, one of the most strict and honourable sects of that religion.

6 Concerning zeal, persecuting the church: touching the righteousness which is in the law, blameless.

6. And if *zeal* for the *law* be of such moment, none was so severe an observer of *ceremonies* and *traditions* as *myself*, nor so violent a persecutor of the *Christian* religion, which came to repeal those *ceremonies*.

7 But what things were gain to me, those I counted loss for Christ.

7. But now the case is justly altered with me: and those external privileges of the *Jewish* profession I so much valued myself upon, I *now* so little esteem, in comparison of the blessings of Christ's religion; that to retain them any longer, while far better and nobler are come in their room, would be the greatest *damage* to me.

8 Yea, doubtless, and I count all things but loss, for the excellency of the knowledge of Christ Jesus my Lord: for whom I have suffered the loss of all things, and do count them but dung, that I may win Christ,

9 And be found in him, not having mine own righteousness, which is of the law, but that which is through the faith of Christ, the righteousness which is of God by faith.

8. & 9. For verily, so excellent and great are the privileges of *Christianity*, that those temporal ones of the *Jewish* dispensation seem perfectly mean and vile things; and I make no difficulty to part with them all for the service and favour of Jesus Christ my great Lord and Saviour; by embracing of whose religion I obtain that perfect pardon and salvation at God's hands, which my strictest observance of the *ceremonial law* could never have procured for me.

10 That I may know him, and the power of his resurrection, and the fellowship

10. & 11. I give them all up, I say, to own *him* for the true *Messiah* and Saviour of mankind; to suffer and die for *his* religion, who suffered

A. D. 62.

lowship of his sufferings, being made conformable unto his death;

11 If by any means I might attain unto the resurrection of the dead *.

suffered for *our* sins; in full hope and assurance to be raised again to eternal life by the same divine power that raised *him* from the dead; not refusing to do and undergo any thing to attain that final blessing of a glorious and happy resurrection.

12 Not as though I had already attained, either were already perfect: but I follow after, if that I may apprehend that for which also I am apprehended of Christ Jesus.

13 Brethren, I count not myself to have apprehended: but *this* one thing *I do*, forgetting those things which are behind, and reaching forth unto those things which are before,

14 I press toward the mark †, for the prize of the high calling of God in Christ Jesus.

12, 13. & 14. *This* is the prize, dear brethren, I, as a *Christian*, hope for, and am assured of, but have not *yet* actually attained. My business in this life is, to strive and run for it; and like a true *racer*, to mind nothing else about me, but keep my eye fixed upon *this*; stretching on towards it with my utmost vigour and activity, in order to gain *that* at last which was the end for which Christ was graciously pleased to convert me to his religion.

15 Let us therefore, as many as be perfect, be thus minded: and if in any thing ye be otherwise minded, God shall reveal even this unto you.

15. Let all those Christians, therefore, who duly understand, and have fully embraced this religion, keep to this maxim, viz. "That this great prize of a glorious and happy resurrection is to be had by Christ's religion, without the *ceremonial* law." Hold to *this*, and then, though you may not be all exactly agreed in

---

* Ver. 11. [If by any means] &c. εἴπως, [that so I might attain,] &c.

† Ver. 14. [I press toward the mark;] or, κατὰ σκοπὸν, [I press forward, according to my view or design.]

A. D. 62. in every notion about this *law*, or our obligation to it, God will *, in due time, bring you all to a complete understanding of the case, and let you see it is perfectly abolished.

16 Nevertheless, whereunto we have already attained, let us walk by the same rule, let us mind the same thing †.

16. In the mean while, let us, that perfectly know it to be so, keep firm and unanimous to the true *Christian* principle.

17 Brethren, be followers together of me, and mark them which walk so, as ye have us for an ensample.

17. Follow *my* example, and my principles in this matter; and take *them* for your patterns, who have relinquished all their *Jewish* privileges for the sake of Christ's religion, as I have done.

18 (For many walk, of whom I have told you often, and now tell you even weeping, *that they are* the enemies of the cross of Christ:

18. As to the *Jewish* zealots, that would persuade you to the contrary, I have always told, and now tell you again, not without tears for their incurable obstinacy, that they are the worst enemies our religion has.

19 Whose end *is* destruction, whose God *is their* belly, and *whose* glory *is* in their shame, who mind earthly things).

19. Their notions and views of religion are all *temporal:* and their chief aim is at the gratification of their sensual appetites and pleasures; they boast in what they ought to be ashamed of, and for such

---

* [God will reveal even this unto you.] Some copies read ἀπεκάλυψε—[God has revealed it.] The sense being thus, [Whoever thinks otherwise is in a plain error; for God hath now expressly declared the Jewish law to be abolished, and no further necessary.] A most agreeable sense indeed: but I keep to our translation, according to the more ancient MSS.

Ibid. [Will reveal.] Thus the abrogation of the ceremonial *law* was *completely* demonstrated by the total destruction of Jerusalem and the temple, about *eight* years after the date of this epistle.

† Ver. 16. [Let us mind the same thing:] or rather, perhaps, τὸ ἀυτὸ φρονεῖν. [To be at unity with one another.] according to Chap. ii. 2. Rom. xii. 16.—xv. 5. As Mr. Pierce well observes.

ſuch irreclaimable prejudices and practices God will deſtroy their whole nation with a moſt exemplary deſtruction. A. D. 62.

20 For our converſation is in heaven, from whence alſo we look for the Saviour the Lord Jeſus Chriſt:	20. Directly contrary to their worldly principles, a *Chriſtian* ought to look further and higher, and conſider himſelf as a citizen of *heaven*, from whence he one day expects to behold Jeſus his Saviour deſcending, to raiſe and exalt him thither.
21 Who ſhall change our vile body, that it may be faſhioned like unto his glorious body, according to the working whereby he is able even to ſubdue all things unto himſelf.	21. To transform theſe frail and mortal bodies of ours into a reſemblance of his own glorious body, enabling them by his Almighty power, for which nothing is too hard, to mount * up after him thither, where we ſhall be for ever happy with him.

* 1 Theſ. iv. 17.

CHAP. IV.

The Encouragements to Chriſtian Conſtancy, Cheerfulneſs, and Reſignation, continued. He expreſſeth the due Senſe he had of the Philippians Kindneſs to him. The Apoſtle's Courage and Contentedneſs under all Conditions of Life. The Salutations and Concluſion.

1 THerefore, my brethren, dearly beloved and longed for, my joy and crown, ſo ſtand faſt in the Lord, *my* dearly beloved.	1. AND thus, my dear Chriſtian converts, in whoſe ſteadineſs to the faith I glory and triumph, continue ſtill firm and unanimous in your profeſſion, from all the foregoing conſiderations.
2 I beſeech Euodias, and beſeech Syntiche, that they be of the ſame mind in the Lord.	2. I particularly entreat Euodias and Syntiche to do thus, and not to be led aſide by the *Jewiſh* zealots.

3. And

A. D. 62. 3 And I entreat thee also, * true yoke-fellow, help † those women which laboured with me in the gospel, ‡ with Clement also, and with other my fellow labourers, whose names || *are* in the book of life.

3. And I beg of you, my true Christian brother * and a fellow apostle, to give your assistance to those † pious women that laboured so heartily to serve me, while I preached in your parts: along with ‡ Clement, and all those my fellow-labourers in the Christian ministry, who, I verily believe, are to be partakers of the reward of everlasting life ||, as truly sincere Christians.

4 Rejoice in the Lord alway, *and* again I say, rejoice.

4. I exhort you again and again, to rejoice and be cheerful under the hopes and privileges of your *Christian* profession.

5 Let your moderation be known unto all men. The Lord *is* at hand.

5. Show an even, patient, and contented spirit toward all that oppose and persecute you: Be not rigorous in insisting upon your utmost right, nor impatient in suffering wrongs. Remember, the Judge is not far off, that will take vengeance on your furious adversaries, and reward your Christian patience.

6. Be

---

* [True yoke-fellow]. Who the apostle particularly means, is not agreed upon by interpreters.

† Ver. 3. [Those women]: Probably he means Euodias and Syntiche, before mentioned.

‡ [With Clement and the rest, &c.] These words may be joined either to συζυγε γνήσιε, [true yoke-fellow] or to αἵτινες συνήθλησαν μοὶ, those who laboured with me and Clement]. The latter seems most probable.

|| [Whose names are written in the book of life]. It is a *Jewish* phrase, and does not at all imply any absolute degree or predestination to eternal life; but signifies their being *registered* in that *corporation* or society where eternal life was the privilege, on condition of faith and obedience to Christ's religion: Alluding to both the *Jewish*, *Greek*, and *Roman* custom of *registering* the inhabitants of every city and great town: and then blotting out their names again as fast as they died. See Exod. xxxvii. 32. with my note on that passage. See also my note on Rev. iii. 5.

A. D. 62.

6 Be careful for nothing: but in every thing, by prayer and ſupplication with thankſgiving, let your requeſts be made known unto God.

6. Be not anxiouſly careful, or ſhow any diſtraction under your greateſt ſufferings. But commend yourſelves and your cauſe to God, in prayer for his aſſiſtance, and in thankſgiving for all his former mercies; and he will not fail to comfort and ſupport you.

7 And the peace of God, which paſſeth all underſtanding, ſhall keep your hearts and minds, through Chriſt Jeſus.

7. For the continual ſenſe of the divine favour and mercy, and the lively hope of the happineſs and reward procured for you by Jeſus Chriſt, will guard you under all trials, and give you that inward ſatisfaction and complacency of mind, that no tongue can expreſs, nor any heart conceive, but ſuch as enjoy it.

8 Finally brethren, whatſoever things *are* true, whatſoever things *are* honeſt, whatſoever things *are* juſt, whatſoever things *are* pure, whatſoever things *are* lovely, whatſoever things *are* of good report; if *there be* any virtue, and if *there be* any praiſe, think on theſe things.

8. In fine; be conſtant in the ſtudy and practice of truth, decency, juſtice, and purity; and of every virtue that is lovely and commendable, or that ſavours of a courageous and manly diſpoſition.

9 Thoſe things which ye have both learned and received, and heard and ſeen in me, do: and the God of peace ſhall be with you.

9. Such virtues I taught you, both by my doctrine and example; follow them, and the God of peace and comfort will never forſake you.

10 But I rejoiced in the Lord greatly, that now at the laſt your care of me hath flouriſhed again, wherein ye were alſo careful, but ye lacked opportunity.

10. I cannot but repeat my ſatisfaction at the care you took to ſupply my wants, now under my confinement. I know you would have done it ſooner, had not my great diſtance from you prevented it.

11 Not

11. Not

A. D. 62.

11 Not that I ſpeak in reſpect of want: for I have learned in whatſoever ſtate I am, *therewith* to be content.

11. Not that I was reduced to abſolute want, or was *uneaſy*, before you ſent Epaphroditus to me; for though I had but little, I have learnt to be contented with any thing.

12 I know both *how* to be abaſed, and I know *how* to abound; every where, and in all things I am inſtructed, both to be full and to be hungry, both to abound and ſuffer need.

22. I am become ſo perfectly maſter of myſelf, as to bear, with an equal mind, the utmoſt degrees either of proſperity or adverſity.

* πάντα.

13 I can do all * things, through Chriſt, which ſtrengtheneth me.

13. I can do or ſuffer any hardſhip in the courſe of my *apoſtolical* * office, through the aſſiſtance of Jeſus Chriſt, who is ever preſent to ſupport me.

14 Notwithſtanding, ye have well done, that ye did communicate with my affliction.

14. However, you did very Chriſtianly and well, in ſending me a ſupply; and in the tokens you have given me, how much you ſympathize with me in my preſent affliction.

15 Now ye Philippians know alſo, that in the beginning of the goſpel, when I departed from Macedonia, no church communicated with me, as concerning giving and receiving, but ye only.

16 For even in Theſſalonica ye ſent once and again unto my neceſſity.

15. & 16. And I muſt acknowledge, to your particular credit, that while I was preaching in your parts, I received contributions from no church but *yours*, and eſpecially at my leaving Macedonia, and while I was at Theſſalonica, you ſent collections to me ſeveral times.

17 Not becauſe I deſire a gift: but I deſire fruit that may abound to your account.

17. Nor do I remind you of this your kindneſs to me, with the leaſt deſign to draw more from you. My acknowledgments for what is done to *myſelf*, are

purely to encourage you in *general* to such excellent acts of Christian charity and beneficence, as will be most amply and gloriously rewarded. A. D. 62.

18 But I have all, and abound: I am full, having received of Epaphroditus the things *which were sent* from you, an odour of a sweet smell, a sacrifice acceptable, well-pleasing to God.

18. What you have *now* sent is abundantly enough for me; and God will accept it as the best sacrifice you could offer up to him.

19 But my God shall supply all your need, according to his riches in glory, by Christ Jesus.

19. And the same God, whose *apostle* I am, will not fail, out of the infinite fulness of divine goodness towards us, in the glorious dispensation of Jesus Christ, to give you a plentiful return of supplies, for your liberality towards me.

20 Now unto God and our Father *be* glory for ever and ever. Amen.

20. Now to him, our supreme Creator and Father, be glory for ever and ever. Amen.

21 Salute every saint in Christ Jesus. The brethren * which are with me greet you.

22 All the saints salute you, chiefly they that are of Cæsar's household.

21. & 22. My hearty love to all the Christians in your parts, as all the Christian brethren here give theirs to you and them; particularly the converts that belong to the emperor's court.

23 The grace of our Lord Jesus Christ *be* with you all. Amen.

23. The love and favour of our Lord Jesus Christ be with you all. Amen.

¶ It was written to the Philippians from Rome, by Epaphroditus.

A PARA-

* Ver. 21. *The brethren;* viz. the *ministers*, in contradistinction to the *saints* here, and in the following *verse*.

A PARAPHRASE ON THE EPISTLE OF ST. PAUL TO THE *COLOSSIANS.*

PREFACE.

IT appears from ſeveral (Chap. ii. 1.) paſſages in this epiſtle, that St. Paul did not *perſonally* preach to, and convert the Coloſſians to the Chriſtian faith; nor had ever ſeen them. Though how near he was to them in his travels, we read, Acts xvi. 6.—xviii. 23. xix. 10. But that he was concerned in their converſion, by ſending *others* to them for that purpoſe, is allowed by all; and that Epaphras was the perſon particularly employed by him there, ſeems probable from Chap. i. 7. Upon hearing their ſteadineſs to the Chriſtian faith, in oppoſition to the *Jewiſh zealots* that would have perſuaded them (as they endeavoured to do all other Chriſtian converts) to a neceſſity of obſerving the *ceremonial law*; and likewiſe to arm them ſtill againſt the mixture of *Gentile philoſophy* (or of ſuch ſpeculations as ſome *Jewiſh zealots* might have learned from *Gentile philoſophers*) with their *Chriſtian* principles, he ſends them

them this epistle; wherein he expresseth his great satisfaction at their constancy in their profession, and confirms them in it, against the insinuations of *each* of those adversaries. It was written at the same time and place with those to the Ephesians and Philippians (*viz* during his confinement at Rome) and in the same strain of expressions. For a clearer notion whereof, the reader may please to see, and compare this with, the preface to the Ephesians.

CHAP. I.

The Title. He congratulates their conversion, and steady Adherence to the Christian Religion. Prays for their Continuance in it. Declares it to have ever been the gracious Purpose of God to bestow on them (the believing Gentiles) the Blessings of Christ's Religion, as well as on the Jewish *nation; and* Himself, *the Apostle especially commissioned to preach it to them and the rest of the* Gentile *World.*

1 PAUL, an apostle of Jesus Christ, by the will of God, and Timotheus *our* brother,

2 To the saints and faithful brethren in Christ, which are at Colosse: Grace *be* unto you, and peace from God our Father, and the Lord Jesus Christ.

3 We give thanks to God, and the Father of our Lord Jesus Christ, praying always for you:

1. & 2. PAUL, called by the express * revelation of God to be an apostle of Jesus Christ, sending this epistle to the steady and faithful Christian church of Colosse. Wishing you all spiritual favours and blessings from God our supreme Creator and Father, and from Jesus Christ our Lord and Governor; as does also Timothy my Christian brother.

3. & 4. Expressing my hearty thanks to God the Father of our Lord Jesus Christ, for your conversion to his true religion, and your extensive charity to all the

A. D. 62.

* Acts ix.

D 62.

4 Since we heard of your * faith in Christ Jesus, and of the love *which ye have* to all the saints;

professors of it (without partial distinction between such as receive *circumcision*, and such as do not receive it) and ever praying for your perseverance in it.

5 For the hope which is laid up for you in heaven, whereof ye heard before in the word of the truth of the gospel;

6 Which is come unto you, as *it is* in all the world, and bringeth forth fruit as it *doth* also in you since the day ye heard *of it* and knew the grace of God in truth.

5. & 6 Blessing God, I say, for the hope and full assurance you now have of the heavenly happiness promised in that gospel of Christ, which is now preached to so considerable a part of the *Gentile* world, and embraced by you in particular, with such good effects on your lives and principles, from your very first conversion to it by Epaphras, my dear fellow-servant in Christ.

7 As ye also learned of Epaphras our dear fellow-servant, who is for you a faithful minister of Christ.

8 Who also declared unto us your love in the Spirit.

7 & 8. Whom I sent to Colosse for that work, and who, like a trusty minister of Christ, has fully performed it; and given me a most comfortable account of your love to Christ, and great charity to all his members, according to the true spirit of the gospel religion.

9 For this cause we also, since the day we heard it, do not cease to pray for you, and to desire that ye might be filled with the knowledge of his will in all wisdom and spiritual understanding:

9. Since my hearing whereof, I have continually made it an article of my most hearty prayers. That God would give you a still larger knowledge of his true religion, and bestow on you greater gifts of his Holy Spirit for that purpose, and bring you to the perfect understanding of its spiritual and excellent nature.

10 That ye might walk worthy of the Lord

10. That you may constantly improve in Christian principles, and in

* Ver. 4. [Since we heard of your faith]—τὴν πίστιν ὑμῶν, *your fidelity* or *steadiness*, viz. to the *Christian* religion, without the observance of the *ceremonial law*.

Lord unto all pleasing, being fruitful in every good work, and increasing in the knowledge of God:

in all such practices as are truly pleasing and acceptable to God. A. D. 62.

11 Strengthened with all might according to his glorious power, unto all patience and long suffering with joyfulness:

11. And, by his great and powerful assistance, may suffer all the hardships your religion brings on you, not only with perfect patience, but with joy and satisfaction.

12 Giving thanks unto the Father, which hath made us meet to be partakers of the inheritance of the saints in light:

12. Giving all praise and glory to God the Father, for vouchsafing you, *Gentile* Christians, the promise of inheriting the happiness of *heaven*, and of glorified saints, as the *Jews* had formerly of the promised land of Canaan.

13 Who hath delivered * us from the power of darkness, and hath translated us into the kingdom of his dear Son.

13. In order to which, he has now, by the revelation of the gospel doctrine, delivered you * from your heathenish state of darkness, ignorance, and vice; wherein you were so miserably subject to the power and delusions of the devil; and has made you members of the church of Christ, the Messiah, his dear and only Son.

14 In whom we have redemption through his blood, *even* the forgiveness of sins:

14. By the sacrifice of whose death, *you* and all the *Gentile* world, as well as the *Jews*, are put into a state of pardon and eternal salvation.

15 Who is the image of the invisible God, the first-born of every creature †.

15. And well may *his* death extend to an atonement for the sins of all mankind, who is the *Son of God*, the express image of the invisible *Father*, and was before all creatures, even the Lord and Governor of all things.

H 2 16. & 17. For

* *Delivered us:* Making *himself* as it were one of the *Gentile* converts, as his usual method is. See Ephes. i. 2, 3.

† Ver. 15. [The first born of every creature.] For the true *original* meaning of this phrase πρωτότοκος. See my note on Gen. xlix. 3.

A. D. 62.

16 For by him were all things created, that are in heaven, and that are * in earth, visible and invisible, whether *they be* thrones, or dominions, or principalities, or powers: all things were created by him, and for him.

17 And he is before all things, and by him all things consist.

16. & 17. For by *him* were all things created in * heaven and earth, angels and archangels, all degrees of spirits *above*, as well as of men here *below*, even the whole visible and invisible world: before all which *he* had an existence with the *Father*, by whose power he created them all at first, and still governs and preserves them.

18 And ‡ he is the head of the body, the church; who is the beginning, the || first-born from the dead, that in all things he might have the pre-eminence.

18. And ‡ *this* glorious *Messiah* is now the Lord and *Head* of the *Christian* church, which has the noble privilege of being *his* spiritual body; and, by his resurrection from the dead, has given *us*, his members, the first and most absolute assurance of *our* resurrection to an immortal life, by him || *who is the Lord both of the dead and of the living*, Rom. xiv. 9.

19 For it pleased *the Father*, that in him should all fulness dwell;

19. It having pleased God the Father thus to invest him with the fulness of divine power and wisdom, for the creation of all things, and for the redemption, government, and preservation of his *whole* church, *viz.* by uniting both *Jews* and *Gentiles* into one body under *him*, the great Saviour and Head of all.

20. And

---

* [In heaven and in earth.] See Ephes. i. 10. note there. Ephes. i. 20, 21, 22.

‡ Ἀυτος, *He* the *same* emphatically.

|| Πρωτότοκος ἐκ τῶν νεκρῶν. [The first-born from the dead,] *i. e.* either is declared and proved to be the *Lord* and *Governor* of the church by his *resurrection*: Or else, The Lord that should *so first* rise from the dead as to give *others* a perfect assurance of *their* resurrection, according to Acts xxvi. 23. I have expressed both senses. See Ephes. i. 10.—20, 21, 22.

A. D. 62.

20 And (having made peace through the blood of his croſs) by him to * reconcile all things unto himſelf, by him, *I ſay*, whether they be things in earth or things in heaven.

20. And by his death upon the croſs hath God procured the * reconcilement of both *Jews* and *Gentiles* to himſelf; giving to them all peace and pardon through his merits; and intending, at laſt, to bring all good and obedient creatures, *men* on earth, and *angels* in heaven, into one bleſſed and happy ſociety ||.

|| See Eph. i. 10.

21 And you that were ſometime alienated, and enemies in your mind by wicked works, yet now hath he reconciled,

22 In the body of his fleſh through death, to preſent you holy and unblameable, and unreproveable in his ſight.

21. & 22. Thus you *Gentile* Chriſtians of Coloſſe are now in a ſtate of pardon and reconciliation with God, and made the pure and holy members of his church; even *you*, who in your *heathen* condition, were utter ſtrangers to his covenant, and, by a habit of idolatrous and wicked courſes, were at perfect enmity with him.

23 If † ye continue in the faith grounded and ſettled, and be not moved away from the hope of the goſpel, which ye have heard, *and* which was preached to every creature which is under heaven, whereof I Paul am made a miniſter.

23. Which glorious privilege you will remember to be upon this condition, viz. your firm adherence, againſt all falſe inſinuations, and under all perſecutions, to the ſame goſpel-doctrine you were firſt inſtructed in; and which is now offered to the whole *Gentile* world; as I Paul am divinely commiſſioned to preach and propagate it.

* Ver. 20. [To reconcile all things unto himſelf]. Note, *This* ſenſe of the word ἀποκαταλλάξαι, is indeed agreeable to the matter of the *Jews* and *Gentiles* being *reconciled* and brought together by Chriſt; [conſonantly to the main ſcope of the epiſtle]; but not to that of *thrones*, *principalities*; viz. *angels* and *men* together. I think, therefore, that in this verſe it is to be moſt truly interpreted by the parallel phraſe ἀνακεφαλαιώσασθαι, Epheſ. i. 10. To *unite* or *ſum up* all under his government.

† Ver. 23. [If ye continue], εἴγε, either *if* ye continue, or *ſince* ye, &c.

A. D. 61.

24 Who now rejoice in my sufferings for you, and fill up that which is behind of the * afflictions of Christ in my flesh for his bodys sake, which is the church,

24. Who, instead of being discouraged, do now glory and triumph in being a prisoner for preaching it to *you Gentiles*; whereby I show Christ to be a truly *suffering* Messiah, by his being still a sufferer in me his apostle, as he was once in his *own person*; for the sake of his body the church.

25 Whereof I am made a minister, according to the dispensation of God, which is given to me for you to fulfil the word of God:

25. Of which church, particularly the *Gentile* part of it, I am (as I have frequently said) a *special* postle, commissioned to preach its doctrines to *you*, and the rest of the world, in common with the *Jewish* nation.

26 *Even* the mystery which hath been hid from ages, and from generations, but now is made manifest to his saints.

27 To whom God would make known what is the riches of the glory of this mystery among the Gentiles,

26 & 27. A thing, indeed, that the former generations of men had little or no notion of, nor had the generality of the *Jewish* nation any understanding of what their own prophets had said about it; but is *now* most expresly and clearly declared to the *Christian* church, as agreeable to the many prophecies of the Old Testament, viz. that God would

* Ver. 24. [And fill up that which is behind of the afflictions of Christ]; καὶ ἀνταναπληρῶ τὰ ὑστερήματα τον θλίψεων του Χριστȣ. Note, The sufferings or *afflictions of* Christ, are, either Christ's *own* sufferings, or those of *Christians* for *his sake*. St. Paul's *filling up*, &c. is not well expressed in our translation. The word is, I, *in my* turn, *fill up*, &c. ἀνταναπληρῶ, &c. i. e. As Christ suffered for *me*, so now (in my *turn*) I suffer for *him*. Or else, as I have exhorted *other Christians* to endure afflictions for Christ, so now I *myself* complete, as it were, that work, by my *own* suffering. The learned and judicious Dr. Clarke rightly also observes, that the phrase *fill up*, signifies the *accomplishment* of what remained to be *fulfilled* of those *prophecies* which foretold, that, after the sufferings of Christ, his *servants* also should therein follow his example—for the good of his church. Serm. Vol. I. page 274, 275.

A. D. 62.

tiles, which is Christ in you the hope of glory.

would, in infinite mercy, bestow upon all *Gentile* believers, the same hopes and conditions of eternal happiness, by Christ the *Messiah*, that the *Jewish* nation was to enjoy.

28 Whom we preach, warning every man, and teaching every man in all wisdom, that we may present * every man perfect in Christ Jesus.

28. Which comfortable doctrine I therefore preach to *all*, without distinction, in order to train them up to that spiritual wisdom, that will make them true and perfect members of his church*.

29 Whereunto I also labour, striving according to his working, which worketh in me mightily.

29. Using my utmost endeavours in the improvement of all those powerful gifts and graces which Christ has endowed me with for that purpose.

CHAP. II.

He repeats his earnest Concern and Prayers for them; the better to warn them against the Error and Subtilty of Heathen Philosophy, *and the vanity of* Jewish Traditions; *encouraging them to depend upon Christ and his* Religion *alone, without any regard to the* Jewish *Ceremonies, or mixing any Part of* Heathen *Devotion with their* Christian *Worship; especially that of the Worship of* Angels *or inferior* Demons, *as Mediators to God, under a Pretence of Religious* Humility.

1 FOR I would that ye knew what great conflict I have

1. THUS, I say, ‡ I strive and labour to make all my converts become true and perfect Christians;

‡ Chap. i. 29.

* [Every man *perfect* in Jesus Christ]; *i. e.* either *perfect* in the understanding of Christianity *here*, or *crowned* with the reward *hereafter*, as the word τέλειος often signifies.

A. D. 62.

have for you, and for them at Laodicea, and for as many as have not ſeen my face in the fleſh.

Chriſtians; but for none more than *you*, and the *Laodiceans*, and all thoſe *Gentile* Chriſtians, whom I converted by other peoples miniſtry under me, but as yet have not perſonally ſeen *them*, nor they *me*;

2 That their hearts might be comforted, being knit together in love, and unto all riches of the full aſſurance of underſtanding, to the acknowledgment of the myſtery of God, and of the Father, and of Chriſt.

2. Continually praying for their cheerful and unanimous progreſs in the true faith, and for their full and complete underſtanding, and free and public profeſſion of all the goſpel-doctrines; particularly this great and unexpected point, *of the* Gentiles *being now called into the Chriſtian covenant*; as God and Chriſt have plainly declared it.

3 In whom are hid all the treaſures of wiſdom and knowledge.

3. In whom * are all the perfections of the divine wiſdom, and by whom the will of God is perfectly and completely revealed to mankind.

4 And this I ſay, leſt any man ſhould beguile you with enticing words.

4. And this perfection, both of the perſon and revelation of Chriſt, I the more carefully obſerve to you, to ſecure you from the enſnaring inſinuations of ſome ‡ men, that lead you into principles that very much derogate from them both.

‡ See Ver. 9, 10.

5 For though I be abſent in the fleſh, yet am I with you in the ſpirit, joying and behold-

5. For though I be at ſuch a diſtance from you, and indeed never ſaw you, yet, by the inſpirations † of the Holy Spirit, I know the condition

---

* *In whom*—it ſeems ambiguous whether ἐν ᾧ refers to Chriſt, or the *myſtery* in the foregoing verſe: But the following verſes, eſpecially the 9th and 10th, make it moſt agreeable to underſtand it of Chriſt.

† [Am with you in the ſpirit.] Τῷ πνεύματι σὺν ὑμῖν εἰμί. It may be rendered, [My mind or heart is with you]. But the former ſenſe is more agreeable to the general acceptation of this phraſe in the New Teſtament. See Acts xx. 22. 1 Cor. v. 3. However, I thought fit to expreſs them both.

A. D. 62.

beholding your order, and the stedfastness of your faith in Christ.

dition you are in, and the temptations you are most liable to; my *heart* and my *authority* is with you, and I think upon your orderly behaviour, and constant adherance to the true faith, with great delight and satisfaction.

6. As ye have therefore received Christ Jesus the Lord, so walk ye in him:

7 Rooted and built up in him, and stablished in the faith, as ye have been taught, abounding therein with thanksgiving.

6. & 7. And I now again exhort you, to keep close to the same rule of Christian doctrine, that Epaphras § first instructed you in. Build your hopes of pardon and happiness upon Christ and his religion only; go on in that profession with a thankful heart, for the honour of being *his* disciples.

§ Chap. i. 7, 8.

8 Beware lest any man spoil you through philosophy and vain deceit, after the tradition of men, after the rudiments of the world, and not after Christ:

8 Taking special care, that neither the *Gentile philosophers* deceive, and make a prey of you, by mixing their vain *speculations* with your *Christian* principles; nor the *Jewish zealots* persuade you to embrace their *traditions* and *ceremonial* observances, those mere external and figurative things, that do not at all belong to the religion of Christ.

9 For in him dwelleth all the fulness of the Godhead bodily.

9. You can have no reason to comply with *either* of these kinds of corruptions; since Christ, by his incarnation, sufferings, and exaltation into heaven, is demonstrated to be invested with all that *power* and * *dominion* over the church of God, which qualifies him and

* Ver. 9. [Fulness of the Godhead]. Τῆς θεότητος of *power* and *dominion*. It is the same with his being made the *Head* or *Lord* over the church, as is most evident from chap. i. 15, 18, 19. which passages, compared with the 18, 19, and 20. verses of this chapter, will show the justness of the other part of my paraphrase on this verse. I understand the phrase *bodily* to signify Christ's *incarnation*, and his whole transaction for us in *our flesh*. But if the reader rather chooseth to understand it to signify *really* and *substantially*, in opposition to *figuratively* and *typically* agreeably, to ver. 17. it will make no alteration in the main sense given of the whole verse.

A. D. 62. and him *alone*, to be our Mediator with the Supreme Father: And therefore by *him only*, and his intercession, ought we to offer up all our prayers and praises to him.

10 And ye are complete in him, which is the head of all principality and power.

10. And you cannot but be absolutely safe, as to all the means of salvation, by *him*, who is the Lord and Governor of all degrees and ranks of creatures whatever. (Compare John i. 14, 16, 17.

11 In whom also ye are circumcised with the circumcision made without hands, in putting off the body of the sins of the flesh, by the circumcision of Christ:

11. And as *circumcision* was the external rite of admitting men into the *Jewish* religion; your *baptism* into Christ's profession, and the reformation of all your sinful principles and practices, make you, in a much higher and better sense, the members of God's true *church*, and entitled to nobler and better *privileges*.

12 Buried with him in baptism, wherein also you are risen with him through the faith of the operation of God, who hath raised him from the dead.

12. For as your being plunged in water, signifies your dying to all sin and vice, in conformity to Christ's death and burial; so your certain belief and assurance of his *resurrection* (denoted by your *rising* again out of the water) gives *you* the certainty of your *own* resurrection to glory and happiness; by the same divine power that raised up *him* from the dead.

13 And you being dead in your sins, and the uncircumcision of your flesh, hath he quickened together with him, having forgiven you all trespasses,

13. And this is now the privilege of you *Gentile*, as well as of the *Jewish* Christians, God having now reduced you from your heathenish and reprobate condition, and granted you the pardon of sin, and the hopes of eternal life by his religion;

14 Blot-

14. For

A. D. 62.

14 * Blotting out the hand-writting of ordinances, that was against us, which was contrary to us, and took it out of the way, nailing it to his cross:

14. For he has now, by the death of Christ upon the cross for all mankind, cancelled and disannulled * the obligation to all those *Jewish ceremonies* that made the difference between you and that people, and kept you at a distance from them.

15 And † having spoiled principalities and powers, he made a show of them openly, triumphing over them in it.

15. And by the same sufferings on the cross, has made Christ the conqueror of sin and Satan, depriving them of their former wicked power and influences over mankind, and leading them, as it were captives in triumph †.

16 Let no man therefore judge you in meat or in drink, or in respect of an holiday, or of the new-moon ||, or of the Sabbath *days*.

17 Which are a shadow of things to come, but the body is of Christ.

16. & 17. Wherefore, it is a vain thing for the Jewish zealots to condemn you Gentile converts, for not observing the Jewish festivals or || Sabbaths, and the ceremonial distinctions between clean and unclean meats. For the *ceremonies* of that law were nothing but figurative and temporary representations of *Christianity;* in Christ they are all now perfectly answered and ceased; and in comparison of *his* religion, they are no more than the *shadow* is to the *substance.*

18. And

* [Blotting out the hand-writing—Nailing it to his cross.] An allusion to the two ancient ways of cancelling a bond or obligation; viz. either by *crossing* the *writing*, or striking it through with a *nail.*

† Ver. 15. [And having spoiled principalities and powers, &c.] *Note*, I have expressed the meaning of this verse agreeably to the general sense of interpreters. That of the learned Mr. Peirce (who interprets the *principalities* and *powers* of the *good angels*) is very particular, but withal exceedingly curious, and worthy of consideration. Let the judicious reader judge for himself.

|| [Or of the Sabbath days.] Perhaps this is not meant of the *seventh-day* sabbath, enjoined by the *moral;* but of the *festivals* appointed by the *ceremonial* law. Let the reader judge for himself.

A. D. 62.

18 Let no man † beguile you of your reward in a voluntary humility, and worshipping of angels, intruding into those things which he hath not seen, vainly puft up by his fleshly mind.

18. And as you are to fence against these notions of the Jewish zealots, so take heed that none of the philosophers, either of the Gentiles, or of those Jews that borrow their philosophy from them, impose upon you, and endanger † your future happiness by any mixtures of false worship with that of God and Christ. Particularly that of addressing to angels, or inferior *demons*, as *mediators* and *intercessors* with God for mankind; under pretence of *humility*, in not addressing to God himself *immediately*. This is the effect of a proud conceit of human reason, that makes men venture to dive into, and determine those divine matters they have no notion of, nor warrant for.

19 And not holding the head, from which all the body by joints and bands having nourishment ministred, and knit together, increaseth ‡ with the increase of God.

19. For to worship any such *beings*, as *intercessors* for us, is the highest disparagement to Christ, our only *Mediator* and all-sufficient *Intercessor*; who being the *Head* of his church, it is by him alone that we have access to God the Father; and from our union to *him* only, do all the members of his body only receive all proper and full ‡ supplies, for their growth and progress in true religion.

20 Wherefore if ye be dead with Christ, from the rudiments of the world, why, as though living in the world, are ye subject to ordinances?

21 (Touch not, taste not, handle not:

20. & 21. As to the nicety of the *Jewish zealots*, about not touching any thing that has been offered to an *idol*; not tasting any forbidden *meats*, and not handling any *unclean* thing, &c. it is plain, that since the death and religion of Christ has freed you from them all,

† Ver. 18. [Let no man beguile you of your reward.] Καταβραβευέτω. *Note.* This word sometimes signifies to *judge* or *condemn*. If it be so taken here, the sense is the same as in ver. 16.

‡ [With the increase of God.] See the note on 2 Cor. viii. 1.

all, it would be the greateſt folly imaginable for you to A. D. 62.
impoſe, or ſuffer others to come under, the ſlavery of
ſuch obſervances.

22 Which all are to periſh with the uſing*) after the commandments and doctrines of men.

22. And to impoſe them *now*, as abſolutely neceſſary, upon no better authority than that of human *traditions*, is ſuch an abuſe* as tends to corrupt and ſpoil the Chriſtian faith.

23 Which things have indeed a ſhow of wiſdom in will-worſhip and humility, and neglecting of the body: not in any honour to the ſatisfying of the fleſh.

23. Thus do they *both* equally err; the heathen *philoſophers*, in pretending *angel* worſhip to be a *religious* act of humanity and reverence; and the *Jewiſh* zealots in recommending their niceties about meats and drinks, &c. as a means to mortify our bodily pleaſures and appetites. It is all *ſhow*, *invention*, and mere *pretence*; nor is there any thing of true religion in either of them, but the gratification of a *carnal* or *Jewiſh* mind.

CHAP.

---

* Ver. 22. [Which things are all to periſh in the uſing.] The literal tranſlation is, [Which things tend to corruption, by the abuſe of them, according to the doctrines and commandments of men.] Or elſe thus: It is the *abuſe* of theſe things, not the mere *uſe* of them, that tends to corrupt or *defile* a man. So referring the following clauſe, [after the doctrines and commandments of men,] to the foregoing verſe; I think the latter is the more natural conſtruction, (though the former be very good ſenſe) agreeable to our Saviour's words, Matth. xv. 11. as interpreted by Grotius and Le Clerc. There is yet another way of rendering theſe words, ἅ ἐςὶ πάντα εἰς φθορὰν τῇ ἀποχρήσει. [All which things are, or were made to be conſumed for our uſe.] Which is very conſiſtent ſenſe, if they be put into a *parentheſis* by themſelves. The judicious reader is to chooſe for himſelf.

CHAP. III.

From the Consideration of the Happiness of a future State, now assured to them by their Christianity, the Apostle exhorts them to renounce all those vicious Practices they were subject to in their Heathenish Condition; among which immoderate Anger, Revenge, and filthy Conversation were the chief. He shows them their great Obligation to Purity, Peaceableness, and Charity; and to an exact Observation of the relative *Duties, notwithstanding any Difference of religious Principles, in the Persons so nearly related to each other.*

A. D. 62.

1 IF ye then be risen with Christ, seek those things which are above, where Christ sitteth on the right hand of God.

2 Set your affection on things above, not on things on the earth.

1. & 2. SINCE then your Christian religion, and particularly that great article of Christ's *resurrection*, has raised you *Gentile* Christians to the hope and assurance of an eternal life in another state; it highly concerns you, no longer to suffer your affections to be immoderately bent upon earthly pleasures and enjoyments, but to fix the main of your thoughts and endeavours after the happiness of heaven; where Christ your *Head* is now set, in the utmost degree of glory and majesty. And, for the same reason, do you *Jewish* Christians raise your minds above carnal and earthly *ceremonies*, and fix them upon *spiritual* and *heavenly* things.

3 For ye are dead, and your life is hid with Christ in God.

3. By your baptism into this religion, you profess yourselves dead to sin, and the world, and them to you. The life you are now to lead is purely *Christian*, and godlike; and though your *future* happiness, consisting in the full enjoyment of God through Christ, be yet at a distance, and its glories invisible; that

that ought by no means to slaken your endeavours. God has it reserved *, and laid up in store for you; and you are sure to enjoy it. A. D. 62.

4 When Christ who is our life shall appear, then shall ye also appear with him in glory.

4. For the *present* life is a state of trial and duty; the season for your *complete* reward is at the great appearance of Christ to *judgment*, when all sincere and good Christians shall shine out with him, in perfect splendor and happiness.

5 Mortify therefore your members which are upon the earth: fornication, uncleanness, inordinate affection, evil concupiscence, and covetousness, which is idolatry †.

5. In order, therefore, to qualify you for this glory, you must be careful to subdue the habits of all those carnal vices you were so addicted to in your heathen state; all those lustful passions and † impure practices, you so freely indulged, in your course of idolatrous religion.

6 For which things sake, the wrath of God cometh on the children of disobedience ‡.

6. Such enormities as these all along have, and do still, bring down the heavy wrath of God upon the wicked and unreformed part of mankind.

7 In the ‡ which ye also walked sometime, when ye lived in them.

7. And you *Gentile Christians*, of *Colosse*, well know, how sad a share you have formerly had in the practice of them, when you conversed among the *heathenish* and wicked part of the world.

8 But now you also put off all these, anger, wrath, malice, blasphemy, filthy communication out of your mouth.

8. But now you are converted to the pure and spiritual religion of the gospel, you must utterly renounce them; and, in like manner, you must carefully reform that temper of furious anger, and bitter

* Ver. 3. *Hid*, κέκρυπται. *Hid*, as *treasures* are said to be hid—ibid. *with Christ in God*. Compare John x. 28—30.

† Πλεονεξία Ephes. iv. 19.—v. 5.

‡ Ἐν οἷς, Among which *children of disobedience*.

A. D. 62. bitter revenge, with all thoſe reproachful * words and filthy expreſſions that flow from it.

9 Lie not one to another, ſeeing that ye have put off the old man with his deeds.

10 And have put on the new man, which is renewed in knowledge, after the image of him that created him.

9. & 10. With the ſame care muſt you forſake that wicked cuſtom of lying to, and deceiving each other in your dealings and expreſſions. Which is a particular inſtance of that former courſe of life, you are engaged by your baptiſm to renounce, in order to live up to thoſe rules of the goſpel that will reduce you to a bleſſed reſemblance of God, after whoſe image you were at firſt created, and of Chriſt, who has reformed you to a new and happy life.

11. Where there is neither Greek nor Jew, circumciſion nor uncircumciſion, Barbarian, Scythian, bond nor free: but Chriſt is all in all

11. In the profeſſion of whoſe religion, God now makes no difference between Jew and Gentile; it matters not of what *country* or *parentage* any man be, whether he be *circumciſed*, or *not*, a *free* man or a *ſlave*; it is ſufficient for his pardon and ſalvation, that he becomes a Chriſtian, and lives up to the precepts and faith of the goſpel.

12. Put on therefore (as the elect of God, holy and beloved) bowels of mercies, kindneſs, humbleneſs of mind, meekneſs, long-ſuffering;

12. Wherefore, being thus made members of the true church of God, make it your principal endeavour to be maſters of thoſe graces and virtuous diſpoſitions, that become perſons ſo highly privileged; ſuch as mercifulneſs, kindneſs, humility, meekneſs, and patient forbearance.

13 Forbearing one another, and forgiving one another, if any man have a quarrel againſt any; even as Chriſt forgave you, ſo alſo *do* ye.

13. In all debates of right, between man and man, let the example of Chriſt, who forgave us all, excite you to bear with the infirmities, and to forgive the injuries of each other.

14. Let

* Αἰσχρολογίαν.

A. D. 62.

14 And above all theſe things, put on charity, which is the bond of perfectneſs.

14. Let *charity*, which conſiſts in a tender regard for the good and welfare of others, and which is the ſum of all the duties of the *ſecond table*, the very bond of all perfect union and happy ſociety, be your principal virtue, and become habitual to you.

15 And let the peace of God rule in your hearts, to the which alſo we are called in one body: and be ye thankful.

15. Let that perfect ſpirit of peace, by which God intends to cement you all into one Chriſtian ſociety, be the rule and umpire to decide all controverſies amongſt you: and, inſtead of envying one another, look *all* up with a thankful heart to him, for his univerſal mercies toward you, in reſtoring you *all*, both *Jews* and *Gentiles*, to peace and reconciliation with him.

16 Let the word of Chriſt dwell in you richly in all wiſdom, teaching and admoniſhing one another in pſalms, and hymns, and ſpiritual ſongs, ſinging with grace in your hearts to the Lord *.

16. Let the doctrine of the *goſpel* be carefully ſtudied, and freely communicated; let Chriſt be the frequent ſubject of your converſation with one another; that God may daily beſtow on you more and more of the ſpirit of wiſdom, and the true knowledge of his word; which will enable you in your Chriſtian aſſemblies, or in your private families, moſt decently and religiouſly to ſing *his* praiſes, in ſpiritual pſalms and divine hymns; inſtead of thoſe lewd and profane ſongs with which you were formerly wont to celebrate your *idolatrous* feſtivals.

17 And whatſoever ye do in word or deed, *do* all in the name of the Lord Jeſus, giving thanks to God and the Father by him.

17. In fine, in all your words and actions, whether in public or private, have a careful and conſcientious regard to the authority and commands of Chriſt, and the juſt limits of your Chriſtian duty; offering up all your prayers and de-

* Ver. 16. [Singing with grace, ἐν χάριτι with or by the (*ſpiritual*) gift, Epheſ. v. 19. James v. 13.

A. D. 62. vout praises to God the Father, through his mediation, and for his sake.

18 Wives, submit yourselves unto your own husbands, as it is fit in the Lord.

19 Husbands love your wives, and be not bitter against them.

18. & 19. Let none of your *Christian* privileges, nor any differences in religious opinions, make any person think himself exempt from the perfect performance of *relative* and *civil* duties. Let the *wife* pay all due submission to the *husband*, and the *husband* use all loving and tender carriage to the *wife*; whether they be both of the same *Christian* * sentiments, or not.

20 Children, obey your parents in all things, for this is well-pleasing unto the Lord.

21 Fathers, provoke not your children to *anger*, lest they be discouraged.

20. & 21. Let children and all young people obey their parents, in every lawful thing, as an essential duty of Christianity. And let all *Christian* parents be especially careful, that, by no severe usage, they discourage their children, either from paying just obedience to themselves, or from embracing the Christian religion, by the badness of their temper or example §.

§ See Eph. vi. 4.

22 Servants, obey in all things your masters according to the flesh: not with eye-service, as men-pleasers, but in singleness of heart, fearing God:

22. Let such Christians as are *slaves* to *heathen* masters, serve them cheerfully and sincerely from a religious principle; carefully discharging their duty, and seeking their interest, as well out of their sight, as while they are under their inspection.

23 And whatsoever ye do, do it heartily, as to the Lord, and not unto men:

24 Knowing, that of the Lord ye shall receive the reward of the inheritance: for ye serve the Lord Christ.

23. & 24. Remembering that a laborious and faithful service to an *earthly* master is in effect to serve Christ our great Lord, whose providence put you into that condition, and who will not fail to reward your patient submission to it, with an inheritance of eternal life.

25 But

25. And

* See Pref. to the Ephesians, § 4. for St. Paul's full meaning in this and the following *relative* duties.

A. D. 62.

25 But he that doth wrong shall receive for the wrong which he hath done: and there is no respect of persons.

25. And let both master and servant consider, that whichever of them does wrong to the other, shall be justly and proportionably punished for it another day, by him who can have no partial regards to any man, upon any account of his external circumstance in this world.

CHAP IV.

The first Verse concludes the Exhortations of the latter Part of the foregoing Chapter, and ought to have been joined to it. Then he exhorts them to constant Prayer for themselves, and for him *their* Gentile *Apostle; to Discretion in their Behaviour towards Infidels, and to Prudence in their words and Expressions to all men. Salutations to and from several Christians. Orders this Epistle to be read to the Laodiceans, and theirs to be read by the Colossians. A Warning to Archippus. His own Salutation, and Conclusion.*

1 MAsters, give unto *your* servants that which is just and equal, knowing that ye also have a master in heaven *.

1. AND as Christian slaves ‖ are obliged to be sincerely observant to even their *heathen* masters; so let all Christian masters be just, and kind toward their servants or slaves, be they of what religious principles soever †; remembering, they themselves have a heavenly Lord, that will reward and punish their behaviour as impartially as he will do that of the meanest servant.

‖ Cap. iii. 22, &c.

I 2 2. AND

* *Note,* This *first* verse does so evidently belong to, and conclude the *foregoing* chapter, that it is amazing it should here be put at the *beginning* of a chapter, which enters upon a quite different argument.

† See Pref. to the Ephesians, § 4.

A. D. 62.

2 Continue in prayer, and watch in the same with thanksgiving:

2. AND NOW, to conclude my exhortation to you all, as you have many difficulties to encounter, many adversaries that strive to draw you from the true faith, be diligent, and constant in earnest prayer to God, for all needful blessings, and in thanksgivings for the mercies you have received.

3 Withal, praying also for us, that God would open unto us a * door of utterance to speak the mystery of Christ, for which I am also in bonds:

4 That I may make it manifest, as I ought to speak.

3. & 4. In which devotions, let me, your apostle, have a continual share; beseeching God to assist and encourage me * in preaching the gospel to the *Gentile* world: a thing so unexpected by them, and so violently opposed by the Jews, that I am now a prisoner for doing it.

5 Walk in wisdom toward them that are without †, redeeming the time.

5. Use the utmost discretion in your carriage toward infidel people; endeavouring as much as lawfully you may, by due circumspection, to avoid † the dangers their obstinacy and malice may expose you to.

6 Let your speech be alway with grace, seasoned with salt, that ye may know how ye ought to answer every man.

6. Let all your discourses in company be mild and courteous, prudent and cautious, so as to answer every question, or objection against your religious principles, and stand any public examination of them before *heathen* magistrates, in such a manner as may conduce to the credit of Christianity, and your own safety in these evil times.

7 All my state shall Tychicus declare unto you, *who is* a beloved brother, and a faithful minister, and fellow-servant in the Lord:

8 Whom

7, 8. & 9. As to my condition here, under my present confinement, of which I conclude you would gladly hear; I have, with this letter, sent Tychicus my beloved Christian brother, and faithful minister of Christ, and along with

* [A door of utterance.] See 1 Cor. xvi. 9. the note there.
† See Ephes. v. 15, 16. And the LXX. in Dan. ii. 8.

8 Whom I have sent unto you for the same purpose, that he might know your estate, and comfort your hearts :

9 With Onesimus a faithful and beloved brother, who is one of you. They shall make known unto you all things which *are done* here.

with him Onesimus *, a faithful member of your own church, on purpose to acquaint you with it, to give you a comfortable account of my circumstances; and to bring me word back how you all do.

A. D. 62.

* See Epistle to Philemon.

10 Aristarchus, my fellow prisoner, saluteth you, and Marcus sister's son to Barnabas (touching whom ye received commandments; if he come unto you, receive him);

10. Aristarchus, my fellow-prisoner, sends his hearty love to your church. And if Mark, nephew to Barnabas, comes to you, entertain him according to the directions you have formerly had about him.

11 And Jesus which is called Justus, who are of the circumcision. These only *are my* fellow-workers unto the kingdom of God which have been a comfort unto me.

11. Those two, and Justus, are the only *Jewish* converts that have assisted me here, in promoting the gospel, and comforted me under my confinement.

12 Epaphras, who is one of you, a servant of Christ, saluteth you, always labouring frequently for you in prayers, that ye may stand perfect and complete in all the will of God.

13 For I bear him record, that he hath zeal for you, and them that are in Laodicea, and them in Hierapolis.

12. & 13. Epaphras, your good Christian teacher, who has a zealous love for your church, and is ever praying for your constancy and perfection in Christianity, salutes you.

14 Luke the beloved physician, and Demas greet you.

14. So does Demas, and Luke the beloved physician.

15 Salute the brethren which are in Laodicea, and Nymphas, and the church which is in his house.

15. My hearty love to the Christians of Laodicea, particularly to Nymphas and his Christian family.

A. D. 62.

16 And when this epiſtle is read amongſt you, cauſe that it be read alſo in the church of the Laodiceans; and that ye likewiſe read † the epiſtle from Laodicea.

16. And, when this epiſtle has been communicated to all your own church, let it be read to the church of Laodicea, and let their † epiſtle be read to your church too.

17 And ſay to Archippus, Take heed to the miniſtry which thou haſt received in the Lord, that thou fulfil it.

17. Warn Archippus, from me, to mind the main duties of his Chriſtian miniſtry, and not trouble himſelf, or other people, with needleſs controverſies and diſputes.

18 The ſalutation by the hand of me, Paul. Remember my bonds. Grace be with you. Amen.

18. I here ſalute you, with my own hand-writing. Remember I am a priſoner for your ſakes, and keep ſteady to my doctrine. The divine love and favour be with you. Amen.

¶ Written from Rome to the Coloſſians, by Tychicus and Oneſimus.

A PARA-

† [The epiſtle from *Laodicea.*] It is not known, for *certain*, what this epiſtle was. Dr. Mills and Dr. Whitby think it to have been St. Paul's Epiſtle to the Epheſians; (which they ſuppoſe in reality, to have been written to the Laodiceans.) See Dr. Mill, Prolegom. § 72, 73, &c. and Mr. Benſon's Hiſt. of the firſt Propag. Goſp. Vol. II. Chap. 10. Sect. 8. Others take it for one written to the Laodiceans, which is now loſt; as no doubt many other apoſtolical papers may be, without any derogation to the ſacred canon; there being as many of them left and providentially preſerved, as are abundantly ſufficient for the end for which they were written.

A

PARAPHRASE

ON THE

FIRST AND SECOND EPISTLES
OF ST. PAUL

TO THE

THESSALONIANS.

PREFACE.

§ 1. IT is agreed on by the most exact chronologers, that there could not pass above a year, between the writing of these two epistles. That they were also written from the same *place*, viz. Corinth; and upon the same argument and occasion, appears by the concurrent suffrage of the best, both of ancient and modern authors. What the chief aim of them was, will be learned partly from the history of the Acts, relating to St. Paul's preaching to this church, and partly from the passages in the epistles themselves.

§ 2. Acts 17. We find St. Paul preaching in a *Jewish* synagogue at Thessalonica. The converts he then made, according to the account there given, consisted of some Jews, but mostly of Greeks, proselyted to their religion. But that some Gentiles also came in, before either of these epistles were sent, and made this, like most others, a church mixed up of both kinds of believers, seems clear from several expressions and advices peculiarly directed to Gentile converts, as in 1 Thess. i. 9. iv. 3, 5, 6.

§ 3. The violent opposition, and implacable malice wherewith the generality of the Jews of this place persecuted the apostle and his doctrine, we read in the forementioned chapter of the Acts. And the whole strain of these epistles, together with the time of their inditement, which was during his stay at Corinth, even in the same year he converted the Thessalonians, shows his design to have been, by an early care, to support and cherish his new Christians, under the furious attacks, and the false and malicious suggestions of these *Jewish* zealots.

§ 4. Those obstinate wretches, not contented to injure the *bodies* and *estates* of such of their brethren as had forsaken the *ceremonial law*, to profess the *Christian* faith, endeavoured to affright and terrify their *minds* also by continually sounding in their ears that confident assertion of theirs, *That none but a circumcised* Israelite *could have any share in the future happiness;* and consequently that all Christians that died without *circumcision*, were eternally lost. To this the apostle refers, 1 Epist. chap. iv. 13, to the end. And, whereas the prophetic writings had spoken much of *the great and terrible day of the Lord*, and the apostles themselves had frequently given notice of a dreadful *appearance of Christ to judgment;* this they understood of the temporal kingdom and conquests of their Messiah; affirming it to be near at hand, and that its greatest terrors were to light upon the head of such Christians as revolted from the *law* of Moses. On the contrary, the sounder Christians, according to St. Paul's doctrine, expected that judgment to fall on the obstinate Jews, and those false Christians that corrupted the gospel religion; though by a common prejudice they seem to have expected it to come sooner than they had any just grounds for. See 1 Epist.

chap. 5,

chap. 5. and 2 Epist. chap. 2. wherein St. Paul seems plainly to include both the day of *final judgment*, and that of the destruction of the *Jewish nation*, under one and the same phrase of the *day of the Lord*; as our Saviour had before done under that of, the *day, or coming of the Son of Man*: Thus, keeping to the general terms of the prophetic scripture, without giving such open and distinct notices of that previous judgment upon Jerusalem, and the temple; which, to have then done, would most probably have exasperated the infidel part of that prejudiced people, into an untimely and incurable degree of rage and bitterness. So then, though the apostle's account of this matter was prudently couched in expressions of a latitude adapted to the times, and persons he wrote to; yet to them who knew his mind, and to us, who have seen the subsequent events so concurring and agreeable, the sum of what he says upon this point in these epistles, is clearly reducible to this; *viz.* That indeed there was a day of dreadful judgment, and wondrous revolutions a-coming, as both the *scriptures* and Christ himself hath foretold: but that neither the day of *universal doom* was any thing near at hand, nor even that of the destruction of the *Jewish nation* was to happen, till some particular occurrences had passed, *viz.* That before the final judgment of the *whole world*, there would be great corruptions, by the violent abuse and impositions of temporal power, even by such as would, in several ages, be governors of *Christian* churches. This is the *grand apostacy*, or *falling-away*, or the *man of sin*, &c. in St. Paul, and the ὁ Ἀντίχριστος, *The Antichrist*, in the most *eminent* sense of that phrase in St. John (1 John ii. 18. 22. 23.) And, moreover, that God would in his due time, and in most terrible manner, scourge and punish all such arbitrary governors, and vile corrupters of the church of Christ. In like manner, the obstinate and infidel nation of the Jews were not to feel the fatal effects of divine wrath upon themselves, their *city* and *temple*, till, by their last and utmost rage against the *Christian* faith, by their persecuting its professors, and their seditious revolt from the *Roman* government, they had began the work of the *great Antichrist*, and might, in a *primary* sense, come under

under his title and character. And thus, as the destruction of *Jerusalem* is allowed by all judicious divines, to be described in expressions common to that of the *final judgment*, and to be a kind of type and emblem of it; so (I think) the *Jews*, and *heretics* spawned from them, were the *Antichrist already come*, the forerunners of that *great Antichrist*, to all whose most eminent characters the church of *Rome* has so undoubted a title. (See and compare Pref. to 1 Epist. John, and 1 John ii. 18. 22. 23. with 2 Peter chap. iii.) See also my Parap. on the *Revelations*.

CHAP.

CHAP. I.

The Title and Salutation. He expresseth his Religious Joy and Satisfaction at their embracing the Christian Faith, by his preaching to them; and their firm and exemplary Adherence to it, against the violent Usage they met with from the Jewish Adversaries.

1 PAUL and Silvanus, and Timotheus, unto the church of the Thessalonians, *which is* in God the Father, and in the Lord Jesus Christ, grace *be* unto you, and peace from God our Father, and the Lord Jesus Christ.

1. PAUL, the apostle of Jesus Christ, sendeth this epistle to the church of *Thessalonica*, converted to the true religion of God the Father, and his Son Jesus Christ; wishing you all divine favours and blessings from them; as do also * *Silvanus* (or *Silas*) and Timothy, who are now with me. A. D. 52.

* See note on Phil. i. 3.

2 We give thanks to God always for you all, making mention of you in our prayers,

2. To let you know how much I bless and praise God for your conversion; and how mindful I am of you in the prayers I put up to him.

3 Remembering without ceasing, your work of faith, and labour of love, and patience of hope in our Lord Jesus Christ, in the sight of God, and our fathers:

3. Religiously and thankfully remembering your steady faith in the gospel, your pious endeavours to promote it, out of pure love to God and to mankind; and the great patience wherewith you suffer for it, from the lively hopes you have in God through Jesus Christ.

4 Knowing, brethren beloved, your election of God.

4. These are my delightful thoughts, dear brethren, while I consider, and assure myself, that God has now made you converted *Gentiles* true members of the church of Christ, by your firm belief of its doctrines, and dutiful observance of its precepts.

5. Especially

A. D. 52.

5 For our gospel came not unto you in word only; but also in power, and in the Holy Ghost, and in much assurance, as ye know what manner of men we were among you for your sake.

5. Especially when I reflect upon myself, as the happy instrument of bringing you to it, by not only delivering its doctrines to you, but demonstrating and confirming the truth of them, by such miraculous powers and evidences of the Holy Ghost, as you know I did.

6 And ye became followers of us, and of the Lord, having received the word in much affliction, with joy of the Holy Ghost:

6. And were so entirely convinced by them, as to imitate our great master Christ Jesus, in suffering for it with a most cheerful mind, assisted with the inward comforts of the Holy Spirit.

7 So that ye were ensamples to all that believe in Macedonia and Achaia.

8 For from you sounded out the word of the Lord, not only in Macedonia and Achaia, but also in every place your faith to God-ward is spread abroad, so that we need not speak any thing.

7. & 8. So that, as your *city* is the metropolis of *Macedonia*, your church has been the first and chief spring of the gospel doctrine in the *Grecian* countries. And I need not say how celebrated and exemplary your Christian principles are become in all those parts.

9 For they themselves show of us, what manner of entering in we had unto you, and how ye turned to God from idols, to serve the living and true God,

9. For every one's mouth is full of it; friends and enemies acknowledge how ready and cheerful a reception you gave me at my first * preaching to you; and how effectually you were converted from *heathen* idolatry to the true *Christian* religion.

* Acts xvii. 1.

10 And to wait for his Son from heaven, whom he raised from the dead, even Jesus, which delivered us from

12. In full hope, and expectation of deliverance from that future punishment, which will fall upon all wicked men; and of eternal happiness, at the great appearance

from the wrath to come.

ance of Jesus Christ the Son of God, our Redeemer and Saviour; an assurance founded on the certainty of his resurrection from the dead.

A. D. 52.

CHAP. II.

He remembers them again of the Powerfulness and Sincerity of his ministry amongst them; and of the good Effects it had on them. The Apostle's *Readiness and Courage to preach to them, as their* Gentile *Apostle; and their Steadiness in his Doctrine, against all the Persecution of the Jews. The Obstinacy and Punishment of that People. St. Paul's Desire to visit the Thessalonians again, out of his great Affection for their Church.*

1 FOR yourselves, brethren, know our entrance in unto you, that it was not in vain.

2 But even after that we had suffered before, and were shamefully entreated, as ye know, at Philippi, we were bold in our God to speak unto you the gospel of God with much contention.

3 For our exhortation was not of deceit, nor of uncleanness, nor in guile:

4 But as we were allowed of God to be put

1. THUS complete * is your conversion to Christianity; and well might it be so, considering with what powerful demonstrations my doctrine was attended.

2. And with what courage and resolution I preached it to your church, against all the furious opposition from the Jews; and after the many contemptuous abuses I had just before suffered for it, as you know, at Philippi †.

3. & 4. And considering how free my arguments to you were of all sinister and selfish designs; void of all deceitful purposes to ingratiate myself with *men*, for the gratification of any sinful passions of

* Chap. i. 5, &c.

† Acts xvi. 12, &c.

A. D. 52. put in trust with the gospel, even so we speak, not as pleasing men, but God, which trieth our hearts.

of my *own*: aiming at nothing but the faithful discharge of the great trust committed to me by God the searcher of hearts.

5 For neither at any time used we flattering words, as ye know, not a cloke of covetousness, God *is* witness;

6 Nor of men sought we glory, neither of you, nor yet of others, when we might have been burthensome, as the apostles of Christ.

5. & 6. Who can testify how perfectly clear I was of all flattering expressions to promote my private interest; how far from seeking popular applause, or temporal profit; insomuch that I refused to be *maintained* by yours, and several other churches, though I could have claimed that privilege belonging to me as a Christian *apostle* and *minister*.

7 But we were gentle among you, even as a nurse cherisheth her children:

7. But, on the contrary, used you with the tenderness of a mother to her child, giving nourishment to you, but receiving none from you.

8 So being affectionately desirous of you, we were willing to have imparted unto you, not the gospel of God only, but also our own souls, because ye were dear unto us.

8. Thus affectionately desirous of your spiritual good, was I ready not only to preach the gospel to you of free-cost, but to die * for you: so dear are you to me.

9 For ye remember, brethren, our labour and travel: for labouring night and day, because we would not be chargeable unto any of you, we preached unto you the gospel of God.

9. For ye cannot but remember, that I and my companions wrought at our trades early and late, to maintain ourselves, and live without any contributions for preaching the gospel to you.

10 Ye *are* witnesses, and God *also*, how holily, and justly, and unblameably we behaved ourselves among you that believe.

10. God, and yourselves, can testify, what care I took to cut off all objections, from every sort of Christian converts, while we conversed among you.

11. & 12.

---

* Our own soul, *τας ψυχας ἑαυτων*, my own life.

A. D. 52.

11 As you know how we exhorted, and comforted, and charged every one of you (as a father doth his children),

12 That ye would walk worthy of God, who hath called you unto his kingdom and glory.

11. & 12. And both by doctrine, and example, treated you, as good and kind parents to their own children, encouraging you all to your duty, confirming you under your affliction, and charging you in the most earnest manner, to live in all respects worthy of this mighty favour of God, in making you members of Christ's kingdom and religion here, in order to your eternal glory hereafter.

13 For this cause also thank we God without ceasing, because when ye received the word of God which ye heard of us, ye received *it* not *as* the word of men, but (as it is in truth) the word of God, which effectually worketh also in you that believe.

13. I am now, therefore, constantly blessing and praising God for the happy effects of my endeavours upon you; that you entertained my doctrine, not as a well-laid scheme of *human philosophy*, but (what it really is) as the pure word and revelation of God, so powerful in its influences on the principles and practices of all that sincerely embrace it.

14 For ye, brethren, became followers of the churches of God, which in Judea are in Christ Jesus: for ye also have suffered like things of your own countrymen, even as they *have* of the Jews:

14. As yourselves are now a plain instance, who are persecuted by the *Jews* of *your* own country *, as the Christians of Judea are by *theirs*, for the sake of this religion; and have courage to bear it patiently, after their example.

* Acts xvii. 5—8.

16 Who both killed the Lord Jesus and their own prophets, and have persecuted us: and they please not God, and are contrary to all men.

15. Being both of you persecuted by that obstinate and malicious people, that crucified Jesus Christ their own *Messiah*, as their forefathers, by the same wicked principles, slew their own prophets that foretold his coming; and so it is no wonder they still persecute us his disciples and followers; being a people that have very few true notions of religion themselves,

A. D. 52. and yet proudly insult, contemn, and scorn all other people that are not of their own nation and persuasion.

16 Forbidding us to speak to the Gentiles, that they might be saved, to fill up their sins alway: for the wrath is come upon them to the uttermost.

16. They are averse to us for preaching the gospel of salvation to the *Gentile* world; utterly refusing to embrace the religion of Christ, unless they can engross all the mercies and privileges of it to themselves. By their incurable obstinacy, in which pride and prejudice they are likely to fill up the measure of their iniquities, and become ripe for a complete and final destruction.

17 But we, brethren, being * taken from you for a short time, in presence, not in heart, endeavoured the more abundantly to see your face with great desire.

* Acts xvii. 5—10.

17. But though, dear brethren, I am, by their malice, * detained from you for the present; be assured my heart is with you; and my desires and resolution to visit your church again, are thereby only heightened and confirmed.

18 Wherefore, we would have come unto you (even I Paul) once and again; but Satan hindered us.

18. Do not, therefore, misinterpret my stay from you. For I had been with you long ago, had not these wicked instruments of Satan prevented me.

19 For what is our hope, or joy, or crown of rejoicing? *are* not even ye in the presence of our Lord Jesus Christ at his coming?

10 For ye are our glory and joy.

19. & 20. And believe me sincere in what I say; for there is nothing I so much delight and rejoice in, nothing I expect so much glory from, at the great day of Christ's appearance to judgment, as from *you* my steady converts to his religion, and from the success of my great labours in converting you to it.

CHAP.

* Ver. 17. [Taken from you,] ἀπορφανισθέντες—It is a most *emphatical* word, [Taken away, as a dying parent is from his orphan children]. See Acts xvii. 5—10.

CHAP. III.

A Testimony of his great Affection for them, in sending Timothy to them, to know how they did, to comfort them under their Persecutions, and confirm their Christian Resolution. The Satisfaction he reaped from the good Account Timothy brought him of their Church. His Prayers for their final Perseverance.

1 WHerefore when we could no longer forbear, we thought it good to be left at Athens alone;

2 And sent Timotheus our brother and minister of God, and our fellow-labourer in the gospel of Christ, to establish you, and to comfort you concerning your faith;

1. & 2. THIS * ardent and sincere affection for your church, put me under such dread and concern at the persecutions you were exposed to, from the malicious *Jews*, that I no sooner left you, and arrived at Athens, but I sent Timothy, that faithful and good minister of Christ, back again to you, to see how you did, to comfort and support you under your distresses. And though I much wanted his assistance there, yet I chose rather to be left only with Silas, amongst those proud † and contentious philosophers, than not to serve you and hear from you.

A. D. 52.

* Chap. ii. 19, 20.

† Acts xvi. 14, 15, 16.

3 That no man should be moved by these afflictions; for yourselves know that we are appointed thereunto.

4 For verily when we were with you, we told you before, that we should suffer tribulation; even as it came to pass, and ye know.

3, 4. & 5. I sent him, therefore, for fear any of you should be discouraged from your profession; and to remind you of what I had often told you, *viz.* That Christianity is, what you have found it to be, a state of trials and sufferings, and those so hard too, that I was under apprehensions the devil, by these his wicked instruments, might succeed in his attempts, and draw

A. D. 52.

5 For this cause when I could no longer forbear, I sent to know your faith, lest by some means the tempter have tempted you, and our labour be in vain.

some of you from the true faith, and so defeat my labours in your conversion.

6 But now when Timotheus came from you unto us, and brought us good tidings of your faith and charity, and that ye have good remembrance of us always, desiring greatly to see us, as we also *to see* you:

7 Therefore, brethren, we are comforted over you in all our affliction and distress by your faith:

6. & 7. But Timothy, at his return, gave me so comfortable an account of your steadiness, constancy, and good affection to me, as made me easy under the worst afflictions that can befal me.

8 For now we live, if we stand fast in the Lord.

8. For your constancy to Christianity is the great comfort of my life.

9 For what thanks can we render to God again for you, for all the joy wherewith we joy for your sakes before our God,

10 Night and day praying exceedingly that we might see your face, and might perfect that which is lacking in your faith.

9. & 10. Nor can I sufficiently bless and praise God for the satisfaction I reap at your conversion, and the progress you have made in the true religion. And am ever wishing and praying for another opportunity to see you again, and perfect those instructions which I could not fully complete, by reason of my short * stay amongst you.

11 Now God himself, and our Father, and our Lord Jesus Christ direct our way unto you.

11. And may God our supreme Creator, and Father, and Jesus Christ, our Redeemer and Governor, so order it that I may soon visit you for that end.

12 And the Lord make you to increase and abound in love one

12. In the mean time, may he graciously assist all your pious dispositions to the same perfect love to

* Acts xvii. 1, 10. and chap. iv. 13. of this epistle.

one towards another, and towards all men, even as we *do* towards you:

to each other, and charity toward all mankind, that I myself bear toward *you*. A. D. 52.

13 To the end he may establish your hearts unblameable in holiness before God, even our Father, at the coming of our Lord Jesus Christ, with all his saints.

13. And may he preserve and confirm you in all holy and acceptable conversation, till the great and solemn appearance of our Lord Jesus Christ to reward you and all good Christians.

CHAP. IV.

He warns the Gentile *Converts of their Church against the Vices they had been most addicted to in their Heathenish Estate; particularly against* Uncleanness. *An Encouragement to mutual* Love *and* Charity, *and to* Industry *in their Callings. A Consolation for the Death of their Christian Friends, from the Assurance of Christ's glorious Appearance and our future Resurrection.*

1 FUrthermore then we beseech you, brethren, and exhort you by the Lord Jesus, that as ye have received of us how ye ought to walk, and to please God, so ye would abound more and more.

1. & 2. THE sum of what I have now further to exhort you to, is, carefully to follow and improve the directions for a holy and Christian life, as I gave you them from the doctrine and authority of Jesus Christ.

2 For ye know what commandments we gave you by the Lord Jesus.

3 For this is the will of God *even* your sancti-

3. I must particularly remind you, *Gentile* converts, of that great

A. D. 52.

|| πορνεία.

ſanctification, that ye ſhould abſtain from fornication:

great duty of *purity* and *chaſtity*, an abſtinence from all kinds of *uncleanneſs* ||; which the goſpel-religion is eſpecially deſigned to reform you *Gentile* Chriſtians from.

4 That every one of you ſhould know how to poſſeſs his veſſel in ſanctification and honour:

5 Not in the luſt of concupiſcence, even as the Gentiles which know not God:

4. & 5. How indiſpenſibly obliged you all now are to preſerve your bodies in temperate and ſober habits, dedicated to the ſervice of God, and free of thoſe luſts and paſſions that are a diſhonour to them; and in which none but ignorant *heathens*, that have no ſenſe and knowledge of the true God, would ever indulge themſelves.

6 That *no man* go beyond and defraud his brother * in *any* matter, becauſe that the Lord is the avenger of all ſuch: as we alſo have forwarned you, and teſtified.

6. That none of you preſume to violate the rights of his neighbour's bed, or abuſe human nature in ſuch luſts as are contrary to it *: Sins that God will moſt ſeverely puniſh, as I have formerly, with great earneſtneſs, forewarned you, as againſt the common vices of the countries † you live in.

7 For God hath not called us unto uncleanneſs, but unto holineſs.

7. For nothing is ſo oppoſite to the *Chriſtian* religion, the very purpoſe whereof is, to cleanſe and reform you from ſuch impurities.

8 He therefore that deſpiſeth, deſpiſeth not man, but God who hath alſo given unto ‡ us his holy Spirit.

8. Whoever of you, therefore, neglects or contemns this advice I give them from the very inſpiration of the Holy Spirit, deſpiſeth God himſelf, by whoſe inſpiration and authority I act.

9 But

9. As

---

* [In any matter,] ἐν τῷ πράγματι. [In ſuch a wicked act;] πράγμα, in a bad ſenſe being the ſame with *facinus* in the *Latin*.

† All hiſtorians are full of the luxury and debaucheries of the Grecians.

‡ Ver. 8. [Unto us his holy Spirit.] Note, all Henry Stephen's MSS. and ſeveral others, read it εἰς ὑμᾶς, *unto you*: And then the

A. D. 52.

9 But as touching brotherly love, ye need not that I write unto you: for ye yourselves are * taught of God to love one another.

9. As to the great duty of *love* and *unity*, I need not repeat my exhortations to you now, who are so truly sensible, from my former apostolical precepts, and from the example of Christ himself, how essential a duty of Christianity this is*.

10 And indeed ye do it towards all the brethren, which are in all Macedonia: but we beseech you, brethren, that ye increase more and more.

10. And I am convinced, how carefully you exercise it toward all the Christians you live amongst. And all I have to do is, to encourage you still further to it.

11 And that ye study to be quiet, and to do your own business, and to work with your own hands (as we commanded you:)

11. And to advise you all to an industrious and peaceable temper, to mind the duties of your several callings, and not intermeddle unnecessarily in what does not concern you.

12 That ye may walk honestly toward them that are without, and that ye may have lack of nothing.

12. Thus approving and showing yourselves to be men of a decent and orderly conversation in the eyes of *infidels*; so as not to be branded with the character of an idle and useless people, or be beholden for your livelihood to men of a contrary religion.

 13. I must

---

the sense is this, "God hath given you his Holy Spirit, on "purpose to cleanse you from impurity, and reduce you to "holiness of life; so that to neglect and despise the advice "I now give, is to despise God, whose Spirit it is." Indeed, the sense will be the same, if by *us* in this verse is meant, not *us* the *apostles*, but *Christians* in general, as in the verse foregoing.

* Ver. 9. [Taught of God]; Θεο διδακτοι—A most *emphatical* word—Not only *taught* by the *precepts*, but by the *example* of God and Christ. Their former *heathen deities* could never be truly supposed to teach them universal benevolence: for those gods are said to have quarrelled *amongst one another*,

A. D. 52.

13 But I would not have you to be ignorant, brethren, concerning them which are asleep, that ye sorrow * not even as others which have no hope.

13. I must also particularly arm you against the proud suggestions and pretences of the *Jewish zealots*, who would fright you into a belief, " That no uncircumcised person, or any that forsake the Jewish religion, can partake of the future happiness, any more than a heathen that has no hope or prospect at all of it || ; whereby they endeavour to discourage your hopes of the good condition of all your Christian friends that have died in the faith of Christ.

|| See the Pref. § 4.

14 For if we believe that Jesus died, and rose again, even so them also which sleep in Jesus, will God bring with him.

14. But be not terrified with such impudence and groundless assertions; for the full assurance you have of the actual death and resurrection of Jesus, your head and Saviour, is demonstration enough to you, that at his second coming to judge the world, God will raise up and fully reward all his true disciples and followers.

15 For this we say unto you by the word of the Lord, That we which are alive, and remain unto the coming of the Lord, shall not † prevent them which are asleep.

15. And, for your further confirmation in this great truth, let me assure you of the following circumstances of this future judgment and resurrection, as I received them from Christ himself; viz. That those good Christians that shall be alive upon earth, at our Lord's appearance, shall not receive their happy change, and glorious reward, till all those that died in his true faith, be raised from their graves, to receive it along with them †.

16. For

* Ver. 13. [That ye sorrow not even as others that have no hope], viz. of a *resurrection*. The apostle means to dissuade the Christians from using those excessive signs of sorrow, those howlings and lamentations over their dead friends, which the *heathens* were known to make.

† Ver. 15. [We which are alive shall not prevent them which are asleep]. Note, I have mentioned the *Jewish zealots* as the persons against whose insinuations this passage, from

A.D. 52.

16 For the Lord himself shall descend from heaven with a shout, with the voice of the archangel, and with the trump of God: and the * dead in Christ shall rise first.

16. For Christ himself shall then, in the most solemn and glorious manner, with a vast retinue of the holy angels, his heralds and ministers, descend from heaven, to summon all mankind to a final judgment; and the first thing then to be done will be, to raise all good and sincere Christians from death ‡.

‡ Rev. xx. 5, 6. 1 Cor. xv. 23.

17 Then we which are alive, and remain, shall be caught up together with them in the clouds, to meet the Lord in the air: and so shall we ever be with the Lord.

17. And then those faithful Christians that are *alive* at the resurrection, shall undergo their blessed *change*; and so all together shall be taken up into the clouds, to meet their Saviour, and be carried with him into a blessed and eternal abode.

18 Wherefore comfort one another with these words.

18. With these considerations, therefore†, fully satisfy and comfort one another, as to the condition of your departed friends, and your own happy state after death.

---

from verse 13. to the end of the chapter, seems to be levelled. Yet I must confess, it seems, probably, to have been spoken against the misunderstandings of some [Thessalonian Christians], concerning the expected [coming of Christ, the day of the Lord], which they took to be [near at hand], 2 Thes. ii. 2, 3. in which they seem to have been of opinion, that those who were then *alive* should enjoy a long and great happiness, before the *resurrection* of such Christians as were *dead* Against this imagination, the several *phrases* of this passage are indeed very much adopted, especially this of the 15th verse—*We which are alive shall not prevent*. ἐ μὴ φθάσωμεν, i. e. *shall have no advantage above, or shall not get the start of them which sleep:* So far from that, says the apostle, That [the dead in Christ shall rise first], ver. 16

* Ver. 16. [The dead in Christ shall rise first]. See Rev. xx. 4, 5, 6. with my paraph. and notes there, and upon the rest of that chapter.

† With these words, ἐν τοῖς λόγοις τέτοις, with these things.

CHAP. V.

The Apostle makes it needless for Christians to know the fixed Time of Christ's Judgment. Only observes to them the suddenness and Terror of it to wicked Men. Exhorts them to such Care, and purity of Conversation, as will prepare them to pay due Value and Respect to their Spiritual Governors. To the Exercise of Unity, Charity, Patience and Forgiveness; to Prayer and Thanksgiving: To a just Regard to Prophetic and Spiritual Endowments; to discretion in entertaining, and Constancy in upholding the Truth. His Prayers, Salutations, and Conclusion.

A. D. 52.

1 BUT of the times and the seasons: brethren, you have no need that I write unto you.

1. BUT as to the particular *time* either of God's judgment upon the *Jewish* nation * in particular, or of Christ's appearance to the great and *general* judgment of the world, there is no occasion for you to know, nor for me, if I could, || to acquaint you with it.

|| Matth. xxiv. 26.

2 For yourselves know perfectly, that the day of the Lord so cometh as a thief in the night.

2. What you know of it already, is sufficient for the state you are in at present; to excite and engage you to prepare for it viz. That (come when it will) it will be very sudden and terrible.

3. It

* Χρόνων καὶ καιρῶν, the *times* and the *seasons*, in the *plural* number; respecting *both* the judgments mentioned in the paraphrase. The *one* was plainly hinted at chap. ii. and the other in the latter part of the foregoing chapter. See the Pref. § 4.

A. D. 52.

3 For when they ſhall ſay, Peace and ſafety; then ſudden deſtruction cometh upon them, as travel upon a woman with child: and they ſhall not eſcape.

3. It will be exceeding dreadful and ſurpriſing to all wicked and irreclaimable men, who, at a time when they are going on thoughtleſs and ſecure in their unrepented impieties, ſhall find themſelves unexpectedly ſeized upon by the moſt diſmal and inevitable deſtruction.

4 But ye, brethren, are not in darkneſs, that that day ſhould overtake you as a thief.

4. But *you*, dear brethren, being reclaimed from your former ſtate of ſin and ignorance, unleſs by your own wilful neglect, are in no danger of being terrified at, and unprepared for, that great day.

5 Ye are all the children of light, and the children of the day; we are not of the night nor of darkneſs.

5. For by your admiſſion into the *Chriſtian* covenant, you have all the means of happineſs and ſalvation, which neither the obſtinate Jew nor infidel Heathen can enjoy.

6 Therefore let us not ſleep as do others: but let us watch and be ſober.

6. You muſt remember, therefore, how highly it concerns you to live a life quite different from either of thoſe ſtupid people; to be active, temperate, ſober, and vigilant, in all inſtances of Chriſtian duty, ſo as to be prepared for that appearance of our great Judge.

7 For they that ſleep, ſleep in the night, and they that be drunken, are drunken in the night.

7. For as night is the ſeaſon wherein drunkards uſually exerciſe their debaucheries, and ſleep and inactivity poſſeſſeth us all; ſo a looſe and unthoughtful life is the beſt that can be expected in a ſtate of ignorance, blindneſs, and prejudice; but in a better and more enlightened condition, we are obliged to better and wiſer courſes.

8 But let us who are of the day be ſober, putting on the breaſt-plate of faith and

8. Which is your caſe now, after your converſion to the *goſpel*-religion. You muſt therefore now be watchful and induſtrious in all

A. D. 52. and love, and for an helmet, the hope of salvation.

all holy* living. Your faith in God, and his promises, your love to him, and to all mankind, must guard you, as the breast-plate does the soldier; and your ardent and firm hopes of eternal happiness must, as the helmet is to his head, be a security against the violent assaults of the devil and wicked men.

9 For God hath not appointed us to wrath: but to obtain salvation by our LORD Jesus Christ.

9. Thus attending therefore to the duties required of you, you may be secure: this day of judgment will be no day of terror, but of salvation to *you*, by Jesus Christ.

10 Who died for us, that whether we wake or sleep, we should live together with him.

10. By virtue of whose death and sufferings, all faithful and sincere Christians are certain to live eternally with him, let him come at what time soever he will *.

11 Wherefore comfort yourselves together and edify one another, even as also ye do.

11. Go on, therefore, in confirming yourselves, and supporting one another, in your Christian profession, by this comfortable assurance.

12 And we beseech you brethren to know them which labour among you, and are over you in the Lord, and admonish you;

13 And to esteem them very highly in love for their works sake. *And* be at peace among yourselves.

12. & 13. And let me particularly exhort you to pay all just respect to the admonitions and instructions of your spiritual governors: esteem them in proportion to the dignity of their office, and the exemplariness of their lives; and live in unity and charity with one another.

14 Now we exhort you, brethren, warn them that are unruly, comfort the feeble-minded, support the weak, be patient toward all men.

14. In order to which, be sure to warn and advise all such as are refractory to theirs and my orders. Relieve and comfort such as are hard pressed with afflictions and persecutions; confirm and restore such as labour under any

* Matth. xxiv. 42. Luke xii. 38.

any doubts and prejudices against our holy religion; A. D. 52.
and bear the infirmities of all sorts of men with an even
and patient carriage.

15 See that none render evil for evil unto any man; but ever follow that which is good, both among yourselves, and to all men.

15. Seek no revenge against such as have injured you; but be kind and forgiving to your fellow Christians, and even to your very persecutors.

16 Rejoice evermore.

16. In all conditions and circumstances, let the hopes you have in Christ, and in the blessings of his religion, be your inward joy and satisfaction.

17 Pray without ceasing.

17. Be diligent and constant in observing all proper seasons of devotion and prayer.

18 In every thing give thanks: for this is the will of God in Christ Jesus concerning you.

18. For whatever mercies you receive, or whatever afflictions befal you, look up with a thankful heart to God, by whose good providence every thing will be turned to your blessing and advantage.

19 Quench not the spirit.

19. Have a just regard to all spiritual *gifts* and *endowments*, improve them in yourselves with diligence, modesty, and prudence; and duly respect others that are qualified with them *.

20 Despise not prophesyings.

21 Prove all things: hold fast that which is good.

22 Abstain from all appearance of evil.

20, 21. & 22. Though there are too many that vent their false doctrines, under pretence of *prophetical* inspiration, yet remember, that God has furnished his church with persons *truly* inspired. Do not therefore neglect the one for the sake of the other; but examine and try them all, by the rule and standard of the Christian † doctrine; keeping close to what you find, by that rule, to be sound and good, and renouncing every thing that upon due examination appears to be false and ill-designed.

* 1 Cor. iii. 1, 3. 1 Cor. xiv. 1 Tim. iv. 14.

† 1 John iv. 1.

23. And

A.D. 52.

23 And the very God of peace sanctify you wholly: And I pray God your whole spirit, and soul, and body, be preserved blameless unto the coming of our Lord Jesus Christ.	23. And may the God of peace and comfort so prosper your endeavours, as to render you true and perfect Christians, in the exercise of all the faculties and powers both of mind and body; that so you may be accepted of him as his true and faithful servants, at the great day of Christ's appearance.
24 Faithful is he that calleth you, who also will do it.	24. Be fully assured that God, who has been so gracious as to call you into the privileges of the

gospel religion, will never fail to do *his* part, for your attaining the final and eternal blessings of it.

25 Brethren, pray for us.	25. Let *me*, dear brethren, your special * *apostle*, have a share in your Christian prayers.
26 Greet all the brethren with an holy kiss.	26. Salute all the Christians in your parts with your usual kiss of charity, for my sake.
27 I charge you by the Lord, that this epistle be read unto all the holy brethren.	27. I charge you, by the authority of Christ, to communicate this epistle to your whole church.
28 The grace of our Lord Jesus Christ be with you. Amen.	28. The love and favour of our Lord Jesus Christ be with you all. Amen.

* Col. iv. 4.

A PARA-

A

PARAPHRASE

ON THE

SECOND EPISTLE OF ST. PAUL

TO THE

THESSALONIANS.

See the Preface to the First Epistle.

CHAP. I.

The Persecutions of the Jewish *Zealots against this Church still, continuing and increasing, and the Apostle being, beyond his expectation, detained from paying them the visit he had promised* (1 Theſſ. ii. 17, 18. iii. 10, 11.) *sends this Second Epistle to revive and back the Encouragements he had given them. He here expresseth his Thankfulness to God for their inviolable Patience and steady Progress in the Christian Faith. Strengthens their Courage and Hopes, from the Consideration of the happy Ends and Effects of their present Sufferings, the Vengeance that would light on their Persecutors, and the glorious Reward they would reap at the great Day of God's Judgment, and Christ's solemn Appearance, to recompense all true Believers, and to vindicate the Honour of his holy Religion.*

1 PAUL and Silvanus, and Timotheus, unto the church of the Theſſalonians, in

1. & 2. PAUL the apoſtle sendeth this second epiſtle to the church of Theſſalonica, which under all preſſures and perse-

Written A. D. 52. the latter end of the year.

A.D. 52.

in God our Father, and the Lord Jesus Christ:

2 Grace unto you and peace from God our Father, and the Lord Jesus Christ.

persecutions that befal them, remain still firm to the true religion of God the Father, and Jesus Christ our Lord and Governor; wishing you all divine favours and blessings from them; as do also * Timothy and Silvanus (or Silas) who are now with me.

3 We are bound to thank God always for you, brethren, as it is meet, because that your faith groweth exceedingly, and the charity of every one of you all towards each other aboundeth:

* ὑπεραυξάνει.

3 Expressing (as in duty and gratitude I am bound) my constant praises to God for the great, and even * unexpected progress you have made in the Christian faith, under all the difficulties attending it, and for your enlarged charity and unanimity with each other.

4 So that we ourselves glory in you in the churches of God, for your patience and faith in all your persecutions and tribulations that ye endure.

4. Of which remarkable degree of faith producing such patience and courage, under what you suffer for your profession, I take notice, and triumphantly boast of to all the Christian churches in these parts.

5 *Which is* a manifest token of the righteous judgment of God, that ye may be counted worthy of the kingdom of God, for which ye also suffer.

6 Seeing it is a righteous thing with God to recompense tribulation to them that trouble you:

5. & 6 Such religious patience, whereby God has enabled you so perfectly to bear such hardships, for his sake, and qualified you for the future glories of his kingdom, does at once fully vindicate the divine wisdom and justice, in calling you to these sufferings, and gives you a complete assurance how justly and fully he will one day take vengeance on those that now so unjustly oppress you.

7, 8, & 9.

* See note on Phil. i. 3.

A. D. 52.

7 And to you who are troubled, reſt with us, when the Lord Jeſus ſhall be revealed from heaven with his mighty angels,

8 In flaming fire, taking vengeance on them that know not God, and that obey not the goſpel of our Lord Jeſus Chriſt.

9 Who ſhall be puniſhed with everlaſting deſtruction, from the preſence of the Lord, and from the glory of his power.

7, 8. & 9 It ſhould highly ſatisfy you, I ſay, what a complete happineſs *you* ſhall then ſhare in with *us* the apoſtles and miniſters of Chriſt; and how terrible ſhall be *their* puniſhment at the dreadful and amazing appearance of the Lord Jeſus from heaven, who by his glorious and powerful preſence, will ſtrike all infidel and obſtinate men into everlaſting miſery and deſtruction.

10 When he ſhall come to be glorified in his ſaints, and to be admired in all them that believe (becauſe our teſtimony among you was believed) in that day.

10. Then will be the time when the divine wiſdom, juſtice, and mercy, in the goſpel diſpenſation, ſhall be fully diſplayed to, and admired by all good creatures, angels and * men; eſpecially by all true Chriſtians, among whom *you*, for this firm and generous adherence to my doctrine, ſhall have a particular and happy ſhare.

11 Wherefore alſo we pray always for you, that our God would count you worthy of this calling, and fulfill all the good pleaſure of *his* goodneſs and the work of faith with power.

11. To which purpoſe, I continually beg of God, ſo powerfully to aſſiſt you in all Chriſtian faith and practice, as may render you truly qualified for thoſe bleſſed ends of your converſion to his holy religion.

12 That

* [In his ſaints.] Ἐν ταῖς ἁγίοις αὐτῦ, *in*, *with*, or *by* his ſaints. It not being clear whether *ſaints* be the ſame with *believers*, or ſignifies the *heavenly ſpirits*, I have expreſſed both acceptations.

A. D. 52.

12 That the name of our Lord Jesus Christ may be glorified in you, and ye in him, according to the grace of our God, and the Lord Jesus Christ.

12. That so Christ may be honoured and glorified by you, and ye made happy in him, according to the wise and gracious design of his gospel.

CHAP. II.

He forewarns them from concluding, either from the confident Assertions of their Adversaries, or from any thing he had himself written or spoken to them, That the Time of Christ's Appearance to judgment was near at hand. The divine Judgment upon Jerusalem and the Jewish Nation, *was not to be fulfilled till that obstinate People had by their last and utmost Malice against the Christian Religion, and their turbulent Rebellion against the* Roman *Government, ripened themselves for a final Destruction. Nor is the* universal *Judgment of the World to come, till after many and great Corruptions be brought into the Christian Church, by the arbitrary Impositions of* temporal *Power among its own Professors. This latter Event is the* Great Apostacy * or falling away. *Those* powerful Corrupters *of Christianity are the* Man of Sin, *in the most* eminent *Sense of that Phrase. The Apostle blesseth God for the safe Condition the Thessalonians were in, by embracing the true Christian Faith; exhorting them to, and praying for their final Perseverance in it.*

* See Pref. to 1 Epist. § 4.

1 NOW we beseech you, brethren, by

1. & 2. THUS have I endeavoured to comfort and support you under your afflictions, from

A. D. 52.

* by the coming of our Lord Jeſus Chriſt, and by † our gathering together unto him.

2 That ye be not ſoon ſhaken in mind, or be troubled neither by ſpirit, nor by word, nor by letter, as from us, as that the day of Chriſt is at hand.

from the conſideration of the great day of *Chriſt's judgment* *. But as you value the bleſſings you are to enjoy at his † glorious appearance, take heed that no confident aſſertions, nor pretended inſpirations of the *Jewiſh zealots*, nor the miſrepreſentation of any thing I myſelf may have ſaid or written ‡ to you upon that head, make you conclude the time of this judgment muſt needs be juſt at hand; for ſuch a falſe perſuaſion, when you ſee the expected event not to anſwer, would tend to ſhake you in your Chriſtian principles, and tempt you to miſtruſt the truth of the whole goſpel religion.

3 Let no man deceive you by any means: for *that day ſhall not come*, except there come a falling away firſt, and that man of ſin be revealed, the ſon of perdition:

3. And, to prevent you from being ſo impoſed upon, I now plainly tell you, that *Chriſt's judgment*, neither upon the *Jewiſh* nation in particular, nor upon the *whole world* in general, is yet near at hand. Jeruſalem is not to be deſtroyed, till that wicked people, by their laſt malice againſt Chriſtianity, and their ſedition againſt the Romans, be ripe for deſtruction. And before the *univerſal* judgment there will be introduced great corruptions of the Chriſtian faith, in ſeveral ages of the church; a *great apoſtacy* from the pure truth, and practice, and worſhip of Chriſtianity, by the arbitary

* Ver. 1. [By the coming of our Lord Jeſus Chriſt] ὑπὲρ —[Concerning the coming, *or* as to the coming.] So Rom: ix. 27. Iſaiah crieth ὑπὲρ τοῦ Ἰσραὴλ, [concerning Iſrael.] And 2 Cor. i. 6. [Our hope concerning you,] ὑπὲρ ὑμῶν. So in Philip. i. 7.

† Ver. 1. Ἐπισυναγωγῆς, [Our gathering together unto him] may ſignify either our being received by him at the laſt *judgment*, or our embracing of his *religion* and *worſhip*, as in Heb. x. 25. The *former* ſenſe is moſt natural in this place.

‡ Chap. iv. 15. and ver. 2. of the Firſt Epiſt.

A. D. 52. arbitrary and violent use of *temporal* power, even among its own pretended professors*.

4 Who opposeth and exalteth himself above † all that is called God, or that is worshipped: so that he as god sitteth in the temple of God, showing himself that he is God.

4. Thus will the Christian religion be dealt by, from a set of haughty and impious men, pretending themselves to be the only true church and people of God; despising all other religious † principles beside their own, trampling upon all human government and authority, and setting up their own inventions and traditions against the plain word of God. Such will be the practice of the obstinate Jews and the heretical Christians, their followers, in *these* times: but much greater and wider will be these corruptions under the *grand apostacy* in the *Christian church* in after ages, by the violence of temporal power in religious matters, under its own pretended heads and governors. [Which *apostacy* in the *latter times* of the Christian church is so plainly foretold by the prophet Daniel.—Dan. xi. and xii. chapters.]

5. You

---

* [That man of sin.] Some copies read τῆς ἀνομίας, [The man of rebellion *or* the lawless man.] So the Jews and those heretical Christians that were tainted with their notions, might truly be styled, both upon account of their impiety towards God, and their incurable proneness to resist those *temporal* powers that Providence had subjected them to. But most *eminently* such is that *Christian church* which takes upon her to excommunicate all Christian *princes*, and absolve their subjects from all allegiance to them that submit not to *her* arbitrary dictates and usurpations. See ver. 4.

† [Against all that is called God, *or* σέβασμα, worship.] Respecting either all other different *religions*, or perhaps the *Roman emperor* that affected to be *deified*, and was styled σέβαστος (*august*); or lastly, *magistrates* in general, who are called *gods* in scripture. It is not very easy to determine the particular sense, and therefore I have expressed them all. See also Le Clerc upon this place, and the learned Dr. Hen. More's Mystery of Iniquity, Book II. Chap. 17. 18 See my Paraph. and Note on Revel. xvii. 12, &c.

A. D. 52.

5 Remember ye not, that when I was yet with you, I told you these things?

5. You cannot but remember, while I was preaching amongst you, I gave you some notices of this matter, though you now seem to have forgot it.

6 And now ye know what withholdeth, that he might be revealed in his time.

7 For the mystery of iniquity doth already work: only he who now letteth, *will let*, until he be taken out of the way.

6. & 7. And you cannot but see a plain reason why this *apostacy* cannot break out *immediately*. The Jews, indeed, for their part, begin already to show great inclinations to persecute the Christians, and rebel against the Romans; but that the many favours conferred on them by the present emperor*, and, at the same time, his strict eye over them, awes them as yet from openly attempting it, till after *his* death, when the troubles and disturbances of the *empire* will prompt them to it †. In like manner, while the government of all countries continues in the hands of none but *heathen* princes, there is no room for the grand *Christian apostacy* which is to come in after the emperors themselves turn Christians, and is to be carried on by the arbitrary use of *temporal* power in religious concerns, by *Christian* governors.

* Claudius.

† Josephus De Bel. Jud. Lib. VI.

8 And then shall that wicked be revealed, whom the Lord shall consume with the spirit of his mouth, and shall destroy with the brightness of his coming:

8. When these things are past, *then* will be the time of God's severe judgment upon the wicked opposers and corrupters of his true religion. The Jews, their temple and city, shall, with a swift destruction, perish by the *Roman* army. But infinitely more dreadful and amazing will be the final punishment of those lawful *Christian* governors and corrupters of the true faith; *whom God will blast with the breath of his mouth*, according to the prophet's expression, Isaiah xi. 4. Compare Revelat. xvii. 12, 13, 14, with my Paraph. there.

A. D. 52.

9 *Even him* whose coming is after the working of Satan, with all power and signs, and lying wonders,

10 And with all deceivableness of unrighteousness in them that perish; because they received not the love of the truth, that they might be saved.

9. & 10. Most exquisite and terrible will be the divine vengeance upon those people, that will give themselves up to diabolical arts, forged miracles, and lying prophecies; abandoned to the pernicious methods of fraud, violence and injustice; and averse to all the clearest evidences of true and saving religion*.

* Josephus and Matt. xxiv 24. and see Pref to 1 John, § 4.

11 And for this cause God shall send them strong delusion, that they should believe a lie.

12 That they all might be damned, who believe not the truth, but had pleasure in unrighteousness.

11. & 12. For which irreclaimable corruptions, God, in just judgment, will let them loose to the prevalent delusions of false prophets and pretenders, so that they will embrace the most absurd and foolish things, and run headlong into such desperate courses as must naturally end in the utter condemnation and destruction of a people, lost to all sense of truth and goodness, and devoted to falsehood and impiety †.

13 But we are bound to give thanks alway to God for you, brethren, beloved of the Lord, because God hath from the beginning chosen you to salvation, through sanctification of the spirit, and belief of the truth.

13. & 14. And, while I am thus representing to you the wretched fate of all such obstinate people, I cannot forbear to express my thankfulness to God for *your* happy condition, dear brethren, who by your firm adherence to the gospel-religion, from the time it was first proposed to you, are now become the true church and people

† See all these predictions exactly fulfilled, with respect to the Jews, in Josephus of the *Jewish* Wars. And they that would see the fullest and most accurate account of the *apostacy* spoken of here, and in other parts of scripture, may read Mr. Mede, Dr. Hen. More, and Sir Isaac Newton. From the works of which learned and great men any honest mind will see to *whom* all these characters principally belong. See my Paraph. on Revelat.

A. D. 52.

14 Whereunto he called you by our gospel, to the obtaining of the glory of our Lord Jesus Christ.

ple of God, and are assured of all its glorious blessings and privileges, by the gifts and graces of the Holy Spirit; agreeably to the gracious purposes of God to mankind, by Jesus Christ.

15 Therefore. brethren, stand fast, and hold the traditions which ye have been taught, whether by word, or our epistle.

15. Continue therefore stedfast to the doctrines * I have delivered to you, whether by word of mouth, or by these my letters.

* παραδοσεις.

16 Now our Lord Jesus Christ himself, and God even our Father, which hath loved us, and hath given us everlasting consolation, and good hope through grace,

17 Comfort your hearts, and stablish you in every good word and work.

16. & 17. And may God the Father, who out of his infinite love, has bestowed these gracious conditions, and sure hopes of eternal happiness, by the *gospel-religion*; and may Jesus Christ, who hath thus redeemed us, and purchased them for us, support you under all your persecution, and keep you stedfast to all the principles and practices of your holy profession.

CHAP. III.

He desires them to pray for his Deliverance from the Malice of the Jews, as he *had prayed for* them. *Renews his Prayer for their Constancy and Patience. Exhorts them, by his own Example, to Industry in their worldly Employments, and to avoid Idleness. Not to suffer any Christians to lead a lazy Life, but to censure them, and avoid their Conversation, in order to reclaim them from it. The Salutation and Conclusion.*

1 FInally, brethren, pray for us, that the word of the Lord may

1. AND now, to conclude my exhortations to you; pray for *me*, brethren, as I have done for

A. D. 52. may have *free* courſe, and be glorified even as *it is* with you.

for *you*, beſeeching God to give the ſame happy ſucceſs to my Chriſtian miniſtry, among other *Gentile* nations, that it has had in your church.

2 And that we may be delivered from unreaſonable and wicked men: for all men have not faith.

2. Entreat God to prevent the malice, and blaſt the deſigns of thoſe obſtinate and unreaſonable Jews, that thus oppoſe his goſpel; of whom, God knows, there are too great a number.

3 But the Lord is faithful, who ſhall ſtabliſh you, and keep you from evil.

4 And we have confidence in the Lord touching you, that ye both do and will do the things which we command you.

3. & 4. But be their infidelity what it will, and their oppoſition never ſo ſtrong, God will not be wanting to ſupport you againſt all the bad effects of it: and I fully perſuade myſelf that your own endeavours will be ſuch as cannot fail, through his aſſiſtance, to keep you firm to the principles and practices I have taught you.

5 And the Lord direct your hearts into the love of God, and into the * patient waiting for Chriſt.

5. And may Chriſt ſo guide and confirm you in the love of God and the true religion, as to render you truly patient under your ſufferings, after his great example *, and in hopes of his glorious appearance to deliver you from, and reward you for them.

6 Now we command you, brethren, in the name of our Lord Jeſus Chriſt, that ye withdraw your-

6. I muſt not forget to warn you, and that by the authority of Jeſus Chriſt himſelf, not to ſuffer any Chriſtian amongſt you to live

* [To the patient waiting for Chriſt,] εἰς ὑπομονὴν τοῦ Χριστοῦ, *i. e.* Either to the ſame kind of *patience* wherewith Chriſt himſelf ſuffered; or elſe, [With the patient expectation of Chriſt's coming.] I have expreſſed both ſenſes.

yourselves from every brother that walketh disorderly, and not after the tradition which he received of us.

live an idle and slothful life, contrary to the express advices I gave you ||.

A. D. 52.

|| Chap. iv. 11. of 1st. Epist.

7 For yourselves know how ye ought to follow us: for we behaved not ourselves disorderly among you.

8. Neither did we eat any mans bread for nought: but wrought with labour and travel night and day, that we might not be chargeable unto any of you.

7. & 8. And to the example you know I myself set you, while I was preaching among you: earning my own living by constant and unwearied labour, at my trade; and taking nothing of any of your church toward my maintenance.

9 Not because we have no power, but to make ourselves an ensample unto you to follow us.

9. Not that I could not have claimed it as the privilege of my office, to be maintained by them I preach to, but I did it on purpose to encourage you all to a diligent and laborious life.

10 For even when we were with you, this we commanded you, that if any would not work, neither should he eat.

10. You remember also, I then gave a particular charge, that no Christian, that was able to work for his livelihood, should be maintained from the public charity.

11 For we hear that there are some which walk among you disorderly, working not at all, but are busy bodies.

11. And I repeat this to you, because I understand there are some of your church, that continue still guilty of this miscarriage, intruding themselves into matters that do not belong to them, instead of minding the proper business of their callings.

12 Now them that are such we command, and exhort by our Lord Jesus Christ, that with quietness they work, and eat their own bread.

12. Wherefore, I now again expresly command all such persons, by the authority of our Lord Jesus Christ, to leave off that idle course, and live upon their own employments.

A. D. 52.

13 But ye brethren, be not weary in well * doing.

* Καλοποιοῦντες.

13. And do you all, dear brethren, go on in that commendable * way of industry and diligence.

14 And if any man obey not our word by this epistle, note that man, and have no company with him, that he may be ashamed.

14. And whoever of those idle persons will not reform, and take warning by what I now say, set a mark upon them, shun their conversation, and make them ashamed of it.

15 Yet count him not as an enemy, but admonish him as a brother.

15. I would not, however, have you utterly reject them like infidels, from your Christian society; but, along with your severities and discouragements, give them brotherly admonition and reproof, in order to reclaim them.

16 Now the Lord of peace himself give you peace always, by all means. The Lord be with you all.

16. Now may God, the Author of our pardon, peace, and happiness, give you all the means of comfort and happiness, by his continual presence with you, and his providence over you.

17 The salutation of Paul with mine own hand, which is the token in every epistle: so I write.

|| See Rom. xv. 25. 1 Cor. xvi 31.

17. I here salute you with my own || handwriting, as a certain sign of the genuineness of my epistles, to all that know my hand.

18 The grace of our Lord Jesus Christ be with you all. Amen.

18. The love and favour of our Lord Jesus Christ be with you all. *Amen.*

A PARA-

A

PARAPHRASE

ON THE

FIRST AND SECOND EPISTLES OF ST. PAUL

TO

TIMOTHY.

THE PREFACE.

§ 1. THOUGH the *place* whence the *first* of these Epistles was written, nor indeed the *time*, be universally agreed on; yet one may most probably conclude the *latter*, with Bishop Pearson and Dr. Mill, to have been Anno Domini 65. about two years after St. Paul's *first* imprisonment and discharge at *Rome*. The chief design of them *both*, pursuant *to his* placing Timothy over the church of *Ephesus*, and those of the neighbouring *provinces*, appears plainly from the characters and false notions of the persons he describes; to suppress whose malicious corruptions, the directions here given are intended. St. Paul's Epistle to this very church of *Ephesus*, three years before, shows the *Jewish zealots* to have been the principal authors of the irregularities and disputes there. And, upon comparing *that* with *these*, to the Bishop, either now actually *resident*, or at least in *commission* there, it seems natural to conclude, that this faction, which had got but little * ground at the date of *that* Epistle, had, by this time, made

* See Pref. to the Eph. § 3.

made ſuch a progreſs, as to call for a vigorous and timely ſuppreſſion: which the attentive reader will, I think, be confirmed in, by obſerving how exactly thoſe characters here given, 1 Tim. iv. 6, 7. chap. iv. and 2 Tim. chap. iii. do agree to zealots for the *Moſaical ceremonies* and traditions; and how juſtly the ſeveral directions in theſe Epiſtles are levelled at the prejudices of a *Jewiſh* doctor, or a *Chriſtian* ſtill tainted with *Jewiſh* prejudices. Thus, *prayer for all men,* and *in every place* (1 Tim. ii.), are clearly oppoſed, the *one* to their contemptuous opinion of all other nations, and even *magiſtrates*, that were of a different extraction from themſelves; the *other* to that fond notion, *That the public worſhip of the true God was* abſolutely confined *to the Jewiſh temple and ſynagogues.* The ſame is to be ſaid of the nice diſtinction of *meats and drinks* (1 Tim. iv.), and of the obligation of *ſervants* or *ſlaves*, ‖ to heathen as well as Chriſtian *maſters* (1 Tim. vi.). To omit ſeveral others.

‖ Pref. to the Epheſ. § 4.

§ 2. Theſe are the people, and theſe the errors the reader will find to have been the occaſion, not only of *theſe*, but indeed of moſt (not to ſay all) of the *epiſtolary* writings. And whatever of the earlieſt heretics, *viz. Nicholaitans, Carpocratians, Corinthians, Ebionites,* &c. (For Dr. Hammond's Gnoſtics were not yet formed into a diſtinct ſect, at leaſt not ſo numerous as to infect *every* church), may be affirmed by the ancients, or ſuppoſed by the moderns, to have been here, or in other Epiſtles referred to; it will be ſufficient to anſwer, that even *their* hereſies were made up of a *Jewiſh* medley; and the *heretics* themſelves were either of *Jewiſh* extraction, or ſet up upon pretence of zeal for *Jewiſh ceremonies* and *traditions.*

§ 3. As to the *ſecond* of theſe Epiſtles, it need only to be obſerved, that the moſt accurate chronologers place it two years after the former, and from ſeveral expreſſions in it, agree it to have been dated from *Rome*, during the apoſtle's *ſecond* confinement under *Nero*, and not long before his martyrdom there. The ſubſtance of it is clearly of a piece with the *firſt;* the prevailing errors above-mentioned, calling yet for freſh advices, and encouragements to *Timothy*, who was ſent to ſuppreſs them.

CHAP.

CHAP. I.

The Title and Salutation. He reminds Timothy of the good End for which he left him at Ephesus; viz. To reduce those Converts, who, by the insinuation of the Jewish Zealots, were intermixing Jewish Doctrines and Traditions with the Christian Faith; and raising warm Disputes about insignificant Matters. Moral Commands of it still perfectly consistent with it, and promotive of it. The Apostle's humble and grateful Sense of the Mercy of his Conversion, and the Honour of his Christian Ministry. His Conversion, a great and Encouraging Example of Divine Favour to all true Penitent Believers, whether Gentiles or Jews. Reminds Timothy of his Call to the Ministry, and exhorts him to the conscientious Discharge of it: Warning him, by the Instances of such as he had severely chastised, for their Insolence and Immoralities.

1 PAUL an apostle
of Jesus Christ,
by the commandment
of * God our Saviour,
and Lord Jesus Christ,
which is our hope;
2 Unto Timothy
my own son in the
faith: grace, mercy
and peace from God
our Father, and Jesus
Christ our Lord.

3 As

1. & 2. PAUL an apostle of Jesus Christ, by the express || revelation of God our Saviour *, and of Jesus Christ our Lord and Governor, the Author of all our hopes of glory and happiness, sendeth this epistle to Timothy, whom I converted, and begat to Christianity; wishing him all divine favour and happiness from God our Supreme Father, and Jesus Christ our Lord.

Written A. D 65.

|| Acts ix.

3. & 4. To

* [God our Saviour]; some good copies read καὶ σωτῆρος ἡμῶν Ἰησῦ Χριστῦ. [And Jesus Christ our Saviour].

A. D. 65.

3 As I besought thee to abide still at Ephesus, when I went into Macedonia, that thou mightest charge some that they teach no other doctrine;

4 Neither give heed to fables, and endless genealogies which minister questions, rather than * edifying, which is in faith: *so do.*

3. & 4. To remind you of the end and design for which I left you at *Ephesus*, viz. To correct and reform several of the *Jewish* converts in that city and the neighbouring parts; to bring them off from mixing their *Jewish* notions with the * *Christian* faith; from the value they set upon their groundless *traditions*, and their frivolous and endless disputes about their *pedigrees* and descent from the *patriarchs*; to the great neglect of their *Christian* faith and practice.

5 Now the end of the † commandment is charity, out of a pure heart, and of a good conscience and of faith unfeigned.

5. For true religion, especially that of the *gospel*, consists in none of these impertinent matters: The grand design of it, and of our † preaching it, being to bring men to the true love of God and their *neighbour*; from a principle of pure conscience, and a firm belief of its *moral* doctrines and precepts.

6 From which some having swerved, have turned aside unto vain jangling.

6. And it is the neglect of this main thing that has turned the heads of them and their *Jewish* teachers to these frivolous disputes, about *traditions* and *pedigrees*; things that are full of uncertainties and void of all advantage to true religion.

7. They

* Ver 4. [Rather than edifying.] It should be rendered μᾶλλον ἢ οἰκονομίαν Θεοῦ τὴν ἐν πίστει. [Which teach men questions, but not the true dispensation of the gospel]. For all MSS. read it οἰκονομιαν, not οἰκοδομιαν. See Dr. Mill.

† Ver. 5. [The end of the commandment]—Or τῆς παραγγελίας. [of our preaching]. I have expressed *both* senses. But perhaps the strict meaning of this word is to be taken from ver. 3. where St. Paul says, [I besought thee still to abide at Ephesus, ἵνα παραγγείλῃς, that thou mightest charge or warn some, &c.]——*Now* he says, *the end of this παραγγελίας, charge* or *caution*, is *charity*, &c.

7 Desiring to be teachers of the law, understanding neither what they say, nor whereof they affirm.

7. They set up for doctors, and expounders of the *Jewish* law; but understand little of the true scope, and ultimate design of the *law* they are so zealous for; nor have any certainty of the *traditions* they so confidently talk of.

A [illegible]s.

8 But we know that the law is good, if a man use it lawfully.

9 Knowing this, that the law is not made for a righteous man, but for the lawless and disobedient, for the ungodly, and for sinners, for unholy and profane, for murderers of fathers, and murderers of mothers, for manslayers,

10 For whoremongers, for them that defile themselves with mankind, for menstealers, for liars, for perjured persons, and if there be any other thing that is contrary to sound doctrine.

8. 9. & 10. And whereas they represent *us* as contemners of the *Mosaical* law in general; it is an ignorant and false suggestion. For we *Christians* allow *that* religion to have been a wise and good dispensation; even the *ceremonials* of it to have had their good purposes, *viz.* To be figurative representations of Christ, and his more perfect religion, and then to cease; and not to be of essential and *perpetual* obligation*, as *they* vainly imagine, contrary to the very design of such kind of institutions. And as to the more substantial part of it, *viz.* the *moral* law, *that* we hold to be perfect and good, and still to remain so: But then, we affirm, *that* law does in no instance condemn a good || *Christian* (as *they* would persuade men); because it was made against those very vices, such as impiety and false *worship*, profanation of *holy things*, *parricide*, *murder*, *uncleanness*, *Sodomy*, *manstealing*, *lying*, *perjury* &c. all which the *gospel* religion severely condemns and punishes, as it does every other instance of immorality, as much as ever the *law* could do.

|| κεῖται.

11. And.

---

* [If a man use it lawfully], νομιμως *i. e.* according to the nature and *design* of the *Jewish ceremonial* law, *viz.* not esteeming *that* to be of the same necessary and eternal obligation with the *moral*; and condemning all people as apostates from the *one*, because they do not think the same of the *other*, as those *Judaizing Christians* do.

A. D. 65.

11 According to the glorious gospel of the blessed God, which was committed to my trust.

11. And, you know, I have always represented the pure and glorious dispensation of the gospel, as destructive of all vice and wickedness: agreeable to the ministerial office with which God has been pleased to intrust me.

12 And I thank Christ Jesus our Lord, who hath enabled me, for that he counted me faithful, putting me into the ministry;

12. And I bless and magnify God, for the great favour of esteeming me worthy of it, and qualifying me for a faithful and sufficient discharge of it by his gifts and graces bestowed on me.

13 Who was before a blasphemer, and a persecutor, and injurious. But I obtained mercy, because I did it ignorantly in unbelief.

13. On *me*, I say, who, for my former rage and blasphemy expressed against Christ and all his professors, did least deserve such a favour. But God had compassion on me, as knowing I did it, not against the *known* dictates of my conscience, but from the fury of misguided zeal and prejudice †.

† See Acts xxvi. 9, 3, 17, 13, 27.

14 And the grace of our Lord was exceeding abundant, with faith and love which is in Christ Jesus.

14. Which eminent degree of divine favour, I have endeavoured to improve into a perfect faith in Jesus Christ, and a zealous love for the promotion of his true religion.

15 This is a faithful * saying, and worthy of all acceptation, that Christ Jesus came into the world to save sinners, of whom I am chief.

15. While, therefore, the *Jewish* disputes ‡, about *traditions* and pedigrees, are built upon nothing but vanity and uncertainty; our *Christian* religion is founded in this undoubted *truth* *, this great and comfortable *fact*, of Jesus Christ's incarnation and sufferings for the salvation of sinful

‡ Ver. 4. 6, 7.

* Ver. 15. [A faithful saying.] πιςος ὁ λόγος, [a true thing.:] For λόγος is the same דבר in the Hebrew, signifying *things* or *facts* as well as *words*. And πιστος *faithful*, signifies being truly or faithfully *represented*, agreeably to the πιστις, the faith or religion of the *gospel*. So *to be found faithful*, is to preach the *gospel truly and faithfully*, in opposition to the *errors* and *misrepresentations* of others.

ſinful mankind, whereof I myſelf am a moſt ſignal example. And if the pardoning mercy of the *goſpel* be extended to ſo remarkable an offender, to ſo notorious a perſecutor of the truth as *I* have been; why ſhould it be thought to be denied to the repenting *Gentiles?* A. D. 65.

16 Howbeit, for this cauſe I obtained mercy, that in me firſt Jeſus Chriſt might ſhow forth all long-ſuffering, for a pattern to them which ſhould hereafter believe on him to life everlaſting.

16. And certainly God has been pleaſed, by this great inſtance of his mercy toward *me*, to ſhow all true penitent believers, of *every* nation, how ready and graciouſly willing he is to accept and reward them with eternal life, upon their ſincere profeſſion of Chriſt's religion.

17 Now unto the king * eternal, immortal, inviſible, the only wiſe God, be honour and glory for ever and ever. Amen.

17. For which, may all honour and glory be for ever aſcribed to God the eternal, inviſible, and all-wiſe Governor of the world, and all the ſeveral diſpenſations * of it.

18 This charge I commit unto thee, ſon Timothy, according to the prophecies which went before on thee, that thou by them mighteſt war a good warfare.

18. Of this excellent and admirable religion, my dear convert Timothy, have I ordained you a *miniſter*, and now conſtituted you *biſhop* over the churches I left you in, as a perſon marked out by the predictions of the Holy Spirit for that office. A very high truſt indeed! take care, therefore, to anſwer thoſe prophetic characters given of you, by a due and conſcientious diſcharge of it.

19 Holding faith and a good conſcience, which ſome having put away, concerning faith have made ſhipwreck.

19. By ſtudying and firmly adhereing to the *Chriſtan* faith, and adorning and confirming that faith by a conſcientious practice, conſidering how much a diſagreeable and impure life will endanger and corrupt the beſt principles.

* The King Eternal, *or* Βασιλεῖ τῶν αἰώνων, the ruler of the ages, or diſpenſations.

A. D. 65.

|| 2 Tim. ii. 17. iv. 14.

20 Of whom is Hymeneus and Alexander, whom I have delivered unto Satan, that they may learn not to blaspheme.

20. As may be seen in the particular instance of Hymeneus || and Alexander, whom for venting their notorious errors, and opposing the doctrine I preach, I have now excommunicated from the Christian church, and delivered up to Satan; till by a sufficient punishment, both of mind and ‡ body, they be brought to repentance and reformation.

‡ 1 Cor. v. 5.

CHAP. II.

Directions to Timothy for the Management of his Church. Prayers to be made for Heathen *Governors, and* Gentile *People, as well as* Christian; *it being the gracious Design of God to give them* all *the Offers of the* Gospel *Covenant and Privileges, without distinction. Christ the Saviour, and God the Creator and Governor both of* Jew *and* Gentile. *The Apostle declares himself a Preacher to* both. *Public Prayer and Worship to be no longer confined to the* Jewish *Temple and Synagogue, but to be performed in the* Christian *Assemblies of* every Nation, *with Reverence and Regularity Charity and Faith. Women enjoined to appear at the Public Assemblies in a decent Garb, with Modesty, Silence, and Subjection, according to the Original Laws of the Creation, and the Circumstances of the first Transgression. Marriage and Child-bearing no way impure and inconsistant with true and saving Religion, as some of the* Jewish *Zealots pretended. Chastity and sobriety the special Duty of Christian Women.*

1 I Exhort, therefore, that first of all, supplications, prayers, intercessions, *and* giving of thanks be made for all men:

1. TO come now to the particular directions I am to give you, for the due discharge of your office. And first, let the public devotions of *Christians* be, not like those of *Jewish zealots*, put

A. D. 65.

put up only for *themselves*, and those of their *own* nation and religion; but let all *mankind* have a share in each part of your prayers; *viz.* In your *deprecations* for averting divine judgments; in your *petitions* for spiritual and temporal blessings; in your *intercessions* for the pardon and salvation of others; and in your *thanksgivings* for mercies already received.

2 For kings, and for all that are in authority; that we may lead a quiet and peaceable life in all godliness and honesty.

2. And, as temporal governors and magistrates, whether they be of the true * religion, or no, are still the ministers of God, for the good of the communities they govern, let the *emperor*, and all officers under him be the special subject of your prayers, beseeching God for a blessing upon their administration, and to incline their minds to give you a quiet and peaceable enjoyment of your *Christian* profession.

* See Romans xiii. 1, &c.

3 For this *is* good and acceptable in the sight of God our Saviour:

3. For, whatever prejudices those *zealots* have against *heathen* governors; the *Christian* religion makes no alteration in *civil* constitutions, but obliges us to pray for their prosperity, and obey their just laws.

4 Who will have all men to be saved, and to come unto the knowledge of the truth.

4. Thus extensive ought our *Christian* prayers to be; since God never intended to exclude any part of mankind from his providence and protection; but especially not from the mercies of the *Christian* covenant; but is desirous to have *all* nations enjoy them, upon their acceptance of the faith, and obedience to the precepts of the *gospel*.

5 For *there is* one God, and one Mediator between God and men, the man Christ Jesus:

6 Who gave himself a ransom for all, to be testified in due time.

5. & 6. For, as God is equally the Creator and Governor ‡ both of Gentiles and Jews, so has he given his Son Jesus Christ as a Saviour and intercessor for them *all*, without distinction. And Christ has, now in the gospel-dispensation, as freely offered up, and demonstrated himself a sacrifice and expiation for the sins of all mankind.

‡ Rom. iii. 29, 30.

A. D. 65.

7 Whereunto I am ordained a preacher and an apostle (I speak the truth in Christ, *and* lie not), a teacher of the Gentiles in faith and verity *.

7. Of which merciful dispensation *I* am appointed a preacher, expressly commissioned to declare and offer it to the *Gentile* world; which, whatever those *Jewish* zealots may think of it, is as certainly true * as the Christian religion itself is.

7 And I will therefore that men pray every where, lifting up holy hands, without wrath and doubting:

8. Wherefore, though the public worship of the true God has hitherto, for a long time, been truly performed only in the *Jewish* temple and synagogues; yet was it not intended to be *absolutely* confined to those places. I order, therefore, that *every* congregation of *Christian* people, whether *Gentile* or *Jewish*, in what country, or place soever, perform their public worship of God, through Christ; assuring them, it will not fail of acceptance, if it be done with true reverence and piety towards God, with charity and forgiveness toward mankind, and without animosities ‡ and contentions among themselves. See Mal. i. 2. John iv. 21---24.

‡ διαλογισμῶ.

9 In like manner also, that women adorn themselves in modest apparel, with shamefacedness and sobriety: not with broidered hair, or gold, or pearls, or costly array:

9. Let all Christian *women* appear in the congregation, in a decent and modest dress; and not set themselves out in a gaudy, costly, and captivating manner.

10 But (which becometh women professing godliness) with good works.

10. But let them esteem *virtue* and *modesty* to be the proper ornaments of *Christian* women.

11 Let the women learn in silence with all subjection.

12 But I suffer not a woman to teach, nor to

11. & 12. And let them be sure to be grave and silent in the church assemblies: For I cannot permit a *woman* to be a public *preacher*; *that* being the proper office of the superior

---

* I speak the truth in Christ, ἀλήθειαν ἐν Χριστῷ, Christian truth. See Rom. ix. 1. *Ibid.* In faith and verity ἐν πίστει καὶ ἀληθείᾳ, in the true faith.

to usurp authority over the man, but to be in silence.

superior ‡ sex, and for *them* to do it, is to usurp upon the laws of the creation. (Gen. iii. 16.)

A. D. 65.

‡ 1 Cor. xiv. 34.

13 For Adam was first formed, then Eve.

13. For the *man* being first created, and the *woman* taken out of him, and being made as a help and assistant to him, bespeaks her beauty of modesty and subjection §.

§ 1 Cor. xi. 8.

14 And Adam was not deceived, but the woman being deceived, was in the transgression.

14. And beside, Eve being first deceived by the tempter, and drawing her husband into a transgression of the divine law, she and all her female posterity were expresly and justly sentenced to an obedience and subjection to *mankind*; as a wise punishment for the ill use of her influence over Adam.

15 Notwithstanding she shall be saved in child-bearing, if they continue in faith and charity, and holiness with sobriety.

15. But whereas some of the *new teachers* endeavour to decry the state of matrimony and child-bearing, as an impure thing * inconsistent with true religion; let not that frighten the most virtuous women from it. Marriage and child-bearing are perfectly consistent with the gospel terms of salvation, and no breach of Christian purity. All that I require of Christian women is, to keep close to their Christian profession, and to remember, that *chastity* and *temperance*, and a freedom from all *unlawful* desires and pleasures are the special duties of their *sex*.

* [She shall be saved in child-bearing.] Διὰ τῆς τεκνογονίας, in the *state of marriage* and *child-bearing*, as well as in that of *virginity*. Τεκνογονία, the same as παιδοποιΐα and παιδοποιέω in the *classics*. By comparing the verse with chap. iv. 3.—v. 10. 14. Heb. xiii. 4. I take the paraphrase to contain the true meaning of it, without any respect either to the *education* of children, or the *pains* of bringing them forth. Each of which senses are attended with difficulties that I humbly conceive are taken off by this interpretation, which I submit to better judgments.

CHAP III.

The Characters and Properties of a good Bishop. Of Deacons and Deaconesses. He gives Timothy these short Rules, till he sees him, and furnishes him with more particular directions. The Truth and Excellency of the Christian Religion.

A. D. 65. 1 THIS is a true saying, If a man desire the office of a bishop, * he desireth a good work.

1. MY next directions to you are, concerning the choice of bishops, and church-governors: Certainly an office the most useful and honourable * that any man can aspire after; and whoever aims at it, ought duly to remember those dispositions and qualifications that are required to render him worthy of that honour.

2 A bishop then must be blameless, the † husband of one wife, vigilant, sober, of good behaviour, given to hospitality, apt to teach:

2. Now the chief of them are such as these; *viz.* He must be a person unexceptionable in his life and morals; one that is guilty neither of the polygamy of the *heathens*, nor of divorcing one wife to marry another, out of lustful or humoursome reasons, as is too customary among the Jews; but one that has had but one wife at a time, and kept constant to her. He must be vigilant in his studies and function, temperate in his passions and pleasures, decent and grave in his habit, words and gestures; ready to entertain strangers, able to teach the true gospel-doctrines, and free in communicating his knowledge, for the instruction of others.

3. He

* [He desireth a good work,] *καλȣ̃ ἔργȣ*, [An honourable office.]

† [The husband of one wife.] Note, The interpreting this passage as a prohibition of *second marriages*. is supported by such slender reasons, that I thought them not worth an annotation. The reader may see them collected together, and fully answered by the learned paraphraser, in Mr. Locke's *manner*, on this *verse*: who agrees with me in the sense here given.

A. D. 65.

3 Not given to wine, no ſtriker, not greedy of filthy lucre, but patient, not a brawler, not covetous;

3. He muſt be given to no exceſs in drinking, nor to violent returns upon any provocation, nor to any ſordid and mean courſes for worldly gains. One that is mild and modeſt, and no way clamorous and abuſive in converſation; nor enſlaved to the love of riches.

4 One that ruleth well his own houſe, having his children in ſubjection with all gravity:

4. One that keeps his children under due diſcipline, and his whole family in a decent order, by exerciſing a prudent authority over them.

5 (For if a man know not how to rule his own houſe, how ſhall he take care of the church of God?)

5. (For no one, that is not a good maſter of a *family*, where his authority is more immediate, direct and clear, can ever be ſuppoſed qualified for a church-governor, which is a much higher province, and requires greater ſkill and pains in its management.)

6 Not a novice, leſt being lifted up with pride, he fall into the condemnation of the || devil.

6. He muſt not be a new convert, a raw and imperfect Chriſtian; but for fear his advancement ſhould puff him up into the ſame pride, and draw him into the ſame condemnation, as that pride once did the fallen *angels*; a juſt condemnation upon one that gives occaſion to the enemies, who are always watching for the faults of Chriſtians, by which to *ſlander* and *reproach* them.

|| Τοῦ διαβόλου, The ſlanderer.

7 Moreover, he muſt have a good report of them which are without; leſt he fall into reproach, and the ſnare of the * devil.

7. Moreover, he muſt be a man of good character among the * unbelieving Jews or Gentiles, with whom he formerly converſed: leſt, by reproaching him with his former life, or preſent immoralities, they

* Ver. 6. & 7. [Condemnation of the devil, reproach and ſnare of the devil, or of the ſlanderer]: And perhaps the ſenſe may be, [Leſt he give occaſion to the adverſaries and calumniators of our religion, to condemn and reproach it, and him]. See Epheſ. iv. 27. John vi. 70. and ver. 11. of this chapter.

A. D. 65. shame him out of his Christian principles, and tempt him to *apostacy*.

8 Likewise *must* the deacons *be* grave, not double-tongued, not given to much wine, not greedy of filthy lucre.

8. And as *bishops* and superior officers of the church, so *deacons*, and all inferior ones ought to be persons of approved gravity and sobriety; no way fraudulent, deceitful, or inconstant in their words and expressions; not given to any intemperance in drinking, nor any base and sordid methods of gain.

9 Holding the * mystery of the faith in a pure conscience.

9. They must be orthodox in the Christian *faith*, and careful to defend and maintain the honour of it by a suitable and conscientious practice.

10 And let these also first be proved; then let them use the office of a deacon, being *found* blameless.

10. In both which points they ought to be thoroughly examined into, and if in either there be found any exception against them, they are not to be admitted to the deacon's office, till it be clearly removed.

Γυναῖκας.

11 Even so *must* *their* wives *be* grave, not slanderers; sober, faithful in all things.

Πιστὰς ἐν πᾶσι.

11. In like manner, all women that are admitted into any church † office, must be such as are remarkable for their gravity and modesty; no way loose and slanderous in their words; sober and temperate in their conversation; steady in all Christian principles, and true to any trust committed to them.

12 Let the deacons be the husbands of one wife, ruling their chil-

12. Be sure to let none be a *deacon*, that keeps several wives at once, or divorceth his wife up- on

* Ver. 9. [Holding the mystery of the faith.] Very probably the apostle means that *particular* divine *discovery* of the Gentiles being partakers of the *gospel*-blessings. Concerning *this* doctrine, they ought not to be *double-tongued*, talking sometimes *for it*, sometimes *against it*, to please the *Judaizers*.

† [Viz. Deaconesses,] that were employed in the baptism of *women*, &c. The manner of baptism, in those times, being to plunge the whole naked body in water.

A. D. 65.

children, and their own houſes well.

on needleſs || occaſions; or, that keeps not good diſcipline in his family.

|| See ver. 2.

13 For they that have uſed the office of a deacon well, purchaſe to themſelves a good degree, and great boldneſs in the faith which is in Chriſt Jeſus.

13. For though the *deacon's* office be but an inferior one, yet it is a ſtep to a higher; the more honourable offices of the church being generally choſen out of the beſt of the lower ones. And therefore, he that has been a good *deacon*, will have the more effectual influence and authority, when he is raiſed to a poſt, in which he is both to teach and *govern*.

14 Theſe things write I unto thee, hoping to come unto thee ſhortly;

14. I thus give you theſe general and ſhort rules, in hopes to ſee you ſoon, and furniſh you with more particular inſtructions.

15 But if I tarry long, that thou mayeſt know how thou oughteſt to behave thyſelf in the houſe of God, which is the church of the living God *, the pillar and ground of the truth.

15. And if I ſhould be detained from you longer than I expect, theſe will ſerve, in the mean time, for the due management of yourſelf, as the governor of a *Chriſtian* church; which is not like the *Jewiſh* temple, famed and magnified for its *outward* fabric; nor is the nurſery of *ignorance* and ſuperſtition, as the *heathen* religions and temples were, but contains a ſociety of men dedicated to the honour and worſhip of the *true* God, and inſtructed in all the great and admirable truths of Chriſt's religion. Behave yourſelf, therefore, like a true * *defender* and *ſupporter* of ſuch important truths.

* [The pillar and ground of truth]. Στύλος καὶ ἑδραίωμα. [As a pillar and ſupport, *or* buttreſs]. It is moſt natural (I think) to refer theſe words neither to ἐκκλησία, *the church*, as the Romaniſts vainly imagine, nor to μυστήριον in the following verſe, as Epiſcopius and others do, but to the perſon of Timothy, to whom the *apoſtle* was ſpeaking: [How thou mighteſt behave thyſelf,—like a pillar of the truth]. Thus James and John are ſtyled *pillars*, Gal. ii. 9. See Rev. iii. 12.

A. D. 65.

16 And without controversy, great is the mystery of godliness: God was manifest in the flesh, justified in the spirit, seen of angels, preached unto the Gentiles, believed on in the world, received up into glory.

16. For, indeed, what religion could ever consist of more noble, comfortable and important articles than these, viz. That the Son of God has taken upon him our human nature, in order to instruct us by his heavenly doctrine, and redeem us by his death: By the wonderful works he wrought by the Holy Spirit, was declared and demonstrated, against all the malice and calumny of the Jews, to be the true Messiah, and Saviour of mankind: That, at his entrance into the world, the *good* angels did worship him, and attend upon him, while the *wicked* spirits were conquered and dispossessed by him: That, upon the most undoubted evidences, his religion was, against the most furious opposition, received by a considerable part of both the *Jewish* and *Gentile* world; being intended as the gracious means of *universal* salvation. Finally, That this Saviour having conquered sin and death, by suffering for us, was raised again, and, in the most open and solemn manner, exalted into heaven; there to remain a powerful advocate, and intercessor with God the Father, for all that truly repent, and embrace his religion?

CHAP. IV.

None ought to be surprised at the great Number of Apostates from the true Christian Faith, since the Holy Spirit had plainly foretold, there would be such a Set of Men. Such were especially the Jewish Zealots of these Times: A Character of them, and their false Doctrines. Timothy warned against them; advised to slight their vain Traditions, and build his Faith on the Scriptures, and to be diligent in the Discharge of his Office.

1. YET

1 NOW * the Spirit ſpeaketh expreſsly, that in the latter times ſome † ſhall depart from the faith, giving heed to ‡ ſeducing ſpirits, and doctrines of devils:

1. YET, notwithſtanding theſe undoubted evidences § of our religion, we muſt not be ſurpriſed to ſee a ſet of men pretending to embrace it, ſeduced from it to quite contrary doctrines, by the influence of wicked ſpirits, or falſe teachers; ſeeing the *Holy Spirit*, both by the old *prophets*, Jeſus Chriſt *, and his inſpired *apoſtles*, has plainly and expreſsly foretold, it would be ſo in the *latter* times of the *Chriſtian* church.

A. D. 65.

§ Chap. iii. 16, &c.

2 Speaking lies in hypocriſy, having their conſcience ſeared with a hot iron;

2. That there would be falſe doctrines broached by hypocritical and deſigning people, men of looſe and profligate conſciences.

3 Forbidding to marry, *and commanding* to abſtain from meats, which God hath created to be received with thankſgiving of them which believe and know the truth.

4 For every creature of God *is* good, and

3. & 4. Such are now thoſe converts that are influenced by the zealots of the *Jewiſh* faction; who, contrary to the clear deſign of *Chriſtianity*, and out of pretended purity, would perſuade us, that marriage || is an impure and unlawful thing, eſpecially to ſome ranks and *orders* of men; and put the main ſtreſs of true religion

|| See chap. ii. 15.

---

* [The Spirit ſpeaketh expreſsly,] which ſome refer to that of Dan. xi. 36, *&c.* But others more probably to that of our Saviour, Matth. xxiv. 11, 12. and of the apoſtles, 2 Theſſ. ii. 3, 9. Jude xvii. 18, 19. and elſewhere.

† Ver. 1. [Some ſhall depart—] Not only *ſome* now in *theſe* times, but even the *generality* in the times of the *grand apoſtacy*. So the word Τινες, is often uſed. See 1 Cor. x. 7. compared with Exod. xxxii. 4. So chap. vi. 10. [Such were ſome of you, *i. e.* all.]

‡ Ver. 1. [Seducing ſpirits.] This phraſe may not ſignify wicked (inviſible) *ſpirits*, but wicked *men*, pretending to the inſpirations of the *true* divine *Spirit*, and thereby ſeducing others into the belief and worſhip of *demons*, or *evil ſpirits*, *as falſe and imaginary deities*. So St. John's [trying of ſpirits,] is to be underſtood, 1 John iv. 1, 2. [Of trying and examining into men pretending to inſpiration.]

A. D. 65. and nothing to be refused, if it be received with thankſgiving: gion upon ſuch indifferent matters, as that of abſtaining from ſuch and ſuch *meats*, formerly forbidden by the *Jewiſh* law: Whereas, the original intent of God's creating all ſorts of creatures, was for the uſe of man; and no *Chriſtian*, that truly underſtands his religion, can be ignorant of the liberty he has of eating them, without diſtinction, in a dutiful and thankful manner.

5 For it is ſanctified by the word of God, and prayer.

5. For, the Chriſtian religion has taken off all difference between clean and unclean meats; rendering them *all* equally * lawful to us to feed upon; and requires nothing of us, but to beg God's bleſſing upon, and return him thanks for our refreſhment from them.

* ἁγιάζεται

6 If thou put the brethren in remembrance of theſe things, thou ſhalt be a good miniſter of Jeſus Chriſt, nouriſhed up in the words of faith, and of good doctrine, whereunto thou haſt attained.

6. It is your duty then, as a faithful miniſter of Chriſt, purſuant to the true doctrines of his religion, you ſo well underſtand, to warn all Chriſtians of theſe things, theſe corruptions already begun, and that are the forerunners of the *great apoſtacy* that will be hereafter.

7 But refuſe profane and old wives fables, and exerciſe thyſelf *rather* unto godlineſs.

7. And be ſpecially careful to daſh and diſcountenance the ſenſeleſs and fabulous ‖ *traditions* of theſe *Jewiſh* teachers; and make the ſubſtantial duties of *Chriſtianity* your chief buſineſs.

‖ See chap. i. 4. 6. Titus i. 15. iii. 19.

8 For bodily exerciſe profiteth little: but godlineſs is profitable unto all things, having promiſe of the life that now is, and of that which is to come.

8. For thoſe external obſervances, they pretend to be ſo ſtrict in, are of no moment in true religion: But the practice of *Chriſtian* virtues and graces, has all poſſible advantage; having the expreſs promiſe of divine bleſſing and protection in this life, and of a certain reward in the next.

9. This

A. D. 65.

9 This *is* a faithful * saying, and worthy of all acceptation.

9. This is the * certain and most important article you should endeavour to possess *Christian* people with.

10 For therefore we both labour, and suffer reproach, because we trust in the living god, who is the Saviour of all men, especially of those that believe.

10. And for this it is that those malicious Jews does thus despise and persecute us; viz. that we forsake their external and *ceremonial* observances, that were intended only for a while, to keep up a distinction between their *nation* and the *rest* of the world; and *preach* up that substantial and spiritual religion of Jesus Christ, which God, who cannot but be thought to intend the salvation of all men, has now graciously offered to *all* mankind, without distinction; and the blessings whereof all true believers, of what nation soever, will most certainly enjoy.

11 These things command and teach:

11. Whatever opposition *they* make, therefore, let it be *your* constant business to inculcate it, and oblige all Christians to the belief of this important doctrine.

12 Let no man despise thy youth, but be thou an example of the believers, in word, in conversation, in charity, in spirit, in faith, in purity.

12. And as you are yet but a young man, be careful, by the soundness of your doctrine, the gravity of your conversation, your charity to all persons, your prudent and industrious improvement of the gifts of the Holy Spirit, by a steadiness in the true faith, and in charity and purity of practice, to be so exemplary to all people, that none may take occasion to despise your *authority* upon account of your *youth*.

13 † Till I come, give attendance to reading, to exhortation, to doctrine.

13. Let reading the holy scriptures of the Old Testament be your constant study †; and, out of them build wholesome instructions and persuasions to your people.

14. Be

* Ver. 9. [A faithful saying.] See the note on chap. i. 15.

† Ver. 13. [Till I come.] See note on Rom. vi. 13.

[Till I come.] ἕως ἔρχομαι. See 2 Sam. vi. 23. 1 Sam. xv. 25. in the Septuagint.

A. D. 65.

14 Neglect not the gift that is in thee, which was given thee by prophecy, with the laying on of the hands of the presbytery.

14. Be no way negligent in the sacred office, the Holy Spirit prophesied you should have *, and which you were consecrated to by the imposition of my hands, and of other church-officers with me. (2 Tim. i. 6.)

* 1 Tim. i. 18.

15 Meditate upon these things; give thyself wholly to them, that thy profiting may appear to all.

15. Consider well and frequently on what you read † and teach to others; that you may show what a proficient you are in the Christian doctrine, by a ready and exact way of instruction.

† Ver. 11, 12.

16 Take heed unto thyself, and unto thy doctrine; continue in them: for in doing this thou shalt both save thyself, and them that hear thee.

16. In fine, be every way careful both of your life and doctrine. Be constant in what I have recommended to you; and, by such a discharge of your office, you will not fail of your own salvation, nor of the best method to secure that of your people too, by the influence of so good an example.

CHAP. V.

Directions for Censuring and Reproving an Elder or Presbyter, and for his Behaviour toward aged, or young Women. For the public Charity to Widows; which of them are fit, and which not to receive it. Good Ministers to be liberally maintained. No Accusation against a Presbyter to be proceeded upon, without due Caution, and full Evidence: but such as are notoriously guilty to be severely and openly reproved. Timothy strictly charged to be impartial in his Government, and to be tenderly cautious who he ordains to the Ministry. Private advice relating to his Health.

1 REbuke not an elder, but entreat *him* as a father, *and* the younger men as brethren;

1. TO come now to ſome other particular directions. Be not haſty and extreme in cenſuring the miſcarriages of any elderly perſon, eſpecially ſuch as are preſbyters of the church, unleſs they be very notorious and ſcandalous; but, as you are a young man, though a governor and biſhop, endeavour to perſuade them with due reſpect to their *age* and *office;* and treat all younger perſons, particularly ſuch as are in any church-office, with brotherly kindneſs, and a friendly temper. A. D. 65.

2 The elder women as mothers, the younger as ſiſters, with all purity.

2. Treat the *deaconeſſes* *, or any other *elderly women,* with juſt regard to their years alſo; and converſe with the younger women, as with Chriſtian relatioms; but with ſuch gravity and decency, as may be ſure to cut off all ſuſpicion of any impure thoughts or behaviour.

* See Chap. iii. 2.

3 Honour widows that are widows indeed.

3. Let ſuch widows as are deſtitute of all friends to relieve them, be liberally and reſpectfully maintained out of the public charities of the church.

4 But if any widow have children or nephews, let them learn firſt to ſhow piety at home, and to requite their parents; for that is good and acceptable before God.

4. But where any widows have children or grandchildren, that are in a capacity to maintain them; let thoſe children know, it is but a juſt return, and one of their prime and ſpecial duties, to provide for their parents; and that God will indiſpenſibly require it at their hands.

5 Now ſhe that is a widow indeed, and deſolate, truſteth in God, and continueth in ſupplications and prayers night and day.

5. Now, a widow ought to have theſe two qualifications, to render her a proper object of the church's charity; viz. ſhe muſt be one entirely deſtitute of relations to relieve her; and one that is remarkable for the ſteadineſs of her *Chriſtian* principles, and the conſtancy of her devotions.

6. For

A. D. 65.

6 But ſhe that liveth in pleaſure, is dead while ſhe liveth.

6. For a looſe and voluptuous widow is to be looked on as a member loſt and dead to the *Chriſtian* church; and ſo incapable of being maintained by its charity.

7 And theſe things give in charge, that they may be blameleſs.

7. Be ſure therefore to divulge and execute their orders carefully, that none but truly good women may be choſen in to partake of the church's maintenance.

8 But if any provide not for his own, and eſpecially for thoſe of his own houſe, he hath denied the faith, and is worſe than an infidel.

8. And none but ſuch as are really deſtitute. For whatever Chriſtian, that is able to do it, neglects to provide for his neareſt relations (eſpecially his parents and children), acts in direct contradiction to one of the eſſential duties of Chriſtianity, and is guilty of a crime, that even a heathen would be aſhamed of.

9 Let not a widow be taken into the number, under threeſcore years old, having been the wife of one man.

9. Let none be choſen into the number of theſe church-widows, under the age of ſixty; nor any that has, upon needleſs and humourſome occaſions, procured a divorce, or for good reaſons been divorced from one huſband, and married another.

10 Well reported if for good works; if ſhe have brought up children, if ſhe have lodged ſtrangers, if ſhe have waſhed the ſaints feet, if ſhe have relieved the afflicted, if ſhe have diligently followed every good work.

10. Nor any, but what are known to have diſcharged their duties of life well; ſuch as the care of their families; the pious education of their children; to have been hoſpitable to ſtrangers, charitable to the poor and afflicted, and ready to do the meaneſt of good offices to any Chriſtian brethren.

11 But the younger widows refuſe: for when they have begun

11. & 12. And be ſure to take in none that are very young, for ſuch women are too apt to grow weary

gun to wax wanton against Christ, they will marry:

weary of the grave and retired life of church-widows; and be tempted to marry into *heathen* * families, and renounce their Christianity; and so be lost, at last, to the great scandal of the church. A. D. 65. * γαμᾶν. See ver. 15.

12 Having damnation, because they have cast off their first faith.

15 And withal they learn *to be* idle, wandering about from house to house; and not only idle, but tatlers also, and busy-bodies, speaking things which they ought not.

13. At least, it is very hazardous; but such young persons, instead of the sobriety and retiredness that become them, will run into idleness, impertinence, and indecency in their words and actions.

14 I will therefore that the younger women marry, bear children, guide the house, give none occasion to the adversary to speak reproachfully.

14. Instead, therefore, of being objects of the public charity, let such young widows marry again, and be duly and honestly employed in breeding and well educating children, and in a discreet management of their families; that so no occasion be given to the adversaries of our religion, to reflect upon it, from their indiscretions, and miscarriages.

15 For some are already turned aside after Satan.

15. And this caution is but too necessary at this time: for, you know, some of these young widows have actually done as † I say, and even renounced their Christian profession. † Ver. 11, 12.

16 If any man or woman that believeth, have widows, let them relieve them, and let not the church be charged; that it may relieve them that are widows indeed.

16. I charge, again ‡, that every Christian, that has wherewithal to do it, maintain the widows that belong to his own family, and not throw them upon the church's charity; that so a large provision may be made for such as are really destitute of other relief. ‡ Ver. 8, 9.

17 Let the elders that rule well, be counted worthy of double honour, especially

17. Take care, that great respect, and very liberal maintenance be given to all our superior officers in the church, especially to such as labour

A. D. 65. cially they who labour in the word and doctrine.

labour hard in the conversion of others to the faith, or in instructing and edifying such as have already received it.

18 For the scripture saith, Thou shalt not muzzle the ox that treadeth out the corn: and, the labourer *is* worthy of his reward.

* See 1 Cor ix. 9, 12, 15.

18. This is but just, according to the rule of the very *Mosaical* law *, that forbids *even an ox to be debarred from feeding upon the corn while he is labouring to tread it out from the straw.* And what you are obliged to from our Saviour's own words, *the labourer is worthy of his hire.* (Matth. x. 10. Luke x. 7).

† Ver. 1.

19 Against an elder receive not an accusation, but before two or three witnesses.

19. But to return to the case of censuring a presbyter † of the church. Entertain no complaint against such officers, so far as to determine and give sentence upon it, but upon the utmost caution, and full evidence of two or three witnesses, at least.

20 Them that sin, rebuke before all, that others also may fear.

20. But, if the evidence given against him plainly prove him to be guilty of any considerable crime, let him be publicly censured, for a warning and restraint to others.

21 I charge *thee*, before God and the Lord Jesus Christ, and the elect angels, that thou observe these things, without preferring one before another, doing nothing by partiality.

‡ See 1 Cor. xi. 10. Heb. i. 4. and Rev. i. 4 with my Paraph. there.

21. And I adjure you by God, and the Lord Jesus Christ, whose minister you are; and by the good *angels*, that are inspectors over, and ministring ‡ spirits to the Christian church to govern the church committed to you, agreeably to the rules I have given you, without the least prejudice or partiality to any person whatever.

22 Lay hands suddenly on no man, neither be partakers of other mens sins: keep thyself pure.

22. Use strict care and examination, before you admit any person into holy orders, or receive any notorious offender into the com-

* communion of the church again. For by granting either of these admissions to unworthy people, you entail a share of their guilt upon yourself: and therefore keep yourself clear. A. D. 65.

23 Drink no longer water, but use a little wine for thy stomachs sake, and thine often infirmities.

23. Though your sacred office obliges you to great temperance in the use of *wine*, yet remember, *wine* was given us for necessary refreshment; and, as you have a weak stomach, and are of an infirm constitution, I advise you to use it as a cordial, and not confine yourself wholly to water.

24 Some mens sins are open beforehand, going before to judgment: and some *men* they follow after.

25 Likewise also the good works *of some* are manifest beforehand; and they that are otherwise, cannot be hid †.

24. & 25. As to the caution I gave you (ver. 22.) you need not understand it of persons whose principles or practices are plain and notorious. Some are so openly scandalous, that there need no witnesses to come in against them; while others are of so good and clear a reputation, that little or no examination will serve to their admission, either into the church as *penitents*, or into holy *orders*. But some there are, that have the art to conceal and varnish over their crimes for the present, and appear fair. But due time and care, will discover and prevent them from imposing themselves upon you; at least, you will have done your part, and discharged your own conscience †.

---

* Which was usually done with [laying on of hands.]

† [And they that are otherwise cannot be hid]: Not, [they cannot be hid at all], but they cannot be hid *long* and *always*.

Ibid. [They that are otherwise]. Perhaps this may refer, not to the *sins of bad men*, in the *foregoing verse*, but to the *good works* of others in *this verse*. So the apostle's similitude is complete and elegant; viz. That neither the secret *vices* of some, nor the hidden *virtues* of others, shall be [long and always concealed]. So the excellent Dr. Clarke's Serm. Vol. I. p. 254.

CHAP. VI.

Christianity exempts none of its Professors from their Natural and Civil Obligations: Not Servants or Slaves from paying due Service and Fidelity even to Heathen Masters, much less to Christian ones. The Reasonableness of being contented in every Condition, where a Competency is to be had; and the Danger of an Immoderate Love of Riches. Rich Men obliged to Courtesy and Charity. The Charge to Timothy renewed.

A. D. 65

1 LET as many servants as are under the yoke, count their own masters worthy of all honour: that the name of God, and his doctrine be not blasphemed.

2 And they that have believing masters, let them not despise *them*, because they are brethren: but rather do *them* service, because they are faithful and beloved, partakers of the benefit. These things teach and exhort.

1. LET all Christians, that are servants (or *slaves*) to *heathen* * masters, respect and serve them diligently; and not, by their disobedience to them, bring a scandal upon the Christian religion; as if it dissolved any man from his *natural* or *civil* obligations.

2. And, as the privilege of *Christianity* exempts none from discharging their duties to *heathen*, much less do it to *Christian* masters: But is a still stronger argument to such *slaves*, not to withdraw their services from *them*, upon account of their being upon the level with them in *religion*, but to serve them the more cheerfully; as considering, they labour for those who are partners with them in the same divi e favours, and common hopes of salvation.

* See Pref. to the Eph. § 4.

3, 4. & 5.

A. D. 65.

3 If any man teach otherwise, and * consent not to wholesome words, *even* the words of our Lord Jesus Christ, and to the doctrine which is according to godliness;

4 He is proud, knowing nothing, but doting about questions and strifes of words, whereof cometh envy strife, railings, evil surmisings.

5 Perverse disputings of men of corrupt minds, and destitute of the truth, supposing that gain is godliness: from such withdraw thyself.

3, 4. & 5. Be sure, therefore, to inculcate this upon all Christian *slaves*. And if any of the *Jewish* converts ‡, contrary to the plain design of the Christian religion, set up *, and plead for an unjust liberty; look on them as a proud and prejudiced people, led away by a perverse fondness for their vain *traditions*, that tend to nothing but mischievous quarrels and disputes: And avoid their conversation, as persons that make religion nothing but a *trade* || for worldly profit and advantage.

‡ Matth. xx. 27. Mark x. 44. Pref. to Ephes. § 4.

|| πορισμόν.

6 But godliness with contentment is great gain.

6. For one of the surest methods of rendering religion truly advantangeous to us in the *next* world, is, to be contented and industrious in the condition that Providence has allotted to us in *this*.

7 For we brought nothing into *this* world, *and it is* certain we can carry nothing out.

7. And good reason we have to be so: For, as we came naked into the world, and are supplied with the necessaries of it, by divine Providence; so, whatever affluence we have here, must be left behind, and the greatest plenty must die with us.

8 And having food and raiment, let us be therewith content.

9. A bare competency, therefore, of the present enjoyments ought to be enough to satisfy any *Christian*.

9 But they that will be rich, fall into temptation, and a snare,

8. And for men to thirst after more, and be bent upon growing rich, by any means whatever, is only

* Ver. 3. [And consent not to wholesome words—μὴ προσέχεται. See Dr. Bentley's remarks on Freethinking, Part I. pag. 72, 73. μὴ προσέχεται, attends not to.

A.D. 65. snare, and *into* many foolish and hurtful lusts, which drown men in destruction and perdition.

only to pamper their foolish lusts and passions; which will destroy their virtuous principles here, and themselves hereafter.

10 For the love of money is the root of all evil, which while some coveted after, they have erred from the faith, and pierced themselves through with many sorrows.

10. For the immoderate love of temporal riches and grandeur, is the inlet to all mischievous principles and practices; as is too plain from the examples of some people, who have already renounced their very *Christianity* for the sake of them, and brought themselves into the most miserable condition.

11 But thou, O man of God, flee these things: and follow after righteousness, godliness, faith, love, patience, meekness.

11. But you, Timothy, as a minister of God, must be perfectly averse to such a temper; and endeavour to become master of that *justice* that will suffer us to defraud no man; that *godliness*, that renders us contented with what we have; that *faith* in God and Christ, that makes us rely upon his good Providence in all estates; that *love* and charity, that obliges us to distribute freely, when we are in plenty; that *patience* that supports us under adversity: and that *meekness* that keeps us kind and forgiving to such as injure and defraud us.

12 Fight the good fight of faith, lay hold on eternal life, whereunto thou art also called, and hast professed a good profession before many witnesses.

12. Thus are you like a good *racer* *, to run and stretch forward, with your eye fixed upon that prize of eternal life, that God has set before you, in the Christian religion: As indeed you have hitherto done and testified your courage in the many sufferings you have publicly undergone for it.

* 1 Cor. ix. 24.

13 I give thee charge in the sight of God, who quickneth all things, and *before* Christ

13. & 14. And I, again, † adjure you, by that God who will raise up all from the dead, that suffer for his sake; and by Jesus Christ,

† Chap. v. 21.

Christ Jesus, who before Pontius Pilate witnessed a good confession,

14 That thou keep this commandment without spot, unrebukeable, until the appearing of our Lord Jesus Christ.

Christ, who openly professed what he was, before Pilate, and sealed and confirmed the truth of his religion, even by his death; that you discharge your office, agreeably to the directions I have given you, and so approve yourself a faithful servant of our great Master, at the great and solemn day of his appearance to judgment.

15 Which in his times he shall show, who is the blessed and only Potentate, the King of kings, and Lord of lords:

16 Who only hath immortality, dwelling in the light which no man can approach unto, whom no man hath seen, nor can see: to whom *be* honour and power everlasting. *Amen.*

15. & 16. A day fixed in God's due time, who is the blessed, and only Supreme Lord and Governor over all things. *He* that is immortal in himself, and has the sole power of giving life to others; dwelling in glory inaccessible, invisible, and unbearable by every mortal eye; to whom be eternally ascribed all honour and power. *Amen.*

17 Charge them that are rich in this world, that they be not high minded, nor trust in uncertain riches, but in the living God, who giveth us richly all things to enjoy.

17. Upon this consideration, warn and dissuade all rich men from proudly over-valuing themselves upon their present transitory enjoyments, and placing their happiness in them. Let God, the eternal Author of all true felicity, be the Supreme object of their hope and confidence.

18 That they do good, that they be rich in good works, ready to distribute, willing to communicate.

19 Laying up in store for themselves a good

18. & 19. Convince them, that a free and cheerful distribution to the needy, is the best improvement of the charitable course of actions, which is the surest foundation * and security of our future

* Θεμέλιον. See 2 Tim. ii. 19. and the Note there.

A. D. 65. good * foundation against the time to come, that they may lay hold on eternal life.

future happineſs, will be their trueſt riches.

22 O Timothy, keep that which is committed to thy truſt, avoiding profane *and* vain babblings, and oppoſitions of ſcience, falſely ſo called:

21 Which ſome profeſſing, have erred concerning the faith. Grace *be* with thee. *Amen.*

20. & 21. And thus, dear Timothy, be diligent in the truſt committed to you, with reſpect to all ſorts of men: Avoiding and deſpiſing the frivolous diſputes, and pretended learning of *Jewiſh traditions* † and *genealogies*; which ſome of thoſe zealous converts are ſo earneſt upon, that they have neglected the ſubſtantials of *Chriſtianity*, and loſt its true principles. The Divine favour and love be with thee. *Amen.*

† Chap. i. 4.

---

* Ver. 19 [A good foundation]; θεμέλιον——The word here is certainly not to be rendered *foundation*, but either a (writing of) *ſecurity*, or rather a *treaſure*; the ſame as θέμα in Tobit iv. 9. where this expreſſion is uſed: The ſame as Κειμήλιον in Homer.

Πολλὰ δ' ἐναφνειῦ πατρὸς Κειμηλια κειταῖ;
Χαλκός τὶ, χρυσος τε——Iliad. Z. l. 46.

See on 2 Tim. ii. 10.

A PARA-

A

PARAPHRASE

ON THE

SECOND EPISTLE OF ST. PAUL

TO

TIMOTHY.

See the Preface to the First Epistle.

CHAP. I.

The Title and Salutation. His great Affection to Timothy, with fresh Encouragements to the diligent and courageous Discharge of the Office. Gentiles as well as Jews to be received into the Christian Covenant. The Apostle specially commissioned to preach to the Former, *for which he is again persecuted and imprisoned by the Malice of the* Latter. *He reminds Timothy, how the* Asian *Christians generally forsook him and his Cause, during his Imprisonment, except Onesiphorus and his Family, whom he mentions, and prays for, with great Respect.*

1 PAUL, an apostle of Jesus Christ, by the will of God, according to the promise of life, which is in Christ Jesus.

2 To

1. & 2. PAUL, an apostle of Jesus Christ, especially commissioned by the express * revelation of God, to declare the gospel-privileges and promises of eternal life, both to Gentiles and Jews;

Written A. D. 67.

* Acts ix.

A. D. 67.

2 To Timothy, *my* dearly beloved son: grace, mercy, *and* peace from God the Father, and Christ Jesus our Lord.

Jews; writeth this epistle to Timothy, my dear convert to Christianity; wishing him all divine favours and blessings from God the Father, and our Lord Jesus Christ.

3 I thank God, whom I serve from *my* forefathers with pure conscience, that without ceasing I have remembrance of thee in my prayers night and day:

3. Expressing my hearty thanks to God, whose religion I have zealously adhered to, as I received it from my forefathers (doing nothing against the *plain* and known dictates of my *conscience*, though I acknowledge it to have been missled by ungoverned prejudices and passions), that I have such happy occasions to remember you in the constant returns of my devotion to him.

4 Greatly desiring to see thee: being mindful of thy tears, that I may be filled with joy.

4. The tears you shed at our last parting, make me very desirous to see you again, that the pleasure of another meeting may recompence for the affectionate concern we were then under.

5 When I call to remembrance the unfeigned faith that is in thee, which dwelt first in thy grandmother Lois, and thy mother Eunice; and I am persuaded that in thee also.

5. Be satisfied, in the mean time, that I have a true and thankful sense of your steadiness and sincerity in the Christian faith; not doubting but those principles will continue as firm in you, as were those of your grandmother and mother before you.

6 Wherefore I put thee in remembrance that thou stir up the gift of God which is in thee, by the putting on of my hands.

6. To which end, I now write again to you, to renew the exhortations I formerly gave you, toward a diligent and vigorous discharge of your office, and the due improvement of the gifts and graces, which, along with it, were conferred on you by the imposition of mine, and other * hands, at your ordination.

* 1 Tim. iv. 14.

7 For God hath not given us the spirit of fear, but of power,

7. And you have no reason to be discouraged from the most violent oppositions you meet withal; for

er, of love, and of a ſound mind.

for the ſpiritual powers and endowments God beſtows on the goſpel miniſters, are ſufficient to ſet us above all ſlaviſh fear and cowardice, and to fix us in an immoveable love to him and his true religion, and in a prudent and diſcreet || exerciſe of our miniſtry.

|| σωφρονισμȣ̃.

8 Be not thou therefore aſhamed of the teſtimony of our Lord, nor of me his priſoner, but be thou partaker of the afflictions of the goſpel according to the power of * God:

8. Go on, therefore, cheerfully, in a religion ſo well atteſted; own and adhere to *me*, though now a priſoner for preaching it, eſpecially to the Gentiles. Suffer along with me, for this good cauſe, agreeably to the great * abilities God has given you, as a *goſpel* miniſter, to ſupport you under it.

9 Who hath ſaved us, and called us with an holy calling, not according to our works, but according to his own purpoſe and grace, which was given us in Chriſt Jeſus, before the world began.

9. Who may juſtly expect we ſhould be ready to ſuffer for him, that has beſtowed eternal happineſs upon us, by calling us into the gracious covenant of the goſpel: A mercy that neither the Gentiles could merit by any performances of theirs, nor the Jews lay the leaſt claim to, by the niceſt obſervance of the *ceremonial* law; but is the pure effect of divine bounty and compaſſion, originally † intended towards *all* mankind, by and for the ſake of Jeſus Chriſt.

10 But is now made manifeſt by the appearing of our Saviour Jeſus Chriſt, who hath aboliſhed death, and hath brought life and immortality to light, through

10. It was not indeed, heretofore expreſsly revealed to the *Gentile* nations, but reſerved to the appearance of Chriſt and his religion; who, now, by dying for our ſins, has reſcued all true believers from the final power of death;

* Ver. 8. [According to the power of God.] I think theſe words ought to be connected to ευαγγελιω. [Be partaker of the affliction, *or* ſuffer thou, τῷ εὐαγγελίῳ κατὰ δύναμιν Θεȣ̃—For the goſpel that is attended with the power of God, Rom. i. 16. See the like phraſe in Rom. i. 4. The note there.

† Ver. 9. [Before the world began, πρὸ χρόνων αἰωνίων. Before any ages or diſpenſations.]

A. D 67. through the goſpel:

death; and by his life and doctrine, has freed them of all the uncertainties they laboured under concerning the future ſtate; and given them a full aſſurance of an eternal and happy life, upon their repentance and ſincere obedience to his commands.

11 Whereunto I am appointed a preacher, and an apoſtle, and a teacher of the Gentiles.

11. Of this comfortable doctrine am *I* a preacher, and an apoſtle; with full commiſſion to declare it to the *Gentile* world, and bring them into the faith and privileges of it.

12 For the which cauſe I alſo ſuffer theſe things: nevertheleſs I am not aſhamed, for I know whom I have believed. and I am perſuaded that he is able to keep that which I have committed unto him againſt that day.

12. For which it is that I am again become a ſufferer, by the pride and malice of the *Jewiſh* people. But not at all diſcouraged; as well knowing it is the truth of God I ſuffer for, who, I am certain, will maintain his own cauſe, and preſerve that life, I commit into his hands, for a glorious recompence at the great and ſolemn day of Chriſt's judgment.

13 Hold faſt the form of ſound words, which thou haſt heard of me, in faith and love which is in Chriſt Jeſus.

13. Do you then join with me in this reſolution, by keeping ſteady to that rule of Chriſtianity I taught; conſiſting in an entire belief of Chriſt's doctrine, and an univerſal love and charity toward mankind, eſpecially toward Chriſtians, without any diſtinction between *Jewiſh* and *Gentile* ones.

14 That good thing which was committed unto thee. keep by the Holy Ghoſt, which dwelleth in us.

14. Remember how much obliged you are by the miniſterial * office you are intruſted with, to maintain and defend the true principles of our holy religion; and how much you are enabled ſo to do by the ſpecial aſſiſtance of the Holy Spirit conferred upon the miniſters of Chriſt.

15. I con-

* Παρακαταθήκην, may refer either to his *office*, or to the *form of ſound words*, in verſe 13.

15 This thou knowest, that all they which are in Asia be turned away from me, of whom are Phygellus, and Hermogenes.

15. I conclude, you cannot but have heard how most of the *Asian* Christians forsook me in my distress here, particularly Phygellus and Hermogenes. A. D. 67.

16 The Lord give mercy unto the house of Onesiphorus, for he oft refreshed me, and was not ashamed of my chain.

16. But Onesiphorus the *Ephesian*, and his family, have always stood close to me, owned me in my worst condition, and refreshed me with his presence and relief.

17 But when he was in Rome, he sought me out very diligently, and found *me*.

17. Particularly, now at Rome, when I was under such close confinement that it was no easy matter to come at me, he made his way to me by indefatigable pains and industry.

18 The Lord grant unto him that he may find mercy of the Lord in that day; and in how many things he ministered unto me at Ephesus, thou knowest very well.

18. And you know how kind and serviceable he was to me while I preached at Ephesus: for all which, may God give him a proportionable recompence at the great day of Christ's judgment.

CHAP II.

Timothy still encouraged by the Apostle's own example of Faith, Hope, and Patience. The good Effects of a Christian's Sufferings, and the Danger of denying Christ in Times of Persecution. Warnings against the immoderate Zeal, the frivolous and violent Disputes of the Jewish Zealots, about their Traditions. The meek and gentle Dispositions of a good Christian Bishop, or Church Governor.

1 THOU, therefore, my son, be strong in the grace that is in Christ Jesus *.

1. WHEREFORE, my dear convert, follow the example of such † as adhere to me, making a continual improvement in

† Chap. i. 16, 17, 18.

A. D. 67. in the uſe of thoſe gifts and graces that were given you, for the due diſcharge of your Chriſtian miniſtry ‡.

‡ χαρις.

2 And the things that thou haſt heard of me among many witneſſes, the ſame commit thou to faithful men, who ſhall be able to teach others alſo.

2. And, as you have received from me a complete ſcheme of the Chriſtian doctrine and diſcipline, be ſure to make choice of able and faithful perſons for the miniſtry, to deliver it down to others pure and unmixed, as I gave it you, and had it myſelf ſo clearly and fully confirmed.

3 Thou therefore endure hardneſs, as a good ſoldier of Jeſus Chriſt.

3. Look upon yourſelf as a *ſoldier* of Chriſt; and approve your valour by enduring all the hardſhips of his ſervice.

4 No man that warreth entangleth himſelf with the affairs of *this* life; that he may pleaſe him who hath choſen him to be a ſoldier.

4. Now, you know, the Roman laws require every one that liſts into the army, to diſengage himſelf of all his former employments, and perfectly to attend the ſervice of his prince, and the commands of his *general*.

5 And if a man alſo ſtrive for maſteries, *yet* he is not crowned, except he ſtrive lawfully.

5. And in the *Olympic* games, no *combatant* wins the prize, unleſs he fights or runs agreeably to the ſtated rules of thoſe games.

6 The huſbandman that laboureth †, muſt be firſt partaker of the fruits.

6. You know too, the *huſbandman* labours in tilling, ſowing, or planting his ground a conſiderable time † before he can expect to reap the crop.

7 Con-

7. Thus

---

* Ver. 1. [In the grace that is in Chriſt Jeſus—εν τῃ χάριτι τῃ ἐν Χριςῷ Ἰησȣ. It may be thus rendered; [Be ſtrong (in aſſerting and propagating) that favour which is (ſhown by God both to Jews and Gentiles) in Jeſus Chriſt.] For *this* appears to have been conſtantly in the apoſtle's eye.

† [Muſt be firſt partaker—κοπιῶντα δεῖ πρῶτον—muſt firſt labour.] If this be the conſtruction, as ſeveral critics take it to be, the word πρῶτον is miſplaced by a metatheſis, pretty common

A. D. 67.

7 Consider what I say, and the Lord give thee understanding in all things.

7. Thus it was with *you*, as a Christian *bishop*; like a true *soldier*, you must be disengaged of all the unnecessary cares of life and business. As a *combatant*, you must throw off every thing that may give the adversary any hold of you. As a *husbandman*, you must labour in planting and promoting the gospel, and wait patiently for your reward. Consider this, and may God give you a just sense of every branch of your duty.

8 Remember that Jesus Christ, of the seed of David, was raised from the dead, according to my gospel.

8. And, for the greater encouragement of yourself and others, remembor yourself, and them, that our Saviour Jesus Christ himself, the true *Messiah*, born of the family of David, as the scriptures foretold, was no *temporal monarch*, as the *Jews* vainly dreamed he was to be, but a *suffering* Saviour; and, after those sufferings, was raised from the dead, and exalted to heavenly glory, according to the true gospel-doctrine, as preached and demonstrated by *me*.

9 Wherein I suffer trouble as an evil-doer, *even* unto bonds; but the word of God is not bound.

6. This is the great truth, for which I am thus, as a malefactor, prosecuted by the *Jewish* people, and am now again a prisoner: But my comfort is, that while I am confined, the *gospel* doctrine is, by my means, spread far and wide, especially in this city ‡.

‡ See Phil. i. 12, 13, 14.

10 Therefore I endure all things for the elects sake, that they may also obtain the salvation which is

10. This makes me undergo all my sufferings with the utmost freedom and cheerfulness; that I may thereby become an instrument to bring other Christians, of

---

common in the New Testament. See an instance of it in the word ὁ πατριάρχης, Heb. vii. 4. or else πρῶτον may be taken *adjectively*, and the sense be thus: The labouring husbandman is to have πρῶτον τῶν καρπῶν, The first and best of the fruits. But the former seems most natural.

A. D. 67. is in Christ Jesus, with eternal glory.

of what nation soever, to the glory and happiness promised by Jesus Christ; by encouraging them to suffer, after my example.

11 *It is* a * faithful saying, For if we be dead with *him*, we shall also live with *him*:

12 If we suffer, we shall also reign with *him*: if we deny him, he also will deny us:

11. & 12. For * this is the comfortable and undoubted truth of the gospel-religion. For, as we figuratively resemble the death of Christ, by being baptized into the death of sin, we shall actually rise with him, to an immortal and happy life. And, upon our readiness to suffer for his religion, as he suffered for our sins, we shall not fail of a glorious reward for it, along with him. But, on the contrary, if we relinquish his profession, for fear of present dangers, he will no longer own us for his disciples, nor reward us as such.

13 If we believe not, *yet* he abideth faithful, he cannot deny himself.

13. And whether we continue steady to his religion, or no, it is certain God is still the same, and cannot but perform the promises he has made, and execute the threats he has denounced.

14 Of these things put *them* in remembrance, charging *them* before the Lord, that they strive not about words, to no profit, *but* to the subverting of the hearers.

14. Inculcate this to all Christians, as the indispensible condition of their profession. And particularly charge the *Jewish* converts, in the name of Christ, to make it their great concern, and not any longer to employ their time in frivolous and eager disputes about *traditions*, that tend to nothing, but to pervert men from the true faith.

15, & 16. En-

* Ver. 11. (It is a faithful saying;) *i. e.* In thus suffering for my endeavours to bring men *of all nations* into the Christian faith and privileges, I act *faithfully*, or agreeably to the design of the *gospel*. See the note on 1 Tim. 15.

15 Study to show thyself approved unto God, a workman that needeth not to be ashamed, rightly dividing the word of truth

16 But shun profane and vain babblings, for they will increase unto more ungodliness.

15. & 16. Endeavour to approve yourself a skilful and unexceptionable minister of Christianity. And, as it was the constant and careful service of the *Jewish* priests, in the temple, to divide the sacrifices, separating the parts that were, from such as were not to be offered upon the altar; so let it be your earnest business to cut off all impertinent disputes, and deliver out nothing but the plain and important doctrines of our religion. A.D 67.

17 And their word will eat as doth a canker: of whom is Hymeneus and Philetus:

18 Who concerning the truth have erred, saying That the resurrection is past already: and overthrow the faith of some.

17. & 18. For that turbulent and disputing temper is of the same dangerous consequence to the Christian *church*, as a gangrene is to the *body*; infecting and eating out all good principles, as you see in the instances of Hymeneus * and Philetus, who have so corrupted those passages of scripture relating to the *resurrection*, with their traditional and allegorical notions, as to give out, That the resurrection of good men is already past, and nothing further to be expected; and so have drawn several Christians from the sound belief of that capital article.

19 Nevertheless, the † foundation of God standeth sure, having this seal, the Lord knoweth

19. But, notwithstanding the surmises of such men, this truth of our future resurrection stands firm, as the main † foundation of all

---

* See 1 Tim. i. 19, 20.

† (The foundation of God.) Θεμέλιος signifies either a foundation of a *building*; or an indenture *writing*: And because the *latter* is more agreeable to the *seal* in this verse, and the *former* to the verse immediately following, I have therefore expressed both senses: But I leave it as conjecture, whether the true reading might not be Κειμήλιον. See the *note* on 1 Tim. vi. 19. Indeed, as the word is there used for *treasure*, so *here* it may most properly signify, not the *foundation*, but the *precious things*, or utensils of a *house*; *treasures* laid up and *sealed* with the *seal* or *mark* of the owner. But let the reader judge.

A. D. 67.

§ Θεμέλιος.

knoweth * them that are his. And let every one that nameth the name of Christ, depart from iniquity.

all our Christian faith and hope, and is an inviolable § indenture of security, that God has sealed and confirmed with a promise, on *his part*, to own and reward all true Christian disciples; and with this condition, on *our* part, that we reform our lives, and live agreeable to the precepts of the gospel.

20 But in a great house there are not only vessels of gold, and of silver, but also of wood, and of earth: and some to honour, and some to dishonour.

20. Nor ought it to surprise and disturb us, to find such factious and unorthodox members in the Christian church. For, as in great mens houses, there is variety and degrees of good and bad, rich, and less costly furniture; so in such a wide society as the church is, it cannot be expected, but some members will prove more ungovernable and degenerate than others.

21 If a man therefore purge himself from these, he shall be a vessel unto honour, sanctified and meet for the masters use, and prepared unto every good work.

21. As therefore, the better, and more sumptuous part of the house's furniture is usually appropriated to the use of the owner and master of the family; in like manner, the only way for any Christian to render himself truly useful and acceptable to Christ, the great Lord of his church, is, To keep himself untainted from the false notions, and impure practices of those deceitful teachers.

22 Flee also youthful lusts: but follow righteousness, faith, charity,

22. & 23. Accordingly, therefore, be you specially careful to avoid all those passions and irregularities, to which

* Ver. 19. (The Lord knoweth them that are his)—— These words are a most emphatical allusion to those of Moses, Numb. xvi. 5. [according to the LXX.] (To-morrow will the Lord show who are his, and who is holy.) A proper application of the case of Korah and his company to that of these *false teachers* before mentioned. *Ibid.*—(depart from iniquity, ἀπὸ ἀδικίας, from falsehood), in opposition to ἀλήθειαν before mentioned. See John vii. 18. Rom. xi. 8. 1 Cor. xiii. 6. 2 Thess. xi. 12. As Moses said, [Depart from the tents of these wicked men.]

charity, peace with them that call on the Lord out of a pure heart.

23 But foolish and * unlearned questions avoid, knowing that they do gender strifes.

which their frivolous and violent disputes may hazard to draw such a young || person as you are: And keep close to the substantial duties of true faith towards God, of perfect justice in your words and behaviour towards all men, and of a charitable and peaceful temper towards all sincere *Christians*.

A. D. 67.

|| 1 Tim. iv. 12.

24 And the servant of the Lord must not strive: but be gentle unto all men, apt to teach, patient:

25 In meekness instructing those that oppose themselves, if God peradventure will give them repentance to the acknowledging of the truth.

26 And that they may † recover themselves out of the snare of the devil, who are taken captive by him at his will.

24, 25. & 26. For it does no way become any *Christian*, much less a ‡ *minister* of the gospel, to strive to gain men over to his religion, by violent disputation, and ill usage; but only by fair and strong reasons proposed to them, and urged upon them, in a candid, free, and peaceable manner; endeavouring to win upon their adversaries, by the meekness and sweetness of their temper, as well as by the strength of their arguments; this being the most likely means to rescue them from that state of ignorance and vice, to which the devil has hitherto enslaved them; and bring them to the knowledge and obedience of God, and of true religion.

‡ δοῦλος Κυρίου.

Vol. II. O CHAP.

* Ver. 23. [Unlearned questions.] ἀπαιδεύτους ζητήσεις, questions that belong not to *Christianity*, the παιδεία, the Christian *institutions* or *instruction*. *Questions* about things *never taught* by Christ, never required of any Christian to believe at his *baptism*.

† Ver. 26. [And that they may recover, &c.] *Note* The learned author of the *Paraphrase and Notes after Mr. Locke's manner*, has translated this verse in a very *new*, and (I think) a very judicious manner—but very agreeably to your sense of my paraphrase; *viz.* Thus: "That when they are tak-" en (or saved) alive out of the snare of the devil by him " (viz. the faithful servant of the Lord), they may be awake " and active to do his (*i. e.* God's) will."

5

CHAP. III.

He again reminds Timothy of the dangerous Times, and wicked People, foretold to be under the Church of the Messiah. *A description of those Men, and their Principles. Encourages Timothy against them, from his own Example, and from the Advantages of his Acquaintance with the Ancient Scriptures.*

A. D. 67.

* 1 Tim. iv. 1.

1 THIS know also that in the last days, perilous times shall come.

1. LET me again * remind you of those predictions of our Saviour and his apostles, concerning the persecutions that would arise in times of the *Christian* church; the better to arm you against being surprised, and moved at them.

2 For men shall be lovers of their own selves, covetous, boasters, proud, blasphemers, disobedient to parents, unthankful, unholy.

3 Without natural affection, truce breakers, false accusers, incontinent, fierce, despisers of those that are good.

4 Traitors, heady, high-minded, lovers of pleasures more than lovers of God.

2, 3. & 4. Those predictions are now in some measure fulfilled in the *Jewish* zealots, that selfish, worldly-minded, proud, and abusive set of men, that are arrived to that degree of ingratitude and impiety, as to break through the most natural and essential obligations, and violate all truth and faith with such as are not of their party; minding nothing but their own ambitious purposes and pleasures, in defiance of the express laws of God.

5 Having a form of godliness, but denying the power thereof: from such turn away.

5. Having nothing to do, therefore with a people that value themselves upon the mere outward name and privileges of religion; and, in their lives, contradict all the noble purposes and designs of it.

6. & 7. These

A. D. 67.

6 For of this sort are they which creep into houses, and lead captive silly women laden with sins, led away with divers lusts.

7 Ever learning, and never able to come to the knowledge of the truth.

6. & 7. These are the men so fond of making proselytes to their own opinions, as to insinuate themselves into all families, and gain upon women, and the weaker sort, that are prepared to their hands, by sinful affections and prejudices; that run after every new teacher, and so are kept in perpetual distraction and ignorance of sound religion.

8 Now as Jannes and Jambres withstood Moses, so do these also resist the truth: men of corrupt minds, reprobate concerning the faith.

8. These people oppose the true doctrines of *Christianity*, with the same obstinate and incurable prejudices, that the magicians of Egypt did the miracles of Moses; against the most evident and convincing demonstrations.

9 But they shall proceed no further: for their folly shall be manifest unto all *men*, as theirs also was.

9. And they are soon like to come to the same wretched end, and show their opposition to be the effect of nothing but woful blindness and malice.

10 But thou hast fully known my doctrine, manner of life, purpose, faith, long-suffering, charity, patience,

11 Persecutions, afflictions which came unto me at Antioch, at Iconium, at Lystra; what persecutions I endured; but out of them all the Lord delivered me.

10. & 11. Be not you, therefore, terrified at their malicious endeavours; but make my doctrine your rule; let my life and conversation, my steady faith, charity, and patience under all my sufferings, particularly those at Antioch, &c. be your example, to encourage you to trust in God for the same powerful deliverances that I had from them all.

12 Yea, and all that will live godly in Christ Jesus, shall suffer persecution.

12. And, indeed, all that will be sincere *Christians*, must now expect, and be prepared for their share of sufferings.

13 But evil men and seducers shall wax worse and worse, deceiving

13. For the successors of these deceitful impostors, instead of reforming, will in the *after times* of Christianity,

A.D. 67. ceiving, and being deceived.

Christianity, still improve in their wicked designs, running into deeper ignorance, drawing others into their errors, and persecuting all that oppose them.

14 But continue thou in the things which thou hast learned, and hast been assured of, knowing of whom thou hast learned *them*:

14. To avoid them, therefore, continue steady to the doctrines I have taught you; and remember you learned them of one, who neither can nor will deceive you.

15 And that from a child thou hast known the holy scriptures, which are able to make thee wise unto salvation; through faith which is in Christ Jesus.

15. And beside what I have particularly instructed you in, the knowledge you have attained from your constant perusal of the scriptures of the Old Testament, from your very infancy, will be of great advantage to you, to show you the truths of Christ's religion, and keep you firm to the faith of it; which will procure your eternal salvation.

16 All scripture is given by inspiration of God, and *is* profitable for doctrine, for reproof, for correction, for instruction in righteousness:

17 That the man of God may be perfect, thouroughly furnished unto all good works.

16. & 17. For * those inspired writings are of great use to discover to us the truth and certainty of our *Christianity*, by showing us the *prophecies* that are now fulfilled, the *types* and *figures* that are now exactly answered in Christ and his religion; and abounding, beside, in most wholesome precepts and prohibitions. By understanding of all which, the Christian minister is completely enabled to correct the errors and misunderstandings of these seducing *teachers*, concerning the nature of Christ's kingdom; and to set forth all the true and saving doctrines of his holy religion.

CHAP.

---

* Ver. 16. [All scripture is given by inspiration of God, πᾶσα γραφὴ θεόπνευστος, &c. All writings that are of divine inspiration are profitable, &c.]—One old *MS.* with the Vulgar Arab. and Syr. Versions, as also some *fathers*, in their quotation of this passage, leave out the καὶ. I make no question, but that *the scriptures by inspiration of God*, have a particular reference to the *prophecies* concerning Christ and his *kingdom*, and the *apostacy* from it.

The Charge to Timothy solemnly renewed. The Jewish Obstinacy and Malice will grow Worse and Worse. The Apostle foretells his own Martyrdom, in full Assurance of his Reward as a faithful Apostle. Tells him how the Christians deserted him: Appoints Timothy to hasten to him. Warns him against Alexander. The Salutations and Conclusion.

1 I Charge *thee*, therefore, before God, and the Lord Jesus Christ, who shall judge the quick and the dead at his appearing, and his kingdom:

2 Preach the word, be instant in season, and out of season; reprove, rebuke, exhort with all long-suffering and doctrine.

1. & 2. TO conclude, then; seeing you are encompassed with such *adversaries, and have such abilities bestowed on you to withstand them, I now again most solemnly adjure you by God the Father, and the Lord Jesus Christ, the judge of all mankind at the great and solemn day of his appearance, to take all opportunities of refuting those false *teachers*, of urging and pressing the truths of *Christianity* upon all people; correcting their errors and immoralities, and endeavouring with the utmost patience and constancy, to reduce them to a sense of true religion.

A. D. 67.

* Chap. iii. 13, 14.

3 For the time will come when they will not endure sound doctrine; but after their own lusts shall they heap to themselves teachers, having itching ears.

4 And they shall turn away *their* ears from the truth, and shall be turned into fables.

3. & 4. My earnest repetition of this charge upon you is but too needful. For, as I † before observed, those ignorant *zealots* are like to be so far from a speedy reformation, that you will find them grow perfectly impatient of the true doctrines of our religion; still more passionately fond of their new *teachers* that sooth them up in their lusts and vices; and run wholly from the *gospel* principles to *Jewish* fables and traditions.

† Chap. iii. 13.

5. But

A. D. 67.

5 But watch thou in all things, endure afflictions, do the work of an evangelist, make full proof of thy ministry.

5. But however irreclaimable and vexatious they may prove, go you on in the work of your *gospel* ministry, and suffer patiently for the conscientious discharge of it.

6 For I am now ready to be offered, and the time of my departure is at hand.

6. I am also *now* the more warm in my exhortations to you, because I expect shortly to be taken from you, and become a sacrifice to their malice and obstinacy.

7 I have fought a good fight, I have finished my course, I have kept * the faith.

7. Nor am I at all discouraged at that prospect: For I have fought and suffered for the *Christian* cause like a hardy soldier: and, as a racer, am at the end of my course: For I have been faithful to my *trust*.

8 Henceforth there is laid up for me a crown of righteousness, which the Lord the righteous judge shall give me at that day: and not to me only, but unto all them also that love his appearing.

8. So that I have now nothing to do, but to wait for that glorious recompense and reward, which the great and righteous Judge of the world will not fail to bestow on me, and on all such who are conscious of having so sincerely performed their duty, as to wish for that happy day of Christ's final judgment.

9 Do thy diligence to come shortly unto me:

10 For Demas hath forsaken me, having loved this present world, and is departed unto Thessalonica: Crescens to Galatia, Titus unto Dalmatia.

9. & 10. Come to Rome to me as soon as possibly you can; for I am left almost quite alone; Demas having preferred the safety of his life before me and my cause, and is retired to Thessalonica; and I have sent away Crescens and Titus upon particular business.

11 Only 11. & 12.

* Ver. 7. [I have kept the faith.] Τὴν πίστιν τετήρηκα, I have preserved my fidelity.

A. D. 67.

11 Only Luke is with me. Take Mark and bring him with thee; for he is profitable to me for the miniſtry.

12 And Tychicus have I ſent to Epheſus.

11. & 12. I have alſo ſent Tychicus to *Epheſus*, ſo that I have now no body with me but Luke. When you come, therefore, bring Mark with you; for he will be very ſerviceable to me in aſſiſting me to promote the goſpel.

13 The * cloak that I left at Troas with Carpus, when thou comeſt, bring *with thee*, and the books, *but* eſpecially the parchments.

13. When I was laſt at *Troas*, I left a parchment * roll, and ſome books there; bring them with you, but eſpecially the *roll*.

14 Alexander the copperſmith did me much evil: the † Lord reward him according to his works.

15 Of whom be thou ware alſo; for he hath greatly withſtood our words.

14. & 15. Alexander the copperſmith has been a great enemy to me: And I † leave him to God to be recompenſed as he deſerves. Take heed of him, for he is a bitter adverſary againſt the *Chriſtian* cauſe.

16 At my firſt anſwer no man ſtood with me, but all men forſook me: *I pray God* that it may not be laid to their charge.

16. When I was brought upon my firſt trial, almoſt ‡ all my Chriſtian acquaintance at *Rome* forſook me: Pray God pity and forgive their cowardice.

17 Notwithſtanding the Lord ſtood with me, and ſtrengthened me; that by me the

17. But, while they relinquiſhed me, I was divinely aſſiſted to defend myſelf; and God was pleaſed to make me the inſtrument

* *The cloak*, φελονην, a parchment *roll*, the ſame with μεμβρανα—*the parchments*. The *Syriac* reads it [a cheſt of books.]

† Ver. 14. [The Lord reward him]—This is not to be underſtood as an *imprecation*, but as a *prophet's* expreſſion: As in like manner, is that dying ſpeech of Zachariah, [The Lord look upon it, and requite it, 2 Chron. xxiv. 22. which is in the *future* tenſe, [God will look upon it].——

‡ [All men forſook me.] Omnibus, id eſt a maxima art e deſertum ſe eſſe conqueritur. Jerom.

A. D. 67. the preaching might be fully known, and *that* all the Gentiles might hear: and I was delivered out of the mouth of the lion.

ment of spreading the gospel doctrine to the *Gentiles* of these parts, by delivering me from the sentence of the cruel * *Emperor* for that time.

18 And the Lord shall deliver me † from every evil work, and will preserve *me* unto his heavenly kingdom: to whom *be* glory for ever and ever. Amen.

18. And, though I am *now* likely to be unjustly condemned, and suffer by him; yet, am I sure, God will still preserve me from doing † or saying any thing unbecoming my religion, or my ministerial office; and carry me through death into the happiness of his heavenly kingdom: To whom, therefore, I ascribe all honour and glory for ever and ever. *Amen.*

19 Salute Prisca and Aquila, and the houshold of Onesiphorus.

19. My hearty Christian love to Aquila and Priscilla, with Onesiphorus and his family.

20 Erastus abode at Corinth: but Trophimus have I left at Miletum sick.

20. If you would know what is become of Erastus, I can only tell you, I left him at *Corinth* in my last || travels thither; and Trophimus falling sick at *Miletus*, in *Crete*, I was forced to leave him in that island.

|| See Pearson, op. Post.

21 Do thy diligence to come before winter. Eubulus greeteth thee, and Pudens, and Linus, and Claudia, and all the brethren.

21. Come to me before winter if you can. Eubulus, Pudens, Linus, Claudia, and all the Christians here salute you.

22 The Lord Jesus Christ *be* with thy spirit. Grace *be* with you. Amen.

22. May the Lord Jesus Christ be your director and guide. His love and favour be ever with thee. *Amen.*

---

* Nero, or else his deputy Helius Cæsarianus.

† [And the Lord shall deliver me.] Et liberabit me inquit (non à vinculus sed) ab omni opere malo. Pearson op. Post. pag. 25.

A PARA-

A

PARAPHRASE

ON THE

EPISTLE OF ST. PAUL

TO

TITUS.

THE PREFACE.

§ 1. THE *time* of St. Paul's being in the iſland of *Crete*, and leaving Titus as biſhop there, is placed, by ſome, in the year 55. viz. in his travels mentioned Acts xx. But our more accurate Biſhop Pearſon has ſhown good reaſons againſt that; and, much more probably, ſtated it in the interval between St. Paul's firſt and ſecond confinement at *Rome*, viz. Anno Domini 63. dating this epiſtle the year following; with which account Dr. Mill differs but in one ſingle year.

§ 2. The occaſion on which it was written is ſo perfectly the ſame with thoſe to Timothy, that the ſubſtance and ſtyle of it may well be, as it appears, of the ſame ſtrain. A church was indeed planted here, but wanted watering, cultivation, and due order. The natives of the iſland were an idle, falſe and luxurious people,

ple, ſay the ancient hiſtorians and geographers, agreeable to St. Paul's deſcriptions of them here, chap. i. but might have made more tractable *Chriſtians*, had not their ill qualities and diſpoſitions been fomented by the *Jewiſh zealots*, abounding in that place. Againſt whoſe ignorant and malicious prejudices the apoſtle moſt clearly levels all the characters he gave of a good biſhop or church governor; and the ſeveral directions for the conduct of people of both *ſexes*, in their reſpective ages, ſtations, and degrees, conformably to the two foregoing epiſtles, and to the general current of the other epiſtolary writings relating to thoſe matters.

CHAP. I.

The Title and Salutation. The Deſign of St. Paul's leaving Titus Biſhop in Crete, and of this Epiſtle to him; viz. To ordain Church Miniſters, and reduce that Church to a regularity in Opinion and Practice; eſpecially the Judaizing part of them, that were more zealous about Jewiſh Traditions and Ceremonies than the ſubſtantial Matters of Chriſtianity. The good Qualifications of a Church Governor. A bad Character of the Cretians, particularly the Jewiſh Inhabitants of that Iſland.

Written A. D. 64.

1 PAUL, a ſervant
of God, and an
apoſtle of Jeſus Chriſt,
according to the faith
of God's elect, and
the acknowledging of
the truth, which is
after godlineſs.
2 In hopes of eternal life, which God,
that cannot lie, promiſed before the
world began:
3 But hath in due
time manifeſted his
word

1. PAUL, a worſhipper of the true God, and an apoſtle of Jeſus Chriſt, ſpecially commiſſioned to preach his religion in its truth and purity, and convert men of *all nations* to the true faith of it.

2. & 3. A religion that gives all true believers, whether *Jews* or *Gentiles*, a full and ſure hope of enjoying that great promiſe of eternal happineſs, made by the God of *truth* himſelf, at firſt to Adam in the

A. D. 64.

word through preaching, which is committed unto me, according to the commandment of God our Saviour:

the beginning of the world, and to Abraham and the *patriarchs* afterward: which, though loſt and forgotten by the far greater part of the *Gentile* nations, through their manifold corruptions, and wilful iniquities; yet is now again revived and declared to them *all*, under the *goſpel diſpenſation* (the proper ſeaſon made choice of by Divine Wiſdom for that purpoſe): and *I* am appointed to publiſh it for the ſalvation of all the world.

4 To Titus, mine own ſon after the common faith, grace, mercy, and peace from God the Father, and the Lord Jeſus Chriſt our Saviour.

4. I Paul ſend this epiſtle to Titus my dear convert to Chriſtianity; wiſhing him all divine favour and happineſs from God the Father, and Jeſus Chriſt our Saviour and Governor.

5 For this cauſe left I thee in Crete, that * thou ſhouldeſt ſet in order the things that are wanting and ordain elders in every city, as I had appointed thee.

5. To remind you of the good end for which I conſecrated and left you biſhop of the church of Crete, viz. to perfect the converſion I had there begun, to give ſuch rules of doctrine and diſcipline as were wanting, and to ordain other church-miniſters in the ſeveral cities of that iſland, to put them in due and conſtant execution.

6 If any be blameleſs, the huſband of one wife, having faithful children, not accuſed of riot, or unruly.

7 For a biſhop muſt be blameleſs, as the ſteward of God: not ſelf-willed, not ſoon angry, not given to wine, no ſtriker, nor given to filthy lucre;

6. & 7. Now a *biſhop* and governor of a Chriſtian church, as a ſteward over God's family, ought in general to be a perſon of an unexceptionable character; and, in particular ought not to be one that has been guilty either of the polygamy of the heathens, or of divorcing his wife for humourſome reaſons, and marrying others, according to the corrupt uſages of the Jews. He muſt be one that has

---

* Ver 5. [That thou ſhouldſt ſet in order the things that are wanting. *Or*, ἵνα τὰ λείποντα διορθώσῃ, to rectify diſorders].

A. D. 64. has educated his family in the Chriſtian faith; that nobody can accuſe of the leaſt debauchery or diſorderly life; not ſtubborn or paſſionate in his words, or violent in his behaviour; addicted neither to drunkenneſs, nor any ſordid practices for worldly gains.

8 But a lover of hoſpitality, a lover of good men, ſober, juſt, holy, temperate,

8. But, on the contrary, muſt be a perſon hoſpitable and charitable, grave in his carriage, juſt in his dealings, devoted to the ſervice of God, and temperate in his pleaſures.

9 Holding faſt the faithful word, as he hath been taught, that he may be able by ſound doctrine both to exhort and to convince the gainſayers.

9. In fine, he muſt be ſteady to the true Chriſtian doctrine, by the truth and ſtrength whereof, he may be able to comfort and ſupport the orthodox, and to confute and reprove the erroneous and obſtinate.

10 For there are many unruly and vain talkers and deceivers, eſpecially they of the circumciſion:

10. Of which latter you have abundance in Crete, whoſe buſineſs is to talk and diſpute, and ſeduce the minds of men; but eſpecially the *Jewiſh* zealots, and ſuch Chriſtian converts as they have corrupted with their notions.

11 Whoſe mouths muſt be ſtopped, who ſubvert whole houſes, teaching things which they ought not, for filthy lucres ſake,

11. Theſe men, however falſe and vain their arguments be, muſt yet be anſwered and confuted; for they gain upon whole families by their unreaſonable ſuggeſtions, which they ſpread about, only for preſent profit and applauſe.

12 One of themſelves, *even* a prophet of their own, ſaid, The Cretians are alway liars, evil beaſts, ſlow bellies *.

12. & 13. When the poet *Epimenides*, a native of their own, deſcribed the Cretians, as a falſe, miſchievous, and luxurious people, he ſaid what was as true of theſe *Jewiſh* inhabitants, as it could be

13 This

* Ver. 12. *Slow bellies*, γαστέρες ἀργαί, not *ſlow* but *ſwift eager* bellies, like that of κακὰ θηρία, *evil wild beaſts*. So in *Homer* κύνες ἀργοὶ are *ſwift dogs*.

A. D. 64.

13 This witness is true: wherefore * rebuke them sharply, that they may be sound in the faith;

be of the original *natives* of the place: and therefore you must keep them under a strict censure and discipline; especially such of either of them as are *Christian* converts, to reduce them again to true Christian principles.

14 Not giving heed to Jewish fables, and commandments of men, that turn from the truth.

14. For they are now addicted to hardly any thing but the study of *Jewish* fables and traditions, that tend to nothing but to corrupt the Christian faith.

15 Unto the pure all things are pure: but unto them that are defiled and † unbelieving is nothing pure; but even their mind and conscience is defiled.

15. Their *Jewish* teachers persuade them to put the stress of religion upon nice distinctions of *meats* and *drinks*, clean and unclean things: whereas, alas! a *Gentile* convert, that lives up to the faith and precepts of *Christianity*, is clean and pure in the sight of God, let him *eat* or *touch* what he will; while *they*, by their obstinate infidelity and immoralities, can perform no acceptable service to God; and their nicest ceremonies signify just nothing †.

16 They profess that they know God; but in works they deny him, being abominable, and disobedient, and unto every good work reprobate ‡.

16. They boast themselves to be the only people in covenant with God, and acquainted with true religion: but their practices are a contradiction to all such pretences, and their stubborn disobedience to the plainest laws of God, has now rendered them odious to him, whose church and people they once were.

CHAP.

---

* Ver. 13. [Rebuke them sharply,] ἀποτόμως, Cut them, *as it were*, to the quick.

† Ver. 15. [And unbelieving.] Ἀπίστοις, unfaithful, treacherous, *though they were pretended* believers.

‡ Ver. 16. [Unto every good work reprobate.] Πρὸς πᾶν ἔργον ἀγαθὸν ἀδόκιμοι, stupid and injudicious as to every good work. See note on Rom. i. 28.

CHAP. II.

Titus's Charge to a prudent and courageous Behaviour againſt the forementioned Perſons and their Principles. Advices concerning elderly *Men and Women; particularly ſuch as were in any* Church-office. *Concerning Servants or* Slaves. *The Chriſtian Religion equally concerns all Ranks and Degrees of People.*

A. D. 64.

1 BUT ſpeak thou the things which become ſound doctrine.

1. BEING, therefore, compaſſed with ſuch a number of falſe teachers, and miſled converts, make it your more earneſt buſineſs to preach, and preſs the true doctrine of Chriſtianity, upon all perſons, in their ſeveral ſtations and degrees.

2 That the aged men be ſober, grave, temperate, ſound in faith, in charity, in patience:

2. Viz. Urge it as the great duty of the *elder* ſort of men, particularly ſuch as are *preſbyters* of the church, to be grave, ſerious, and temperate in their converſation, ſound in Chriſtian principles, charitable to all, and patient under the ſufferings that befal them.

3 The aged women likewiſe, that *they be* in behaviour as becometh holineſs; not falſe accuſers, not given to much wine, teachers of good things;

3. And that all elderly *women*, particularly ſuch as are employed by the church *, in the baptiſm of women, and in other offices of like nature, uſe ſuch habit, geſture, and behaviour, as become Chriſtians; no way addicted to ſlander or drunkenneſs, but to be exemplary in all the virtues that adorn their *ſex*.

* Deaconeſſes, See 1 Tim. iii. 11.

4 That they may teach the young women to be ſober, to love their huſbands, to love their children.

4. & 5. That, by their good example, the younger women may be influenced to a ſober, modeſt, diſcreet, and chaſte behaviour; to mind the buſineſs of their families,

5 To

5 To be discreet, chaste, keepers at home, good, obedient to their own * husbands, that the word of God be not blasphemed.

lies, to respect their husbands, and take due care of their children; and so, on their part, cut off all occasions from any to think or speak reproachfully of our holy religion.

* See Pref. to the Ephesians, § 4.

6 Young men likewise exhort to be sober-minded.

6. In like manner, exhort all young *men* to a due and careful government of their passions.

7 In all things showing thyself a pattern of good works: in doctrine *showing* uncorruptness, gravity, sincerity.

8 Sound speech that cannot be condemned; that he that is of the contrary part may be ashamed, having no evil thing to say of you.

7. & 8. And thus, in relation to all ranks of people, do your utmost to become truly exemplary in the purity and simplicity of your *doctrine*, and the sincerity of your *practice;* that so neither *Jewish* nor *Gentile* adversary may find any reasonable objection against you.

9 *Exhort* servants to be obedient unto their own masters, *and* to please *them* well in all things: not answering again.

10 Not purloining, but showing all good fidelity; that they may adorn the doctrine of God our Saviour in all things.

9. & 10. And, whereas the *Jewish* zealots would persuade *men*, that their religious privileges exempt them even from *civil* and *natural* † obligations to men of different and false religions; be the more earnest to warn all such Christians, as are servants or *slaves* (though it be to *heathen* masters) against so false a principle. Exhort them to serve their respective masters, in every lawful thing, diligently and faithfully, without rudely contradicting their commands, or defrauding them by the least neglect or injustice: by which they will become a credit to their profession, even in the low station wherein Providence has placed them.

† See Pref. to the Ephesians, § 4.

11 For the grace of God, that bringeth salvation, hath appeared unto all men.

11. & 12. For the gracious religion of the gospel lays the same excellent duties of piety, justice, and sobriety, upon the lowest *slave*,

12 Teach-

as

A.D. 64.

as much as upon the highest *master*, equally respecting all ranks and degrees of mankind.

12 Teaching us, that denying ungodliness and worldly lusts, we should live soberly, righteously, and godly in this present world.

13 Looking for that blessed hope, and the glorious appearing of the great God, and our Saviour Jesus Christ:

13. And as *all* have the same *duties* and conditions, so have they the same comfortable *hope* and expectation of a glorious reward for their obedience, at the appearance of the great God, and our Saviour Jesus, to judge the world.

14 Who gave himself for us, that he might redeem us from all iniquity, and purify unto himself a peculiar people, zealous of good works.

14. Even of that Saviour, who gave his life a sacrifice for the redemption of *all* mankind, to procure the pardon of their sins, and restore and oblige all to that sincere practice of piety and virtue, which makes us the true and beloved members of his church.

15 These things speak and exhort, and rebuke with all authority. Let no man despise thee.

15. These are the truths you ought to declare and urge upon men, in the most authoritative manner: and, with so prudent a severity, to censure and punish such as openly contradict them, that they may not slight and undervalue your authority.

CHAP.

CHAP. III.

Of Duty to Magiſtrates, againſt Railing, and Evil ſpeaking. The Goſpel-religion intended for the Reformation and Happineſs of both Gentile and Jew. Pardon and Salvation not to be attained by the niceſt Obſervation of the Ceremonial *Law, but is the Effect of the pure Mercy of God, on Condition of our ſincere Obedience to the* Goſpel *Commands. Againſt* Jewiſh *Traditions and Genealogies. A Heretic not to be excommunicated, till after juſt and due Admonition. Charitableneſs recommended. The Salutations and Concluſion.*

1 PUT them in mind to be ſubject to principalities and powers, to obey magiſtrates, to be ready to every good work,

1. ANother prejudice you muſt carefully warn the *Jewiſh* zealots againſt, is, *That no heathen governors have any obedience due to them from God's people;* † *nor any magiſtrates that are not of their nation and religion.* Remind them often, that Chriſtianity alters no civil rights; and that they ought to pay all juſt ſubmiſſion to the emperor, and all due ‡ and cheerful reſpect to all their ſuperiors.

A. D. 64.

† See Rom. xiii. 1.

‡ πᾶν ἔργον ἀγαθόν.

2 To ſpeak evil of no man, to be no brawlers, *but* gentle, ſhowing all meekneſs unto all men.

2. Warn them alſo againſt that prevailing temper of reviling, and furiouſly contending with all that are not of the ſame religious ſentiments with themſelves.

3 For we * ourſelves alſo were ſometimes fooliſh, diſobedient,

3. All Chriſtians, both *Gentile* and *Jewiſh*, ought to be the more patient and condeſcending in their behaviour

* Ver. 3. [We ourſelves.] St. Paul either mixes himſelf with the *Gentile* Chriſtians (as in ſeveral other paſſages) or, perhaps, ſpeaks of *himſelf ſtrictly*, denoting what temper he was of before his *converſion*.

A.D. 64. deceived, ſerving divers luſts and pleaſures, living in malice and envy, hateful *and* hating one another.

behaviour toward their adverſaries, when they conſider this turbulent, ſelfiſh, and quarrelſome diſpoſition ſavours too much of that unregenerate ſtate, wherein they all lately were, before their converſion.

4 But after that the kindneſs and love of God our Saviour toward man appeared.

5 Not by works of righteouſneſs which we have done, but according to his mercy, he ſaved us, by the waſhing of regeneration, and renewing of the Holy Ghoſt;

6 Which he ſhed on us abundantly, through Jeſus Chriſt our Saviour:

7 That being juſtified by his grace, we ſhould be made heirs according to the hope of eternal life.

4, 5, 6. & 7. And that it was the deſign of this great mercy of God in the goſpel revelation, and in receiving them into the happy privileges of the Chriſtian covenant by baptiſm, and the gracious influences of the Holy Spirit attending their admiſſion into it, to reform them from ſuch a temper: and to prevent all further diſputes about the neceſſity of their *external* matters of religion; they ought to remember they were *all* thus redeemed, and put into a capacity of eternal life and happineſs, by the pure and ſole mercy of God through Chriſt; a mercy which neither the Gentiles could in the leaſt merit, by virtue of any thing they did, or could have done; nor the Jews lay any claim to, by the moſt exact obſervance of their *ceremonial* law.

8 *This is a* * faithful ſaying, and theſe things I will that thou affirm conſtantly, that they which have believed in God, might be careful † to maintain good works: theſe things are good and profitable unto men.

9 But

8. Theſe are the * certain and moſt ſubſtantial points of *Chriſtianity;* and it is of infinite importance to *you* and *them*, to perſuade them to be chiefly bent upon poſſeſſing themſelves of ſo gentle and charitable a temper, and upon ſuch practices as are the indiſpenſable conditions of theſe mighty bleſſings and privileges.

9. Where

---

* Ver. 8. [A faithful ſaying.] See the notes on 1 Tim. xv. 2 Tim. ii. 11.

† Ver. 8. [Might be careful to maintain good works.] καλῶν ἔργων προΐστασθαι, to prefer, to excel in, good works.

A. D. 6..

9 But avoid foolish * questions and genealogies, and contentions, and strivings, about the law; for they are unprofitable and vain.

9. Wherefore reject and discountenance all the frivolous and contentious disputes about *Jewish* traditions, pedigrees, and ceremonies; as being of no manner of advantage, but the greatest obstacles to the Christian profession.

10 A man that is an heretic, after the first and second admonition, † reject:

11 Knowing that he that is such, is subverted, and sinneth, being condemned of himself.

10. & 11. Whatever pretended Christian is obstinately and incurably bent upon maintaining such doctrines, or practices, as are directly contradictory to the known rules of our religion *; and such as, upon sufficient admonition, he cannot but, *himself*, know to be so; and all this out of a *factious* temper, to set himself up as *head* of a *party*, ready to join with any *sect* whatever, for promoting some *worldly* end and purpose; let him † be expelled from the Christian church, as one that acts against the plain dictates of his own conscience; and is to be looked on as a lost and profligate person, and his conversation avoided.

* αἱρετικὸς ἄνθρωπος.

† αὐτοκατάκριτος.

12 When I shall send Artemas unto thee, or Tychicus, be diligent to come unto me to Nicopolis: for I have determined there to winter.

12. As soon as I send either Artemas, or Tychicus, to supply your place, make it your business to meet me at Nicopolis, for I intend to stay there the winter season.

13 Bring Zenas the lawyer, and Apollos, on their journey diligently, that nothing be wanting unto them.

13. Supply Zenas and Apollos with all necessaries for their voyage to me.

14 And let ours also learn ‡ to maintain good works for necessary

14. And be careful to exhort all Christians, but especially the *Jewish* ‡ converts (who most want the

‡ ἡμέτεροι.

* Ver. 9. [Foolish questions.] See 2 Tim. ii. 23.

† Ver. 10. [An heretic—reject, παραιτοῦ, avoid him, have nothing to do with him.]

‡ Ver. 14. [Let ours learn.] Some learned persons think that by *ours*, he means the *Gentile* converts. Let the reader judge.

A. D. 64. cessary uses, that they be not unfruitful.

the advice) to the exercise of charity and * beneficence, wherever there is occasion for it, without distinction, upon any account of different sentiments and opinions.

* καλῶν ἔργων.

15 All that are with me salute thee. Greet them that love us in the faith. Grace *be* with you all. Amen.

15. All the Christians with me send their hearty love to you. Do the same from us to all that bear us any Christian respect. The Divine love and favour be with you all. Amen.

A PARA-

A

PARAPHRASE

ON THE

EPISTLE OF ST. PAUL.

TO

PHILEMON.

THE PREFACE.

ONESIMUS was servant (or *slave*) to Philemon the *Colossian*, one of St. Paul's converts. He had robbed, and ran away from his master. The better to lie undiscovered, he gets to Rome, where the *apostle* then lay, under his *first* (see ver. 22.) confinement. St. Paul providentially happens upon this man; converts him to the Christian faith; and now sends him back to his *master*, with this epistle of reconciliation: wherein are so many lively strokes of generous humanity and Christian compassion to a reformed *sinner*; of such *justice*, mixed with so much *sweetness* and *condescension*, along with the *authority* of an *apostle*, toward one that was both a *friend* and a *disciple*, as may render it a just wonder, to find some people of opinion, that *this* epistle contained so little in it, as to be unworthy to be ranked among St. Paul's writings. For more particular moral reflections from this letter, the curious reader may be referred to the excellent preface of St. Chrysostome.

PHILEMON.

Written A. D. 62.

1 PAUL a prisoner
of Jesus Christ,
and Timothy *our* brother,
unto Philemon
our dearly beloved,
and fellow-labourer,
2 And to *our* beloved
Apphia, and Archippus,
our fellow-soldier,
and to the
church in thy house:
3 Grace to you, and
peace from God our
Father, and the Lord
Jesus Christ.

‡ Theodoret.

|| See Philip. i. 1.

1, 2. & 3. I PAUL, that am now a prisoner at Rome for the sake of Jesus Christ, and his religion, send this epistle to my dear convert, and fellow-labourer Philemon, and to my dear friend Apphia ‡ his wife, not forgetting Archippus, my brother minister, and all your Christian family: wishing you all divine favours and blessings from God the Father, and the Lord Jesus Christ. As doth || Timothy also, who is now with me.

4 I thank my God,
making mention of
thee always in my
prayers,
5 Hearing of thy
love and faith which
thou hast toward the
Lord Jesus, and toward
all saints;

4. & 5. Expressing my hearty thanks to God (which indeed I never omit to do whenever * I mention you in my prayers) for your steadiness to the Christian religion, and your charity to all its professors, which I hear to be so exemplary and remarkable.

6 That the communication
† of thy
faith may become effectual
by the acknowledg-

6. & 7. For it cannot but be a matter of the deepest satisfaction to me, to have such ample testimonies of your Christian sincerity in

* [Making mention of thee alway in my prayers.] Or thus, εὐχαριςῶ τῷ Θεῷ πάντοτε, μνείαν σε ποιέμενος. [I always thank God when I mention you in my prayers.

† Ver. 6. [The communication of thy faith—ἡ κοινωνία τῆς πίςεως σε, your sharing or partaking of the (Christian) faith.

Ibid. [By the acknowledging of every good thing—ἐν ἐπιγνώσει, By your manifesting every good thing to be in you.

ledging of every good thing which is in you in Chriſt Jeſus.

your generous relief of the indigent and ſuffering members of that holy profeſſion. A. D. 62.

7 For we have great joy and conſolation in thy love, becauſe the bowels of the ſaints are refreſhed by thee, brother.

8 Wherefore, tho' I might be much bold in Chriſt, to enjoin thee that which is convenient,

9 Yet for love ſake I rather beſeech thee, being ſuch a one as Paul the * aged, and now alſo a priſoner of Jeſus Chriſt.

8. & 9. Wherefore, with a perſon of a good and generous diſpoſition, I ſhall have no occaſion to inſiſt upon the reſpect and reverence he owes me, as his *apoſtle* and firſt converter; but hope, it may be ſufficient for gaining your compliance with a requeſt I am now going to make to you, to apply myſelf to you as a *friend*, as an *aged* friend, and a *priſoner* for the faith you ſo much eſteem and value.

10 I beſeech thee for my ſon Oneſimus, whom I have begotten in my bonds:

11 Which in time paſt was to † thee unprofitable: but now profitable to thee and to me:

10. & 11. My ſuit is not in my *own* behalf, but of the bearer, your ſervant Oneſimus; who, though once ſo treacherous, † as to rob and run away from you; yet, now that I have converted him to the *Chriſtian* religion, will, I doubt not, make you the utmoſt amends, by a diligent and faithful ſervice for the future, and become a profitable ſervant to *you*, and a credit to *me*.

12 Whom I have ſent again: thou therefore receive him that is mine own bowels.

12. In full aſſurance of which, I now ſend him back to you, and beg you would entertain him again; if not for his *own*, yet for *my* ſake,

13 Whom ... as

* Ver. 9. Paul *the aged*—Or perhaps Παῦλος πρεσβεύτης, Paul *the ambaſſador*, agreeably to 2 Cor. v. 20. Eph. vi. 20. Indeed it does not appear that St. Paul was a very *aged* man when this epiſtle was written; though it may well be allowed, that the many *fatigues* and *hardſhips* he had undergone, might bring an *earlier* old age upon him than upon the generality of mankind.

† [To thee unprofitable, ἄχρηστον, injurious]. See Rom. i. 28. Eph. v. 11. *Thus* inutilis *among the* Latins *is* injurious.

A. D. 2. as a perſon now exceeding dear to me: For remember I had the pleaſure to make him a convert in my *bonds* and the ſon of my *old age*.

13 Whom I would have retained with me, that in thy ſtead he might have miniſtered unto me in the bonds of the goſpel.

14 But without thy mind would I do nothing, that thy benefit ſhould not be as it were of neceſſity, but willingly.

13. & 14. Indeed I could willingly have kept him here, to do me thoſe good offices, in my confinement, which I know yourſelf would gladly perform, if you could: But, as you have a right to him, I would reap the benefit of no one's ſervant, without his maſter's leave.

15 For perhaps he therefore departed for a ſeaſon, that thou ſhouldeſt * receive him for ever:

15. And I think, you may well look on it as an act of *Providence*, that his leaving you, for a while, ſhould prove ſo happy an occaſion of improving him into a faithful ſervant, for his * whole life after.

16 Not now as a ſervant, but above a ſervant, a brother beloved, ſpecially to me, but how much more unto thee, both in the fleſh, and in the Lord?

16. Entertain him, therefore, now, not only in the character of a good *ſervant*, but alſo of a Chriſtian *brother*. Conſider how dear he is to *me* in that relation; and look upon him not only as your *domeſtic*, but as a fellow member of the ſame Chriſtian *church* with us both.

17 If thou count me therefore a partner, receive him as myſelf.

17. And ſhow the reſpect you bear to *me*, by the generous reception you give *him*.

18 If he hath wronged thee, or oweth *thee ought*, put that on mine account.

19 I Paul have written it † with mine own hand, I will repay it: albeit I do not ſay to thee, how thou oweſt unto me even thine own ſelf beſides.

18. & 19. As to any damage he has done you, though I could balance that account, by remembering you owe your very ſalvation to *me*, as the inſtrument of your converſion; yet I wave that at preſent, and here give you, under my own hand-writing, † to make good whatever you have loſt by him.

20. Do

* [Receive him again forever αιωνιον] [A ſervant for life.]

† [With my own hand]. See Rom. xvi. 26. 1 Cor. xvi. 21. 2 Theſſ. iii. 17.

20 Yea, brother, let me have joy of thee in the Lord: refresh my bowels in the Lord.

20. Do not, therefore, dear brother, deny the Christian pleasure and comfort you will do me, by your forgiveness and compassion to one so near and dear to me.

21 Having confidence in thy obedience, I wrote unto thee, knowing that thou wilt also do more than I say.

21. The great opinion I have of your dutiful respect toward me, suffers me not to doubt of a compliance from you, even beyond what I have requested.

22 But withal, prepare me also a lodging, for I trust that through your prayers I shall be given unto you.

22. I must desire lodgings at your house, intending to visit you when my *trial* is over; in which I doubt not but to be cleared, by the concurrence of yours, and other good Christians prayers.

23 There salute thee Epaphras, my fellow prisoner in Christ Jesus.

24 Marcus Aristarchus, Demas, Lucas, my fellow labourers.

23. & 24. Epaphras, my fellow prisoner for the same cause of Christ, as also Mark, Aristarchus, Demas and Luke, that labour with me in promoting the gospel in these parts, send their hearty Christian love to you.

24 The grace of our Lord Jesus Christ be with your spirit. Amen.

25. The love and favour of our Lord Jesus Christ be with you, and direct your mind. *Amen.*

A PARA-

A

PARAPHRASE

ON

THE EPISTLE

TO THE

HEBREWS.

PREFACE.

THE testimony of all ancient copies and translations, with the concurrent suffrage of the best writers, both ancient and modern, give such evidence for St. Paul's * being the author of this excellent epistle, that the objections, or rather scruples, brought to the contrary are of no weight. His mentioning himself as lately a prisoner, chap. x. 34. and in *Italy*, chap. xiii. 24. with Timothy's enlargement, and a promise to visit the *Hebrews* along with *him*, chap. xiii. 23. do sufficiently clear the *time* of its *date* to have been just after his deliverance from his first *trial* at *Rome*, viz. Anno Domini 63. as both Bishop Pearson and Dr. Mill have adjusted it. All, therefore, that will be further needful to let the reader into the main spirit of this writing, is, to observe something concerning the *persons* to whom, and the *occasion* upon which it was written.

§ 1. I

* See Dr. Mill's Prolegom. § 83, &c. and Mr. Hallet's Introduction to his Supplem. to Mr Pierce *on the* Hebrews.

§ 1. I have formerly obſerved the *Hebrews* to ſignify the native inhabitants of the *Jewiſh land*, as diſtinguiſhed from the *foreign Jews* diſperſed in other countries; who went under the name of *Helcniſts*, or *Greeks*; though, moſt properly, the *converts* or *proſelytes* to the *Jewiſh* religion were called by this name. (See Acts x. 2. and vi. 1). With theſe *believing Jews* of *Paleſtine*, St. Paul held a conſtant intimacy and correſpondence, had a free acceſs to them in his writings and arguments, from the obligations he had laid them under, by the charitable collections he had made, and the conſtant care he took for their poor, Acts xxiv. 17. 1 Cor. xvi. 2 Cor. viii. and ix. So that though it be no queſtion but that this epiſtle was intended for the conviction of the *Jews* of *all* nations, and the confirmation of the *Jewiſh converts*, wherever diſperſed, yet it was thus prudently directed to them of the *Holy Land*: to *them* firſt who were the immediate and conſtant attendants on thoſe religious *ordinances* and *ceremonies*, the inſufficiency and aboliſhment whereof was the chief argument of this letter, and to that *place* that was the *centre* of the *circumciſion*, from whence his epiſtle might, the ſooner and better, be communicated to the whole circumference of their *diſperſion*. (See Sir Iſaac Newton's *Obſervations on the Apocalypſe*, chap. i). Hebrews who?

§ 2. St. Paul in his ſecond epiſtle to the * *Theſſalonians* had foretold a great *apoſtacy*, which, ſo far as it related to the *Jewiſh* people, may be interpreted, either of the general revolt of their nation from the *Roman* government, or of their *Chriſtian converts* from the religion of Chriſt, agreeably to our Saviour's prediction, Mat. xxiv. 12. In the *latter* of theſe ſenſes, it began now to be fulfilled by a too general deſertion of the *Jewiſh Chriſtians*, frighted from their profeſſion by the furious perſecution of the infidel *Jews*. To arm ſome, and to recover others from this *apoſtacy*, was the purpoſe of this epiſtle: The ſubſtance whereof, may, I think, be reduced to the following arguments.

* The occaſion of it, chap. ii. 3.

Firſt, The ſuperlative excellency of Chriſt's *perſon*, not only above that of Moſes, but above the very *angels* too, by the miniſtration of whom the *Jewiſh* law was delivered. This is the argument of the *two firſt* chapters.

Secondly,

Secondly, The dignity and perfect efficacy of Chriſt's *prieſthood*, and the inſufficiency of the *Levitical* one, together with the wiſdom and advantage of his being not a *temporal monarch*, but a *ſuffering* Meſſiah, make up the diſcourſe from the *third* to the *ninth* chapter.

Thirdly, The mere figurative nature, and utter inſufficiency of the legal *ceremonies* and *ſacrifices*, and the perfect ſufficiency of Chriſt's *death*, for the redemption and pardon of mankind, is the purpoſe of the *ninth* and *tenth* chapters.

And, *Fourthly*, To obviate that prejudice and bold aſſertion of the *Jews*, *That to forſake the Moſaical religion was to apoſtatize from God*, the *eleventh* chapter is ſpent in ſhowing, the faith of *Chriſtians* to be the exerciſe of the ſame virtuous *principle*, whereby all holy men of old rendered themſelves acceptable to God, and ſtand upon record as his true and eminent ſervants.

Theſe are ſeverally intermixed with their proper inferences and exhortations, all tending to ſhow the *Jewiſh* Chriſtians the unreaſonableneſs, folly, and danger of falling off again from the *Chriſtian* faith to the *Jewiſh* religion; and to ſupport and ſpirit them under the perſecution that tended to draw them from it.

§ 3. It is of no great moment to know the true reaſon, why the apoſtle thought not fit to prefix his *name* to this epiſtle: The moſt probable one ſeems to be, that he might give the leſs offence to the *infidel Jews* of that country, who were enraged at him as a preacher to the *Gentiles*; or that, having owned himſelf the *apoſtle* of the *circumciſion*, he concealed his *name*, to give the leſs diſguſt to ſuch *Jewiſh Chriſtians* as were not fully weaned from their prejudices in that matter. (See Dr. Mill's *Prolegom.* § 99, 100.

I ſay nothing concerning the original *language* in which this epiſtle was written by St. Paul. I reſt myſelf contented in the opinion of thoſe who, upon the ſupport of the beſt of ancient tradition, conclude it to have been written in the *Syriac* (commonly, at that time, called the *Hebrew*) language; and tranſlated into *Greek* by St. Luke. In confirmation of which ſentiment, I cannot do better than refer my reader to the ingenious and learned Mr. Hallet's Introduction to his *Supplement to* Mr. Pierce *on the* Hebrews.

CHAP.

The Apostle's first Argument for dissuading the Jewish *Christians from Apostizing from Christianity to the* Jewish *Religion,* viz *The Truth and Certainty of Christ's Religion, and the superlative Dignity of his* Person, *not only above* Moses, *but even those very* Angels *by whom the* Jewish *Law was delivered.*

1 GOD, who at sundry * times, and in divers manners, spake in time past unto the fathers by the prophets,

2 Hath in these last days spoken unto us by *his* Son, whom he has appointed heir of all things, by whom also he made the worlds.

1. & 2. TO preserve you, dear brethren, from that general apostacy from the Christian faith, to which the false doctrines, and furious persecutions of the *Jews*, are now so prevalent to draw the believers of that nation: Let me request you seriously to consider, that your Christian religion is a revelation from the same God, who, in several times, manners, and degrees, revealed his will to your forefathers, down from Adam, Abraham, Moses, and all the *Jewish prophets*, to this day; wherein he has made the *last* and complete discovery of his divine will to us and all mankind, by Jesus Christ, the promised *Messiah:* A person of most superlative dignity and excellence, being that *Word* † and *Son of God*, by whom the Father created the whole world, ‡ and governs all the dispensations of it, and has constituted him the Lord and Governor over all created beings.

Written A. D 63.

† John i. 1. &c.

‡ τὰ αἰῶνας the ages or dispensations.

3 Who being the brightness of his glory, and the express image of his person, and upholding all things

3. Whose origination is not like that of other prophets and lawgivers, of mere human and mortal extraction, nor produced into being by the agency of any subordinate

---

* Ver. 1. At sundry times. πολυμερῶς, *or* in sundry parts, parcels.

A. D. 63.

§ ἀπαύγασμα.

things by the word of his power, when he had by himself purged our sins, sat down at the right hand of the majesty on high:

ordinate power, as *instrumental* in his production; he being an immediate ray § of the divine majesty itself; the perfect image and resemblance of God the *Father*, by whom the Father made and preserves all things. Nor did he, after the great sacrifice of himself in the flesh, for the perfect redemption of mankind, die and leave us, like other *priests*; but was exalted to the highest degree of heavenly glory and majesty, to become a most powerful and constant *intercessor* with the *Father* for all true believers.

4 Being made so much better than the angels, as he hath by inheritance obtained a more excellent name than they.

4. Thus is Christ, in dignity of nature and character, far superior, not only to all mankind, but even to the very *angels*, by whose ministry the *Mosaical* law was delivered to your nation. As may most clearly be seen from all those scripture passages that describe the person, office, and authority of the *Messiah*.

‖ Acts xiii. 33.

5 For unto which of the angels said he at any time, Thou art my Son, this day have I begotten thee? And again, I will be to him a Father, and he shall be to me a Son?

5. Thus (in *Psal.* ii.), He is styled, the ‖ *Son*, the peculiarly *begotten Son of God*. And (in 2 *Sam.* vii. 14. 1 *Chron.* xxii. 10.), *God declares himself his Father, by way of special eminence.* Which expressions, as they could no way be applicable * to the persons of David or Solomon (though the most famous princes), so neither were such distinguished characters ever given to the highest *angel* or *archangel* whatever; but must be meant of Christ, of whom David was a *type* and *figure*.

6 † And again, when he bringeth in the first-begotten

6. Again, The scripture, in other passages, speaking † of the triumphant

---

* See the learned Dr. Pierce's note upon this *verse*.

† [And again, when he bringeth in]—εἰσαγάγῃ may refer either to the *scripture*, or to God the *Father*. [The bringing him again into the world], may signify either the *scripture* speaking *again of Christ's coming into the world*, or the *Father's* bringing Christ into the world again at his *resurrection*, say some, or at the last day of *judgment*, as others. I have expressed it as agreeably as I could to each of these acceptations.

begotten into the world, he ſaith, And let all the angels of God worſhip him.

phant reſurrection of Chriſt, and his being made the Saviour, Lord, and Judge of the whole world, repreſenting God the Father as commanding *all angels to reverence him*, (Pſal. xcvii. 7.*) A. D. 63.

7 And of the angels he ſaith, Who maketh his angels ſpirits, and his miniſters a flame of fire.

7. Whereas, the lofticſt titles the ſcriptures ever give to the *angels*, are no higher than thoſe of *meſſengers* and *miniſters* of God; comparing them, for their ſwiftneſs and efficacy in their office, to *winds* and *flames*, (Pſal. cxxiii. 20. 21.)

8 But unto the Son *he ſaith*, Thy throne, O God, *is* for ever and ever, a ſceptre of righteouſneſs is the ſceptre of thy kingdom;

9 Thou haſt loved righteouſneſs, and hated iniquity; therefore God, *even* thy God, hath anointed thee with the oil of gladneſs above thy fellows.

10 And thou, Lord, in the beginning haſt laid the foundations of the earth: and the heavens are the works of thine hands.

11 They ſhall periſh, but thou remaineſt: and they all ſhall wax old as doth a garment.

12 And as a veſture ſhalt thou fold them up, and they ſhall be changed; but thou art the ſame, and thy years ſhall not fail.

8. 9. 10. 11. & 12. But, in a quite different ſtrain, does David repreſent the *Meſſiah*, *viz*. As the *only Son of God, the Creator, Lord and Governor of the whole world; as a perfectly wiſe, juſt, and righteous Governor over all created beings; and not, like them, of a created, finite, and temporary exiſtence, at leaſt of a finite and temporary authority, but of a nature and dominion truly divine, eternal, and immutable.*

13 But to which of the angels ſaid he at any

13. So alſo, when the Pſalmiſt (Pſal. cx. 1.) introduceth God the *Father*

---

* Deut. xxxii. 43. according to the *LXX*; and to *that* paſſage, in all probability (as ſome think) the apoſtle refers; that of Pſal. xcvii. 7. being, not as it is here, *all the angels of God*, but *all ye gods*. But, as *angels* are often ſtyled *gods* in ſcripture, there is no weight in that argument. See Mr. Pierce upon this place.

A. D. 63. any time, Sit on my right hand, until I make thine enemies thy footstool?

Father speaking to Christ his *Son*, *to take possession of his utmost height of heavenly glory and majesty, and get the entire conquest over sin, Satan, death, and all the enemies of his kingdom:* It is in such expressions as are infinitely too great to be meant of the most exalted *angel* or created spirit.

14 Are they not all ministring spirits, sent forth to minister for them who should be heirs of salvation?

14. In fine, the highest of *angels* are but *ministers* and *messengers* of God; they were but *ministers* in delivering the *law* the *Jews* so much boast of; and they are still the same to the *Christian* church; assisting and ministring to *us*, in such measures as God is pleased to appoint: But Christ is the Lord and *Head* over both *us* and them *.

CHAP. II.

An Inference from the foregoing Argument: viz. *That Christians are obliged to the utmost Care and Constancy in their Religion, as being delivered by a Person of greater Dignity than the very* Angels *that conveyed the* Mosaical Law. *The Excellency of Christ's* Person *further illustrated. His being a* Suffering *Saviour no* Objection; *but the utmost Testimony of the Wisdom and Goodness of the Christian Dispensation, for the Benefit of sinful Mankind.*

1 THerefore we ought to give the more earnest heed to the things which we have heard, lest at any time we should let them slip.

1. THE superlative dignity then of the *person* of Jesus Christ, ought to render you the more regardful of the religion, and the more resolute to adhere to the doctrines he has revealed to us; so as never to be drawn, or tempted from them.

2 For 2. 3. & 4.

---

* *Note*, For a more complete understanding of the force of the apostle's argument in these passages, I can do nothing better than to refer the reader to the learned *notes* of Mr. Pierce.

2 For if the word ſpoken by angels was ſteadfaſt, and every tranſgreſſion and diſobedience received a juſt recompence of reward:

3 How ſhall we eſcape if we neglect ſo great ſalvation, which at the firſt began to be ſpoken by the Lord, *and* was confirmed unto us by them that heard *him*;

4 God alſo bearing them witneſs, both with ſigns and wonders, and with divers miracles, and gifts of the Holy Ghoſt, according to his own will?

2. 3. & 4. For if God did in ſo exact and ſevere a manner, vindicate the honour of the *Jewiſh law*; that was conveyed to that people by the miniſtry of *angels* only; inſomuch that every contemptuous violation of it was puniſhed with immediate death*, and had no ſacrifices to atone for it: How much more dreadful muſt be the puniſhment of ſuch as wilfully neglect and forſake the mercies of the *Chriſtian* religion, that were revealed and brought down to us from heaven by the very *Son* of God himſelf; the truth whereof was, in ſuch ample manner, demonſtrated to us his *apoſtles*, by the powers of the Holy Ghoſt; and by us to the reſt of mankind?

A. D. 63.

* Chap. vi. 2.

5 For unto the angels hath he not put in ſubjection the world to come, whereof we ſpeak.

5. Remember, I ſay, that your religion was conveyed to mankind by one that is ſuperior to all *angels*; and that the *Chriſtian* church has the happineſs to be under the immediate conduct and government of the *Son of* God himſelf.

6 But one in a certain place teſtified, ſaying, What is man that thou art mindful of him: or the ſon of man that thou viſiteſt him?

7 Thou madeſt him a little lower than the angels, thou crowneſt him with glory and honour, and didſt ſet him over the works of thy hands.

8 Thou haſt put all things in ſubjection under his feet. For in that he put all in ſubjection under him, he left nothing that is not put under him. But now we ſee not yet all things put under him.

6. 7. & 8. Of whom thoſe words of the Pſalmiſt (Pſal. viii. 4. &c.) [tho' we ſhould ſuppoſe they were] primarily ſpoken of Adam, and his poſterity in general; yet, in their *full* and *complete* ſenſe, could not be true of *them*; becauſe they expreſsly repreſent a *perſon as perfect Lord and Governor over all created beings; a complete Conqueror over all the enemies of God's kingdom*; which can never be ſaid of Adam, or of any branch of human race.

A. D. 63.

9 But we see Jesus, who was made a little * lower than the angels, for the suffering of death, crowned with glory and honour, that he by the grace of God should taste death for every man.

9. Whereas they exactly answer to Jesus our Messiah, the Second Adam, who though in his human state*, while by the wise and merciful dispensation of God, he was to suffer death, for the redemption of *mankind*. He was indeed in a state inferior to that of *angels*; yet in reward of those sufferings, is that *human* nature of his now exalted to the highest degree of heavenly glory and majesty; and this *God-man* become the Lord, and Governor, and Saviour of all men.

10 For it became him, for whom are all things, and by whom are all things, in bringing many sons unto glory, to ‡ make the Captain of their salvation perfect thro' sufferings.

10. The generality of the *Jews*, indeed, expected Christ under the character of a *temporal* monarch, and a conqueror for their particular nation, and think it a great objection against our Jesus, that he was a suffering † *Messiah*: But the Divine Wisdom saw further and better. The happiness he was to bestow on his disciples, was not *temporal*, but *spiritual* and heavenly: And, for the encouragement and support of such as were to go through a world of sufferings and temptations, as the condition of that happiness; this (among others) was one instanee of the Divine Wisdom, that he that was to be both our *Saviour* and *example*, should work our salvation by, and be himself crowned and rewarded for, his *sufferings*.

† See 2 Cor. i. 18. 23, 24, 25. and chap. ii. 2.

11 For both he that sanctifieth, and they who are sanctified, are all

11. 12. & 13. Thus it pleased God, that the Redeemer of mankind should condescend to take on him the

* Ver. 9. [Made a little lower than the angels]—— Βραχύ τι, [for a little while lower than the angels].

‡ [Make the Captain——perfect through suffering]. τελειῶσαι, in a *sacrificial* sense, is either to *consecrate*, or to *purge perfectly* from *sin*. In an *agonistical* sense, it is to *crown* and *reward*. I shall distinguish them as clearly as I can, by the connection of the several passages in which it occurs in this epistle.

A. D. 63.

all of one: for which cause he is not asham- ed to call them bre- thren.

12 Saying, I will declare thy name unto my brethren, in the midst of the church will I sing praise unto thee.

13 And again, I will put my trust in him: and again, Be- hold, I, and the chil- dren which God hath given me.

the same nature with those he was to redeem: according to those pro- phetical expressions of scripture, concerning the *Messiah;* wherein "He vouchsafes to own us for his brethren," *as in* Psal. xxii. 22. and is represented as "paying the same humble duties to God the Father" with the rest of the holy and truly religious part of man- kind; and in another place calling us *his children,* as in Isaiah viii. 17, 18. "I will wait upon the Lord—Behold I and the children which God hath given me, are for signs and for wonders in Is- rael, from the Lord of hosts."—

14 Forasmuch then as the children are partakers of flesh and blood; he also him- self likewise took part of the same, that through death he might destroy him that had the power of death, that is the de- vil:

15 And deliver them who through fear of death were all their lifetime subject to bondage.

14. & 15. Thus it seemed good to the Divine Wisdom to recon- cile and make us his children, by the sufferings of Christ in that very nature that had transgressed; as the most proper way of conquer- ing that prevailing power of the devil, that had tempted us to sin, and draw us into death; and, by this means, to give to all mankind (especially the Gentile world, that were enslaved with the sense of guilt, and the fear of death, with- out any prospect of a recovery from it), the certain hope of a future and happy life.

16 For verily he took not on him *the nature of* angels; but he took on *him* the * seed of Abraham.

17 Wherefore in all things it behoved him to be made like unto his

16. & 17. For Christ is to be con- sidered, not as a Redeemer of *an- gels* and fallen *spirits,* but of *man- kind**; of all those, who like true children of Abraham, are subject to temptations and sufferings, and are to be advanced to pardon and happiness

* Ver. 16. [But the seed of Abraham], according to the great promise, [in thy seed shall all the nations of the earth be blessed.]

A. D. 63.

his brethren, that he might be a merciful and faithful high prieſt, in things pertaining to God, to make reconciliation for the ſins of the people:

happineſs by imitating him, in a patient ſubmiſſion to that Divine Will which they had tranſgreſſed. Upon which account, it was highly expedient for Chriſt, our great Prieſt and Sacrifice, to live and ſuffer in our nature, as the moſt perfect method both to atone for our ſins, and to ſupport and encourage us under *our* preſent ſufferings for *his* religion; whom we know to have had a fellow-feeling with us, and ſo to bear a compaſſionate regard towards us.

18 For in that he himſelf hath ſuffered, being tempted, he is able to ſuccour them that are tempted.

18. For nothing is ſuch an immediate comfort to a *Chriſtian*, as to know he ſuffers for the ſake of a *Saviour*, who is touched with the experience of what he undergoes, as well as with a full power to relieve and ſupport him.

CHAP. III.

The Second Branch of the Apoſtle's firſt Argument for their Steadineſs to the Chriſtian Profeſſion; viz. The Dignity of Chriſt, as a Lawgiver, above Moſes. A Warning from thence againſt Infidelity and Apoſtacy. As alſo from the Inſtance of the Obſtinate Iſraelites, that were denied Entrance into the Land of Canaan, for the ſame Miſcarriage.

* Chap. ii. 11, 12, 13.

† μέτοχοι.

1 WHerefore holy brethren, partakers of the heavenly calling, conſider the Apoſtle and High Prieſt of our profeſſion, Chriſt Jeſus.

1. WHerefore, dear * brethren, *brethren* of Chriſt, and children of Abraham, members of the holy church of God (though you only *partake* † of it with *other* people) conſider well the exceeding great dignity of Chriſt's *perſon*,

person, who as a *Prophet* has given you the most complete rules of life; as a *High Priest*, by suffering in your own nature, has procured the perfect pardon of your sins; and by his religion, obtained such spiritual and heavenly blessings for you, as far surpasses those of the *Jewish law*. A. D. 63.

2 Who was faithful to him that appointed him, as also Moses was faithful in all his house.

2. Remember that God the Father has appointed and established him the Lord and only High Priest over his church: And that he has as perfectly performed every part of his great * office for the *Christian* church, as you can imagine, or the scripture declare, Moses to have done toward the *Jewish* one, when it styles him *Faithful in all his house*; i. e. the church of God. (Numb. xii. 7.)

* πιςὸν ὄντα.

3 For *this* man was counted worthy of more glory than Moses, in as much as he who hath builded the house, hath more honour than the house.

4 For every house is builded by some man, but he that built all things is God.

3. & 4. But you must consider too, that as a substitute and *deputy* † governor, who is himself but a *member* of the house or society he governs, is inferior to the lord ‡ that appoints him; so much is Moses inferior to Christ: For Moses acted in the *Jewish* church only as a *servant* of God; whereas Christ, as the *Son of God*, is Lord and Governor both of the *Jewish* and *Christian* church; and the *supreme* Governor or householder over all is God the Father §.

† Κατασκευάσας.

5 And Moses verily was faithful in all his house, as a servant, for a testimony of those things

5. & 6. Moses indeed had a commission to manage that church, and faithfully || discharged it; but still it was in the capacity of a *servant* and

|| πιςὸς.

‡ Κατασκευάζω—signifies either to *build*, or to *order* and *govern*. The *former* sense is most commonly received, but the *latter* seems, in this place, to be most natural. Moreover οἶκος the house, here seems clearly to signify not the *material* house, but the *inhabitants* or *family* dwelling in it.

§ Compare 1 Cor. xi. 3. 12.

A. D. 63. things which were * to be ſpoken after.

and *deputy*, employed to deliver a diſpenſation that plainly pointed out *another* more perfect one, that was to ſucceed it.

6 But Chriſt as a ſon over his † own houſe, whoſe houſe are we, if we hold faſt the confidence, and the rejoicing of the hope firm unto the end.

But we *Chriſtians* are now under the immediate government of Chriſt himſelf, † the Lord over all churches and divine diſpenſations, as the *Son of God:* And ſhall not fail to enjoy the final fruits of ſo great a privilege, on condition of our ſteady adherence to his religion, under all our preſſures and perſecutions.

7 Wherefore as the Holy Ghoſt ſaith, To-day, if ye will hear his voice,

8 Harden not your hearts, as in the provocation, in the day of temptation in the wilderneſs:

9 When your fathers tempted me, proved me, and ſaw my works forty years.

7. 8. & 9. Let therefore that inſpired leſſon of the Pſalmiſt (Pſal. xcv.) be heartily conſidered by you now: Wherein he exhorts the *Jewiſh* people, "To hearken to the divine command while opportunity was afforded them; and not to harden their hearts and become incurable, by an obſtinate and wilful diſobedience, as their forefathers did in the wilderneſs; where they diſtruſted the divine power and Providence, and provoked the wrath of God, for forty years together."

10 Wherefore I was grieved with that generation, and ſaid, They do always err in their hearts, and they have

10. & 11. The conſequences of which habitual courſe of impiety, was, "That they became utterly unworthy of the countenance of the divine favour and protection, and

---

* Ver. 5. [For a teſtimony of thoſe things that were to be ſpoken after] that is, the *religion* or *diſpenſation* of Chriſt; as appears moſt clearly from John v. 46, 47. Luke xxiv. 44. Acts xxvi. 22. and many like paſſages.

† Ver. 6. [Chriſt as a ſon over his own houſe.] A very wrong tranſlation. It is, *over his*, viz. *God's houſe; ἐπι τὸν οἶκον ἀυτοῦ*; the ἀυτοῦ plainly is to be referred to Θεοῦ God, (ver. 4.) as it is in the 5th verſe; agreeably to 1 Tim. iii. 15. 1 Cor. iii. 9. *ye are God's building*,

have not known my ways.

11 So I ſware in my wrath, They ſhall not enter into my reſt.

and cauſed God to ſwear by himſelf, that they ſhould never enter into the promiſed land. A. D. 63.

12 Take heed, brethren, leſt there be in any of you an evil heart of unbelief, in departing from the living God.

12 Take heed then, that *their* caſe in reſpect of that *temporal* bleſſing of Canaan, be not *yours*, now, in reſpect to the eternal bleſſings of Chriſt's religion. Remember, that by forſaking *Chriſtianity*, you apoſtatize from the *ſame* God, who lives eternally to reward the faithful, and puniſh the diſobedient.

13 But exhort one another daily while it is called To-day, leſt any of you be hardened through the deceitfulneſs of ſin.

13. To prevent which, make it your immediate endeavour ſo to encourage one another to patience and perſeverance, that none, if poſſible may be drawn from their profeſſion, by the ſubtle inſinuations, or moſt violent perſecutions from their adverſaries.

(14 For we are made partakers of Chriſt, if we hold the beginning of our confidence ſteadfaſt unto the end.)*

[14. Remember, that the great privileges of Chriſtianity are to be enjoyed only upon condition of a reſolute perſeverance in *that* religion, to which you have engaged yourſelves.]

16 While it is ſaid, To-day if ye will hear his voice, harden not your hearts, as in the provocation.

15. Conſider how much it concerns you to lay hold of the *preſent* time afforded for it; and the danger of neglecting it, as the Jews did in the wilderneſs.

* Ver. 14. Note, This verſe being included in a *parentheſis*, makes the cleareſt connection between the 13 and 15 verſes; which, otherwiſe, is much interrupted.

A. D. 63.

16 * For some when they had heard, did provoke: howbeit not all that came out of Egypt by Moses.

17 But with whom was he grieved forty years? *was it* not with them that had sinned, whose carcasses fell in the wilderness.

18 And to whom sware he that they should not enter into his rest, but to them that believed not?

16. 17. & 18. And let it move you the more, to observe how infectious and epidemical their dissatisfactions and disobedience was, * "That the whole congregation were drawn to murmer against Moses and Aaron, except Caleb and Joshua (Numb. xiv.)." Nor did their *numbers* prevent the certainty of that punishment God had sworn to inflict upon them; for they all, except these two, died in the wilderness.

19 So we see that they could not enter in because of unbelief.

19. As therefore infidelity and a revolt from the divine commands lost them the *promised* land; so will your renouncing the *Christian profession*, for any persecutions whatever, forfeit you all the blessings of this *new* and gracious *covenant*.

---

* [For some, when they heard, &c. τινὲς γὰρ ἀκούσαντες παρεπίκραναν; ἀλλ᾽ οὐ πάντες—; Who did provoke? Did not all that came out of Egypt?] Interrogatively, as the two following verses are; or else the sense is this,—Though your apostacy from Christianity be now too general, as theirs was then—yet remember you have Caleb and Joshua for your example and encouragement; who were preserved for their singular obedience, while all the rest were destroyed.

CHAP.

CHAP. IV.

The same Exhortation to Constancy and Patience continued. Christianity promises a future and better State of happiness, than the Land of Canaan was. That there is such a State provided for good and faithful men, proved from the ancient Scripture of the Old Testament. Christ a severe and terrible Governor to the obstinate and disobedient. No concealing our Cowardice and Infidelity from Him. The Exhortation of Chap. ii. 10. *renewed.*

1 LET us therefore fear, lest a promise being left *us* of entering into his rest, any of you should * seem to come short of *it.*

2 For unto us was the gospel preached as well as unto them, but the word preached did not profit them, not being mixed with faith in them that heard *it.*

3 For we which have believed, do enter into rest, as he said, As I have sworn in my wrath, If they shall enter into my rest: although the works were finished from the foundation of the world.

4 For

A. D. 63.

1. BE exceedingly careful therefore, || I say, that by a revolt from the true religion, you lose * not the celestial happiness of the *gospel*, as the murmuring Jews did that of the terrestrial Canaan.

|| Chap. iii. 18, 19.

2. You have now the substantial religion and promises of Christ as fully declared and confirmed to you, as they had their *law*, and the promise of the land of Canaan; and may, through your own default, forfeit the blessings of it, as they did theirs.

3. 4. 5. & 6. For that there is a future and eternal state of rest and happiness reserved for God's faithful servants, beside, and far exceeding that of the *Jewish* Canaan, is plain, by comparing the several passages of scripture where that phrase of *the rest of God* is mentioned. When God had finished the

* [Seem to come short of it.] Δοκῇ in the same sense as in Luke viii. 18.

A. D. 63.

4 For he ſpake in a certain place of the ſeventh day on this wiſe, And God did reſt the ſeventh day from all his works.

5 And in this place again, If they ſhall enter my reſt.

6 Seeing therefore it remaineth that ſome muſt enter therein, and they to whom it was firſt preached, entered not in becauſe of unbelief:

the works of the creation he is ſaid to have *reſted from his work**. And when the Pſalmiſt (Pſal. xcv.) mentions the entrance into *God's reſt*; it is indeed ſo far as it refers to the Jews in the *wilderneſs*, meant of their entering into the *land of Canaan*, as a *reſt* from their travels in the *wilderneſs*, reſembling that of God's *reſting* from his *creation*: but, as it relates to the Jews of his *own* time, to whom David ſpoke them, it muſt have a *higher* meaning than the *reſt of Canaan*, which thoſe murmurers loſt by their infidelity.

* Gen. ii.

7 Again, he limiteth a certain day, ſaying in David, To-day, after ſo long a time; as is ſaid, To-day if ye will hear his voice, harden not your hearts.

8 For if Jeſus had given them reſt, then would he not afterward have ſpoken of another day.

9 There remaineth therefore a reſt to the people of God.

7. 8. & 9. For as that exhortation of David, *not to harden the hearts*, was directed to the people *then* living, who had for a long time been poſſeſſed of the land of Canaan, into which Joſhua brought their forefathers; the *reſt of God* propoſed to *them* could not be *that*, but muſt ſignify a future *ſtate* of *heavenly* happineſs; the ſame that the goſpel promiſeth to us Chriſtians.

10 For he that is entered into his reſt, he alſo hath ceaſed from his own works, as God *did* from his.

10. Nor indeed could the happineſs and reward of a true ſervant of God be properly compared to *God's reſt from all his work*, unleſs it be a *final* and *complete* deliverance from the labours and troubles of this life.

11 Let us labour therefore to enter into that reſt, leſt any man fall after the ſame example of unbelief.

21. Strive therefore to attain this *perfect* ſtate of felicity, and not loſe it by apoſtacy, as the Iſraelites did their Canaan.

12 For

12. & 13. And

A. D. 63.

12 For the word of God *is* quick and powerful, and sharper than any * two-edged sword, piercing even to the dividing asunder of soul and spirit, and of the joints and marrow, and *is* a discerner of the thoughts and intents of the heart.

13 Neither is there any creature that is not manifest in his sight: but all things are naked and open unto the eyes of him with whom we have to do.

12. & 13. And consider how exquisitely wise, all-knowing, and terribly powerful this Jesus, the *Son* and *Word of God* is: that there is no way to conceal your cowardice and hypocrisy from him, the searcher of hearts; who is both your *Saviour* and your *Judge* *. Consider also what a powerful and effectual thing the *Word of God* is (viz. his *promises* and *threatenings*) when duly believed and attended to in the minds of men.

14 Seeing then that we have a great High Priest, that is passed into the heavens, Jesus the Son of God, let us hold fast *our* profession.

14 Look on him and adhere to his profession, to his *word* and *promise*, as your Great *High Priest*, that hath both atoned for your sins, and, by his exaltation into heaven, is become your powerful and constant *Intercessor* with God.

15 For we have not an high † priest which cannot be touched with the feeling of our infirmities; but was in all points tempted like as we are, *yet* without sin.

15. Embrace him, as a far more able and sufficient High Priest than† the *Mosaical* one could be; as in all other respects, so particularly in this, That he has not only perfect power to help and assist you, but is one that must be most compassionately willing and free to do it; as having himself been exposed to sufferings, and felt the miseries of human life, as you do; only with this difference, that those miseries *we* feel, are the result of *sin*, while *he* suffered in pure and unspotted *innocence* ‡.

† Chap. ii. 17.—iii. 1. 3, 6.

‡ Chap. vii. 26. 1 John ii. 1, 2.

16. Relying

* See Rev. i. 16. and ii. 12. 16. and xix. 13. and 15. with my paraphrase on those passages. And let the reader compare the *notes* of the learned Mr. Pierce; and then judge for himself. I thought it proper to express *both* senses; each of them having its favourers amongst the learned.

A. D. 63. 16 Let us therefore come boldly unto the throne of grace, that we may obtain mercy, and find grace to help in time of need.

16. Relying therefore on the power and compaſſion of ſuch an Interceſſor, you may addreſs to God with a much more comfortable aſſurance, than the Jews could to the *mercy ſeat*: and cheerfully depend upon him, for a ſeaſonable deliverance from all the perſecutions you ſuffer for his ſake.

CHAP. V.

The Dignity and Excellency of Chriſt's Prieſthood *above the* Levitical. *The Efficacy of it proved from his Reſurrection and Glorification. It is compared to that of Melchiſedec. The Wiſdom and Advantage of the Sufferings of the* Son of God. *The ſmall Progreſs of the* Jewiſh *Chriſtians complained of.*

* See Chap. iv. 14, 15, 16, 17.

1 FOR every * high prieſt taken from among men, is ordained for men in things *pertaining* to God, that he may offer both gifts and ſacrifices for ſins:

1. YOU may now, I ſay, as you are Chriſtians, addreſs yourſelves to God with a clearer and more comfortable aſſurance of acceptance with him than the Jews could do; as having Chriſt for your High Prieſt, whoſe office is of far more dignity and prevalence than that of *their* high prieſt could ever be: as may be ſeen by comparing them in any reſpect whatever. As firſt, The *Jewiſh* high prieſts, though employed in divine ſervice, and mediators between God and the people, were yet but mere frail and mortal *men*.

2 Who can have compaſſion on the ignorant, and on them that are out of the way; for that he himſelf alſo is compaſſed with infirmity:

2. & 3. And though they could not but bear a compaſſionate regard to the frailties and infirmities of the people, in whoſe behalf they miniſtered; yet was this their compaſſion of a much inferior and leſs effectual kind than that of Chriſt to *us*.

3 And *They*

A. D. 63.

3 And by reaſon hereof he ought, as for the people, ſo alſo for himſelf, to offer for ſins.

They could not but have a fellow-feeling with the reſt of the congregation, becauſe they were *men* and *ſinners* themſelves: And for that reaſon, upon the great *expiation day*, they offered a particular ſacrifice for their *own* offences: Whereas Chriſt lived and ſuffered in perfect *innocency*, and was pleaſed, for our great comfort and aſſurance, to ſympathiſe with our infirmities, miſcarriages and ſufferings, while he had not the leaſt ſin of his *own*.

4 And no man taketh this honour unto himſelf, but he that is called of God, as *was* Aaron:

5 So alſo Chriſt glorified not himſelf to be made an high prieſt: but he that ſaid unto him, Thou art my Son, to-day have I begotten thee.

6 As he ſaith alſo in another *place*, Thou *art* a prieſt for ever after the * order of Melchiſedec.

4. 5. & 6. Then again, our Lord excels *the Levitical* high prieſts, in the divine *demonſtrations* given of the greatneſs and authenticneſs of his high office. For as *they* were expreſsly ordered to be of the line of Aaron, and ſometimes the *perſon* ſpecially appionted by God; ſo was Chriſt of the family of David, according to the prophecies concerning him. And while he did not affect † to appear and ſhow himſelf in the form of a *divine* and heavenly Mediator, while he lived upon earth, he was by his glorious reſurrection from the dead, in a much more ſolemn manner, declared and demonſtrated to be the *Son of God*, the great *High Prieſt* and *Saviour* of mankind. According to thoſe words of the Pſalmiſt, ſpoken of the || reſurrection of the *Meſſiah*, by God the *Father* (Pſal. ii.) *Thou art my Son, this day have I begotten thee.* And upon the ſame account in another *pſalm* (Pſal. cx.) he is called *A Prieſt for ever after*

† See Philip. ii. 5—11.

|| Acts xiii. 33.

* [After the order of Melchiſedec,] κατὰ τὴν τάξιν· According to the likeneſs or reſemblance of Melchiſedec]; as the following paſſages, and thoſe of the ſeventh chapter, plainly ſhow it, eſpecially ver. 15. of that chapter. Accordingly the Syraic renders it by דמותא *ſimilitude.*

A. D. 63. *after the order of* Melchisedec, *i. e.* an eternal and powerful one; a *King* to govern and save, as well as a *Priest* to *sacrifice* for his people.

7 Who in the days of his flesh, when he had offered up prayers and supplications, with strong crying and tears, unto him that was able to save him from death, and was heard, in that he feared.

8 Though he were a Son, yet * learned he obedience, by the things which he suffered:

7. & 8. So also the prayers and tears, the agonies and sufferings of our Jesus, were a service of infinitely more acceptance and prevalency with God, than the prayers and sacrifices of a *Jewish* high priest could possibly be. The obedience and sufferings of one, who was the very *Son of God*, making him at once both a complete atonement for our sins, and a most perfect and encouraging * example of obedience and resignation to the Divine Will.

9 And being made perfect, he became the author of eternal salvation unto all them that obey him;

|| Τελειωθεὶς.

10 Called of God an high priest after the order of Melchisedec.

9. & 10. And as his sufferings thus rendered him a perfect *High Priest* for our reconciliation to God, so his resurrection || and glorification in *heaven* has demonstrated him to be the powerful Saviour of all his true disciples; giving them a perfect assurance of eternal happiness: According to the true meaning of the forementioned scripture, *Thou art a Priest for ever after the order of* Melchisedec †.

† See ver. 6.

11 Of whom we have many things to say, and hard to be uttered; seeing ye are dull of hearing.

11. I have several things particularly to observe to you, concerning this analogy between the priesthood of Melchisedec, and that of Christ; in order to convince you of its great excellency above the *Levitical* priesthood, the *Jews* so much boast of. But I fear your prejudices are still such, that

* [He learned obedience by the things, *&c.*] ἔμαθεν may signify, not only to be instructed one's *self*, but to learn *others*, answering to the Hebrew לָמַד rendered both by ἔμαθεν and διδάσκειν, in the Septuagint.

that you will hardly * underſtand and reliſh them, though A. D. 63.
the things themſelves are intelligible and eaſy enough.

12 For when for the time ye ought to be teachers, ye have need that one teach you again which *be* the firſt principles of the oracles of God; and are become ſuch as have need of milk, and not of ſtrong meat.

12 For indeed, though one would think you have had time enough, from your firſt converſion, (eſpecially the *Jewiſh* converts, who have long before enjoyed the advantage of the *law*, and the *prophets*) to underſtand your Chriſtian religion ſo well, as to be able to teach the higheſt doctrines of it to others; yet I find your *Jewiſh* notions and prejudices have made your improvement ſo ſmall, that inſtead of that, I had need go over with you again, teach you the firſt rudiments of it, and treat you not like *men* but *children*.

13 For every one that uſeth milk, is unſkilful in the word of righteouſneſs: † for he is a babe.

14 But ſtrong meat belongeth to them that are of full age, *even* thoſe who by reaſon of uſe have their ſenſes exerciſed to diſcern both good and evil ‡.

13. & 14. And, as milk is the proper food for children, ſo, I am afraid, the firſt and plaineſt articles of Chriſtianity would be fitter for ſuch ſlender proficients as you, than the higher doctrines of it, which ought to be communicated only to ſuch as have already attained to a good underſtanding ‡ of the firſt and fundamental points of their profeſſion.

CHAP.

---

* [Hard to be uttered] λόγος δυσερμήνευτος. Hard for ſuch prejudiced people to underſtand. The ſame with St. Peter's δυσνοητα. 2 Peter iii. 16.

† Ver. 13. [The word of righteouſneſs,] *or* λόγου δικαιοσύνης, *the* [doctrine of juſtification]—viz. by Chriſt, in oppoſition to that of or by the *law*.

‡ Ver. 14. [Both good and evil]—is an Hebraiſm to ſignify *things in general*. *To know good and evil*, is to have a very *large knowledge*, Gen. iii. 5. To ſpeak *neither good nor evil*, is to ſay *nothing at all*. But the phraſe is here confined to a particular *ſubject* in religious matters, as the context ſhows, and as in the paraphraſe.

CHAP. VI.

The Apostle promiseth them farther instructions, particularly in the Comparison between Christ and Melchisedec. But, before he enters upon that Point, renews his Exhortation to Constancy and Perseverance, from the great Danger and Hazard of ever recovering a Christian Apostate; *and from the Example of the Faith and Reward of Abraham, and the Truth of the Divine Promises.*

A. D. 63.

1 THerefore, leaving the principles of the † doctrine of Christ, let us go on unto perfection; not laying again the foundation of repentance from dead works, and of faith towards God.

2 Of the doctrine of baptisms, and of laying on of hands, and of resurrection of the dead, and of eternal judgment.

* Chap. v. 11, 12, 13.

1. & 2. BUT, notwithstanding that the small proficiency you have made would make it not amiss for me, * as I said, to teach you, over again, the first principles of Christianity; such as the necessity of *repentance* and reformation of life; of belief in God and Christ; of being baptized with *water* and the Holy Ghost; the imposition of the apostles *hands*, for receiving the Holy Ghost after *baptisms;* of the belief of a *future state* and a *future judgment*, and the like; yet, for the better encouragement of those that still adhere to their profession, in these general and fundamental points, I shall wave them, and pursue my proposal of instructing you further and higher, particularly in the forementioned analogy between the priesthood of Christ, and that of Melchisedec.

3. (Which

† Ver. 1, 2. The principles of the doctrine of Christ—the foundation of repentance—faith—baptisms, &c.

Note, Whoever, looks into the *comments* upon these two verses, will find to what a great uncertainty the learned are reduced in their interpretations of these *phrases;* viz. Whether they be *principles* and *fundamentals* of the *Jewish* religion (originally designed to lead men to the doctrines of Christ) or doctrines of *Christianity itself.* I have followed the *latter* sentiment; the reader may consult Mr. Pierce for the arguments that countenance the former.

A. D. 63.

3 And this will we do if God permit.

3. (Which I shall partly now do in the sequel of this epistle, and more fully (God willing) when I see you again.)

4 For *it is* impossible for those who were once enlightned, and have tasted of the heavenly gift, and were made partakers of the Holy Ghost,

5 And have tasted the good word of God, and † the powers of the world to come;

6 If they shall fall away, to renew them again unto repentance: seeing they crucify to themselves the Son of God afresh, and put *him* to an open shame.

4, 5. & 6. I will do this, I say, for the sake of those who still persevere in their *Christian* profession. For indeed, it would be a vain * and endless undertaking for me to begin again and reconvert those among you, who, against the most solemn engagements of their *baptism*, and the happy experience of the gifts of the Holy Ghost, conferred from *heaven* upon them; against all the sense they had of the great mercies of the laws and privileges of the *gospel*; and, in defiance of all those powerful † demonstrations, whereby the whole religion of Christ has been so amply conferred to them; have wilfully revolted, and thrown off their Christianity, to embrace the *Jewish* and *heathenish* religion again. Because such people have already resisted the utmost evidences that can ever be offered for their conviction, and done as perfect and public a ‡ dishonour to Christ and his religion, as if they had crucified him anew as a *malefactor*.

‡ παραδειγματίζοντας, Exposing him to infamy.

7 For the earth which drinketh in the rain that cometh oft upon it, and bringeth forth herbs meet for them by whom it is dressed, receiveth blessing from God:

7. & 8. So that, as that ground only which is likely to answer the cost bestowed on it, by bearing a good crop, is worth a man's pains to manure and cultivate; whereas, that which spoils the seed thrown into it, and returns the husbandman nothing but rubbish instead

* ἀδύνατον. Not strictly *impossible*, but only highly *improbable* or *difficult*.

† [The powers of the world to come]—Δυνάμεις τε τοῦ μέλλοντος αἰῶνος. Not of the *future state*, but the *miracles* (Δυνάμεις) wrought in confirmation of the *religion* of the Messiah, who was to come in the *future* or *last age* of the *world*.

A. D. 63.

8 But that which beareth thorns, and briers, *is* rejected, and *is* nigh unto curſing: whoſe end *is* to be burned.

of corn, is fit for nothing, but to be left wild and barren, or elſe to be ſtubbed up and burnt: ſo theſe obſtinate and wilful *apoſtates* deſerve no further means of conviction, but are to be left to the effects of their ingratitude and incurable infidelity.

9 But beloved, we are perſuaded better things of † you, and things that accompany ſalvation, though we thus ſpeak.

† Compare 2 Theſſ. ii. 12, 13. Epheſ. iv. 20. Rom. viii. 9.

9. But I hope, dear brethren, this is not *your* caſe, at leaſt, not of many of you; and therefore I give you this, only as a very earneſt and neceſſary caution of the great danger of falling from your Chriſtian profeſſion.

10 For God is not unrighteous to forget your work and labour of love, which ye have ſhowed toward his name, in that ye have miniſtered to the ſaints, and do miniſter ‡.

‡ Chap. x. 33, 34.

10. And be aſſured, that whatever our preſſures and afflictions may at preſent be; if you be not wanting to yourſelves, God will ſupport you under them all. And I am the more confident of his ſpecial aſſiſtance towards you, as a juſt reward for that eminent degree of charity, which you formerly have, and ſtill do ſhow to the poor diſtreſſed Chriſtians of your country.

11 And we deſire, that every one of you, do ſhow the ſame diligence, to the full aſſurance of hope unto the end.

11. Let me, therefore, exhort you all conſtantly to perſevere in that good diſpoſition and practice, in full aſſurance of ſo glorious a reward.

12 That ye be not ſlothful, but followers of them who through faith and patience inherit the promiſes.

12. To be diligent and courageous in every branch of your Chriſtian duty, and patient under all ſufferings for the ſake of it; in imitation of all thoſe great and holy men, who have reaped the promiſed bleſſings of God, by the ſame means.

13 For when God made promiſe to Abraham, becauſe he could ſwear by no greater,

13. & 14. Remember, in particular, how punctually true God was in his great promiſe made to Abraham, of a numerous poſterity,

A. D. 63.

greater, he ſware by himſelf,

rity, from whom Chriſt, the Saviour of mankind (the promiſed *ſeed*) was to come.

14 Saying, Surely, bleſſing, I will bleſs thee, and multiplying, I will multiply thee.

How ſolemnly he was pleaſed to confirm it, by ſwearing by himſelf; Gen. xxii. 16, 17. "By myſelf have I ſworn, That in bleſſing, I will bleſs (i. e. moſt aſſuredly and greatly bleſs) thee, and in multiplying, I will multiply (i. e. moſt aſſuredly and greatly multiply) thee."

15 And ſo after he had patiently endured, he obtained the promiſe.

15. And accordingly, Abraham actually lived to ſee a numerous (at leaſt a very proſperous) family † of his own, as a *preſent* reward of his faith and patience. But the promiſe was *further* performed, by God's merciful and wondrous diſpenſations toward the *Jewiſh* church; and is now *abſolutely* completed to all mankind, by the bleſſings of the *Chriſtian* religion.

† Gen. xxiv. 1—35.

16 For men verily ſwear by the greater, and an oath for confirmation is to them an end of all ſtrife.

17 Wherein God willing more abundantly to ſhow unto the heirs of promiſe the immutability of his counſel, confirmed *it* by an oath.

16. & 17. Thus God was pleaſed to condeſcend to the manner of us *men*, for our greater and more perfect ſatisfaction. For an *oath* is the higheſt and moſt deciſive evidence that can be given or deſired, in any human court. And becauſe God could not appeal to any greater than himſelf, as *men* do when *they* ſwear by *himſelf* as the Author and Fountain of truth. (ver. 13.)

18 That by two immutable things, in which it was impoſſible for God to lie, we might have a ſtrong conſolation, who have fled for refuge to lay hold upon the hope ſet before us.

18. So that the aſſurance we Chriſtians have of a future and eternal ſalvation, on condition of our faith and patient obedience, is upon the ſureſt grounds that Heaven itſelf can give; being founded both upon the *promiſe* and the *oath* of God: In either of which it is impoſſible for *him* to deceive us, who is *truth* itſelf.

19 Which *hope* we have as an anchor of the ſoul, both ſure and ſtedfaſt,

19. This aſſured hope of ours, like a ſtrong anchor to a ſhip, holds up our minds againſt all the ſtorms

A. D. 63. stedfast, and which entereth into that within the vail,

and billows of this world; mounting our thoughts, and raising our views above its present cares and fears; and presenting us with a lively prospect of *future* and eternal felicity.

20 Whither the forerunner is for us entered, *even* Jesus, made an high priest for ever, after the order of Melchisedec.

20. Even of that glorious happiness, to which Jesus Christ our *Head* is now exalted, as an earnest, that we his true members are hereafter to follow him, who is thus become our *High Priest;* not like those mortal and temporary ones among the Jews; but, like Melchisedec, an *eternal* Intercessor, Prince and Saviour to us. The particulars of which comparison, I come now, according to my proposal, to explain.

CHAP. VII.

In what Respects the Priesthood of Christ resembles that of Melchisedec. Thence the Dignity and Excellency of it above the Levitical. And by the Change of the Priesthood is demonstrated the Suspension of the Jewish Religion, and of the Obligation to the Ceremonial Law.

* 1 FOR this Melchisedec king of Salem, priest of the most high God, who met Abraham returning from the slaughter of the kings, and blessed him;

2 To whom also Abraham gave a tenth part of all: first being

1. & 2. TO show you, then, the particular analogy between the priesthood of Christ and that of * Melchisedec, and from thence the dignity of it above the *Levitical* priesthood: Now the first part of the resemblance lies in their *titles* and *characters;* the word Melchisedec signifying as, *a just and righteous king;* and *Salem* the place whereof

---

* [For this Melchisedec, &c.] or thus οὗτος γὰρ ὁ Μελχισεδὲκ. For *he* (*i. e.* Christ) is the Melchisedec—*i. e.* The antitype of that Melchisedec who was king of Salem.

ing by interpretation king of Righteousness, and after that also, king of Salem, which is king of peace;

whereof he was king, denoting PEACE. He was also a *priest* over his people, as well as a *king*; a sincere worshipper of the true God, and approved of by him in that high office; and was in such esteem and authority, that the great patriarch Abraham, at his return from the slaughter of the four kings (Gen. xiv.) received his blessing, and paid him a tenth of the spoils he had taken. And thus he was a proper type and figure of *Christ the Lord our Righteousness*, our *Justifier*, *Peace-maker*, and Great *High Priest*. A. D. 63.

3 * Without father, without mother, without descent, having neither beginning of days, nor end of life; but made like unto the Son of God, † abideth a priest continually.

3. Again, the scripture records give no account of Melchisedec's pedigree. He had no descent from ‖ Abraham, or was born of any *priestly* family. The *scriptures* say nothing either of the beginning or end of his life; nor of the time when he entered on his *priesthood*, or when he left it. And thus he, so far, figuratively represents our *Jesus*, *the Son of God*, *who was in the beginning* ‡, *before all things*, who *abideth for ever*; and who, by his *resurrection* and *ascension* into heaven, is become the *Eternal Lord* and Governor of his church, an everlasting *High Priest* and *Intercessor* for all true believers.

‖ See verse 6.

‡ John i. 1. and viii. 55, 58.

R 3 4. Now

---

* 'Αγενεαλόγητος,—Without any *catalogue* or *register* of ancestors. [Without father, without mother.] The care that men of figure, in all ancient countries, took in registering their *ancestors* (and the Jews for particular reasons above any other), made it a common mode of speech, to call such persons, whose pedigree was either *obscure* or *lost*, *fatherless* and *motherless*. Thus,

Patre Nullo. Matre Servâ. Liv. Lib. IV.

—Nullis Majoribus ortus. HORAT. Serm. Lib. I. Sat. 6.

Duos Romanos Reges esse quorum alter patrem non habet, alter matrem—Nam de Servii Matre dubitatur, Anci Pater nullus. SEN. Epist. 108.

† [Abideth a priest for ever.]—Not Melchisedec *abideth a priest for ever*, but Melchisedec resembles Christ (who) abideth, &c. It is an *ellipsis* and ὅς is understood. Revel. i. 4, 5. where the like *ellipsis* may be seen.

A.D 63.

4 Now consider how great this man *was*, unto whom even the patriarch Abraham gave the tenth of the spoils.

4. Now, if you consider what great respects were paid to this Melchisedec, even by your great father Abraham himself, the very head of the *Jewish* nation; you cannot but conclude Christ (of whom *he* was but a mere *type*) to be a priest of far greater dignity than any *Jewish* priest can pretend to be.

5 And verily they that are of the sons of Levi, who receive the office of the priesthood, have a commandment to take tithes of the people according to the law, that is, of their brethren, though they come out of the loins of Abraham:

6 But he whose descent is not counted from them, received tithes of Abraham, and blessed him that had the promises.

5. & 6. For observe, the *Jewish* priests were appointed to take tithes of their *brethren*, the people that were descended from Abraham as well as they; and so in all other respects on the level with them. Whereas Melchisedec, who was not of that family, had yet these honours paid him, by the very *head* and father of it, even by Abraham himself, that *friend of God*, that had such noble promises made to him.

7 And without all contradiction, the less is blessed of the better.

7. From whence it is clear, he must be a greater person than Abraham (for it is an undoubted maxim, *That he that receives a solemn blessing from another person, must be inferior to him*) and if so, then how much more excellent must Christ be, above all other priests, when even Melchisedec himself was but his mere *type* and resemblance?

8 And here men that die receive tithes: but there he *receiveth them*, of whom it is witnessed that he liveth.

8. Again, the *Jewish* priests, you know, are but mortal *men*, and their priesthood of a short duration. Whereas, of Christ (the perfect Melchisedec) it is said, *That he is a priest for ever*, Psal. cx. 4.

9 And

9. & 10. And

9 And * as I may ſo ſay, Levi alſo who receiveth tithes, paid tithes to Abraham.

10 For he was yet in the loins of his father when Melchiſedec met him.

9. & 10. And * indeed all the A. D. 63.
Jewiſh prieſts that ever were, may properly enough be ſaid to have paid tithes to, and received bleſſing from Melchiſedec, when Abraham did it, whoſe deſcendants they all were. And conſequently muſt, in their office, be inferior to him; and therefore much more to Chriſt.

11 If therefore perfection were by the Levitical prieſthood (for under it the people received the law) what further need *was there* that another prieſt ſhould riſe after the order of Melchiſedec, and not be called after the order of Aaron?

11. Now, from all this it plainly appears, that the *Moſaical* prieſthood, and the ſacrifices of the *Jewiſh* law, were not deſigned by God as the only and ſufficient means of pardon, and expiation for the ſins of mankind; no, nor for that of the Jews themſelves: for if ſo, it was to no manner of purpoſe for God to appoint *another* Great High Prieſt like Melchiſedec, when the *Levitical* prieſts and ſacrifices would have done without him.

12 For the prieſthood being changed, there is made of neceſſity a change alſo of the law.

13 For he of whom theſe things are ſpoken, pertaineth to another tribe, of which no man gave attendance at the altar.

14 For *it is* evident that our Lord ſprang out of Juda; of which tribe Moſes ſpake nothing concerning prieſthood.

12, 13. & 14. And whereas there is now ſuch a change for the better made in the *prieſthood*, that the ſucceſſion in the *Aaronical* family, and the tribe of Levi is quite out of date (as it is clear from Chriſt, the new and Great High *Prieſt's* not being born of the tribe of Levi, but Judah) it muſt thence follow, that God muſt be thought to make a proportionable alteration in the religion too.

* Ver. 9. [As I may ſo ſay: *or* ὡς ἔπος εἰπεῖν, to ſpeak the truth.] See Le Clerc, Art. Crit. Part II. chap. 2. But our own tranſlation is very agreeable.

A. D. 63.

15 And it is yet far more evident; for that after the ſimilitude of Melchiſedec there ariſeth another prieſt,

16 Who is made, not after the law of a ca al commandment, b..t after the power of an endleſs life.

15. & 16. For nothing can be more abſurd, than to ſuppoſe ſo conſiderable a change and advancement in the nature of the *prieſthood*, without a *proportionable* excellency and improvement in the *ſervices* to be performed: that God, in the room of a ſet of frail and imperfect Levites, ſhould ſolemnly appoint *one* completely *perfect*, *powerful* and *immortal High Prieſt*, as Chriſt is; and yet, that the *ſacrifice* he offers, and the *religion* he inſtitutes, ſhould be of no better kind than the *Moſaical* one was.

17 For he teſtifieth, Thou *art* a prieſt for ever after the order of Melchiſedec.

17. To ſuppoſe this, would be to loſe all the importance of the forementioned prophecy concerning Chriſt: *Thou art a Prieſt for ever after the order of Melchiſedec*. (See chap. v. 6, 9, 10.)

18 For there is verily a diſannulling of the commandment going before, for the weakneſs and unprofitableneſs thereof.

19 For the law made nothing perfect, but the bringing in of a better hope *did*; by which we draw nigh unto God.

18. & 19. So that the very appointment of Chriſt, as a *prieſt*, is an evident declaration that the *Levitical* prieſthood is to be now aboliſhed, as too imperfect to anſwer the great end of expiating for the ſins of mankind: and that the *Moſaical* ſacrifices and ceremonies were nothing but figures and introductions to that great ſacrifice of Chriſt, that procures us a perfect redemption and acceptance with God; and to *his* religion, which conſiſts of complete laws, hopes and promiſes.

20 And in as much as not without an oath *he was made prieſt*.

21 (For thoſe prieſts were made without an oath: but this with an oath, by him that ſaid unto him, The Lord ſware, and will not repent, Thou *art* a prieſt

20, 21. & 22. And indeed that ſolemn oath whereby God is ſaid to have confirmed and ratified the prieſthood of Chriſt (a thing never uſed at the conſecration of Aaron or any of his ſucceſſors), ſufficiently proves, that he was to be a prieſt of greater dignity, and a mediator of a covenant and religion far more excellen

a prieſt for ever after the order of Melchiſedec).

22 By ſo much was Jeſus made a ſurety of a better teſtament.

excellent than that of Moſes. For no leſs than this can be implied in that expreſſion, " The Lord ſware, and will not repent, Thou art a prieſt for ever after the order of Melchiſedec," Pſal. cx. 4. A. D. 63.

23 And they truly were many prieſts, becauſe they were not ſuffered to continue by reaſon of death:

24 But this man, becauſe he continueth ever, hath an unchangeable prieſthood.

23. & 24. And when you conſider the *Jewiſh* prieſts to be mere mortal *men*, dying and ſucceeding one another; but Chriſt, on the contrary, to be exalted into *heaven*, there to remain our *eternal* High Prieſt, and *conſtant* Interceſſor with God; this will convince you of the mighty difference in point of excellency, between one and the other.

25 Wherefore he is able alſo to ſave them to the uttermoſt, that come unto God by him, ſeeing he ever liveth to make interceſſion for them.

25. This will abundantly ſatisfy you in how happy a ſtate we Chriſtians are above the Jews, in having the ſame Saviour that died for our ſins now ſitting at the right hand of God, as the perfect Saviour and eternal Interceſſor for all his true diſciples.

26 For ſuch an high prieſt became us, *who is* holy, harmleſs, undefiled, ſeparate from ſinners, and made higher than the heavens;

26. And thus is Chriſt a High Prieſt moſt exactly ſuited to the great purpoſe of atoning for the ſins, and procuring the ſalvation of mankind. Which could never have been accompliſhed by the *external* ſervice of a mortal and ſinful *man*, offering up the blood of a *beaſt* in our behalf. But is completely effected by *him*, who, by the undefiled purity of his life, and the ſpotleſs innocency of his death, is our perfect *High Prieſt*; and by his exaltation to the utmoſt height of heavenly glory and majeſty, is become our powerful and conſtant *Interceſſor*.

27 Who needeth not daily, as thoſe high prieſts, to offer up ſacrifice firſt for his

27. Such a one muſt the Saviour of mankind be, who has no ſins of his *own* to expiate for, before he atones for *others*; nor, that

A. D. 63. his own fins, and then for the peoples: for this he did once, when he offered up himfelf.

that offers fuch a facrifice as need to be repeated again and again; but one that completely redeems us *once for all*; as Chrift did, by the facrifice of *himfelf*.

28 For the law maketh men high priefts which have infirmity; but the word of the oath which was fince the law, *maketh* the Son, who is confecrated for evermore.

28. And accordingly, you fee the wide difference in point of excellency, between thofe infirm and mortal priefts of the *Jewifh* law, and *him* the *Son of God*, whom the *Pfalmift* (in words fpoken long after the law was given) declares God the Father to have made the only and all-fufficient Prieft, the Eternal Saviour and Interceffor of mankind.

CHAP. VIII.

The foregoing Arguments, with the Inferences from them fummed up, viz. *that the Priefthood and Sacrifice of Chrift do exceedingly much excel, and confequently have fuperfeded and difannulled thofe of the* Mofaical Law. *That it was defigned to be fo, further proved from the Prophecies of the Old Teftament.*

1 NOW of the things which we have fpoken, *this is* the fum: We have fuch an high prieft, who is fet on the right hand of the throne of the Majefty in the heavens:

2 A minifter of the fanctuary, and of the true tabernacle, which the

1. & 2. THE fum* then of what we are to infer from the foregoing comparifon between Chrift and Melchifedec, is this; that we Chriftians are exceedingly more happy than the Jews could be, in having Chrift for a High Prieft; not like thofe weak and mortal men, that ferved in the figurative fabrics of the tabernacle and temple, built by the hands

* Ver. 1. This is the fum: or κεφαλάιον, the chief and principal thing.

the Lord pitched, and not man.

hands of *men*; but one that is exalted into *heaven*, the very throne and habitation of God, there to intercede for us.

3 For every high priest is ordained to offer gifts and sacrifices: wherefore it is of necessity that this man have somewhat also to offer.

4 For if he were on earth, he should not be a priest, seeing that there are priests that offer gifts according to the law:

3. & 4. Thus is he, in the most effectual and happy sense, our High Priest *still*. For as the *Jewish* priests are daily and yearly repeating their imperfect sacrifices in the *temple* here below; so does he *there*, continually and most prevailingly offer himself to God the Father for *us*. A service of infinitely greater necessity and advantage than the offering of those earthly gifts and sacrifices: a service to be performed in *heaven*, not upon *earth*, like the *Jewish* services; for *Jewish* priests are sufficient enough for such kind of performances, as are so imperfect as to leave the *conscience* of the sinner still guilty and impure.

5 Who serve unto the example * and shadow of heavenly things, as Moses was admonished of God when he was about to make the tabernacle. For see (saith he) that thou make all things according to the pattern showed to thee in the Mount.

5. These *Jewish* priests minister in a tabernacle that was only an imitation* and shadow of what God showed to Moses from heaven, on the Mount. And as this tabernacle was but a mere *copy* of something shown before; so the services performed in it can, at farthest, be no more than a mere shadow of something better to be hereafter.

6 But now hath he obtained a more excellent ministry, by how much also he is the mediator of a better covenant, which was established upon better promises.

6. Well, then, may this Priesthood of Christ be more excellent, and his intercession more effectual than the Mosaical, as he is the Mediator of a covenant, and the Author of a religion, so much greater in its promises, blessings and privileges.

---

* Ver. 5. Unto the example and shadow, ὑποδείγματι καὶ σκιᾷ, or in the copy or shadow.

A. D. 63.

7 For if that first *covenant* had been fruitless, then should no place have been sought for the second.

7. For, that the *Mosaical* religion was an imperfect and temporary dispensation, is demonstrable from this, that if it had not been so, there had been no occasion for God to have so expresly promised to introduce *another* and a *better*.

8 For finding* fault with them, he saith, Behold, the days come (saith the Lord) when I will make a new covenant with the house of Israel and the house of Judah:

9 Not according to the covenant that I made with their fathers in the day when I took them by the hand to lead them out of the land of Egypt, because they continued not in my covenant, † and I regarded them not, saith the Lord.

8. & 9. Whereas the prophet Jeremy (Jer. xxxi. 31.) after having reproached the *Jewish* nation for their irregularities, in plain words promised them, "That in after times God would give them a new and more perfect dispensation of religion, far superior to that external and figurative service appointed at Mount Sinai, which they had so often neglected, and thereby forfeited the protection † and favour of God.

10 For this is the covenant that I will make with the house of Israel after those days, saith the Lord, I will put my laws into their mind, and write them in their hearts: and I will be to them a God and they shall be to me a people.

10. "A religion that should consist of laws and privileges purely moral and spiritual, and perfectly agreeable to rational minds; by obedience to which, they should obtain the perfect favour of God, and become his true church and beloved people.

11. A

---

* Ver. 8. [For finding fault with them he saith]—Or, perhaps, more truly, and agreeable to the foregoing verse—μεμφομενος γὰρ, αυτοις λεγει, finding fault (with that *first covenant*) *he saith to them* (to the Jews).

† [And I regarded them not.] So the Septuagint, which the apostle follows. We translate the Hebrew—Though *I was a husband unto them*. The same word בעלתי being taken in both senses. Pocock Miscal. Chap. i. and in Micah, pag. 3.

A. D. 63.

11 And they ſhall not teach every man his neighbour, and every man his brother, ſaying, Know the Lord? for all ſhall know me from the leaſt to the greateſt.

11. " A religion that ſhould be neither difficult to underſtand, nor encumbered with ſuch numerous ceremonies as would render it hard, coſtly, or tedious to practiſe; but by its purity and plainneſs, ſhould be natural and agreeable to every mind, and condeſcending to men of all circumſtances and capacities.

12 For I will be merciful to their unrighteouſneſs, and their ſins and their iniquities will I remember no more.

12. " In fine, a religion, the ſervices whereof would not leave the conſciences of its worſhippers uncleared of guilt, as the *Jewiſh* ſacrifices did; but would provide for the full and complete expiation for the ſins of all true penitent believers."

13 In that he ſaith, A *new covenant*, he hath made the firſt old. Now that which decayeth and waxeth old is * ready to vaniſh away.

13. Now, it is moſt evident, that by promiſing a *new* and better diſpenſation, God muſt intend to abrogate the *old* and more imperfect one. And accordingly the *ceremonial* religion of the Jews is now going to be * quite laid aſide, and the *Chriſtian* to ſucceed in its room.

CHAP.

* [Ready to vaniſh away.] Which was *perfectly* fulfilled at the deſtruction of Jeruſalem, and the temple; about *ſeven* years after the date of this epiſtle.

CHAP. IX.

The Argument of Chap. viii. 5. &c. *continued,* viz. *Proving the* Jewish *Tabernacle and Temple, with the Services performed therein, to have been figurative of Christ, his Sufferings and Religion. The comparison between them enlarged upon, and the excellence of one above the other farther demonstrated.*

A. D. 63. 1 THEN verily the first *covenant* had also ordinances of divine service, and a worldly sanctuary.

1. BUT to proceed. That the *Mosaical* * covenant and religion was only typical, temporary, and introductory to Christ, and his more perfect dispensation, is apparent from the nature of the whole service, and the *tabernacle* wherein it was performed.

2 For there was a tabernacle made, the first wherein was the candlestick, and the table, and the shew-bread; which is called the sanctuary.

2. Which tabernacle (and so the *temple* afterward), consisted of two principal parts; the first whereof had the golden candlestick, and the table with the shew-bread on it: and this was called the *holy place, i. e.* the common place of public worship, (Exod. xxvi. Numb. vii.)

3. And after the second vail, the tabernacle, which is called the holiest of all;

4 Which had the golden censer, and the ark of the covenant overlaid round about with gold, wherein *was*

3, 4. & 5. In the second, which was parted from the former by a large curtain, were placed the golden censer (made use of only upon the great day of expiation) and the ark, plated over with gold; in the side chests whereof were put the two tables of the

* Some copies read Σκηνὴ, others Διαθήκη, without any material difference in the sense.

was the golden pot
that had manna, and
Aaron's rod that bud-
ed, and the tables of
the covenant *;
5 And over it the
cherubims of glory
ſhadowing the mercy-
ſeat: of which we
cannot now ſpeak par-
ticularly.

the law, the golden pot of man- A. D. 63.
na, and Aaron's rod that budded (Numb. xvii. Exod. xxv.) Over which ark were placed the *cherubims*, that covered the mercy-ſeat with their wings (from whence God was pleaſed to make the ſeveral manifeſtations of himſelf in a *cloud* and light of *fire*). The figurative ſignifications of all which particulars I have no time now to explain. And this *ſecond* part of the tabernacle was called the *Holy of Holies*, i. e. The *moſt holy*, or the place of *extrordinary* worſhip.

6 Now when theſe
things were thus or-
dained, the prieſts
went always into the
firſt tabernacle, ac-
compliſhing the ſer-
vice of God.
7 But into the ſe-
cond went the high
prieſt alone once eve-
ry year, not without
blood, which he of-
ferred for himſelf, and
for the errors of the
people.

6. & 7. The *firſt* of theſe (anſwering to the *Iſraelites* court in the *temple*) was the place where the prieſts performed the *daily* ſacrifices and ſervices: But the *latter* (and the ſame in the *temple*) was never uſed but one day in a year, the great day of *expiation*, by the high prieſt alone; who there offered up the blood of a ſacrificed beaſt, firſt for *himſelf*, and then another for the whole congregation.

8 The

8. Now,

* Ver. 4. [Wherein was the golden pot that had manna.] *Note*, By the word *wherein*, cannot be meant within the body of the *ark* itſelf. For, beſide other plain reaſons, the copy of the law muſt then have been cloſed up, and never taken out more; contrary to the very deſign of laying it there, as an authentic *original*. It muſt, therefore, mean the *ſide* of the *ark*, as the word (*mitzzad*) in Deut. xxxi. 26. ſignifies, as appears by comparing it with 1 Sam. vi. 8. and paraphraſed by the Chaldee Paraphraſe, in that very place of Deuteronomy. See the excellent Dr. Prideaux's Connexion of the Old and New Teſtament, Book III. p. 146, 147. 1ſt Edit. But indeed the word *wherein*, ἐν ᾗ may very well ralate not to κιβωτῷ *the ark*, but to the σκηνὴ ἡ λεγομένη ἅγια before mentioned, *the ſecond tabernacle called the moſt holy*; in which all theſe ſacred utenſils were; and whereby all objections are obviated.

A. D 63.

8 The Holy Ghost thus signifying, that the way into the holiest of all, was not yet made manifest, while as the first tabernacle was yet standing:

8. Now, that *most holy* place may be an emblem of *heaven*. And the meaning of the *high priest's* being suffered *alone*, and but *once* a year to enter that solemn apartment, and the rest of the priests and people being wholly excluded from it, could be only this, *viz*. That the true and perfect manner of mens attainment of *heaven* and true happiness by the full pardon of their sins, and the complete dispensation of religion, was not yet clearly manifested under the *Jewish economy*.

9 Which *was* a figure for the time * then present, in which were offered both gifts and sacrifices, that could not make him that did the service perfect, as pertaining to the conscience.

10 *Which stood* only in meats and drinks, and divers washings, and carnal ordinances imposed on them until the time of reformation.

9. & 10. And for the same reason, neither is it so *now*, * under the *temple* service, which is nothing but a more splendid continuation of that of the *tabernacle*, consisting of external and figurative sacrifices and ceremonies, that have nothing in them to expiate the guilt, and clear the conscience of a sinner; but are only *introductions* to that *great* sacrifice, and most perfect dispensation of Jesus Christ the *Messiah*.

11 But Christ being come an high priest of good things to come, by a greater and more perfect tabernacle, not made with hands; that is to say, not of this building;

12 Neither

11. & 12. For *he*, indeed, by shedding his own precious and innocent blood for us, has perfected that expiation for our sins, which the blood of all the beasts upon earth, could no way have obtained: And by being *exalted* into *heaven* itself, and become our *Intercessor* there, he is a high priest of that dignity, and eternal

* ἥτις παραβολὴ εἰς τὸν καιρὸν τὸν ἐνεστηκότα. Which figure ramains to *this present* time.

12 Neither by the blood of goats and calves: but by his own blood he entered in once into the holy place, having obtained eternal redemption for us.

eternal prevalency, which the *Jewish* priest, in his little *earthly* fabric, with his figurative services, can bear no comparison with: The difference being as wide as that between the *shadow* and *substance*, or as *heaven* is from *earth*.

13 For if the blood of bulls and of goats, and the ashes of an heifer, sprinkling the unclean, sanctifieth to the purifying of the flesh;

14 How much more shall the blood of Christ, who through the Eternal * Spirit offered himself without spot to God, purge your conscience from dead works to serve the living God?

13. & 14. For if those merely external and typical performances of *sacrificing*, *washings*, *sprinklings*, &c. were allowed sufficient to cleanse the *Jews* from *legal* defilements, and procure them re-admission to the service of the *tabernacle* and *temple* (which was the utmost they could do); How much more available, in proportion, must be the sacrifice of Christ's blood, a person of the highest dignity, and unspotted innocence, raised from the dead by the power of the Eternal Spirit: The Spirit under whose conduct and direction he was, and by which he was demonstrated to be indeed *the Son of God with power;* lived a spotless life, offering himself an immaculate sacrifice to God; and then, by the power of the same *Spirit*, was exalted into *heaven*, there presenting himself as an *Intercessor* with the Father, to expiate all those sins that render us obnoxious to death and misery, and to make us the true church and servants of God, worthy to serve him here, and to enjoy him in his heavenly sanctuary hereafter?

15 And for this † cause he is the mediator of the New Testament, that by means of death, for the redemption of the transgressions that were under

15. Thus † is Christ the Mediator of the new and better covenant than that of Moses. By *his* death are all those transgressions forgiven, which would have entailed death upon us, notwithstanding the expiation of the *Jewish*

† διὰ τοῦτο. By this *blood.*

* Ver. 14. [The Eternal Spirit.] See and compare Gen. xlix. 26. Habak. iii. 6. Note also, that many MSS. read it ἁγίου, *the Holy Spirit;* and so the Vulgar Latin.

A. D. 63. under the first testament, they which are called, might receive the promise of eternal inheritance.

ish sacrifices; and all true *Christian believers, viz.* whether *Jews* under the *first* testament or covenant, or *Gentile* believers under this *second*, are blest with the promise of eternal life and happiness.

16 For where a testament is, there must also of necessity be the death of the testator.

17 For a testament *is* of force after men are dead: otherwise it is of no strength at all while the testator liveth.

|| Διαθήκη as כרת in the Hebrew.

16. & 17. To his *death*, I say, is all this owing; nor could we enjoy it, till his sufferings were past, any more than the last *will* and *testament* of any man can be valid, till the testator be dead. For thus may the blessings of Christianity be considered, either as a || *covenant* of God the *Father*, that was to receive its *ratification* by the blood of Christ: Or as the *will* and *testament* of Christ *himself*, that could not take place but at, and by his *death* *.

18 Whereupon, neither the first testament was † dedicated without blood.

18. And in this it agrees with the *Mosaical* covenant, which was confirmed † and ratified by sprinkling the people with the *blood* of slain beasts: *Thereby figuratively showing the necessity of Christ's blood for the redemption of mankind.*

19 For when Moses had spoken every precept to all the people, according to the law, he took the blood of calves and of goats, with water and scarlet wool, and hyssop, and sprinkled both the book and all the people.

19. & 20. According to that account in Exod. xxiv. " That after Moses had read over the law to the people, he took the blood *of calves* and *goats*, *mixing* the blood with water (to keep it from congealing); and taking scarlet wool (to imbibe); *and hyssop* (to sprinkle it); and with it he sprinkled the book of the law, and had it (by degrees ‡) sprinkled

* Ver. 15, 16, 17, &c. *Note*, I have here expressed the *two* acceptations whereof the words Διαθήκη, *covenant* or *testament*, and Διαθέμενος, the *testator* or *pacifier*, are capable of in this difficult passage. The more critical reader may consult the learned Mr. Pierce.

† Not *dedicated* without blood, ἐγκεκαίνισται, i. e. Βεβαία γέγονεν ἐκυρώθη, Chrysostom. So the Syraic Version.

‡ Josephus Archæol. Lib. III. p. 89.

20 Saying, This is the blood of the testament which God hath enjoined unto you.

led upon all the people, *at least all the chief* heads *and* representatives of them; saying, "This is the blood of the covenant which God hath enjoined to you;" *i. e.* by this ceremony used in making covenants and contracts, God on *his part* engages to perform the *promises*, and on *your* part to observe the *laws* of this covenant.

21 Moreover, he sprinkled with blood both the tabernacle, and all the vessels of the ministry.

21. "In like manner, *after the* tabernacle *was built*, he sprinkled the whole tabernacle, and all the utensils of divine service belonging to it *."

22 And almost all things are by the law purged with blood: and without shedding of blood is no remission.

22. And, you know, that according to *that* law, all kinds of vessels and appurtenances of the tabernacle whatever, were purified and consecrated by being sprinkled with blood (excepting some vessels of *metal* that would abide the *fire*, and *clothes* that were washed in *water*.) And that no person whatever was cleansed, and *legally* absolved from his sins or defilements, without a *bloody* sacrifice.

23 It was therefore necessary that the patterns of things in the heavens should be purified with these, but the heavenly things themselves with better sacrifices than these.

23. Thus men obtained admission to that sanctuary here *below*: But as to *heaven* itself, we can gain no entrance into *that*, but by being redeemed and purified by the *great* sacrifice of Christ, in a *perfect* and *effectual* manner, as *Jewish* things and persons were in a *figurative* one.

24 For Christ is not entered into the holy places made with hands, which are the figures of the true, but into

24. And this Christ has done, by his ascension into *heaven*, and becoming our Advocate with the *Father* there; in comparison of which, the entrance of the high priest into

* Ver. 21. [Sprinkling the tabernacle.] See and compare what is said in Exod. xxiv. and xl. chapters; in which *last* chapter, ver. 9—11. the word *sprinkling* is not indeed expressed, but is (most probably) included in the phrases *hallowing*, *sanctifying*, &c.—Compare also ver. 12. & 13. of that chapter, with Exod. xxviii. 40, xxix. 1—20, 21. and Levit. xvi. 16—20.

A. D. 63. into heaven itself, now to appear in the presence of God for us.

to the *second* tabernacle, the *most holy place*, was nothing but a mere shadow, and a figurative resemblance.

25 Nor yet that he should offer himself often, as the high priest entereth into the holy place every year with the blood of others:

26 For then must he often have suffered since the foundation of the world: but * now once in the end of the world, hath he appeared to put away sin by the sacrifice of himself.

25. & 26. And so effectually sufficient is this his entrance into *heaven*, to present himself to God for us, that neither it, nor his death in order to it, need ever be repeated, as those of the *legal* priests were, every year. For the *one* attonement he has made, in this last * and great dispensation of the *gospel*, by the sacrifice of himself, is abundantly enough for the pardon and salvation of all mankind.

27 And as it is appointed unto men once to die, but after this the judgment:

28 So Christ was once offered to bear the sins of many; and unto them that look for him shall he appear the second time, † without sin unto salvation.

27. & 28 And thus, so far, the death of Christ is like that of all other *men*, *viz*. That as *they* die but *once*, and are then to receive an eternal recompense for what they have done in this life; so Christ, after *once* dying for our sins, has no more sufferings to undergo, no further *sacrifice* † to make, and is to appear no more upon earth, till, at the solemn day of judgment, he comes to crown and reward all his true disciples.

CHAP

* [Now in the end of the world:] ἐπὶ συντέλεια τῶν αἰώνων. In the last *age* or *dispensation*.

Ibid. Ver. 26. [Now once: ἅπαξ, once for all;] in the same sense with ἐφάπαξ, it being so used in this, and in many other passages of the New Testament and *LXX*, with this *emphasis*, not taken notice of by interpreters. Compare 1 Pet. iii. 20. Jude ver. 3. Heb. vi. 4.—vii. 27.—x. 10. Psal. lxxxix. 36. Job xl. 4. Esther iv. 11.

† Appear—*without sin*; χωρὶς ἁμαρτίας, without any further *offering* for sin. As in 2 Cor. v. 21. Or else referring these words to ἀπεκδεχομένοις, [Those that look for him without sin, *are* good and pure Christians,] if this be not too hard a transposition. Beside that, χωρὶς ἁμαρτίας, is naturally connected to ἐκ δευτέρου, as ἀνενεγκεῖν ἁμαρτίας is to ἅπαξ foregoing.

CHAP. X.

The second Argument still continued, viz. Judaiſm *was but a figurative Introduction to* Chriſtianity. *The Inſufficiency of the legal Sacrifices, for the complete Atonement of Sin. The Death of Chriſt, the full and final Sacrifice further proved from the Old Teſtament. It gives all good Chriſtians a full Aſſurance of Heavenly Happineſs, and is the moſt comfortable Argument for their final Perſeverence in their Profeſſion. The* Jewiſh *Chriſtians again particularly exhorted to Conſtancy and Patience under their Sufferings; from the great Danger of wilful Apoſtacy; from the ſenſe of their former Courage, and the Proſpect of their certain and ſpeedy Deliverance from their Perſecutions.*

1 FOR the law having a ſhadow of
good * things to come,
and not the very image
of the things, can never
with thoſe ſacrifices
which they offered
year by year
continually, make the
comers thereunto perfect.

2 For then would
they not have ceaſed
to be offered? becauſe
that

A. D. 63.

1. WELL then, it plainly appears by what I have already * ſaid, that the *Moſaical* prieſthood and ſacrifices were nothing but *types* and ſhadows of a future and more perfect atonement for the ſins of mankind: and therefore, though never ſo often repeated, they could not of *themſelves*, cleanſe any *Jewiſh* worſhipper from his ſins, and open the way to *heaven* for him.

* Cap. viii. 5. ix. 8, 9. 23, 24.

2. & 3. For indeed, had thoſe ſacrifices (particularly that upon the great *expiation* day) any real vir-

* [Of good things to come—] That is, ſay moſt interpreters, [Of the bleſſings of the goſpel-religion;] Some underſtand it of *Heaven*, the true *Holy of Holies*. I have expreſſed *both* ſenſes.

Ibid. Not the very image: αὐτὴν τὴν εἰκόνα, the original, *the* very truth of the thing.] Chryſoſ. Syr. Verſ. Rom. i. 23.

A. D. 63.

that the worſhippers once purged, ſhould have had no more conſcience of ſins.

3 But in thoſe *ſacrifices there is* a remembrance again *made* of ſins every year.

virtue to that effect, they need not have been * repeated ſo often; when the thing was *once* perfectly done, had been done for *ever*. And again, if that *repetition* were effectual, there could be no occaſion to abrogate them, and introduce another in their room. Whereas, upon that great *annual* day, the high prieſt commemorates and deplores the paſt ſins, both of that and the *foregoing* years; a plain demonſtration that they were not perfectly atoned for by the *former* ſacrifices.

4 For *it is* not poſſible that the blood of bulls and of goats ſhould take away ſins.

4. And the truth is, there is nothing in the blood of any *beaſt*, that can anſwer the Divine Wiſdom and Juſtice in demanding an atonement for the ſins of *mankind*.

5 Wherefore when he cometh into the world, he ſaith, Sacrifice and offering thou wouldſt not, but ‡ a body haſt thou prepared me.

6 In burnt offerings and *ſacrifices* for ſin thou haſt had no pleaſure:

7 Then ſaid I, Lo, I come (in the volume of the book it is written of me) to do thy will, O God.

5, 6. & 7. Accordingly the *Pſalmiſt* (Pſal. xl.), prophetically repreſenting Chriſt, as coming into the world, brings him in thus addreſſing to God the Father: "That whereas the ſacrifices of the *Jewiſh* law were but mere figures, no way acceptable to him as a propitiation for the ſins of mankind; the time was now come, wherein *he* (the Son of God) was now fully to accompliſh it *by being made man, and* by yielding *himſelf* to ſuffer, in perfect ſubmiſſion and obedience to the Divine Will of the *Father*: and that he was actually moſt ready, and free to do it, as the ſcriptures had foretold ‡."

8. & 9. Now

---

* [For then would they not have ceaſed to be offered.] The ἂν is not in ſome copies; but it makes no material alteration in the ſenſe, which I have expreſſed both ways.

‡ [A body haſt thou prepared me.] See Dr. Allix's ſenſe of the Jewiſh Church, &c. Chap. 27. And Biſhop Kidder, Dem. Meſſ. Vol. II. p. 268, 269, &c. for a full vindication of this paſſage, from the exceptions of the Jews. See alſo the note on Chap. xi. 21.

8 Above, when he said, Sacrifice, and offering, and burnt offerings, and *offering* for sin thou wouldst not, neither hadst pleasure *therein* (which are offered by the law):

8. & 9. Now these words are a plain declaration of the utter insufficiency of the *Jewish* sacrifices; when Christ puts his *own* sufferings and sacrifice to supply their defects. And, by doing the *one*, he abrogates all further use of the *other*.

9 Then said he, Lo, I come to do thy will, O God. He taketh away the first, * that he may establish the second.

10 By the which will we are sanctified, through the offering of the body of Jesus Christ once *for all* †.

10. And, consequently, we are not to regard *them* as the means of our justification and happiness; but to rely upon this obedient act of Christ suffering in our flesh; an act that need never be repeated; having, once † and for ever, procured the pardon and salvation of all true believers.

11 And every priest standeth daily ‡ ministring and offering oftentimes the same sacrifices, which can never take away sins:

12 But this man after he had offered one sacrifice for sins, for ever sat down on the right hand of God;

13 From henceforth expecting till his enemies be made his footstool.

11, 12, 13. & 14. Consider again, therefore, the great difference between the happy and glorious effects of this office of Christ and that of the *Jewish* priests. *They* were obliged to repeat their sacrifices every day or year. A clear evidence that their efficacy for the perfect pardon of sin was but small: whereas Christ, by *once* offering his *own* life, was so acceptable to God, as to be raised again from the dead, exalted to the highest degree of heavenly glory and majesty, invested with the full dominion over all his and

* Ver. 9. [Taketh away the first]; i. e. He abrogates the first will or law of God, viz. the law of Jewish sacrifices, and establishes the second will, viz. the sacrifice of Christ—[By the which will we are sanctified, &c.] in the following words. Thus the ingenious Mr. Pierce has connected the sense; with which my paraphrase fully agrees, though the emphasis be not laid upon the same substantive.

† Note, [Once for all.] See Chap. ix. 26.—vi. 4.—x. 10. 1 Pet. i. 12.—iii. 18, 20. Jude, ver. 3.

‡ Ver. 11. [Daily ministring Καθήμεραν, from time to time,—i. e. *yearly* upon the *great expiation day*.

A. D. 63.

14 For by one offering he hath perfected for ever them that are sanctified.

our enemies, ſin, Satan, wicked *men*, and *death* itſelf; and ſo is the *complete* Redeemer of all that embrace his religion.

15 *Whereof* the Holy Ghoſt alſo is a witneſs to us: for after that
|| Cap. viii. 8, 9, &c. he had ſaid before,

16 This is the covenant that I will make with them after thoſe days, ſaith the Lord, I will put my laws into their hearts, and in their minds will I write them:

17 And their ſins and iniquities will I remember no more.

15, 16. & 17. For this and no other, is the ſenſe of that forementioned || divine prophecy (Jer. xxxi.), where, *after having expreſſed the excellency, plainneſs, and ſimplicity of the* goſpel *religion*, it is added, "and their ſins and iniquities will I remember no more;" i. e. There ſhall be one perfect and complete atonement made for them.

18 Now where remiſſion of theſe *is*, *there is* no more offering for ſin.

18. And if ſo, there can be no further occaſion for theſe *legal* ſacrifices and ceremonies which the Jews and many of the *Jewiſh* Chriſtians are ſo exceſſively zealous for.

19 Having, therefore, brethren, boldneſs to enter into the holieſt by the blood of Jeſus,

20 By a * new and living way † which he hath conſecrated for us through the vail, that is to ſay, his fleſh;

21 And *having* an high prieſt over the houſe of God:

19, 20. & 21. Wherefore, dear brethren, ſince our pardon and entrance into the heavenly ſtate of happineſs is thus fully procured, by ſo wiſe and effectual a method as this of Chriſt's *death*; ſince he has taken down the partition, † and prepared the way by ſuffering upon earth, and by being exalted into heaven, and becoming the High Prieſt, Governor and Interceſſor for the Chriſtian church;

22. & 23.

---

* Ver. 20. [By a new and living way.] A moſt emphatical expreſſion to denote the happy difference between the *Jewiſh entrance* into the *moſt holy* place of the *temple*, and a *Chriſtian's* entrance into *heaven*. If any Iſraelite, beſide the *high prieſt*, dared to enter into that *inner* ſanctuary, he ſuffered *death*: every *Chriſtian's* entrance into *heaven* gives him eternal *life*.

† [Which he hath conſecrated;] ἣν ἐνεκαίνισεν, which he hath *prepared*, ἣν κατεσκεύασεν, ἧς ἤρξατο. Chryſoſt. and which he himſelf began to enter by.

22 Let us draw near with a true heart, in full assurance of faith, having our hearts sprinkled from an evil conscience, and our bodies washed with pure water.

23 Let us hold fast the profession of our faith without wavering (for he *is* faithful that promiseth.)

22. & 23. How steadily ought we to embrace *his* religion, whereby so perfect a reconciliation is obtained for us; worshipping God through *him*, with full and unshaken confidence in those promises that can never fail and deceive us?

24 And let us consider one another, to provoke unto love, and to good works:

24. And, as this ought to establish your faith in God and Christ, under all your persecutions; so ought it to make you, by your exemplary practice, to encourage and spirit up one another to perfect love and charity towards all your Christian *brethren;* without any further partial distinction between *Jewish* and *Gentile* believers.

25 Not forsaking the assembling of ourselves together, as the manner of some is; but exhorting *one another:* and so much the more as you see the day approaching.

25. In fine, it ought to be a preservative against the cowardice, the *Jewish* Christians now too commonly discover, by forsaking the profession and || worship of *Christianity*, and returning to that of the *synagogue* and *temple*, for fear of persecution; and cure them of that prejudice against the *Gentile* Christians, which they carry so far as to refuse to join with them in their worship and devotion. And it should be the stronger argument upon them to remember how near the time is drawing, wherein our Lord himself has declared there should be an end put even to the *temple*, and the whole *Jewish dispensation* ‡.

|| ἐπισυναγωγήν.

‡ See Matt. xxiv. Job xiv. 23, 24.

26 For if we sin wilfully after that we have received the knowledge of the truth, there remaineth no more sacrifice for sins,

27 But a certain fearful looking for of judgment and fiery indignation, which shall

26. & 27. Let me again * remind you of the fatal consequence of wilfully and deliberately renouncing a religion so clearly attested and confirmed to you. If you slight, and once neglect the means of salvation now offered you by Christ, you lose the last and only method God will ever propose for your redemption; and must

* Cap. vi. 4. 5, 6, 7.

A. D. 63. ſhall devour the adverſaries.

muſt expect to periſh by that divine wrath and vengeance, that awaits the obſtinate adverſaries of true religion.

28 He that deſpiſed Moſes law, died without mercy, under two or three witneſſes:

* Cap. ii. 3.

29 Of how much ſorer puniſhment, ſuppoſe ye, ſhall he be thought worthy, who hath trodden under foot the Son of God, and hath counted the blood of the covenant wherewith he was ſanctified, an unholy thing, and hath done deſpite unto the Spirit of grace?

28. & 29. And how great *that* will be, you may conclude from God's dealing with *apoſtates*, and preſumptuous * offenders againſt the *Jewiſh* law. Whoever was convicted of ſuch a crime by the teſtimony of two or three witneſſes, was ordered to be *ſlain without mercy*, Numb. xv. Deut. xvii. How much more dreadful and exemplary do you think, muſt be that *final* deſtruction of thoſe, who now, contemptuouſly, and againſt the cleareſt evidences, reject the authority of Chriſt the *Meſſiah*, the very *Son of God*, profaning and treating his precious blood, that ratified this gracious covenant of their redemption, as the blood of an *ordinary* perſon, nay, of a *malefactor*; and doing the utmoſt contempt to the *Holy Spirit* ſo graciouſly given; by undervaluing the great and miraculous powers, which ſo amply demonſtrated the truth of their holy profeſſion?

30 For we know him that hath ſaid, Vengeance *belongeth* unto me, I will recompenſe, ſaith the Lord. And again, The Lord ſhall judge his people.

30. Remember thoſe ſevere words (Deut. xxxii. 35, 36.), wherein God declares, that "To him belongeth vengeance and recompence." And again, "The Lord will judge his (diſobedient) people."

31 *It is* a fearful thing to fall into the hands of the living God.

31. Conſider duly, and in time, how fearful a thing it is to fall under the final diſpleaſure of an infinite Governor, whoſe *juſtice*, upon obſtinate and incurable offenders, is eternally durable, as his *exiſtence* is.

32 But call to remembrance the former days, in which after ye were illuminated, ye endured

32. And, the better to ſupport yourſelves under your preſent perſecutions, recollect and comfort your ſpirits with a ſenſe of that

endured a great fight of afflictions:

that generous Christian courage that carried you through the sufferings which befel you || at your first conversion.

|| Acts viii. 2. 1 Thes. ii. 14.

33 Partly whilst ye were made a gazing-stock, both by reproaches and afflictions; and partly whilst ye became companions of them that were so used.

33. When you were exposed, vilified and abused, by the raging malice of the Jews; and bravely adhered to us the *apostles* of Christ, that were then treated in the same manner, Acts v. 41.—Chap. xiv. 5, 19. and—Chap. xvii. 10, 14, 15.

34 For ye had compassion of me in my bonds, and took joyfully the spoiling of your goods, knowing in yourselves * that ye have in heaven a better and an enduring substance.

34. When you were so truly courageous, as to own and relieve those *apostles* (and *me* in particular) that were imprisoned in Judea for Christ's religion; and were so entirely convinced of the certainty of that eternal happiness of heaven, promised in the gospel, as cheerfully to part with all you had in this world for the sake of it.

35 Cast not away therefore your confidence, which hath great recompence of reward.

35. After such signal instances, therefore, of courage and resolution, in owning a religion you know to be attended with such ample and glorious rewards; how little and mean would it *now* be, to shrink back and forfeit such hopes!

36 For ye have need of patience; that after ye have done the will of God, ye might receive the promise.

36. Consider, that *courage* and patience is the only thing that is to carry you through, and bring you to the heavenly state; which is the recompence for submitting to the Divine Will and Providence.

37 For

37. Nor

---

* Ver. 34. [Knowing in yourselves, *or rather* knowing that you yourselves (that are thus persecuted) have in heaven a better—substance.] So the Alexand. MSS. read it ἑαυτοὺς, as also the Syr. Arab. and Clem. Alexandrinus.

A. D. 63.

37 For yet a little while, and † he that shall come, will come, and ‡ will not tarry.

37. Nor be discouraged, that you are not *immediately* rescued from your persecutions; for though it be not *immediate*, yet be assured, your deliverence will not only be certain, but speedy enough too. According to those words of the prophet, Hab. ii. 3. spoken of the coming of Christ, "Though he tarry, wait for him. For he that cometh (i. e. † Christ) will come, and will not tarry ‡ long."

38 Now the just shall live by faith, but if any man draw back, my soul shall have no pleasure in him.

38. And forget not the following words, ver. 4. "Now the just shall live by his faith," i. e. By a firm and resolute belief of, and adherence to the revelation of God's will, when sufficiently made to him, and by a *faithful* perseverance in a practice agreeable to such belief. "But if any man draw || back, my soul shall have no pleasure in him," i. e. Whoever, after the entertainment of divine truth, hypocritically conceals, or cowardly renounces the profession of it, shall forfeit all the blessings to which it entitled him.

* Cap. vi. 9.

39 But we are not of them who draw back unto perdition: but of them that believe, to the saving of the soul.

39. And, brethren, I hope the generality of * you, that have thus far stood out, under your former persecutions, will not now at last be lost for want of courage, but will reap the final salvation promised in the gospel, by a steady perseverance in its faith and principles.

---

† [He that cometh]. See Mat. xi. 3. Luke vii. 19.

‡ [Will not tarry: οὐ χρονιεῖ, *will not* stay too long.] Sept.

|| ἐὰν ὑποστείληται, *if*, or *whenever*, he draws back.

CHAP. XI.

The Apostle's Third *Argument, for encouraging the Christians of Judea to Perseverance in their Profession, under all their Persecution,* viz. *The numerous Examples of all the* Patriarchs *and holy Men recorded in* Scripture, *or in the* Apocryphal *Writings, as the most eminent Servants of God. That they all were justified by the* same *Principle of* Faith in God's Revelation; *for suffering under the same Hopes of future and invisible Blessings, that* Christianity *now proposeth: and for the very* same, *shall they, and all good Christians, be finally and completely rewarded together at the Great Day of* Judgment.

1 NOW faith is the substance * of things hoped for, the evidence of things not seen.

1. I Said †, it was a steady faith in Christ, and a resolute profession of his *religion*, that must procure your salvation. And whereas the *Jewish zealots* are wont to affright you, by confidently affirming, "That to embrace Christianity, is to apostatize from Moses and from God:" it will be enough to silence that vain pretence, to consider, that to be a Christian, is the exercise and result of no other principle of *faith*, but what justified all the *patriarchs*, and holy men of old; *viz.* "Such a rational and steady belief," either of things long since past, "or of the invisible blessings of a *future* life, proportionable to the evidences God has given us of them, as will actuate us into obedience, and make us ready to suffer for the profession of such a belief."

A.D. 63.

† Chap. x. 29.

2. For

* Ver. 1. [The substance of things hoped for: ὑπόστασις, The firm assurance, *or* expectation.] So this word is truly rendered, Psal. xxxix. 7. Ruth i. 12. Ezek. xix. 5. in the LXX. and Chap. iii. 14. of this epistle.

A. D 63.

2 For by it the elders obtained a good report.

2. For *this* great virtue the ancestors of your nation stand recorded, as such eminent examples of piety and true religion.

* τὺς αἰῶνας.

† Ῥῆμα.

‡ Gen. i. 2. &c. John i. 2. 3. 4. λόγος.

3 Through faith we understand that the worlds were framed by the word of God, so that things which are seen were not made of things which do appear.

3. What is it, but divine *revelation*, that makes us absolutely certain, that the world * was not by *chance*, nor a fortuitous jumble of pre-existing *matter*, but made in *time*, by the power and command † of God, and put into this beauteous form wherein we now see it, by Christ ‡ the *Word*, and *Son of God*, who governs all the dispensations of it?

4 By faith Abel offered unto God a more excellent sacrifice than Cain, by which he obtained witness that he was righteous, God testifying of his gifts: and by it he being dead, yet speaketh.

4. The serious belief of divine *revelation* rendered the sacrifice of Abel acceptable, and the want of it caused Cain's to be rejected. God demonstrating his acceptance of him as a pious and good man, by causing fire from ‖ heaven to consume his sacrifice. And though Abel be dead, yet is his sacrifice a standing evidence, *That this is the principle that makes our services acceptable to God.*

5 By faith Enoch was translated, that he should not see death, and was not found, because God had translated him: for before his translation he had this testimony, that he pleased God.

5. As a reward of this very same virtue, was Enoch translated from earth, without dying according to the common course of nature. Gen. v. 22. 24.

§ See ver. 1.

6 But without faith it is impossible to please him: for he that cometh to God, must believe that he is, and that he is a rewarder of them that diligently seek him.

6. And indeed, nothing is plainer, than that a firm persuasion of the *existence of God* (though he be § invisible to us), and a lively hope and assurance, proportionable to the knowledge men have of his nature and will, that he will reward

‖ Ἐνεπύρισε. Version. Theodos. See Gen. xv. 17. Lev. ix. 24. Psal. xx. 3.

reward all his true and ſincere worſhippers (though that A. D. 63.
reward be *future* and at a diſtance), is the firſt and moſt
neceſſary principle of all true religion.

7 By faith Noah being warned of God of things not ſeen as yet, moved with fear, prepared an ark to the ſaving of his houſe, by the which he condemned the world, and became heir of the righteouſneſs which is by faith.

7. Upon *this* it was, that Noah prepared the ark, ſaved himſelf from the deſtruction of *this* world, and obtained the happineſs of the *next;* while the reſt of mankind were juſtly left to periſh in their unreaſonable infidelity.

8 By faith * Abraham when he was called to go out into a place which he ſhould after receive for an inheritance, obeyed, and he went out, not knowing whither he went.

9 By faith he ſojourned in the land of promiſe, as in a ſtrange country, dwelling in tabernacles with Iſaac and Jacob, the heirs with him of the ſame promiſe.

8. & 9. By *this* Abraham left his native country, went and dwelt as a ſtranger, in a mean and obſcure manner, in a foreign land; even before he knew what the land was, or was acquainted with the *promiſe*, that his poſterity ſhould fully poſſeſs and enjoy it, Gen. xii. 1. with Gen. xxvi. 3. xxviii. 13.

10 For he looked for a city which hath foundations, whoſe builder and maker is God.

10. It was ſufficient to that reaſonable and good man, that God had promiſed him, in general, *To be his ſhield and exceeding great reward*, Gen. xv. 1. And *his* eye was upon the certain and unchangeable ſtate of *future* happineſs.

11 Through faith alſo Sarah herſelf received ſtrength to conceive ſeed, and was delivered of a child when ſhe was paſt age, be-

11. & 12. In reward of the ſame *faith* in the repeated *promiſe of God*, Sarah was enabled to conceive and bear a ſon, when both ſhe and her huſband were naturally incapable of ſuch a thing, through

---

* Ver. 8. [Abraham when he was called, *or* ὁ καλούμενος Ἀβραὰμ, he that was called Abraham.] The words have a great emphaſis; he whom God was pleaſed to call The Great Father, The Father of many Nations, The Father of the Faithful. See Gen. xvii. 3, 4, 5, 6. with my paraphraſe

A. D. 63. because she judged him faithful who hath promised.

12 Therefore sprang there even of * one, and him as good as dead, so many as the stars of the sky in multitude, and as the sand which is by the sea shore innumerable.

through their great age: And from them came an innumerable posterity, which, without an extraordinary act of divine power, could no more have been expected from two such superannuated people, than if they had been actually dead *.

13 These all died in faith, not having received the promises, but having seen them afar off, and were persuaded of them, and embraced them, and confessed that they were strangers and pilgrims on the earth.

13. & 14. All these forementioned worthies died in *this* noble principle; full of the hopes, and possessed with the prospect of *future* and eternal felicities. Upon these *distant* joys they acted; for *these* they gave up all worldly enjoyments, and looked upon the present life as nothing but a passage into a better.

14 For they that say such things, declare plainly that they seek a † country.

15 And truly if they had been mindful of that country, from whence they came out, they might have had opportunity to have returned:

16 But now they desire a better country, that is an heavenly: wherefore God is not ashamed to be called their God; for he hath prepared for them a city.

§ See Mat. xxii. 32.

15. & 16. For it is very clear, it could not be *temporal* hopes, these great souls were acted by; because Abraham, for instance, had a much more fair and natural prospect of *that* kind, in his own native country, than he could be supposed to have in a foreign land, among a barbarous and uncultivated people. Nor could it amount to much, for God to style himself *their* God§, *i. e.* in an *eminent sense*, their Great Protector and *Rewarder;* if he had nothing

---

* Ver. 12. [Even of one, ἀφ᾽ ἑνὸς, from that single person, and from him in a manner dead.]——So the word εἷς is used, Gal. iii. 20. and in many other passages.

† Ver. 14. [That they seek a country.]—A very flat translation! It is Πατρίδα, [A country of their father's, their native and proper home]: So *heaven* is the *proper country* or habitation of *good men*, the place where (God) their Father dwells.

nothing to beſtow on them but a few *temporal* bleſſings, A. D. 63.
and thoſe too mixed up with many troubles and afflictions common to human life. All their proceedings, therefore, beſpeak their main and ultimate hopes to have been in the *future* and inviſible glories of another world, even the very ſame that the *goſpel* now more explicitly propoſes to us *Chriſtians*.

17 By faith Abraham, when he was tried, offered up Iſaac: and he that had received the promiſes, offered up his only begotten ſon:

18 Of whom it was ſaid, that in Iſaac ſhall thy ſeed be called.

17. & 18. To proceed, therefore: This ſerious perſuaſion of the divine truth and Providence, made Abraham, at the inſtance of the divine command, ready, with his own hands, to ſacrifice the very *ſon*, in whom alone he expected to ſee the *great promiſe* fulfilled to him.

19 Accounting that God was able to raiſe him up, even from the dead: from whence alſo he received him in a figure.

19. Moſt dutifully and rationally conſidering that the ſame Divine Power that cauſed Iſaac to be conceived and born, in a manner as wonderful as that of raiſing the dead to life again, could either reſtore him to him again, or elſe fulfil the promiſe in ſome other way, that would be as good and happy for him. And accordingly, as the birth of Iſaac from the dead womb of Sarah was a gift of new and miraculous life; ſo the reſcue of Iſaac, by the voice of an *angel*, was the ſame thing to Abraham as if he had been actually ſlain, and then reſtored to life.

20 By faith Iſaac bleſſed Jacob and Eſau concerning things to come.

21 By faith Jacob, when he was dying, bleſſed both the ſons of Joſeph, and worſhipped * leaning upon the top of his ſtaff.

20. & 21. With this firm aſſurance, That God would make good all his benedictions (though perhaps he knew not preciſely *when*) did Iſaac, in a prophetical way, and with religious reverence, pronounce the bleſſings on his ſons Jacob and Eſau; as Jacob did afterwards upon Ephraim and Manaſſes †. † Gen. xlvi. 32.

 22. So

* Ver. 21. [Leaning upon the top of his ſtaff.] In the Hebrew it is, " Iſrael bowed himſelf upon his bed's head." The word מטה, by the change of one *point*, ſignifying either

A. D. 63.

22 By faith Joſeph, when he died, made mention of the departing of the children of Iſrael: and gave commandment concerning his bones.

22. So did Joſeph, juſt before his death, foretel the deliverance of the Iſraelites out of Egypt, and ordered his own bones to be carried with them into Canaan, as a teſtimony how fully he aſſured himſelf of their arrival there, according to the *divine* promiſe.

23 By faith Moſes, when he was born, was hid three months of his parents, becauſe they ſaw he was a proper child, and they were not afraid of the kings commandment.

23. Thus Moſes's parents, in defiance of that barbarous edict of Pharaoh, reſolved not to deliver up ſo lovely and beautiful a child, but hid him three months by the ſide of the river Nile, in hopes that God would providentially provide for his eſcape.

24 By faith Moſes, when he was come to years, refuſed to be called the ſon of Pharaoh's daughter:

25 Chooſing rather to ſuffer affliction with the people of God, than to enjoy the pleaſures of ſin for a ſeaſon:

26 Eſteeming the reproach * of Chriſt greater

24, 25. & 26. Thus Moſes, when he came at age, refuſed the great privilege of being adopted into the royal family of the Egyptian monarchs, owned himſelf to be a Hebrew born, and not Pharaoh's grandchild; chooſing rather to ſhare in all the difficulties the Iſraelites, * whom he knew to be God's true *church* and people, were to undergo, than to enjoy the vicious and temporary

---

ther a *bed*, or a *ſtaff*, the *LXX.* read it in the *latter* ſenſe: And it was that *verſion* the writers of the New Teſtament generally made uſe of. Of their method of quoting the Old Teſtament paſſages, though not abſolutely *verbatim*, yet ever ſo as to make no alteration in the *ſenſe* and *purpoſe* they are quoted for. The learned reader may conſult Glaſſius Philog. Sac. p. 1472, *&c.* edit Francof. 1653. But indeed the more true rendering ſhould be "worſhipping upon the top of his ſtaff." See Mr. Hallet's Supplement to Mr. Pierce on the Hebrews, *in loc.*

* [The reproach of Chriſt:] τοῦ Χριστοῦ; of the *anointed* (people) *i. e.* the Iſraelites, Pſal. cv. Or rather thus, *of Chriſt*, i. e. ſuch reproaches as *Chriſtians* now ſuffer for the ſake of Chriſt and his religion; or ſuch reproaches as Chriſt himſelf ſuffered while he was upon earth; or, *laſtly*, the reproach Moſes was likely to ſuffer for thus acting from a principle of *faith* in the *Meſſiah* to come.

A. D. 63.

greater riches than the treaſures in Egypt: for he had reſpect unto the reward.

rary pleaſures of the Egyptian court. And, with what view was this? Not of any *worldly* advantage or *preſent* happineſs: for Moſes refuſed the higheſt of *theſe*, by ſlighting the glories of Egypt. And as for the land of Canaan, he ſaw it at a diſtance, but never enjoyed it. His aim, therefore, was at *heaven*, *then*, as that of all good Chriſtians is *now*.

27 By faith he forſook Egypt, not fearing the wrath of the king, for he endured, as ſeeing him who is inviſible.

28 Through faith he kept the paſſover, and the ſprinkling of blood, leſt he that deſtroyed the firſt-born ſhould touch them.

29 By faith they paſſed through the Red Sea, as by dry land, which the Egyptians aſſaying to do, were drowned.

27, 28. & 29. With this religious *faith* in the *revelations* of the inviſible † God, he led the Iſraelites out of Egypt; dreaded not the powerful army that purſued him; kept the paſſover, ordered the blood to be ſprinkled on the door-poſts of each houſe, as a ſure token of their exemption from the plague that raged around them; had the Red Sea miraculouſly divided for his paſſage; and the return of the waters to deſtroy his purſuers.

† See ver. 1.

30 By faith the walls of Jericho fell down after they were compaſſed about ſeven days.

31 By faith the harlot Rahab periſhed not with them that believed not, when ſhe had received the ſpies with peace.

30. & 31. God, in reward of the Iſraelites *faith* in the divine *promiſes*, made the walls of Jericho fall (Joſh. vi. 5.) And by *owning the true God*, upon ſufficient *teſtimonies* given her, the very harlot Rahab ſaved her life.

32 And what ſhall I more ſay? for the time would fail me to tell of Gideon, and of Barak, and of Sampſon, and of Jephthah, of David alſo and Samuel, and of the prophets.

32, 33, 34, 35, 36, 37. & 38. In fine, it would be endleſs for me to go through the numberleſs inſtances of the like kind, recorded in the Old Teſtament. The miraculous victories obtained by ſome, the marvellous deliverances of others, and the wonderful and divine courage expreſſed by the reſt, under the moſt terrible afflictions, and moſt exquiſite ſufferings for the ſake of God and religion; being all the reſult of this very ſame principle "of a reaſonable faith in the divine revelation and promiſes;" the very thing now required to make you Chriſtians *.

A. D. 63. 33 Who through faith ſubdued kingdoms, wrought righteouſneſs, obtained promiſes, ſtopped the mouths of lions.

34 Quenched the violence of fire, eſcaped the edge of the ſword, out of weakneſs were made ſtrong, waxed valiant in fight, turned to flight the armies of the aliens.

35 Women received their dead raiſed to life again: and others were tortured, not accepting deliverance: that they might obtain a better reſurrection †.

36 And others had trials of cruel mockings, and ſcourgings, yea, moreover, of bonds and impriſonment.

37 They were ſtoned, they were ſawn aſunder, were tempted, were ſlain with the ſword: they wandered about in ſheepſkins, and goat-ſkins, being deſtitute, afflicted, tormented:

38 Of whom the world was not worthy: they wandered in deſerts, in mountains, and in dens and caves of the earth.

39 And theſe all having obtained a good report through faith, received not the promiſe: ‡ Ver. 11.

39. Thus all your pious *anceſtors* ſtand upon record as *ſuch*, by the firm and rational belief of *future* ‡ and inviſible bleſſings. Things they actually ſaw not, while they lived; and though they have all been, long ſince, in a ſtate of reſt and happineſs, it is but a ſtate of bleſſed *expectation*. They have not, as yet, the full and complete enjoyment of that *celeſtial* glory.

40 God having provided ſome better thing

40. It being the good pleaſure, and wiſe appointment of God, to defer

* Ver. 32, &c. [Of Gideon, and Barak, and Sampſon, &c. For the particular *inſtances* of the *faith* and *exploits* of the ſeveral perſons named or not named in theſe verſes, to the 39th verſe, let the reader conſult Mr. Hallet's Supplement to Mr. Pierce, *in loc.*

† Ver. 35. [A better reſurrection,] i. e. a *future* reſurrection to *eternal life*, far better than the reſurrection of the *women's children*, before-mentioned, or than that of the perſons *tortured*, would have been. The *one* being a reſtoration to the preſent *ſhort* life, the *other* to an *eternal* one.

thing for us: that they without us should not be made perfect.

defer *that*, till the perfect and complete || revelation of the *gospel* were made to us Christians, and the last and great dispensation of the *Messiah* be past: that so, both they *patriarchs*, *prophets*, *apostles*, and all sincere Christians, whether *Jewish* or *Gentile* ones, may for the courageous exercise of the same excellent and virtuous *principle*, be all rewarded and crowned together, with the happiness both of body and soul, at the final day of judgment.

A. D. 63.

|| Κρεῖττόν τι.

CHAP. XII.

The Inference from the foregoing Argument; viz. That as the Behaviour of the Patriarchs *and Holy Men of old, do vindicate the Reasonableness of the* Christian Faith, *so ought it to be the most exemplary Encouragement, to spirit up all Christians under their Sufferings for it. The same Encouragement further enforced, from the Example of Christ himself. The great Reasonableness and Advantage of suffering for true Religion. The Danger of relapsing from* Christianity: *especially to the* Jewish *Converts, from the apparent Excellency and Greatness of the* Christian Religion, *when compared with the* Jewish *Law.*

1 WHerefore, seeing we also are compassed about with so great a cloud of witnesses, let us lay aside every weight, and the sin which doth so easily beset *us*, and let us run with patience the race that is set before us,

1. HAving therefore such * abundant testimonies, "that your Christian faith is the exercise of the same virtuous principle for which all your pious ancestors stand so famously recorded;" let such numerous and excellent examples ‡ raise you above all fears and peplexites, spirit you on in your Christian course, and keep you from that cowardly apostacy, † to which your present sufferings are so apt to tempt and draw you.

* Chap xi.

‡ νέφος μαρτύρων.

† εὐπερίστατον ἁμαρτίαν.

2. And

A. D. 63.

2 Looking unto Jeſus the author and finiſher of *our* faith; who for the joy that was ſet before him, endured the croſs, deſpiſing the ſhame, and is ſet down at the right hand of the throne of God.

2. And, for your ſtill higher encouragement, conſider the moſt perfect example of Jeſus Chriſt, himſelf, the author of your religion, and the great rewarder of its true profeſſors; who for the joyful proſpect of being exalted as the Redeemer and Saviour of mankind, with abſolute patience endured the pains, and with inexpreſſible height of mind deſpiſed the ſcandal of dying like a *malefactor* upon the croſs: and is now accordingly rewarded for it with the utmoſt degree of heavenly glory and majeſty.

|| ἀναλογίσασθε.

3 For conſider him that endured ſuch contradiction of ſinners againſt himſelf, leſt ye be wearied and faint in your minds.

3. Weigh || and compare *his* ſufferings with your *own;* and ſee if the blaſphemies againſt *his* doctrine, the reproaches upon *his* perſon, and the malicious attempts upon *his* life, be not ſufficient to buoy *you* up under all the conflicts you endure for his ſake.

4 * Ye have not yet reſiſted unto blood, ſtriving againſt ſin.

4. Remember you have not yet ſuffered the worſt, * from thoſe malicious adverſaries; and to give out before you have done as much as thoſe great *worthies*, and Chriſt himſelf has done before you, would be to come ſhort, and loſe the power of their examples.

5 And ye have forgotten the † exhortation, which ſpeaketh unto you, as unto children, My ſon, deſpiſe not thou the chaſtening of the Lord, nor faint when thou art rebuked of him.

5. & 6. Thoſe converts among you, that ſhrink and faint, already under their perſecutions, ſeem to have forgotten the wiſe purpoſes, and great advantages the ſcriptures mention of God's permitting afflictions to befal his true ſervants: particularly that of Prov.

6 For

* [Not yet reſiſted unto blood.] Perhaps it may be an *agoniſtical* term: it being the moſt ſcandalous thing for any combatant to give out before any blood was drawn: as Jacobus Lydius obſerves, Agoniſt. Sat.

† Ver. 5. [And ye have forgotten the exhortation—] It may perhaps be beſt to take theſe words *interrogatively*; Καὶ ἐκλέλησθε τῆς παρακλήσεως, [Have ye forgotten the exhortation?

6 For whom the Lord loveth, he chaſteneth, and ſcourgeth every ſon whom he receiveth.

Prov. iii. 11, & 12. "My ſon, A.D. 63.
deſpiſe not thou the chaſtening of the Lord, nor faint when thou art rebuked of him: for whom the Lord loveth he chaſteneth, &c."

7 If ye endure chaſtening, God dealeth with you as with ſons: for what ſon is he whom the father chaſteneth not?

8 But if ye be without chaſtiſement, whereof all are partakers, then are ye baſtards, and not ſons.

7. & 8. In laying preſent afflictions on us, God acts only the part of a prudent *father;* training us up, by ſuch methods, as may beſt work our tempers into a dutiful and patient obedience. And, ſhould he wholly neglect theſe means, and indulge us in uninterrupted eaſe, and preſent proſperity, he would be wanting in one of the proper inſtances of a careful and tender father.

9 Furthermore, we have had fathers of our fleſh which corrected us, and we gave *them* reverence: ſhall we not much rather be in ſubjection unto the Father of ſpirits, and live?

9. You all own, that the prudent ſeverities and ſtrict diſcipline of a *natural* parent are ſo far from diſcouraging, that they gain greater reſpect and reverence from the child. How infinitely more advantageous, then, muſt it be for us *men*, but eſpecially Chriſtians, to be under the preſent diſcipline of a wiſe and good *Creator*, that will reward our ſufferings with *eternal* life and happineſs?

10 For they verily for a few days chaſtened *us* after their own pleaſure; but he for our profit, that we might be partakers of his holineſs.

10. For, while the corrections of our earthly parents may, through human weakneſs, be ſometimes paſſionate and humourſome, and, at beſt, do chiefly tend to our conduct in a ſhort and tranſitory life; the chaſtiſements of God are full of reaſon, and levelled at our higheſt advantage; being deſigned to work thoſe diſpoſitions in us, that will render us like to God, and for ever happy in the enjoyment of him.

11 Now no chaſtening for the preſent ſeemeth to be joyous, but

11. Be not, therefore, diſcouraged at the ſharpneſs of your preſent ſufferings. Afflictions indeed

A. D. 63.

but grievous; nevertheless, afterward it yieldeth the peaceable fruit of righteousness unto them which are exercised thereby.

deed are always troublesome, and sometimes press very hard; but the great advantage a good Christian may reap from a wise and courageous behaviour under them, is infinitely able to balance that account.

12 Wherefore lift up the hands which hang down, and the feeble knees.

13 And make straight * paths for your feet, lest that which is lame be turned † out of the way, but let it rather be healed.

12. & 13. Wherefore, like true combatants, hold out and stand firm to the last. Encourage the faint-hearted, and support such as you find weak and feeble under their afflictions. Remove all objections * and obstacles out of the way of such as you find apt to be prejudiced, and drawn aside; and, by a prudent behaviour toward them, endeavour to rectify their judgments, uphold their spirits, and keep them firm to their profession.

14 Follow peace with all men, and holiness, without which no man shall see the Lord:

14. Be careful to practise that *chastity* and *purity* of life, without which none can enjoy the favour of God, nor be happy in his presence. And remember that a peaceable carriage, and a gentle disposition toward all mankind, is one of the main branches of our Christian duty.

15 Looking diligently, lest any man fail of the grace of God; lest any root of bitterness springing up, trouble *you*, and thereby may be defiled:

‡ ἐπισκοποῦντες.

|| See Deut. xxix. 18.

15. Have a careful eye to yourselves, and to one ‡ another, to prevent, if possible, any from relapsing from Christianity, and forfeiting all its blessings; for fear any such *apostate* should prove like a poisonous herb; and so taint || and infect others with his cowardly and base principles.

16 Lest

16. For

* Ver. 13. [Make straight paths: *or rather* τροχιὰς ὀρθὰς, smooth, even paths.]

† [Be turned out of the way: ἐκτραπῇ, should be put quite out of joint.—]

16 Lest there be any fornicator, or † profane person, as Esau, who for one morsel of meat sold his birth-right.

16. For fear any *Christian*, for A. D. 63.
the gratification of any * sinful lusts, or securing his *worldly* advantages, should prove as thoughtless and profane † as Esau was, when, to satisfy his present hunger, he resigned up his *birth-right*, to which such excellent privileges were annexed.

17 For ye know how that afterward when he would have inherited the blessing, he was rejected: for he found no place of repentance, though he sought it carefully with tears.

17. Let them learn by *his* example, that blessings, once lost, may not be recoverable by the utmost importunity and concern. And as *his* tears could avail nothing toward retrieving the *birth-right* he had fooled away; so it will be an exceeding hard, || if || Chap. vi. 4, 5, 6.
not impossible thing, for wilful *apostates* from *Christianity*, to be ever reduced again to true religion and happiness.

18 For ye are not come unto the mount that might be ‡ touched,

18, 19, 20. & 21. And this danger will appear the greater, by considering, they forsake a religion so much

---

* Ver. 16. Any fornicator: μή τις πόρνος. That there be no whoremonger, of any kind, amongst you.

† Ver. 16. [Profane persons as Esau:] for resigning the chief *priesthood*, which was the office and privilege of the *eldest* of the family, say most interpreters. Or else, for slighting the solemn *prayers* and *benedictions* of his *father*, with which the birth-right of the eldest son was conferred upon, and confirmed to him, as Mr. Le Clerc thinks. But the true and immediate notion of this *profaneness* of Esau appears best from the words of the history, Gen. xxv. 23. " He did eat and drink, and rose up, and went his way," i. e. careless and unconcerned; *thus Esau despised his birth-right—despised;* the Hebrew word signifies *profanely contemned.* And the *privilege* of the birth-right seems very plainly to have been the *rule* or *headship* of the family, according to those words of Gen. xxvii. 28, 29. " Be lord over thy brethren, &c."

‡ Ver. 18. [Unto the mount that might be touched,] i. e. an *earthly*, *corporal* and *sensible* one, denoting the external and carnal nature of the *ceremonial law*, from thence delivered. Yet I make a *query*, whether the true reading should

A. D. 63. ed, and that burned with fire, nor unto blackness, and darkness, and tempest.

19 And the sound of a trumpet, and the voice of words, which *voice* they that heard, entreated that the word should not be spoken to them any more:

much more mild and gracious; privileges and blessings so much nobler than those of the *Jewish* law. That *law* was delivered to your forefathers in a manner so dreadful, and with circumstances so tremenduous and affrighting, that neither the people nor Moses himself could bear them, without horror and astonishment.

20 (For they could not endure that which was commanded: And if so much as a beast touch the mountain, it shall
be stoned, or thrust through with a dart.
21 And so terrible was the sight, that Moses said, I exceedingly fear and quake.)

22 But ye are come unto mount Sion, and unto the city of the living God, the heavenly Jerusalem, and to an innumerable company of angels.

23 To the general assembly and church of the first-born which are written in * heaven, and to God the judge of all, and to the spirits of just men † made perfect,

24 And to Jesus the mediator of the new covenant, and to the blood of sprinkling

22, 23. & 24. On the contrary, you *Christian* religion, without any such terrible introductions, upon only the gracious and reasonable conditions of *repentance*, and true *faith*, makes *you* members of that spiritual and heavenly society, whereof all good and holy men * (whether *circumcised* or *uncircumcised*), glorified saints, and even *angels* themselves are a part, under Christ their universal Head, the Mediator of this new and gratious covenant of the *gospel*; who has redeemed and cleansed us by the sacrifice of his blood. A sacrifice infinitely more pleasing to God than that of Abel, though offered with the most

---

should not be μὴ ψηλαφωμένῳ ὄρει, "the mountain that might "not be touched." This being perfectly true, as to the *time* of the delivery of the *law*, and a circumstance exactly agreeable to the rest, as mentioned by the *apostle*, in this passage. But finding no copies to warrant this reading, I leave it only as a conjecture.

* [Whose names are written in heaven.] See Phil. iv. 3. the note there.

† Ver. 23. [The spirits of just men made perfect; *that is*, who have perfected and finished their course,] having escaped all the dangers and temptations of the present world.

ling, that ſpeaketh better things * than that of Abel.

perfect faith *; and a bloodſhed directly oppoſite in its effects to *his;* procuring *us* perfect *mercy* and *forgiveneſs;* while Abel's called for nothing but *vengeance.* A. D. 63.

25 See that ye refuſe not him † that ſpeaketh: For if they eſcaped not who refuſed him that ſpake on earth, much more *ſhall not* we *eſcape*, if we turn away from him that *ſpeaketh* from heaven:

25. Take heed then that you fall not off from the religion of the *Son of God.* For if *apoſtates* from the *law* delivered only from mount || Sinai, and by Moſes, who was but a *man*, were ſo ſeverely puniſhed with death; how more terrible will be *their* puniſhment, who renounce a religion that was immediately revealed by the *Son of God* from *heaven?*

|| τοῦ ἐπὶ τῆς γῆς χρηματίζοντα.

26 Whoſe voice then ſhook the earth: but now he hath promiſed, ſaying, Yet once more I ſhake not the earth only, but alſo heaven.

26. For, as great a deſpenſation as the *Jewiſh* law may ſeem to be, by the *ſolemnity* wherewith it was at firſt delivered; yet it is not comparable, either for its *greatneſs* or *duration*, to that of Chriſt. At the giving of that *law* indeed, *the earth was ſaid to tremble,* Pſal. lxviii. 8. And the moſt remarkable dealings of God toward the *Jewiſh* people, are expreſſed in *ſcripture*, by *his ſhaking the earth.* But when the prophets deſcribe the great changes and revolutions that ſhould forerun, and the mighty power that ſhould accompany the laſt and perfect diſpenſation

* [Than that of Abel: παρὰ τὸν Ἄβελ, than Abel.] It not being agreed on by interpreters, whether theſe words relate to the *ſacrifice* offered by Abel, or his *blood* ſpilt by Cain; I have expreſſed both ſenſes.

† Ver. 25. [Him that ſpeaketh—and him that ſpeaketh from heaven—] Note, I interpret this of the *Son of God:* The learned Mr. Pierce thinks it was *God the Father.* The difference cannot be great; ſince we all allow, it was the ſame God who ſpake by the *angels* and Moſes, at mount Sinai on *earth*, and by his Son from *heaven.* And the words of the prophet Haggai expreſs no more than the *degree* of the *ſolemnity* or *change* made by either of theſe *voices.* But let the reader judge.

A. D. 63. tion of Christ the *Messiah*, they represent it by God's *shaking both heaven and earth*, Hag. ii. 7, 8. *Yet once more* (says God) *and I will shake heaven and earth*; i. e. make a *thorough* revolution, and establish a lasting dispensation of religion to all mankind *.

27 And this *word*, Yet once more, signifieth the removing of those things that are shaken, as of things that † are made, that those things which cannot be shaken may remain.

27. Now these words, *yet once more*, are a plain declaration, that the *Jewish* religion was to be altered and abolished, and a more perfect and *lasting* one to succeed in its room.

28 Wherefore we receiving a kingdom which cannot be moved, let us have ‡ grace, whereby we may serve God acceptably, with reverence and godly fear.

28. Seeing, therefore, we *Christians* are actually become members of this excellent and unalterable religion, let us keep firm and ‡ steady to it; and worship God with that religious reverence, which cannot fail to make us acceptable to him.

29 For our God *is* a consuming fire.

29. Remembering that, if we do otherwise, he will, one day, consume and destroy us, in a more terrible manner than he did the rebellious *Israelites*, Deut. iv. 24. and chap. ix. 3.

CHAP.

---

* See Matt. xxiv. 30. Mark xiii. 25. Luke xxi. 26.

† Ver 27. [Of the things that are made—ὡς πεποιημένων, Of the things appointed]; i. e. *formerly* appointed, but *now* to be *changed* and *abolished*. See Mr. Pierce.

‡ Ver. 28. [Let us have grace: ἔχωμεν χάριν, Let us hold fast the grace,] i. e. the *gospel religion* ἔχω being often the same with κατέχω, as in 1 Cor. vii. 2. 2 Tim. i. 13. See Glassius Philolog. Sac. Tract. *de Verbo* Can. 1.

CHAP. XIII.

The Apoſtle concludes with Exhortations to ſeveral Chriſtian Duties, *ſuch eſpecially as the* Jewiſh *Chriſtians wanted moſt to have inculcated upon them; viz. to Charity, Hoſpitality, and Beneficence to their Fellow-Chriſtians in impriſonment. To a due Eſteem of the lawfulneſs of* Marriage, *and to abſtinence from all* Uncleanneſs. *To Contentment in their wordly Condition. To a juſt eſteem and imitation of their Spiritual* Guides. *In fine, to Conſtancy in the true Doctrine, and Worſhip of* Chriſtianity, *as far ſurpaſſing the External Ceremonies of the* Jewiſh *Religion. Deſires their Prayers for him. Prays for them. The Salutation and Concluſion.*

1 LET brotherly love continue.

1. HAving thus ſhown you the great obligations and advantages of reſolutely adhering to your profeſſion, I ſhall conclude with exhorting you to the practice of ſuch of its eſſential *duties*, as you *Jewiſh* Chriſtians are moſt apt to be wanting in. Remembering, then, in the firſt place, that univerſal love and charity to *all* your fellow Chriſtians, is one of the ſpecial duties of the *goſpel*. No partial diſtinction ought to be made between *Jewiſh* and *Gentile* brethren. A. D. 63.

2 Be not forgetful to entertain ſtrangers: for thereby ſome have entertained angels unawares.

2. In particular be mindful of that part of charity, that conſiſts in hoſpitality to *ſtrangers*. Remember how happy Lot and Abraham were, in entertaining *angels* *, whom they at firſt took to be but *men*.

* Gen. xvii, and xix.

3 Remember them that are in bonds, as bound with them; *and*

3. Have a ſpecial regard and compaſſion to ſuch Chriſtians as are under impriſonment for their religion,

A. D. 63. *and* them which suffer adversity, as being yourselves also in the body *.

religion. Consider yourselves as liable to the same afflictions.

||See 1 Tim. iv. 3. and chap. iii. 15.

4 † Marriage *is* honourable in all, and the bed undefiled: but whoremongers and adulterers God will judge.

4. And whereas the || *Jewish zealots* would persuade you, under pretence of greater purity, that *marriage* is an *unclean* state, and inconsistent with the perfection of religion: be assured there is no such matter. God condemns none but irregular and unlawful pleasures; and the *marriage-bed* is † as honourable and pure to a *Christian* as to any other man.

5 Let your conversation be without covetousness: and be content with such things as ye have. For he hath said, I will never leave thee nor forsake thee.

5. Discover no immoderate desire of worldly gain in your dealings and conversation: But rest yourselves contented with what Providence and your own honest industry provides for you. For *Christians*, while they do their duty, may, with still greater reason, depend upon that promise of God to his church and people, Deut. xxxi. 6. Jos. xv. *He will not fail thee nor forsake thee.*

6 So that we may boldly say, The Lord is my helper, and I will not fear what man shall do unto me.

6. And may with the Psalmist confidently say, *The Lord is my helper, I will not fear what man shall do unto me.*

7 Re- 7. Pay

* Ver. 3. [In the body: ὡς καὶ αὐτοὶ ὄντες ἐν τῷ σώματι—or considering yourselves as (*members*) of the same body,] as some think it should be rendered. But this is not the use of the phrase in other passages, 2 Cor. xii. 3. and elsewhere.

† [Marriage is honourable, &c.] The phrase seems to me to be the most natural sense of the apostle: But, if the reader like it not, he may understand the verse as *imperative*, like the preceding and following ones, ἔστω being understood, "Let marriage be kept honourable, and the bed undefiled. For whoremongers, &c. δέ." The like expression is found in the following verse—"let your conversation be, &c." ἀφιλάργυρος ὁ τρόπος; where ἔστω is plainly understood.

A. D. 63.

7 Remember them which have the rule over you *, who have ſpoken unto you the word of God: whoſe faith follow, conſidering the end of their converſation.

7. Pay a due reſpect to the memory, and follow the example of ſuch as have been our ſpiritual guides and governors. Remember with what conſtancy they profeſſed and taught you the Chriſtian faith, with what patience and courage they died, and how they are now crowned and rewarded for it.

8 † Jeſus Chriſt the ſame yeſterday, and to-day, and for ever.

8. And conſider, that as Jeſus Chriſt is for ever ſteady and unchangeable in the promiſes he has made, † ſo you ought to be immutably conſtant in preſerving the doctrines of his religion pure and untainted: Remembering that his *goſpel* is the *ſame* goſpel to your teachers at *firſt*, and to *you* now, and to all generations that are to come *hereafter*.

9 Be not carried about with divers and ſtrange doctrines: for ‡ it is a good thing that the heart be eſtabliſhed with || grace, not meats, which have not profited them that have been occupied therein.

9. Be not, therefore, deceived, and led away by the ſalfe notions of the *Jewiſh* doctors, about the abſolute neceſſity of their *ceremonial* law. For it is of much ‡ greater advantage to be firm and ſteady in the practice of the moral rules of the || *goſpel*, than to be never ſo ſtrictly obſervant of the *Jewiſh* ceremonies and ſacrifices, that render a man not a whit *inwardly* better than he was without them.

10. Certainly

---

* Ver. 7. [Who have had rule over you, &c.] It is very probable that the *perſons* here meant, and recommended as examples of faith and conſtancy, were, in general, the *elders* of the church at Jeruſalem, and in particular St. James their biſhop, lately martyred there. See Mill. Prolegom. § 83. 84.

† [Jeſus Chriſt the ſame yeſterday, &c.] That this is not meant of the *perſon*, but the *promiſes* and *doctrine* of Chriſt, is not only agreeable to the *context*, but to many other paſſages of like nature. See Acts v. 42. 2 Cor. iv. 5. 1 Cor. i. 24, &c.

‡ [It is good, κάλον, much better.] See Matt. xviii. 8, 9.

|| [With grace.] See 1 Tim. vi. 3. Where *ſound words*. and the doctrines of Chriſt, are oppoſed to *ſtrange doctrines*, as *grace* is in this place.

A. D. 63.

10 We have an altar whereof they have no right to eat which serve the tabernacle.

10. Certainly the benefits we Christians receive, by the great sacrifice of Christ's death, are infinitely preferable to the exter-
† τῇ σκηνῇ nal services of the *Jewish* law, or the privileges of its †
λατρεύοντες. *priests*. But such as still adhere to *that law*, must lose
all the blessings and advantages of this religion of Christ.

11 For the bodies of those beasts, whose blood is brought into the sanctuary by the high priest, for sin, are burnt without the camp.

12 Wherefore Jesus also, that he might sanctify the people with his own blood, suffered without the gate.

11. & 12. For, as the flesh of those beasts, whose blood was offered upon the great day of *expiation*, was ordered to be wholly burnt without the *camp* (whilst the tabernacle stood) and afterwards without the gates of the *city*; and none of the priests or people permitted to eat it: So in like manner, Christ our great Sacrifice was for our redemption, crucified without the *gates* of Jerusalem; and accordingly none can partake of the blessings of his sacrifice and religion, till they come entirely off from the *Jewish ceremonies*, and become true *Christians*.

13 Let us go forth therefore unto him * without the camp bearing his reproach.

13. Let us, therefore, leave the *Jewish camp*, i. e. * the Jewish *ceremonial* religion, and entirely embrace his more excellent *dispensation*. Let us carry his cross, and after his example, patiently suffer the reproaches and persecutions of our adversaries.

14 For here have we no continuing city, but we seek one to come.

14. Nor be discouraged, though at present, you live in an unsettled condition, and are persecuted from place to place. This world, at best, is not designed as a constant residence; it is *heaven* we are to look on as our eternal city, and lasting home.

15. By

---

* [Without the camp:] ἔξω τῆς κατὰ νόμον γενώμεθα πολιτείας, *i. e.* we ought to think ourselves under the *Jewish* dispensation no longer. Theodoret.

A. D. 63.

15 By him therefore let us offer the ſacrifice of praiſe to God continually, that is, the fruit of *our* lips, giving thanks to his name.

15. By him therefore, as your perfect *High Prieſt* and *Interceſſor*, offer up your conſtant prayers and thankſgivings to God; which the prophet calls, "The calves, or fruits of our lips," Hoſ. xiv. 2.

16 But to do good and to communicate, forget not, for with ſuch ſacrifices God is well pleaſed.

16. And, to your Chriſtian prayers and praiſes, be ſure to add that great duty of *charity* and *beneficence* toward each other, without partiality and diſtinction; a ſacrifice far better and more acceptable to God than all the burnt-offerings upon the *Jewiſh altar*.

17 Obey them that have the rule over you, and ſubmit yourſelves: for they watch for your ſouls, as they that muſt give account, that they may do it with joy, and not with grief: for that is unprofitable for you *.

17. Pay all juſt regard to the rules and admonitions of your preſent || biſhops and ſpiritual guides. Remember how great their charge over you is. Be therefore ſo tractable under their diſcipline and admonitions, that they may have the comfort of giving a good account of you, at the great day of judgment; and not ſee all their pains loſt upon you; which would be a moſt fatal * thing to *yourſelves*, as well as a mortification to *them*.

|| See Ver. 7.

18 Pray for us: for we truſt we have a good † conſcience in all things, willing to live honeſtly.

19 But I beſeech you the rather to do

18. & 19. Let *me* have a ſpecial ſhare in your prayers. Beſeech God for ſucceſs in my miniſtry, and deliverance from my adverſaries. And though I make no queſtion, but to go through my *apoſtleſhip*,

* [For that would be unprofitable for you;] ἀλυσιτελὲς, very flatly tranſlated, it bears the ſame ſenſe with τὰ μὴ καθήκοντα, Rom. ii. 28. As *that* is to be rendered *abominable things*, ſo *this* ſignifies a moſt *dangerous and fatal thing*. See Epheſ. v. 11. the note there. And compare Rom. iii. 12.

† Ver. 18. [We truſt we have a good conſcience—] It is a very elliptical expreſſion. His meaning is thus to be ſupplied; viz. "In preaching both to Jews and Gentiles, I aſſure myſelf, I act agreeably to my apoſtolic commiſſion; whatever hard cenſures ſome *zealots* may paſs upon me."

A. D. 63. this that I may be restored to you the sooner.

apostleship, with a good conscience, and an undaunted courage; yet I desire the concurrence of your prayers, which may tend to procure my deliverance from several approaching dangers, and bring me the more speedily to you.

20 Now the God of peace, that brought again from the dead our Lord Jesus, that great Shepherd of the sheep, through the blood of the everlasting covenant,

21 Make you perfect in every good work to do his will, working in you that which is well pleasing in his sight, through Jesus Christ, to whom be glory for ever and ever. Amen.

20. & 21. And, in the mean time, may God, the Author of all peace and happiness, who raised up our Lord Jesus Christ from the dead, and thereby declared him the Saviour and Governor of his church, accepting of his blood as the ratification of the new and gracious covenant of the *gospel*, for our perfect pardon and redemption: may he confirm and strengthen you in all true obedience, giving you all the means and advantages of saving religion, by Jesus Christ; to whom be ascribed all honour and glory for ever. Amen.

22 And I beseech you, brethren, suffer the word of exhortation, for I have written a letter unto you in a few words.

22. I request, dear brethren, you would not think the arguments I have here used, for your constant perseverance in *Christianity*, too long and tedious. I have couched them in as short a compass as the importance of the matter, and my great affection to you would permit.

23 Know ye that our brother Timothy is set at liberty, with whom if he come shortly, I shall see you.

23. Take notice, that our Christian brother Timothy is released from his confinement: and I am in hopes, we may shortly come together, and pay a visit to your church.

24 Salute all them that have the rule over you, and all the saints. They of Italy salute you.

24. My hearty Christian love to all your spiritual governors. All the Christians of Rome, and other parts of Italy, salute you all.

25 Grace be with you all. Amen.

25. The Divine Love and favour be with your whole church. Amen.

A PARA-

A

PARAPHRASE

ON THE

GENERAL EPISTLE

OF

St. JAMES.

THE PREFACE.

§ 1. THE *clearest* accounts from antiquity, ascribe this epistle to James the son of Alpheus, or Cleopas, the brother of Jude, and consequently cousin-german to our blessed Lord, being called the Lord's *brother*, as that word in the *Jewish* language was usually appropriated to all *near* relations. He was, moreover, styled James the *Less*, to distinguish him from the other James, who, from his great age, was denominated James the *Greater*, or *Elder*. And, lastly, From his extraordinary sanctity and devotion, he went under the character of James the *Just;* and was by the apostles, chosen *bishop* of Jerusalem. The Author.

§ 2. The exact distinction of the *person*, helps much to determine the *date* of his *epistle:* it being certain, from Josephus, that this James suffered martyrdom, under the high-priesthood of Ananus, and procuratorship of Albinus, viz. in the year of Christ LXII. This epistle must bear date before that time; and is most probably placed by Dr. Mills in, or just before, the year LX. The Time.

The Occasion. § 3. About this time the predictions of our Saviour, and of St. Paul, in his second epistle to the Thessalonians, concerning the temper and behaviour of the *Jewish* nation, as tokens of their approaching destruction, were growing on apace towards an accomplishment. False *prophets* and pretended *Messiahs* were numberless; their furious persecution against the Christians was either actually begun, or drew very near; and as *their* rage improved to its utmost heat, "the love of many Christians began to wax cold." In fine, they had so corrupted their own religion, became so furious against all other people, and so malicious, even to one another, that it could not but be a certain conclusion, "The Judge was not far from the door." These circumstances gave occasion to this *apostle* the *residentiary* of the *circumcision* in Judea, to indite this epistle, partly to the *infidel*, and partly to the *believing*, Jews. With the *former*, his purpose was, to correct their haughty errors, soften their ungoverned zeal, and reform their indecent usages in religion. The *latter* he was to comfort, under the hardships they then did, or shortly were to suffer for their Christianity; to warn them from several of the prejudices and practices of their persecutors; to which their former education, or present afflictions might render them too prone; and to spirit them up to a pure and patient profession of the *gospel*. The several turns and applications of his argument to *one*, or the *other*, of these parties, shall be observed, with as much clearness, as can be gathered from the context of each passage; several whereof, after the manner of *eastern* writing, may, at first, seem directed to them *both*, promiscuously, and without distinction.

There is one particular passage (Chap. ii. 14. to the end) that seems clearly levelled against the doctrine of the heretics, called Simonians, or followers of Simon Magus, who, as Irenæus tells us (Lib. II. cap. 20.) affirmed, "Liberos eos esse agere quæ velint; secundum enim Gratiam Salvari Homines non secundum justas Operas;" i. e. "That they might live and act as they pleased, because men were to be saved by *grace*, and not according to their good *works*."

To whom? § 4. It was directed to the Jews and *Jewish converts* of the *dispersion*: yet, as that to the Hebrews was intended

tended for the general benefit of all the *scattered* tribes, * though directed to the natives of the Holy Land; so, no doubt, *this* had an equal respect to *them*, over whom St. James immediately presided in the special character of their bishop.

* See Pref to the Heb § 1.

Why called General?

§ 5. And lastly, As this, and the following epistles were written, not to any *one*, but to *several* Christian churches; it is upon that account, commonly thought, they are called *catholic*, or *general* epistles.

CHAP. I.

The Title and Salutation, to the foreign Jews, and Jewish *Christians. He begins with the* latter, *exhorting them to a cheerful and good Improvement of present Troubles and Persecutions, as the highest Perfection of a* Christian *Life. Prayer, with steady Faith in God, through Christ, the means to attain that Perfection. Advice to the Poor, and to such as are despoiled of their Riches, for the sake of* Christianity. *The Uncertainty of Riches, and the Benefit of well improved Trials and Temptations. A Warning not to impute any Sin (particularly that of* Apostacy*) to God, who permits Temptations to befal them; but to the wilful Indulgence of their own worldly and vicious Inclinations. God, the Author of all spiritual Blessings, cannot be answerable for the Cowardice and Defaults of Men. An Inference from thence, against the furious Temper, and violent Disputes of some* Judaizing *Christians. Against the pernicious Error of the* Jewish *Zealots, about the Efficacy of mere* Faith, *or* external *Profession of Religion without a suitable* Practice. *Against Railing and Contention. Charity in Words and Actions, a principal Branch of true Religion.*

1 JAmes a servant of God, and of the Lord Jesus Christ, to the twelve tribes which are

1. JAmes, bishop of Jerusalem, a worshipper of the true God, and an apostle of Jesus Christ our Lord and Saviour, sendeth this epistle

Written A. D. 60.

A. D. 60. are ſcattered abroad, greeting.

piſtle to the Jews and the *Jewiſh* Chriſtians, particularly to thoſe of the diſperſion in foreign countries, wiſhing you all bleſſing and happineſs.

2 My brethren, count it all joy when ye ſhall fall into divers temptations.

3 Knowing this, that the trying of your faith worketh patience.

2. & 3. My dear brethren, I am truly ſenſible of the hardſhips and perſecutions that are to be undergone by ſuch of you as have embraced the *Chriſtian* faith. And I earneſtly exhort you, not to be diſcouraged at them; as being the happy means and opportunities of improving your patience, and working you up to that noble diſpoſition of a perfect ſubmiſſion to the Divine Will and Providence.

4 But let patience have her perfect work, that ye may be perfect and entire, wanting nothing.

4. This is the temper that renders us complete diſciples, and is the perfection of a *Chriſtian* life.

* σοφια.

5 If any of you lack wiſdom, let him aſk of God, that giveth to all men liberally and upbraideth not, and it ſhall be given him.

5. In order to attain * which, let every perſecuted Chriſtian have recourſe to God, in prayer, as to a moſt bountiful and free benefactor, that will not fail to grant him all ſeaſonable aſſiſtance toward a prudent and courageous behaviour under his diſtreſs.

‡ ἐν πίστει.

6 But let him aſk in faith nothing wavering: for he that wavereth is like a wave of the ſea, driven with the wind, and toſſed.

7 For let not that man think that he ſhall receive any thing of the Lord.

8 A double minded man is unſtable in all his ways.

6, 7. & 8. But theſe prayers muſt be offered up with a full perſuaſion of, and reliance upon, the Divine Power and Goodneſs ‡, with a firm conviction of the fitneſs and lawfulneſs of the things he prays for—an entire ſubmiſſion to the heavenly Providence, and a ſincere purpoſe of adhering to the duties of your *profeſſion*. For a man that is divided in his thoughts and religious principles, has really no ſolid principle at all, will ſtick cloſe to no meaſures of duty and virtue; which will defeat all the ſucceſs of his prayers.

9. With

9 Let the brother of low degree rejoice in that he is exalted:

9. With this ſteady faith and resolution, let the *poor* Christian, that has * always lived in mean circumstances, think his poverty abundantly compensated by the excellent privileges the *goſpel*-religion has advanced him to, and the opportunities he is furniſhed with, for the advancement of his faith and virtue.

A. D. 60.

* ὁ ταπεινός.

10 But the rich, in that he is made low: because as the flower of the graſs he ſhall paſs away.

11 For the ſun is no ſooner riſen with a burning heat, but it withereth the graſs; and the flower thereof falleth, and the grace of the faſhion of it periſheth; ſo alſo ſhall the rich man fade away in his ways.

10. & 11. And let ſuch, who for the ſake of their religion are fallen ‡ from a wealthy and proſperous condition, be well pleaſed with a change, that gives them a title to ſubſtantial and *eternal* bleſſings, inſtead of that *temporal* proſperity, which, in itſelf, is as liable to be deſtroyed by a thouſand accidents of human life, as a tender flower is by the heat of the ſun.

‡ ὁ πλούσιος.

12 Bleſſed is the man that endureth temptation: for when he is tried, he ſhall receive the crown of life which the Lord hath promiſed to them that love him.

12. Happy therefore is the Chriſtian that perſeveres in his integrity, though at the expence of all his worldly enjoyments; ſince he is ſo certain of that future and complete reward, which the God of truth has engaged to beſtow upon all his ſincere and courteous ſervants.

13 Let no man ſay when he is tempted, I am tempted of God: for God cannot be tempted with evil, neither tempteth he any man.

13. Let no perſon then, that is drawn into the commiſſion of any known ſin (eſpecially that of ‖*apoſtacy* from his religion, for fear of perſecution) preſume to attribute his miſcarriage to God, for ſuffering temptations or aſſlictions to befal him. For, as God cannot poſſibly commit any moral evil *himſelf*, ſo it is equally abſurd and impious to imagine he ſhould be the *cauſe* of ſin in any of his creatures.

‖ πειραζόμενος.

A. D. 60.

14 But every man is tempted, when he is drawn away of his own luſt, and enticed.

14. Certainly the only *proper cauſe* of a man's forſaking his profeſſion, or tranſgreſſing the precepts of it, is, his wicked indulgence of ſome worldly and vicious principle.

15 Then when luſt hath conceived he bringeth forth ſin; and ſin when it is finiſhed, bringeth forth death.

15. It is nothing but his deliberate approbation of, and free conſent to, ſuch irregular paſſions, that draws him into the commiſſion of ſuch actions as bring him to death and condemnation.

16 Do not err my beloved brethren.

17 Every good gift, and every perfect gift is from above, and cometh down from the Father of lights, with whom is no variableneſs; neither ſhadow of turning.

16. & 17. Do not therefore ſo groſsly impoſe upon yourſelves, as to aſcribe your wilful failings to *him*, to whom we owe all that is, or can be, good in us; who has given ſuch ample aſſiſtance, and propoſed ſuch infinite rewards, for our virtue and perſeverance. To *him* alone we owe all that light and influence, that guides the *mind*; as much as the *world* does the lights of the *ſun* and *moon*. Nay, more excellent are his heavenly gifts to the *ſoul*, than is the light of the heavenly bodies to the *world*: for, while *theſe* have their turns and periods varying, and removing nearer, or farther off from us; God is always the ſame, and *his* bleſſings ever at hand to us.

18 Of his own will begat he us with the word of truth, that we ſhould be a kind of firſt-fruits of his creatures.

18. In fine, ſo infinitely far is God from being the author of evil, or from neceſſitating us to any ſin, or leaving us to the wild direction of *chance* or *deſtiny*; that he has diſplayed the moſt wonderful inſtance of divine care, and free mercy towards us, in beſtowing on us the bleſſings and privileges of the *goſpel* doctrine and religion to guide our practices, and to actuate our endeavours: making *us* of the *Jewiſh* nation *firſt* converts to it, as an earneſt of his calling the *reſt* of mankind, after us, to the ſame bleſſings: ſo that *we*, like the firſt *fruits* under the *law*, ought to ſtrive

to

to be the *beſt* of our kind, and moſt exemplary Chri- A. D. 60.
ſtians, as being *firſt* dedicated to his ſervice.

19 Wherefore, my beloved brethren, let every man be ſwift to hear, ſlow to ſpeak, ſlow to wrath.

19. And if you deſire ſo to approve yourſelves, you muſt be entirely weaned from that pride and affectation of *teaching*, and imperiouſly *dictating* to other men; from that fierceneſs in diſputing for your own opinions (a thing the *Jewiſh* doctors and zealots are ſo addicted to) and be of a tractable, meek, and peaceable diſpoſition.

20 For the wrath of man worketh not the righteouſneſs of God.

20. For the violence of human *zeal* is but a hindrance, inſtead of an advantage, to thoſe principles and practices that are to juſtify and ſave us.

21 Wherefore lay apart all filthineſs, and ſuperfluity of naughtineſs, and receive with meekneſs the ingrafted word, which is able to ſave your ſouls.

21. Strive, therefore, to get rid of all thoſe exorbitant paſſions, that, like a multitude of proud ſuckers from a tree, will ſpoil your growth in Chriſtian virtues, which are always beſt received and improved by a calm and humble ſpirit.

22 But be ye doers of the word, and not hearers only, deceiving your own ſelves.

22. And, whereas the *Jewiſh* zealots are wont to put all the ſtreſs of religion in mere *outward* profeſſion, and *external* obſervances; do not you treat the *Chriſtian* religion in that manner; which would be to put the moſt fatal cheat upon yourſelves.

23 For if any be a hearer of the word, and not a doer, he is like unto a man beholding his natural face in a glaſs:

24 For he beholdeth himſelf, and goeth his way, and ſtraightway forgetteth what

23. & 24. For the *goſpel* doctrine is of the ſame uſe to the *mind* and *conduct* of men, as a glaſs is to the *face*. And as the glaſs is of no benefit to one that ſees the ſpots of his face in it, but takes no care to wipe them off; ſo the *goſpel* precepts can be of no manner of advantage to a Chriſtian,

A. D. 60. what manner of man he was.

stian, that only externally professes and hears them, but neglects to reform his practice, and leads his life agreeable to them.

15 But whoso looketh into the perfect law of liberty, and continueth *therein*, he being not a forgetful hearer, but a doer of the work, this man shall be blessed in his deed.

25. He therefore is the only person that truly edifies by the *Christian* doctrine, who embraceth and useth it as a rule of *action*. Then, indeed, it becomes a *law* to him, a law that sets him *free* from the slavish observance of *Jewish ceremonies*; and that man will experience the *gospel* to be a dispensation of more excellent liberties, immunities, and privileges, than all that the zealot Jew can boast of his *Mosaical* institution.

26 If any man among you seem to be religious, and bridleth not his tongue, but deceiveth his own heart, this mans religion is vain.

26. Certainly, the most specious and loud pretences of external religion are but vain and insignificant things, while a man gives himself up to uncharitable slanders, revilings, and reproaches against his brethren.

27 Pure religion, and undefiled before God and the Father, is this, to visit the fatherless and widows in their affliction, *and* to keep himself unspotted from the world.

27. For the habitual practice of *charity* and bounty toward the afflicted, the conquest over all sensual, worldly and partial inclinations, and such like *moral* duties, are the things in which true religion does chiefly and principally consist.

CHAP.

CHAP. II.

The Argument of the latter Part of the foregoing Chapter continued; viz. That the External *Profession of Religion is wholly fruitless, where Men live in the Breach of its* Moral *and Substantial Duties. This shown in the Instance of* Partiality, *and respect of* Persons, *especially in Public and* Judicial *Causes.* Jewish Christians *are taxed with this Vice, so common among the* Jews. *The evil and dangerous Consequence of any* one *such known and wilful Sin. Moral* Practices *the best, and only Evidence of Good* Principles, *proved from the Examples of Abraham aud Rahab. All is nothing without them.*

1 MY brethren, have not the faith of our Lord Jesus Christ *the Lord* of glory, with respect of persons.

1. THE Jews, that now so much value themselves, and despise all other people in point of religion, are become so corrupt in their morals, in their private and public dealings, that hardly any justice is to be found, even in their courts of *judicature.* All is carried amongst them by wealth and *interest:* But for *you,* dear brethren, that profess the more perfect and glorious religion of Jesus Christ, how monstrous must it be to be guilty of a partiality so directly opposite to its spirit and precepts? A. D. 60.

2 For if there come unto your * assembly a man with a gold ring, in goodly apparel, and there come in also a poor man in vile raiment:

3 And ye have respect to him that weareth the gay clothing, and say unto him, Sit

2. 3. & 4. For *you* to distinguish your respects, and be partial in your proceedings with any, but especially a *Christian* brother, in a public *court,* * or in your *church assemblies,* upon account of his higher or lower fortunes in the world, his circumstances and outward figure; to caress the rich, and slight the poor; would be to make

* συναγωγή.

A D. 60. Sit thou here in a good place: and say to the poor, Stand thou there, or sit here under my footstool:

make a most unreasonable distinction, where there ought to be none; and to show yourselves most unthoughtful and unjust judges.

4 Are ye not then partial in yourselves, and are become judges of * evil thoughts?

5 Hearken, my beloved brethren, Hath not God chosen the poor of this world, rich in faith, and heirs of the kingdom which he hath promised to them that love him?

5. Consider seriously, dear brethren, upon this matter. Does God make such partial differences in his dealings with mankind, as *you* do with one another? How many, that are mean in their outward circumstances, but humble in their tempers, have made the best *Christians*? Did not God choose the very *apostles* out of that number? And have not *they*, and all their poor, but humble *followers*, the surest title to eternal life and happiness?

6 But ye have despised the poor. Do not rich men oppress you, and draw you before the judgment-seat?

7 Do not they blaspheme that worthy name by the which ye are called?

6. & 7. On the contrary, while you are thus guilty of neglecting your *poor* brethren, how forgetful are you, that the *rich* men, to whose rank and quality you are so partial, are the persons most apt to oppose your holy religion! Who are they, but the *richer* sort, of both *Jews* and *Gentiles*, that most commonly blaspheme † the name of Christ, and his religion?

8 If ye fulfil the royal law, according to the scripture, Thou shalt love thy neighbour as thyself, ye do well.

8. Had you any just regard to that noble and comprehensive duty, of *doing as you would be done by*, you would act at another rate.

9 But

9. Whereas

* Ver. 4. [Judges of evil thoughts: *or* διαλογισμῶν πονηρῶν, judges that use wicked and unjust arguments.]

† [That holy name by which you are called.] τὸ ἐπικληθὲν ἐφ' ὑμᾶς; that is, called *over* you, or *given to* you.

A. D. 60.

9 But if ye have respect to perſons, ye commit ſin, and are convinced of the law as tranſgreſſors.

9. Whereas, by ſuch an unjuſt and partial proceeding, you violate and ſtand convict, breaking the *whole* law reſpecting your neighbour.

10 For whoſoever ſhall keep the whole * law, and yet offend in one *point*, he is guilty of all.

10. For, the wilful and habitual breach of any *one* ſuch *principal* command, renders a man, in a juſt ſenſe, a tranſgreſſor of that * *whole table* of the divine law, though he were not guilty in other particular inſtances.

11 For he that ſaid, Do not commit adultery, ſaid alſo, Do not kill. Now if thou commit no adultery, yet if thou kill, thou art become a tranſgreſſor of the law.

11. Becauſe the ſame divine *authority* that forbids us any *one* act of violating the rights of our neighbour, forbids us *all* the reſt. The ſame divine authority (for inſtance) that reſtrains us from invading the property of our neighbour's *bed*, reſtrains us from *killing* him. So that, though you do not actually attempt his *life*, yet, if you commit *adultery* againſt him, you break in upon the *whole* divine authority, that eſtabliſheth *all right* between man and man.

12 So ſpeak ye, and ſo do as they that ſhall be judged by the law of liberty.

12. Deal by one another, therefore, both in words and actions, as men that expect hereafter to be judged by the pure and perfect rule of *Chriſtianity*. A religion that while it is moſt ſtrict in its *moral* obligations, debarring us from all thoſe licentious practices the *Jewiſh* zealots † think† themſelves privileged in; yet, as I ſaid, chap. i. 5. it is attended with immunities and bleſſings far exceeding what the *Moſaical* diſpenſation can pretend to.

† ἐλευθερία.

13 For he ſhall have judgment without mercy, that hath ſhowed no mercy; and mercy

13. For certainly, the man, of what profeſſion ſoever, that ſhows no tenderneſs and impartiality towards his brethren, ſhall find ſeverity

---

* [The whole law—he is guilty of all :] ὅλον τὸν νόμον, the ſame as νόμον Βασιλικὸν in verſe 8. *viz.* the *royal law* reſpecting our *neighbour.*

A. D. 60. mercy rejoiceth againſt judgment*.

ſeverity of juſtice, without mercy, at God's hands. And no perſon can ſo ſecurely and cheerfully ſtand the great trial of *divine* judgment, as he that has been kind, impartial, and merciful to other *men*, without any unreaſonable diſtinctions.

14 What *doth it* profit, my brethren, though a man ſay he hath faith, and have not works? can faith ſave him?

14. Thus, I ſay, the actual and careful practice of *moral* virtue, is the ſubſtance and life of true religion. Mere *faith*, and *external profeſſion*, without this, is of no effect to any man's ſalvation.

15 If a brother or ſiſter be naked, and deſtitute of daily food;

16 And one of you ſay unto them, Depart in peace, be you warmed, and filled: notwithſtanding ye give them not thoſe things which are needful to the body; what *doth it* profit?

15. & 16. Thus, when an indigent brother preſents himſelf to you, as an object of your *charity;* to feed him with good *words* and kind *wiſhes*, without giving him any thing to clad his body, or ſatisfy his hunger, is to do juſt nothing at all for him.

16 Even ſo faith, if it hath not works, is dead, being alone.

17. The caſe is the very ſame with God, in all other inſtances of religion; the moſt loud pretences to *faith*, and the warmeſt zeal for *external* acts of his worſhip, is to pay him no real ſervice, while the practice of thoſe *duties* are wanting, that are the main purpoſes of all religion.

18 Yea, a man may ſay, Thou haſt faith, and I have works: Show me thy faith without thy works, and I will ſhow thee my faith by my works.

18. To ſay you are the true members of God's *church*, becauſe you believe his word and revelation, and are a mere *profeſſor* of his inſtituted religion, is to take a thing for granted, without full proof, and to give only your

---

* Ver. 13. [Mercy rejoiceth againſt judgment:] Κατακαυχᾶται ἔλεος κρίσεως, Mercy triumphs over condemnation; *or* The merciful man triumphs at his judgment, or at his trial. Mercy *for the* merciful man, *as* circumciſion *is put for the* circumciſed perſon, Rom. ii. 26, 27.

your *own* word for it. Whereas, he that shows the sincerity of his *faith* and profession, by the good influences it has in the conduct of his *life*, concludes very rightly; as the *cause* is demonstrated by the *effect*. A. D. 60.

19 Thou believest that there is one God; thou doest well: the devils also believe and tremble.

19. The Jew magnifies himself above the Gentile, for his knowledge and belief of the *one true God*. If *that* be all, the very devils themselves are upon the level with him; for they believe the same, and tremble at the apprehensions of his divine power and justice. And, if your faith be no better than theirs, you have the same reason to tremble as they have.

20 But wilt thou know, O vain man, that faith without works is dead?

21 Was not Abraham our father justified by works, when he had offered Isaac his son upon the altar.

20. & 21. But to convince *you* and *them* of the utter falsity of this principle; let the Jew tell me what it was that justified Abraham, the father of his nation, and of all faithful people? You cannot but know, by the express words of the history, it was not his mere *belief* and persuasion, that God had ordered him to offer up his son, or his confident reliance upon God's *promise*, and his being in *covenant* with him, but his *actual* entrance upon the *performance* of what God had commanded him.

22 Seest thou how faith wrought with his works, and by works was faith made perfect?

23 And the scripture was fulfilled, which saith, Abraham believed God, and it was imputed unto him for righteousness: and he was called the Friend of God.

22. & 23. Thus, that great *patriarch* demonstrated the excellence and sincerity of his inward *principle*, by the *practice* of the noblest virtue. It was this procured him that great character, "Abraham believed God, and it was imputed to him for righteousness, and he was called the Friend of God." Gen. xv. 6.

24 Ye see then how that by works a man is justified, and not by faith only.

24. And if this was Abraham's case, it is in vain for any Jew or *Christian* to expect to be saved, upon a different foot from that of the *father* of the faithful.

25. Again,

A. D. 60.

25 Likewiſe alſo, was not Rahab the harlot juſtified by works, when ſhe had received the meſſengers, and had ſent them out another way?

|| Joſh. ii. 1. vi. 23. Heb. ix. 31.

25. Again, what was it that rendered the harlot Rahab ſo acceptable to God, as to ſave her life? Not her mere *conviction* that the God of the Jews was the *true God*||; but her actual *reception* of the ſpies, as his meſſengers; as the genuine effect of ſuch a perſuaſion.

26 For as the body without the ſpirit is dead, ſo faith without works is dead alſo.

26. From which inſtance, as a confirmation of the reaſon of the thing itſelf; it is exceeding plain, that bare *external* privileges, and *outward* profeſſion can no more make a true *Iſraelite* (much leſs a true *Chriſtian*) than a *body* without a *ſoul* can make up a *man*.

CHAP. III.

The Jewiſh *Chriſtians are again particularly diſuaded from the Pride and Ambition of being called* Doctors, *and* Teachers; *and from that Spirit of Contemning, Reviling, Curſing, and Calumniating, to which the* Jewiſh *Zealots were ſo much addicted. The great Advantage of a gentle and peaceful Temper, and the fatal Effects of a Cenſorious and Unbridled* Tongue.

‡ Chap. i. 19. See 1 Tim. i. 7. Rom. ii. 19, 20.

1 MY brethren, be not many maſters, knowing that we ſhall receive the greater condemnation.

1. I Have already‡ obſerved to you, that you can never anſwer the character of true *Chriſtians*, while you harbour that ambition of the *Jewiſh* zealots, of imperiouſly ſetting up for *teachers*; of uſurping an authority over the conſciences of others, and be guilty of the calumny and cenſoriouſneſs that is conſequent to ſuch pride and affectation. Againſt *this* notorious *vice* I muſt now more particularly warn you. Conſider then, the more knowledge and underſtanding you pretend to, the more heinous

A. D. 60.

2 For in many things we offend all. If any man offend not in word, the same *is* a perfect man, *and* able also to bridle the whole body.

2. The very best of us have their slips and failings. But the liberties of the *tongue*, are what most men are too apt to transgress in, above all measure. And were those *zealots* but free of the vices of that very *member*, wherewith they pretend to teach others, they had much better pretence to the religious perfection than now they have. The government of the *tongue* has a general good influence upon the conduct of human life.

3 Behold, we put bits in the horses mouths, that they may obey us; and we turn about their whole body.

4 Behold also the ships, which though they be so great, and are driven of fierce winds, yet are they turned about with a very small helm, whithersoever the governor listeth.

5 Even so the tongue is a little member, and boasteth great things. Behold how great a matter a little fire kindleth.

3. 4. & 5. And, as horses are managed by the bit, and ships steered by the rudder, that is, but a small piece, in comparison of the bulk of the vessel; so the whole conversation of a man is, in a manner, guided and well-ordered by the temperate use of that *little* member. Which, whenever it flies out into extravagant, uncharitable and abusive expressions, becomes like a spark amongst combustible matter; blows up and consumes all before it.

6 And the tongue *is* a fire, a world of iniquity: so is the tongue amongst our members, that it defileth the whole body, and setteth on fire the course of nature; and it is set on fire of hell.

6. Well may such a *tongue* be compared to *fire*, for its desperate and destructive quality: It puts the whole world into confusion and disorder, and destroys like a conflagration, begun from hell itself.

7 For every kind of beasts, and of birds, and of serpents, and things in the sea, is tamed, and hath been tamed of mankind:

7. & 8. When it once obtains, and has got the mastery over a man's conduct, it is unruly beyond the most savage creature we know of: Its fierceness exceeds that of the

A. D. 60.

8 But the tongue can no man tame, it is an unruly evil: full of deadly poiſon.

the *lion* and *tiger*; and its venom beyond the worſt of *ſerpents*.

9 Therewith bleſs we God, even the Father: and therewith curſe we men, which are made after the ſimilitude of God.

10 Out of the ſame mouth proceedeth bleſſing and curſing. My brethren, theſe things ought not ſo to be.

9. & 10. It runs men into practices the moſt abſurd as well as impious; cauſing them to uſe that *very* member, that was given us to celebrate the praiſes of God, to throw out curſes and imprecations againſt their *brethren* that were created like themſelves in the *image* of God. Bleſſing and curſing out of the ſame mouth! How irrational and monſtrous a thing to be guilty of!

11 Doth a fountain ſend forth at the ſame place ſweet *water* and bitter?

12 Can the fig-tree, my brethren, bear olive berries? either a vine, figs? ſo can no fountain both yield ſalt water and freſh.

11. & 12. A thing as utterly inconſiſtent with true religion, as it is to ſuppoſe the ſame water, from the ſame part of a ſpring, ſhould be ſalt and freſh at the ſame time; that a fig-tree ſhould bear olives, or a vine produce figs, i. e. a perfect contradiction in the nature of things.

13 Who is a wiſe man and endued with knowledge amongſt you? let him ſhow out of a good converſation his works with meekneſs of wiſdom.

13. Whatever Chriſtian convert, or *Jewiſh* zealot, therefore, would be indeed a maſter of religious wiſdom, let him ſhow his wiſdom, firſt in the ſuppreſſion of this wretched habit, and in reducing himſelf to a meek and charitable diſpoſition toward his brethren.

14 But if ye have bitter envying and ſtrife in your hearts, glory not, and lie not againſt the truth.

15 This wiſdom deſcendeth not from above, but is earthly, ſenſual, deviliſh.

14. & 15. For as long as ever this haughty and contentious ſpirit in *religious* diſputes, vents itſelf through the *tongue*, his boaſting is but vanity, and his pretences hypocriſy. The wiſdom he pretends to, is the effect of nothing but ſenſual and worldly principles, and a perfect imitation of the *devil* and wicked ſpirits.

A. D. 60.

16 For where envying and ſtrife is, there is confuſion and every evil work.

16. For nothing but wickedneſs and diſtraction can be the reſult of a proud, cenſorious, and contentious diſpoſition.

17 But the wiſdom that is from above is firſt pure, then peaceable, gentle, and eaſy to be entreated, full of mercy and good fruits, without partiality, and without hypocriſy.

17. Directly contrary to this, the wiſdom and temper of *true religion* exerts itſelf in a freedom from ſenſual and worldly inclinations, in rendering a man mild and courteous, and perſuadable by reaſon, kind and charitable to the indigent, generous, juſt, and impartial to *all* mankind, and ſincere in all religious pretences.

18 And the fruit of righteouſneſs is ſown in peace of them that make peace.

18. And whoever is of this peaceable and good temper, and endeavours to perſuade others to it, will not fail to reap the happy fruits and bleſſed effects of it.

CHAP. IV.

The Apoſtle illuſtrates the woful Effects of a turbulent and malicious Temper, from the then preſent State and Condition of the Jewiſh People. A ſad Account of them. He endeavours to work their Cure, by perſuading them to Repentance, and true Religion. Then diſſuades the Chriſtian Converts from the notorious Vice of Slander and Calumny; and from an immoderate and confident Purſuit of worldly Projects, without any pious Regard to, or Reliance upon, Divine Providence.

1 FROM whence come wars, and fightings among you? come they not hence, even

1. WHAT I have * hitherto obſerved, of the wretched effects of a turbulent and contentious ſpirit, is, but too wofully demonſtrable,

* Chap. iii. 16.

A. D. 60

even of your luſts, that war in your members?

monſtrable, from the preſent ſtate and condition of the *Jewiſh* people. Let any Jew tell me the real cauſe of all thoſe calamities and deſolations, thoſe foreign, civil, and domeſtic broils, that are now the general plagues of *that nation*. What is it, but the ſenſual and ambitious temper I have been deſcribing?

2 Ye luſt, and have not: ye kill, and deſire to have, and cannot obtain: ye fight and war, yet ye have not, becauſe ye aſk not.

2. Your hearts are entirely bent upon temporal pleaſure, and temporal dominion; you are impatient under the *government* Providence has ſubjected your nation to. This puts you upon *ſeditious* practices, that can never gain your ends; and your inteſtine diſcords make your caſe ſtill worſe. Nor can God be ſuppoſed to proſper a people, ſo eſtranged from all true religion and devotion toward him.

3 Ye aſk and receive not, becauſe ye aſk amiſs, that ye may conſume it upon your luſts.

3. It is true, you keep up the external profeſſion, and the *form* of worſhip and prayer. But this can avail you little, while the ſtreſs of your deſires is fixed on *worldly* pleaſures, and the view of all your very *prayers* is the gratification of luſtful and ambitious principles.

4 Ye adulterers and adultereſſes, know ye not that the friendſhip of the world is enmity with God? whoſoever therefore will be a friend of the world, is the enemy of God.

4. O faithleſs and perverſe *nation*! How can you be ſo ignorant, as to imagine, the love of God and true religion can ever be conſiſtent with this immoderate thirſt after *temporal* riches and grandeur! You muſt give up one, or the other.

5 * Do ye think that the ſcripture ſaith in vain, the ſpirit that dwelleth in us luſteth to envy?

6 But he giveth more grace; wherefore he ſaith, God reſiſteth

5. & 6. How contrary have the ſcriptures of the Old Teſtament deſcribed the temper of God's true ſervants, to that envious and contentious ſpirit that now reigns in the generality of *your* nation? Do you perceive any ſuch diſpoſition and

* Ver. 5. [Do you think the ſcripture ſaith—the ſpirit in us—] Theſe words are, by ſome interpreters, thought to refer

sisteth the proud, but ‡ giveth grace unto the humble.

and practice in us *Christians?* So far from it, that you behold nothing but peaceableness and humility, the genuine fruit of God's Spirit, and to which his special favour and blessing is annexed; according to those words of Solomon, (Prov. iii. 34.) *Surely he scorneth the scorners, but he giveth grace ‡ (or favour) to the lowly.* A. D. 60.

7 Submit yourselves therefore to God: resist the devil, and he will flee from thee.

8 Draw nigh to God, and he will draw nigh to you: cleanse your hands, ye sinners, and purify your hearts, ye double minded.

9 Be afflicted, and mourn, and weep: let

7. 8. 9. & 10. And if you would be cured of those wretched habits, that are the causes of your present calamities, and partake of the same blessings with *us*, you must serve God in the same true and sincere manner as *we* do; sue to him for pardon and salvation, by reforming all your towering and proud conceits, by hearty repentance for the violences and injustice you have committed; and endeavouring to rectify

---

fer to [Numb. xi. 29. Enviest thou for my sake?] i. e. should the gifts of the Spirit, conferred upon *one*, move *another* to envy? But as those words are very different from St James, who was not here speaking of *gifts* and spiritual pre-eminence at all; I judge the paraphrase to be the most agreeable and coherent sense. For I think it will clear this passage of all difficulties, if we divide the *fifth verse* into two *interrogations;* viz. [Do you think that the scripture speaks in vain?] *i. e.* the scripture quoted in the *sixth verse;* or any of those *scriptures* that speak against *pride* and *envy*. Then [The spirit that is in us lusteth (or lusteth it) to envy? in *us;* i. e. in us apostles, or Christians. No; far from it; it puts us into a far better way of obtaining God's *grace* or *favour;* viz. by *peaceableness* and *humility*. [Wherefore (not *he*, but) *it*, the scripture saith, God resisteth the proud, &c.

‡ Ver. 6. [Giveth grace,] i. e. Favour or blessing. χάρις answers to חן in the *Hebrew:* its primary sense is *favour;* which in the New Testament is branched out into several acceptations, including either the *blessings of the gospel in general*, or any *principal branches* of them. But is rarely (that I can find) used to signify any *inward motions, or secret operations of the Holy Spirit on the mind*, unless when it expresseth the *extraordinary* gifts, and *miraculous* endowments on the apostles and *first* Christians.

A. D. 60.

let your laughter be turned to mourning, and your joy to heaviness.

10 Humble yourselves in the sight of the Lord, and he shall lift you up.

rectify those corrupt inclinations, that have hitherto divided you between God and the world: by thus striving against the temptations of the devil, you shall be enabled to overcome them; and upon condition of so thorough a humiliation and repentance, God will be reconciled to you, avert the judgments that hang over you, and make you again, his beloved *church* and *people*.

11 Speak not evil one of another (brethren) he that speaketh evil of his brother, and judgeth his brother, speaketh evil of the law, and judgeth the law: but if thou judge the law, thou art not a doer of the law, but a judge.

11. As to *you*, dear brethren, that are already converted to *Christianity*, be sure to avoid that pernicious custom of *slander* and rash *censure*. Remember, that whoever hastily and unjustly condemns another man, reflects upon *religion* itself, sets up for a *judge*, and makes himself wiser than the divine *law*. And such a one must not pretend to be a true disciple of that *law*, while he sets himself *above* it.

12 There is one law giver, who is able to save, and to destroy: who art thou that judgest another?

12. Consider, that God alone, * who gives us his laws, has the right to judge and condemn us for the breach of them: and how dare any man take *his* work out of his hands!

* Rom. xiv. 4, 10.

13 Go to now, ye that say, To-day or to-morrow we will go into such a city, and continue there a year, and buy and sell, and get gain:

13. Another thing, I would correct in you all is, that *confidence*, and unthoughtful *assurance*, with which you are apt to pursue your worldly projects; without a due sense of, and pious dependence upon divine Providence. Some of you *Christian* converts, I find, are too much tainted with the *Jewish* spirit of worldly mindedness. You cut out business, and conclude upon the success, as if *time* and *events* were at *your* disposal.

14 Whereas ye know not what *shall be* on the morrow: for what

14. & 15. You forget what changes and disappointments a single *day* may produce: and that life

A. D. 60.

what is your life? It is even a vapour, that appeareth for a little time, and then vanisheth away.

life itself is as fleeting as a vapour. A consideration, that ought to fill us with the most humble dependance upon the divine will, in all events and expectations.

15 For that ye ought to say, If the Lord will, we shall live, and do this, or that.

16 But now ye rejoice in your boastings: all such rejoicing is evil.

16. And, therefore, such eager designs, and confident proposals, in your temporal affairs, look as if you thought yourselves independent of divine blessing and protection.

17 Therefore to him that knoweth to do good, and doth it not, to him it is sin.

17. Now *this* or any *other* crime, must be greater in a *Christian*, than in any other man; because *he*, by the clear revelation of the *gospel*, has (or ought to have) better notions of his duty, and a stronger sense of his religious obligations.

CHAP. V.

He turns himself to the Jews, *reproaching them with the just and miserable Effects of their Avarice, Cruelty, Lust, and Injustice. Then returns to the* Jewish Christians, *exhorting them to Patience and good Temper, under their Persecutions from the* Jews, *in hopes of a speedy Deliverance, by a just Judgment upon that* Nation. *Warns them from the Sin of rash* Swearing, *so common among the* Jews. *Recommends Prayer to the Afflicted, and Divine Praises to such as are in easy and cheerful Circumstances. Adviseth* Anointing *and the devout Prayer of Inspired Ministers, to be used for the Recovery of such as are struck with Sickness, as a Punishment for some notorious Sins. Such are enjoined to make special Confession of the Sins they take to have been the* Cause *of their Distemper. The great Effect of the Prayers of Holy and Inspired Ministers, for the Recovery of such People. The happy Advantage of bringing a Sinner from Ignorance and Vicious Courses, to true Repentance.*

A. D. 60.

|| Chap. iv. 13, 17.

1 GO to now ye rich men, weep and howl for your miseries that shall come upon you.

2 Your riches are corrupted, and your garments moth-eaten.

3 Your gold and silver is cankered, and the rust of them shall be a witness against you, and shall eat your flesh as it were fire: ye have heaped treasure together for the last days.

1. 2. & 3. IT is not without good reason that I warn || you all against a too eager and confident pursuit after worldly riches. For let the worldlings of the *Jewish* nation consider now, and behold, to what a lamentable end those principles are likely, in a short time, to reduce them; when their riches shall perish, their grandeur be eclipsed, and themselves be destroyed, by a judgment most dreadful and exemplary.

4 Behold, the hire of the labourers, which have reaped down your fields, which is of you kept back by fraud, crieth, and the cries of them which have reaped, are entered into the ears of the Lord of Sabaoth.

4. *You* that to enrich yourselves, have defrauded and oppressed others, even robbing the hireling of his wages, will shortly feel the effects of such injustice, in the resentments of a just and all-powerful God.

5 Ye have lived in pleasure on the earth and been wanton: ye have nourished your hearts as in a day of slaughter.

5. *You* that have abused the plentiful provisions of Providence, to riot and excess, will find you have been but fatting yourselves up, like sacrifices, for the day of slaughter *.

6 Ye have condemned and killed the just, and he doth not resist you †.

6. *You* that have crucified your own innocent Messiah and Saviour; and still, with unrelenting hearts, are persecuting his *disciples*, from the

* Ver. 5.—[As in a day of slaughter.] Note, This phrase may, perhaps, more properly signify, *As men do in a time of feasting upon slain sacrifices.*

† Ver. 6. [And he doth not resist you, or else interrogatively, ὐκ ἀντιτάσσεται ὑμῖν; Doth he not (in return) now set himself against you?] A much more consistent and clearer sense; agreeable to chap. iv. 6. and 1 Pet. v. 5. See also Dr. Bentley's *Remarks upon Free Thinking;* where there is given, by that admirable critic, a most ingenious conjecture, for a yet clearer sense of this passage.

the ſame wicked principles, by which your forefathers A. D. 60.
ſlew the ancient *prophets*; will ſoon experience the direful conſequences of ſuch incurable malice and ingratitude.

7 Be patient therefore, brethren, unto the coming of the Lord: behold, the huſbandman waiteth for the precious fruit of the earth, and hath long patience for it, until he receive the early and latter rain.

8 Be ye alſo patient: ſtabliſh your hearts, for the coming of the Lord draweth nigh.

7. & 8. Wherefore, my dear brethren, that are *converted* to his perſecuted *religion*, bear all your preſent ſufferings with courage and patience. Imitate the induſtrious huſbandman, that patiently waits the ſeaſons of the year, to produce him the fruits of his coſt and labour. With infinitely better aſſurance, may you depend upon Chriſt for * a ſpeedy deliverance from theſe your perſecutors, and a glorious reward for your perſeverance.

9 Grudge not one againſt another, brethren, leſt ye be condemned: behold * the judge ſtandeth before the door.

9. Diſcover no fretful impatience, no thirſt of revenge againſt your enemies, or one another. For that would be to incur the ſame puniſhment due to *them*. God himſelf will very * ſhortly be your juſt avenger, and you have no need to prevent him, in what he will ſo ſoon and certainly perform for you.

10 Take, my brethren, the prophets, who have ſpoken in the name of the Lord, for an example of ſuffering, affliction, and of patience.

11 Behold, we count them happy which endure. Ye have heard of the patience of Job, and have ſeen the end of the Lord: that the Lord is very pitiful, and of tender mercy.

10. &. 11. Let the courageous examples of God's true *prophets* in all ages, ſpirit and ſupport you. Remember Job, that moſt afflicted of all men; how deeply he ſuffered, and how amply he was recompenced. And from hence aſſure yourſelves, God can never fail, in due time, to reſcue and reward *every* faithful ſervant.

12. And

* [The coming of the Lord draweth nigh. The Judge ſtandeth before the door;] viz. The deſtruction of Jeruſalem, which was but a few years after this epiſtle was written.

A. D. 60.

12 But above all things, my brethren, ſwear not, neither by heaven, neither by the earth, neither by any other oath: but let your yea, be yea, and your nay, nay, * leſt ye fall into condemnation.

12. And let me particularly warn you, that no examples, no provocations whatever draw you into the vice of common ſwearing, and invoking the name of God upon light and needleſs occaſions. Swear not ſo much as by any *creature* of God, in common converſation, as the Jews accuſtom themſelves to do, and vainly pretend there is no evil in ſuch kind of * oaths. For no oath can be made by any *creature* *, but muſt have an *ultimate* reſpect to the *Creator*, whoſe creature it is. Be therefore careful, always to ſpeak truth, and uſe no other means to gain belief, than a modeſt *affirmation* or plain *denial*. For every degree beyond this, beſpeaks ſome ‡ falſe deſign, and is ſinful ‡ and condemnable.

13 Is any among you afflicted, let him pray: Is any merry, let him ſing pſalms.

|| κακοπαθεῖ.

§ εὐθυμεῖ.

13. Improve every condition of life to a religious advantage. Let *prayer* be the refuge of the || afflicted; and devout *praiſes*, the exerciſe of them that are in eaſe § and proſperity.

14 Is any ſick among you? let him call for the elders of the church, and let them pray over him, anointing him with oil in the name of the Lord:

15 And the prayer of faith ſhall ſave the ſick, and the Lord ſhall raiſe him up; and if he have committed

14. & 15. When any Chriſtian is viſited with ſickneſs, eſpecially any diſeaſe inflicted on him for ſome *notorious ſin*; let no *charms* and conjurations be uſed over him, as the Jews are † now a-days wont to do, when they anoint their ſick with oil: But let the Chriſtian *miniſters* be ſent for, to intercede with God, by fervent prayer. They may indeed, uſe the *anointing* as a *natural* remedy, but not in a *ſuperſtitious*

---

* [Nor by any other oath, μήτε ἄλλον τινὰ ὅρκον. Nor by any ſuch kind of oath.] So in Mark iv. 41. Luke viii. 25. Τίς ἄρα οὗτός ἐστιν, What *manner* of perſon is this. See Matth. v. 34. 35.

‡ [Leſt ye fall into condemnation, or εἰς ὑπὸ κρίσιν, as ſome copies read it.

† See Lightfoot Harm. N. T. Burnet Artic. p. 289.

mitted ſins, they ſhall be forgiven him.

ſtitious way. Let them lay all the A. D. 60.
ſtreſs in the devout *prayers* of *inſpired* miniſters, put up in Chriſt's name, for a bleſſing upon that means. And thoſe prayers ſhall become effectual for the recovery of a true penitent, and the forgiveneſs of thoſe ſins that were the cauſe of his diſtemper *.

16 Confeſs your faults one to another, and pray one for another, that ye may be healed: the effectual fervent prayer of a righteous man availeth much.

16. In all ſuch *extraordinary* ſickneſſes as theſe, let the ſick perſon freely acknowledge and confeſs to his *miniſter* the *particular* ſins he hath reaſon to conclude brought the diſtemper as a *ſpecial* puniſhment upon him. And then let the miniſter appoint and pray for him, as before preſcribed, ver. 14. for God will have great reſpect to theſe prayers of ‡ *miniſters*, which now, in the *firſt* times of the *goſpel*, are directed and aſſiſted by the inſpirations || of the *Holy Ghoſt*.

‡ δικαίου.
|| δέησις ἐνεργουμένη. See 1 Cor. 4, 5, and Chap. xiv. 15, 17.

17 Elias was a man ſubject to like paſſions as we are, and he prayed earneſtly that it might not rain: and it rained not on the earth by the ſpace of three years and ſix months.
18 And he prayed again, and the heavens gave rain, and the earth brought forth her fruit.

17. & 18. And, as the prayers of Elijah who was but a mortal *man*, any more than many Chriſtian *miniſters* are now), availed to ſtop the rains upon the land of Iſrael, for three years and ſix months together, in the days of Ahab; and then to bring them again; So ſhall theſe prayers of men inſpired by the *Holy Spirit*, now under the *goſpel*, be as available for the cure of theſe diſtempers, or any ſuch miraculous event, as God ſhall think convenient, for the promotion and encouragement of his true religion.

19 Brethren, if any of you do err from the

19. & 20. And, to conclude, let all Chriſtians whatever (eſpecially *miniſters*,

* [The ſick.]—The ſame *ſickneſs*, and the ſame kind of *ſins*, as in Matth. ix 2, 6, 7.—x. 8. Mark vi. 13 1 Cor xi. 32. See the paraphraſe fully vindicated, in the excellent Dr. Clagett, in his diſcourſe of *Extreme Unction*, Part I. Printed in 1687.

A. D. 60. the truth, and one convert him,

20 Let him know, that he which converteth the sinnerfrom the error of his way, shall save a soul from death, and shall * hide a multitude of sins.

ministers, whose * special office it is), remember, that for them to be instrumental in thus reducing a sinner to the sense of his miscarriages, and to true repentance for them, is the noblest office they can perform. Let them value themselves as instruments of saving a *soul* from destruction, and covering all its sins; an act of infinitely greater value than the restoring a sinner to his *bodily* health; and as much preferable, as *eternal* is to *temporal* good, and, as the *soul* is to the *body* †.

---

* ἀδελφοί—τίς—See Dr. Claget, Sup. p. 40, 41.

† [Shall hide a multitude of sins.] Both Dr. Hammond and Dr. Whitby makes this refer to the sins of the person who *does*, not who *receives* the charitable office of conversion. But, as I have chosen to follow the sense of Dr. Claget, as much more natural, I refer the reader to his own choice, when he has seen how judiciously he has cleared the sense of these verses. Extreme Unction, pag. 40, 41.

A PARA-

A

PARAPHRASE

ON

THE FIRST EPISTLE GENERAL

OF

St. PETER.

THE PREFACE.

§ 1. CONCERNING the *author* of these two Epistles, there can be no doubt, all ages having ascribed them to the Apostle St. Peter. Author

§ 2. In the year of Christ 67 or 68, in the latter end of Nero's reign, St. Peter and St. Paul are agreed on to have suffered martyrdom at Rome. They having, therefore, both of them declared their deaths, to be near at hand, St. Paul, in 2 Tim. iv. 6. and St. Peter here, 2 Epistle i. 14. makes it most natural to conclude, the *date* of these two *epistles*, with that of 2 Tim. to have been in the year 66 or 67, as judiciously stated by Dr. Pearson, Dr. Mills, and Dr. Whitby; to the eternal confutation of the Romanists, who in favour of their darling notion of St. Peter's being at Rome, and for 25 years *bishop* there, would place it in the year 44, in direct contradiction to the history of the Acts, and the most evident passages in these *epistles* themselves. Time.

§ 3. They are dated from Rome, which, for its notorious degree of *idolatry*, vice, and superstition, is figuratively styled Babylon here, and in Rev. xvii. and xviii. (see note on cap. v. ver. 13.) Place.

§ 4. The design of the apostle, with relation to the Christians of these provinces, is evidently the same with that Occasion.

that of St. Paul to the Hebrews, and of St. James, to their whole *dispersion*, viz. The Jews being now, from Judea to the utmost bounds of their dispersion, arrived to the utmost degree of impiety, lust, rage, and distraction; their aversion to the Roman government prompting them to *sedition*; and their unbounded zeal for the *ceremonial* law exciting them to persecute all *Christians*, without any relentings of mercy or humanity, and to hearken to the pretences of every *false prophet*; gave occasion to St. Peter's advices here directed, chiefly to the *Jewish* converts, but not excluding such *Gentile* Christians as had been either formerly proselyted to the *Jewish* religion, or were newly converted from * *heathenism* to Christianity. To support them under their heavy persecutions; to persuade the *Jewish* converts particularly to have no hand in the rebellion against Cæsar, or his officers; and to spirit them *all* to perseverance in the pure and peaceable profession of their *Christianity*, against the false doctrines, and impure practices of the *Jewish* zealots, or of such *heretics* as were then spawned from those people, as was Nicholas of Antioch (Acts vi. 5.) whose lewd *sect* is taken notice of by St. John, Revel. ii. 15. and is generally thought to be referred to, in some passages of these *epistles*.

* See cap. i. 18.—ii 10. —iv 3. and 2 Pet. i. 1.

§ 5. I shall only add, That the destruction of Jerusalem drawing now very near, St. Peter presents it in the same expressions, taken in the same latitude with those of the ancient *prophets*, our Saviour and St. Paul, upon the same prudential reasons: those phrases, *the day of the Lord*, *the coming*, *or revelation of Jesus Christ*, referring both to the *particular* judgments on the *Jewish* nation, and to that of the whole *world* in *general*. For which I refer the reader to the *Preface* to the Thessalonians: and for what is here urged in the *relative* duties, I refer him to the *Preface* of the Ephesians, § 4. Let the learned reader also consult the great and learned Sir Isaac Newton's Observat. on the Apoc. cap. 1. where he will see still a clearer light into the *time*, *date*, and *design*, of this and other *epistles*.

CHAP.

CHAP. I.

The Direction and Salutation. The Apostle blesseth God for the great Mercies and Privileges of the Gospel Religion. Comforts both Jewish and Gentile Christians under their present Persecutions, from the Sense of those happy Blessings, is the Truth and Certainty of them, as foretold by the Ancient Prophets, and now exactly fulfilled. Exhorts them to the pure and steady Practice of their Religion, from the great Consideration of their Redemption by the Blood of Jesus Christ.

1 PETER an apostle of Jesus Christ, to the strangers scattered throughout Pontus, Galatia, Cappadocia, Asia, and Bithynia,

1. PETER, an apostle of Jesus Christ, sendeth this epistle to the converted Jews of the ancient *dispersion*, in Pontus, Galatia, Cappadocia, the provinces of the Lesser Asia, and Bithynia. Not forgetting the *Gentile* * Christians of those parts.

Written A. D 66.

* See chap. i. 18. ii. 10. iv. 3, 4, 5. & 2 Pet. i. 1.

2 Elect according to the foreknowledge of God the Father, through sanctification of the spirit unto obedience, and sprinkling of the blood of Jesus Christ: Grace unto you, and peace be multiplied.

2. To all you that have embraced the gracious covenant of the *gospel*; a covenant that is ratified ‡ and confirmed by the blood of Christ, and entitles you to the gifts and graces of the *Holy Spirit*; privileges that God originally designed, and by his prophets formerly promised, to the *Christian* church. Wishing you the abundance of divine favour and happiness.

‡ ῥαντισμοῦ. See Heb. xii. 24 Exod. xxiv. 8.

3 Blessed *be* the God and Father of our Lord Jesus Christ, which according to his abundant mercy, hath begotten us again unto a lively hope, by the resurrection of Jesus Christ from the dead,

To an inheritance incorruptible, and undefiled, and that fadeth not away, reserved in heaven for you,

3. & 4. Expressing my humblest thanks to God, the Father of our Lord Jesus Christ, for the inexpressible mercy of giving us Christians so sure a prospect of the never-fading and eternal happiness of heaven, by the resurrection of Jesus Christ, our Lord and Head.

5. And

A. D. 60.

5 Who are kept by the power of God through faith unto salvation, ready to be revealed in the last time.

|| ἐν καιρῷ ἐσχάτῳ.

5. And for preserving and supporting us, by his almighty power, under all our afflictions and temptations, to persevere in the faith of this his last || and great dispensation of the *gospel*, whereby we shall not fail of complete glory and happiness, at the final day of judgment.

6 Wherein ye greatly rejoice, though now for a season (if need be) ye are in heaviness through manifold temptations.

7 That the trial of your faith being much more precious than of gold that perisheth, though it be tried with fire, might be found unto praise, and honour, and glory, at the appearing of Jesus Christ:

6. & 7. This is what *you*, as good Christians, cannot but make the subject of your utmost joy and satisfaction. Looking on the worst of present evils as only so many happy opportunities of exercising your faith, improving your virtue, and brightening that future crown you are then to receive; and consequently to be of more real advantage to you than all the riches and fading glories this world can afford.

8 Whom having not seen, ye love; in whom, though now ye see *him* not, yet believing, ye rejoice with joy unspeakable, and full of glory.

9 Receiving the end of your faith, *even* the salvation of *your* souls.

8. & 9. Thus upon reasonable and sufficient evidence, you embrace a Messiah you never *personally* knew; and believe the doctrine and promises of a Saviour you never *actually* saw. This fills you with the inexpressible and glorious hopes of that eternal salvation which is the sure reward of such as are possessed with a faith so rational and well-grounded.

10 Of which salvation the prophets have inquired and searched diligently, who prophesied of the grace *that should come* unto you:

10. & 11. This is that gracious dispensation of religion for the future happiness of mankind, so exactly described and punctually foretold by the ancient prophets, men inspired by the Spirit of

11 Searching what, or what manner of time the Spirit * of Christ which was in them did signify, when it testified before-hand the sufferings of Christ, and the glory that should follow.

* of this very Christ, to foretel both the *time* and glorious *fruits* of his sufferings in relation to himself, and all his true disciples.

12 Unto whom it was revealed, that not unto themselves, but unto us they did minister the things which are now reported unto you by them that have preached the gospel unto you, with the Holy Ghost sent down from heaven; which things the angels desire to look into.

12. For, as to the *time*, they knew and expresly declared it was not to be transacted in *their* days, but spoke of it as *future*, representing it just as it has now been actually revealed by Christ himself, and declared to you and all Christians, by us his *apostles*, endowed with the same Holy Spirit for that purpose. And this dispensation of the *gospel* is so abundant in divine wisdom, justice and mercy toward mankind, that not only *prophets* foretold it with pleasure, but the very *angels* themselves cannot but contemplate upon it with delight and astonishment.

13 Wherefore gird up the loins of your mind, be sober, and hope to the end, for the grace that is to be brought unto you at the revelation of Jesus Christ;

13. Let this consideration then arm you with vigilance, courage, and constancy in a profession attended with such blessings as these of the *Christian* * religion are, which you are so certain to enjoy at the final appearance of * Christ to judgment.

* ἐν ἀποκαλύψει Ἰησῦ Χριςῦ.

14 As obedient children, not fashioning yourselves according to the former lusts in your ignorance:

15 But as he which hath called you is holy, so be ye holy in all manner of conversation;

14. & 15. Show yourselves true disciples of Christ, by reforming the irregularities of your former notions and practices, and imitating the divine Author of your religion in holiness and purity of life.

* Ver. 11. [The spirit of Christ which was in them.] The meaning is, either the same Spirit of God, which inspired the *prophets* formerly, and dwelt in Christ more fully afterward: Or else, the Spirit by whose inspirations the *prophets* foretold the time and circumstances of Christ's sufferings, and is therefore called the *Spirit* of Christ. The *former* seems to be the more natural sense.

A. D. 66.

16 Becauſe it is written, Be ye holy, for I am holy.

16. For thoſe expreſſions (Lev. ii. 44.---xix. 2.—xx. 7, 26.) wherein the *Jewiſh* people are exhorted *to be holy as God is holy*, are much more engaging upon us of the *Chriſtian* church.

17 And if you call on the Father, who without reſpect of perſons judgeth according to every man's work, paſs the time of your ſojourning here in fear:

17. And this does moſt ſpecially concern ſuch of you as are newly converted from the *heathen* to the *Chriſtian* religion, from the worſhip of *idols* to that of the *one true God*. Now that you are received into the true *church* of God, with the ſame goodneſs and mercy as the *Jews* themſelves are, and ſhall be judged and rewarded equally with *them; you* are obliged to particular care and watchfulneſs over your future conduct.

18 Foraſmuch as ye know that ye were not redeemed with corruptible things, *as* ſilver and gold, from your vain converſation received by tradition from your fathers:

19 But with the precious blood of Chriſt, as of a lamb without blemiſh and without ſpot.

18. & 19. You ought to conſider yourſelves as captives redeemed from a ſtate of ignorance and *idolatry*, wherein you were originally educated. And that the purchaſe was not procured by the moſt valuable thing *this* world could afford, but coſt the blood even of Chriſt himſelf *the Son of God*; a perſon of moſt exalted dignity and perfect innocence.

20 Who verily was fore-ordained before the foundation of the world, but was manifeſt in theſe laſt times for you;

21 Who by him do believe in God that raiſed him up from the dead, and gave him glory, that your

20. & 21. Even that *Meſſiah*, originally deſigned by God for the redemption of all mankind; but, though promiſed from the firſt, and all along deſcribed by the *Jewiſh prophets*, to that people; yet was not *actually* ſent into the world for that purpoſe, till this laſt and great diſpenſation of the *goſpel*; wherein his religion was intended to be propoſed equally to *you* † and *them*, by his *apoſtles*, and demonſtrated to us all, by his reſurrection from the dead, as a ſure pledge of *our* future happineſs, upon our ſincere obedience. So that, by being *Chriſtians*, you do not forſake

† δι ὑμᾶς.

God

faith and hope might be * in God.

God (as the obstinate *Jews* vainly pretend) but do most effectually .* believe in him.

A. D. 66.

22 Seeing ye have purified your souls in obeying the truth through the Spirit, unto unfeigned love of the brethren; *see that ye* love one another with a pure heart fervently:

22. And since you have engaged to reform your lives, by obedience to this pure and *spiritual* religion, one of the chief duties whereof, is an universal love and charity to *all* your Christian *brethren;* be sure to practise that *principal* virtue with the utmost ardour and sincerity.

23 Being born again, not of corruptible seed, but of incorruptible, by the word of God, which liveth and abideth for ever.

23. Remember that by embracing this profession, you become the *church* and people of God, in a sense much more excellent than the Jews were by their natural descent from Abraham and the *patriarchs;* or than any *proselyte* could be, by joining himself to their external and *ceremonial* worship. You are regenerated and made the children of God, by the belief of those *gospel* doctrines, the habitual practice whereof will work in you those excellent graces and divine virtues, that will for ever adorn and make you happy ||.

|| See John i. 12, 13. and here ver. 42.

24 For all flesh *is* as grass, and all the glory of man, as the flower of grass. The grass withereth, and the flower thereof falleth away:

25 But the word of the Lord endureth for ever. And this is the word which by the gospel is preached unto you.

24. & 25. Those privileges of natural *descent* the Jews so much boast of, the succession in rich and noble families, by any civil relation or institution, are mere *external* and fading blessings: As Isaiah formerly represented them. But the blessing of being taken into God's *church*, by embracing the revelation of Jesus Christ, is of the utmost and everlasting consequence to us. And thus the gospel we preach to you is truly what Isaiah there described it, "The word of the Lord that endureth for ever," Isa. xl. 6, 7, 8.

* Ver. 21. [That your faith and hope might be in God, ὥςε τὴν πίςιν ὑμῶν—εἶναι εἰς Θεόν. So that your faith—is in God.]

CHAP. II.

The Loving and Charitable Temper spoken of chap. i. 22. *further and particularly recommended, from the great Example of Christ; and the Blessings of his Religion. The believing* Gentiles *are received into its Privileges, while the infidel* Jews *are rejected; according to the Scripture* Prophecies. *The* Jewish *Christians exhorted to pay all due Obedience to the* Emperor *and his* Officers; *as obliged thereto by their* Christianity, *and as the only Means to avoid the scandalous Character of being* Seditious, *as the* Gentiles *were apt to represent the* Christians, *in common with the rest of the* Jewish *Nation. Christian Servants or* Slaves *obliged to serve and respect even their* Heathen *Masters, though severe toward them for their* Religion's *sake: Encouraged thereto by the Example of Christ's Meekness and Patience under his Sufferings.*

A. D. 66.

1 WHerefore laying aside all malice and all guile and hypocrisies, and envies, and all evil speakings,
2 As new born babes desire the sincere milk of the word, that ye may grow thereby:

1. & 2. THus are you * regenerated by the *Christian* faith. And therefore, as new born children are to be fed with the most simple and harmless diet; so ought *you*, now, most carefully to avoid all those principles of treachery, hypocrisy, envy, and calumny, to which the *Jewish* † people are so miserably prone, and to put in practice the pure and ‡ reasonable precepts of the *gospel*, whereby you may improve in all virtue and holiness.

* Chap. i. 23, 24, 25.
† Josephus. Jam. i. 21.
‡ τὸ λογικὸν γάλα. Rom. xii. 1.

3 If so be ye have tasted that the Lord is gracious.

3. Those contrary graces of a gentle, meek, || and kind disposition, being so fully recommended to you by Christ your merciful Redeemer and great example.

|| χρηστὸς.

4. & 5. Look

A. D. 66.

4 To whom coming, as unto a living stone, disallowed indeed of men, but chosen of God, and precious,

5 Ye also, * as lively stones, are built up a spiritual house, an holy priesthood to offer up spiritual sacrifices, acceptable to God by Jesus Christ.

4. & 5. Look upon yourselves as members of *his* religion; both *Jewish* and *Gentile* Christians being equally parts of that noble fabric, the *church*; of which *he* is the foundation and corner-stone, uniting you both into one building, far exceeding that of the *Jewish temple*. And, though the *Jewish* council rejected and despised him, yet has God demonstrated him to be the true *Messiah*; and *you*, as members of his church, are capable to offer such truly spiritual services to God, as infinitely surpass their legal and *ceremonial* sacrifices; and are invested with such honours and privileges as *their* imperfect dispensation have no pretence to*.

6 Wherefore it is contained in the scripture, Behold, I lay in Sion a chief corner-stone, elect, precious; and he that believeth on him shall not be confounded.

6. Agreeably to that prophecy of Isa. xxviii. 16. concerning Christ: "Representing him as the Head of a new and more perfect religion, attended with more valuable promises and privileges, undoubtedly to be bestowed on all the Jewish people that would embrace and obey him."

7 Unto you therefore which believe he is precious; but unto them which be disobedient, the stone which the builders disallowed, the same is made the head of the corner.

8 And a stone of stumbling, and a rock of offence, even to them

7. & 8. Which character of him is now fulfilled to you *Christian* believers, that enjoy the privileges of the *gospel*. But, to the obstinate unbelievers of *that nation*, are as justly applicable those words of the Psalmist, relating to the same *Messiah*; Psal. cxviii. 22. "The stone which the builders (*i. e.* the Jewish council) rejected, is become the head of the corner," i. e. the head and foundation

* [Lively stones, a spiritual house, a holy priesthood,] Expressions all alluding to the *Jewish* temple and priesthood, and intended to show the excellency of the *Christian* above the *Jewish* religion.

A. D. 66.

them which ſtumble at the word, being diſobedient, whereunto alſo they * were appointed.

tion of God's true church. In them alſo is completed that prediction of Iſa. viii. 14. repreſenting Chriſt as a "ſtone of ſtumbling, error, prejudice and deſtruction," to which God has in ſo juſt judgment, given *that* people over, for their incurable malice and ingratitude*.

9 But ye are a choſen generation, a royal prieſthood, an holy nation, a peculiar people; that ye ſhould ſhow forth the praiſes of him who hath called you out of darkneſs into his marvellous light;

10 Which in time paſt were not a people, but are now the people of God: which had not obtained mercy, but now have obtained mercy.

† See ver. 5.

9. & 10. As much, therefore, as the *Jewiſh* zealots are apt to deſpiſe you *Gentile* Chriſtians, as a people that never were in covenant with God, nor belonged to his ancient *church*; yet even *you* may now aſſure yourſelves, that, by your embracing *Chriſtianity*, your condition is as much different from what it was, as light is from darkneſs; and all the ſacred *characters*, † great *titles*, and religious *privileges*, *that* nation ſo much value themſelves upon, are *yours* now in a much better and truer ſenſe than ever they were *theirs*. So that you are capable of offering up a ſervice to God more pure and acceptable than *they*, by their *ceremonial worſhip*, can pretend to.

11 Dearly beloved, I beſeech you as ſtrangers and pilgrims, abſtain from fleſhly luſts, which war againſt the ſoul.

11. Wherefore, dear brethren, whether *Gentile* or *Jewiſh* Chriſtians, make it your utmoſt endeavour to anſwer this excellent deſign of your religion, for the glory of God, and your own happineſs,

* Ver. 8. [Whereunto alſo they were appointed:] Or elſe εἰς ὃ καὶ ἐτέθησαν—[To which (*prejudice and infidelity*) they were wilfully and habitually diſpoſed:] In the ſame ſenſe with τεταγμένοι εἰς ζωὴν αἰώνιον, [Men well diſpoſed for eternal life,] Acts xiii. 48. But it is, perhaps, moſt natural to refer the εἰς ὃ καὶ ἐτέθησαν, to the τῷ λόγῳ, [the word]. Thus—"They, being diſobedient, ſtumbled at that word to which "they were appointed, viz. for light and inſtruction."

pinefs, by the conqueft of all thofe fenfual appetites A. D. 66.
that corrupt the true principles of the mind. Place not your aims and hopes upon *temporal* pleafures: Look upon the prefent *world* only as a paffage toward the more certain and durable happinefs of *heaven*.

12 Having your converfation honeft among the Gentiles, that whereas they fpeak againft you as evil doers, they may by your good works which they fhall behold, glorify God in the day of vifitation.

12. I warn the *Jewifh* converts efpecially, to confult the credit and intereft of their profeffion, by a prudent and decent behaviour among the *Gentile* people; and particularly by paying all due obedience to the government of the *country* you live in. This will be the beft means to take off that prejudice and mifreprefentation you lie under, among the Romans, as a people as feditious * and averfe to their laws, as the reft of the † *Jewifh* nation is. And, by thus expreffing your peaceable fubjection to their government, you will avoid the vengeance of God, wherewith the reft of the finful world will be feverely ‡ chaftifed; and, whenever you are called to account before the Roman ‡ judicatures, will be able to give an honourable account of yourfelves, and caufe all people to think and fpeak well of your religion.

* κακοποιῶν

† Jofeph. de Bel. Jud. Lib. II. Cap. 8.

‡ ἡμέρα ἐπισκοπῆς.

13 Submit yourfelves to every ordinance of man for the Lord's fake, whether it be to the king as fupreme,

14 Or unto governors, as unto them that are fent by him for the punifhment of evil doers, and for the praife of them that do well.

13. & 14. Nor let your own *private* fafety be the only motive of obedience to the government under which Providence has placed you; but know, you are bound to it by the law of *Chriftianity*, which makes no alteration in *civil rights*. As therefore, the Roman Emperor and his deputy *officers*, are placed over you, for the fame good purpofes as *Jewifh* princes or governors were formerly appointed over the *Jewifh* nation, viz. the prefervation of the public peace, the fecurity of the rights and properties of the people committed to their charge, by fuitable re-

wards

wards and punishments; *all* ought to pay them a just obedience and subjection *.

* See Rom. xiii. 1. &c.

† οὕτως ἀγαθοποιοῦντες.

‡ See verse 12.

15 For so is the will of God, that with well doing we may put to silence the ignorance of foolish men.

15. Thus † you will at once promote your own safety, obviate the prejudices ‡ your character is aspersed with, and discharge a most principal duty of your holy religion.

16 As free, and not using your liberty for a cloak of maliciousness, but as the servants of God.

|| As free; See John viii. 32, 33, —36.

16. The Jews indeed, under the notion of being the seed of Abraham, and under the immediate government of *Heaven*, || proudly disdain to be subject to any *powers* but those of their *own* nation and religion. You *Christians* are now entitled to liberties || and privileges much nobler than *theirs*. But these privileges are purely *spiritual;* and you ought by no means to abuse them into a pretence for seditious practices, and disturbance of the *civil government* you live under, as the Jews do.

17 Honour all men. Love the brotherhood. Fear God. Honour the king.

17. In fine, therefore, give all ranks of men the respect due to their character. Bear an affectionate regard to all your fellow *Christians*, of what denomination soever. Adhere firmly to your religion, and reverence the *emperor* and his *ministers*, with the honours due to temporal governors.

18 Servants be subject to your masters with all fear, not only to the good and gentle, but also to the froward.

18. Let all Christians that are servants or *slaves*, to *heathen* masters, continue to serve them with all fidelity and respect; not only submitting to their *reasonable* commands, but also patiently bearing their frowardness toward them on account of their *religion*. Think not that *Christianity* exempts any one from his *natural* and *civil* obligations, as the *Jewish* zealots are apt to imgine §.

§ See Pref. to the Eph. § 4.

19 For this is thank-worthy, if a man for conscience toward

19. & 20. Not to repine at the punishments you *really* deserve, by neglecting your master's business,

A. D. 66.

toward God endure grief, ſuffering wrongfully.

20 For what glory is it, if when ye be buffeted for your faults, ye ſhall take it patiently? but if when ye do well, and ſuffer for it, ye take it patiently: this is acceptable with God.

neſs, has no great virtue in it: but to endure, with an even and contented mind, the hardſhips they lay on you for being Chriſtians, and diſcharging your conſcience towards God, this is a true inſtance, and will be rewarded by God as a generous act of obedience.

21 For even hereunto were ye called: becauſe Chriſt alſo ſuffered for us, leaving us an example, that we ſhould follow his ſteps.

21. This is indeed agreeable to your *religion*, which you are now to conſider as a ſtate of ſuffering and diſcipline. Your very *profeſſion* is, to imitate the meekneſs of Chriſt, your great *head* and *example*; and to ſuffer for *his* ſake, who has undergone ſo much for *you*.

22 Who did no ſin, neither was guile found in his mouth.

23 Who when he was reviled, reviled not again; when he ſuffered, he threatened not, but committed himſelf to him that judgeth righteouſly.

22. & 23. For thus did the innocent and unſpotted Jeſus, while he ſuffered for the ſins of others, having no blemiſhes of his own, return none of the reproaches caſt upon him, nor flung out ſo much as one impatient threat againſt his mercileſs crucifiers; but perfectly reſigned himſelf and his cauſe to God, the great and righteous Judge.

24 Who his own ſelf bare our ſins in his own body on the tree, that we being dead to ſin, ſhould live unto righteouſneſs; by whoſe ſtripes ye were healed.

24. So complete an example have you in a Saviour, who ought the moſt ſtrongly to engage you to an imitation of him, in this, and all other inſtances of true virtue; ſince the very ſufferings and patience propoſed to you were the means whereby he redeemed you from ſin and death.

25 For ye were as ſheep going aſtray, but are now returned unto

25. In ſhort, both *Jewiſh* and *Gentile* Chriſtians are to reflect upon themſelves to have been in ſuch a ſtate

A. D. 66. unto the Shepherd and Bishop of your souls.

a state of ignorance and vice, before their conversion, as might well bear the comparison of the *prophet*, resembling you to "sheep that were lost and gone astray," (Isaiah liii. 6. See also Jerem. l. 6, 17.) But now, by the *Christian religion*, you are recovered again, and put under the conduct of a *Saviour* and *Governor*, whom it is your utmost happiness, as well as duty, to imitate and obey.

CHAP. III.

Differences in Religious Principles ought to be no Pretence for Christian Husbands *or* Wives *to withdraw the Duties of that Relation even from* Heathens, *to whom they are married. The Christian* Wife *ought to endeavour to win over such* Husband *to the Christian* Faith, *by the singular Kindness of her Behaviour, her modest Garb, and virtuous Conversation. The Christian* Husband *to do the same toward such* Wife, *by Expressions of the utmost Tenderness and Affection, Unanimity, Candour, Peace, and Justice recommended, upon the same Reasons of Interest and Duty, as in the foregoing Chapter, especially that of the Example of Christ, who is now exalted to be our powerful Head and* Saviour. *A Comparison between the* Ark *of Noah, and the* Baptism *of Christians.*

* See Chap. ii. 13—18.

1 LIkewise, ye wives, be in subjection to your own husbands, that if any obey not the word, they also may without the word be won by the conversation of the wives:

2 While they behold your chaste conversation

1. & 2. TO proceed then: * the same reasons that oblige Christians to be peaceable *subjects*, even under *heathen* governments, and faithful *servants*, even to *infidel* masters, are equally strong for your discharge of all other *relative duties*, under the same circumstances. Thus, all Christian

versation coupled with fear.

Christian *wives* ought to pay all due submission and respect to their *husbands*, though *unconverted*; ‡ endeavouring, if possible, by a meek, chaste, loving, and modest behaviour, to win them over to the *Christian faith*, that hath so visible good effects upon their conduct.

A. D. 66.

‡ See 1 Cor. vii. 12, 13, 14, 15, 16.

3 Whose adorning, let it not be that outward adorning, of plaiting the hair, and of wearing of gold, or of putting on of apparel:

4 But let it be the hidden man of the heart, in that which is not corruptible, even *the ornament* of a meek and quiet spirit, which is in the sight of God of great price.

3. & 4. Let these *women* strive to recommend themselves to their *husbands* affections, not by the nicety and sumptuousness of their dress, and outward gaiety of their persons; but by the virtue of their lives, and sweetness of their tempers: those lovely ornaments of the mind, that infinitely surpass all external beauty and artificial accomplishments, and render them amiable in the eyes of God.

5 For after this manner in the old time, the holy women also who trusted in God adorned themselves, being in subjection unto their own husbands.

6 Even as Sarah obeyed Abraham, calling him Lord, whose daughters ye are as long as ye do well, and are not afraid * with any amazement.

5. & 6. In this you will truly imitate those famous women, that were wives of the *patriarchs*, and *mothers* of your *nation*: you will approve yourselves the genuine daughters of Sarah, that dutiful spouse of faithful Abraham, so long as you keep firm to your duty *, and be discouraged from no instance of it by any dangers and inconveniences.

7 Likewise ye husbands, dwell with them according to knowledge, giving honour

7. In like manner, let all Christian *husbands* treat their *wives* in a tender and condescending manner, as the weaker *sex*; performing all conjugal

* [With any amazement;] alluding, perhaps, to that passage of Sarah, Gen. xx. 20. or Gen. xviii. 15.

A. D. 66.

* See 1 Cor. vii. ut supra.

nour unto the wife as unto the weaker vessel, and as being heirs together of the grace of life, that your prayers be not hindered.

conjugal duties to them *, as Christianity requires; looking upon a *Christian* wife in the notion of an heiress of the same heavenly happiness with himself, and endeavouring to render an *unbelieving* one so, by converting her to the *faith*, by this virtuous and obliging carriage toward her: that so their religious devotions be not hindered, by any differences in principles, or disagreement of tempers.

8 Finally, be ye all of one mind, having compassion one for another; love as brethren, be pitiful, be courteous:

8. In fine: be all unanimous in your principles, compassionate to the infirmities of each other; and let your whole conversation run in that strain of charity, tenderness, and courtesy that becomes Christian *brethren*.

9 Not rendering evil for evil, or railing for railing: but contrariwise blessing, knowing that ye are thereunto called, that ye should inherit a blessing.

9. Seek no revenge against your persecutors, but return prayers and good wishes to such as revile and reproach you: remembering that the blessings you enjoy by your *Christian* profession, are the strongest argument to make you desire the good and happiness of all your fellow-creatures.

10 For he that will love life, and see good days, let him refrain his tongue from evil, and his lips that they speak no guile.

11 Let him eschew evil and do good, let him seek peace and ensue it.

12 For the eyes of the Lord are over the righteous, and his ears are open unto their prayers: but the face

10. 11. & 12. Consider the blessings annexed to an even, just and peaceable disposition (Psal. xxxiv. 12, 13, &c.) " What man is he that desireth (a happy life) and loveth to see (many) good days? Keep thy tongue from evil (speaking) and thy lips from speaking deceit. Depart from evil (or mischief) and do good, seek and pursue peace. The eyes of the Lord are upon the righteous (the just, or merciful), and his ears are open to their prayers. But the face

face of the Lord is against them that do evil.

face (i. e. displeasure) of the Lord is against them that do evil. A. D. 66.

13 And who is he that will harm you, if ye be followers of that which is good?

13. And, as this *providentially* tends to procure you the *divine* blessing, so does it *naturally* prove the best means to preserve you from the malice of *mankind*. For there are scarce any people of so savage a temper, as without any provocation, to injure a person of a kind * and inoffensive behaviour.

* τȣ̃ ἀγαθȣ̃.

14 But and if ye suffer for righteousness sake, happy are ye; and be not afraid of their terror, neither be troubled:

14. But, whenever it shall happen, that you suffer for the sake of your *religion*; look upon *that* as your happiness. Be not discouraged at any threats, or the worst that can befal you of that kind.

15 But sanctify the Lord God in your hearts, and be ready always to give an answer to every man that asketh you a reason of the hope that is in you, with meekness and fear:

15. Be but possessed of a religious fear of offending God, believe his truth, depend upon his power, justice and goodness; and you need not fear to own, and be ready to defend your *Christian* principles, in a modest and humble way, upon either private or public examination.

16 Having a good conscience, that whereas they speak evil of you, as of evil doers, they may be ashamed that falsely accuse your good conversation in Christ.

16. For, thus to demonstrate the innocence and peaceableness of your carriage, is the most direct way to shame and confound those that would represent you as men of turbulent and ‡ seditious principles.

‡ ὡς κακοποιῶν. See Chap. ii. 12, &c.

17 For it is better, if the will of God be so, that ye suffer for well doing, than for evil doing.

17. And whether it succeeds in securing you from *their* malice, or no; yet you will have the inward satisfaction of suffering with a good conscience, and for a good cause; without which your afflictions would indeed be insupportable.

18. You

A. D. 66.

18 For Christ also hath once suffered for sins, the just for the unjust: (that he might bring us to God) being put to death in the flesh, || but quickned by the Spirit:

|| 2 Cor. xiii. 4.

18. You will, then, copy after the great example, and share in the glories of your innocent Saviour, who laid down his spotless life to procure the pardon and salvation of a guilty world; and in reward of those sufferings, was raised again from the dead, by the power of the Holy Spirit.

19 By which also he went and preached unto the spirits in prison: *

20 Which sometime were disobedient, † when once the long suffering of God waited in the days of Noah, while the ark was a preparing, wherein few, that is, eight souls, were ‡ saved by water.

§ τοῖς ἐν φυλακῇ πνεύμασι.
|| Gen. vi. 3.

19. & 20. Even of that Divine *Spirit* wherewith he inspired Noah to preach repentance and reformation to the wicked people, before the flood; those dissolute wretches, that were enslaved to § their brutish lusts; and after the merciful space of a hundred years || given them to repent in, and Noah persuading them to it, with particular earnestness, all the while he was preparing the *ark*; were, at last, like *condemned * prisoners*, justly sentenced to destruction, for their incurable impiety; and none saved in the § *ark*, beside Noah, and seven more of his family ‡.

§ Gen. vii. 13.

21 The like figure whereunto even baptism, doth also now save us (not the putting away of the filth of

21 & 22. Now our *baptism* is the same to us, as the *ark* was to Noah, and his family, viz. a means of our salvation from sin and eternal death, as the *ark* saved them from

* Ver. 19. [By which (ἐν ᾧ) he went and preached—] Not that Christ *himself* preached, but preached by the *Spirit*, i. e. by sending the *Spirit* upon Noah; agreeably to 2 Pet. ii. 5. and 1 Pet. i. 11.

† Ver. 20. [When once, ὅτε ἅπαξ, when once for all.] See the Note on Heb. ix. 26.

‡ [Saved by water.] A quite wrong translation: δι' ὕδατος, is *out of*, or *from* the water; in the same manner as διὰ πυρὸς, saved by *fire*, should be rendered, *As out of the fire*, 1 Cor. iii. 15.

of the flesh, but * the answer of a good conscience towards God) by the resurrection of Jesus Christ,

22 Who is gone into heaven, and is on the right hand of God, angels, and authorities, and powers being made subject unto him.

A. D. 66.

from the *flood*. For Christian *baptism* is not a mere external *ceremony* of washing and cleansing the *body*; but its nature and advantage lies in its being a solemn * *engagement* on *our* part, to dedicate ourselves to the service of Christ; and the *promise* of eternal life, on God's part, on condition of our performing that engagement. A promise we are certain to see performed, as having now a perfect pledge and earnest of it, by the resurrection of Christ from the dead, and his glorious exaltation into heaven, to the utmost degree of glory and majesty; whereby angels and archangels, men and devils, all ranks and degrees of creatures are put under his government and dominion.

* [The answer of a good conscience:] επερώτημα signifies either a *question* or an *answer*. It most probably alludes to the *questions* put to, and *answered* by the person baptized, and so signifies the *stipulation* of baptism.

CHAP.

CHAP. IV.

The Gentile *Christians again exhorted to Purity of Life, and Constancy in their Profession, from the Consideration of Christ's Sufferings for them, and their Engagement to imitate* him. *They are warned from the former Vices of their* Heathen *State. The Apostle turns his Argument again to the* Jewish *Converts, telling them the Dissolution of the* Jewish *State and Religion, with the exemplary Destruction of that People, was near at hand; exhorting them to great Sobriety, Devotion, Charity, and Hospitality, for their Preservation from the Effects of that Calamity. Advices for the due Use of Spiritual* Gifts, *and the Exercise of Sacred* Offices. *The dreadful Judgment upon the* Jewish *Nation, and the happy Security of good* Christians.

A. D. 66.

* Chap iii. 18, &c.

1 FOrasmuch then, as Christ hath suffered for us in the flesh, arm yourselves likewise with the same mind: for he that hath suffered * in the flesh, hath ceased from sin.

2 That he no longer should live the rest of his time in the flesh, to the lusts of men, but to the will of God.

1. & 2. THUS * you are to consider how great an obligation the sufferings of Christ, on your behalf, lays on you to renounce all your former vicious principles and carnal practices, and that the very design of your *Christianity* is, to engage you to live by the purity of *his* pattern, and whenever you are called to it, to *suffer* too, after his example.

3 For the time past of our life may suffice us to have wrought the

3. You *Gentile* converts must especially know, you are now to bid adieu to all the drunkenness, impure

* Ver. 1. [He that hath suffered in the flesh.] A Christian's *suffering* in the flesh is, in this place, evidently the same with his *mortifying* the flesh, and its *lusts*; as appears by the *second* and *third verses*.

A. D. 66.

the will of the Gentiles, when we walked in laſciviouſneſs, luſts, exceſs of wine, revellings banquettings, and abominable idolatries:

impure debaucheries and abominable practices, ſo uſual in your former courſe of *heathen* worſhip.

4 Wherein they think it ſtrange that you run not with them to the ſame exceſs of riot, ſpeaking evil of you:

4. Thoſe impious cuſtoms being become branches even of their *religious worſhip*; your *heathen* neighbours will, it is like, wonder at your relinquiſhing them, and point you out for men of novelty and affectation, with the utmoſt indignity and reproach.

5 Who ſhall give an account to him that is ready to judge the quick and the dead.

5. But let not *that* diſhearten you. A time is coming when God will ſeverely recompenſe them, and all that have given themſelves up to obſtinate and irreclaimable wickedneſs.

6 For, this cauſe was the goſpel preached alſo to them that are dead, that they might be judged according to men in the fleſh, but live according to God in the ſpirit *.

6. Remember the bleſſed advantages your *Gentile* Chriſtians, who were *dead in treſpaſſes and ſins*, now enjoy by the *goſpel* revelations engaging you to condemn * and mortify your former vicious and ſenſual habits, and live a new and divine life. A thing which, though your *heathen* neighbours may reproach * and condemn you for, yet the preſent comforts of this *ſpiritual life*, and the aſſurance of being raiſed to an immortal happineſs, by the power of the *divine Spirit*, will demonſtrate *your* wiſdom and *their* folly.

7 But the end of all things is at hand: be ye therefore ſober and watch unto prayer.

7. Let the *Jewiſh* converts now take notice, the *ceremonial* religion, ſome of them are ſo fond of, is drawing near to an end; and the

* [Judged according to men in the fleſh, but, &c.] I have joined the two moſt natural interpretations of theſe phraſes, and leave the reader to take which he thinks to be the moſt ſtrictly agreeable to the context.

A. D. 66. *Jewiſh* ſtate and people to be deſtroyed, by a moſt exemplary judgment. To prevent their ſharing in which common calamity, it behoves them to betake themſelves to great ſobriety, temperance and devotion, according to our Saviour's advice, Matth. xxi. 34, 36.

8 And above all things have fervant charity among yourſelves: for charity ſhall cover the multitude of ſins *.

9 Uſe hoſpitality one to another without grudging.

8. & 9. Remember, too, that a charitable, kind, and hoſpitable temper, free of all partial diſtinctions and animoſities againſt ſuch as are not of your opinion, will do you particular ſervice in the preſent caſe, will contribute much to atone for your *former* miſcarriages of *that* kind *; and procure you the divine protection from the miſeries now coming upon your obdurate *nation*.

† χάρις, χάρισμα.

10 As every man hath received the gift, even ſo miniſter the ſame one to another, as good ſtewards of the manifold grace of God.

10. Whatever extraordinary † gift of the *Spirit* any Chriſtian is endowed with, or whatever † *office* he is intruſted withal, let him not overvalue himſelf and deſpiſe others upon that account; but look upon himſelf as a *ſteward* to whom God has committed a talent to be liberally and cheerfully improved to the *church's* good.

‡ λαλεῖ.

§ ὡς λόγια Θεοῦ. See Rom. xii. 6.

|| διακονεῖ.

11 If any man ſpeak, *let him ſpeak* as the oracles of God; if any man miniſter, let *him do it* as of the ability which God giveth, that God in all things may be glorified through Jeſus Chriſt: to whom be praiſe and dominion for ever and ever. Amen.

11. Thus, he that has the gift of *explaining* ‡ *ſcripture prophecies*, let him preſume to carry that explanation no further § than his *inſpiration* reaches. He that is a ſteward of the church's *charities* for the poor, or is ſent on any charitable || meſſage to any church, let him perform thoſe offices with diligence and heartineſs. And ſo, for all other employments in the miniſtry, let your chief aim be to the glory of God, through Jeſus Chriſt; to whom be aſcribed all praiſe and dominion for ever. *Amen.*

12. Once

* See James v. 9—20. and the note there.

A. D. 66.

12 Beloved think it not ſtrange concerning the fiery trial, which is to try you, as though ſome ſtrange thing happened unto you:

12. Once more let me entreat you, dear brethren, not to be ſurpriſed and diſheartened at the ſevere perſecutions that befal you, for the ſake of your profeſſion. Think it not ſtrange, that *Chriſtianity* ſhould be a ſtate of trials and ſufferings.

13 But rejoice, in as much as ye are partakers of Chriſt's ſufferings; that when his glory ſhall be revealed, ye may be glad alſo with exceeding joy.

13. Look on it, rather as an *honour* to be ſharers in the ſufferings of your Lord, who accounts all *your* afflictions as his *own*. And rejoice in it as your greateſt happineſs, that, as you are to reſemble him in ſuffering here, you are one day to ſhine with him in eternal ſplendor and felicity.

14 If ye be reproached for the name of Chriſt, happy *are ye*; for the Spirit of glory, and of God reſteth upon you: on their part he is evil ſpoken of, but on your part he is glorified.

14. Whenever, therefore, you are vilified for your Chriſtian religion, it is a happy token of your being the true diſciples of God and Chriſt; entitled to thoſe endowments of the Holy Spirit, that are the earneſt and pledge of your future glory, and will enable you to triumph and ſing the praiſes of him, whom your adverſaries ſo ignorantly deſpiſe.

15 But let none of you ſuffer as a murderer, or as a thief, or as an evil doer, or as a buſy-body, in other mens matters.

15. Only take ſpecial care, that none of you commit, and ſo juſtly ſuffer for, any acts of violence, theft, ſedition, or intruding into matters that do not belong to you: vices that the *Jewiſh* * zealots are now ſo very prone to.

* Joſephus.

16 Yet if *any man ſuffer* as a Chriſtian, let him not be aſhamed, but let him glorify God on this behalf.

16. But, ſo far as you innocently ſuffer for the peaceable profeſſion of *Chriſtianity*, bleſs God for ſuch happy opportunities of diſplaying and perfecting your ſubmiſſion to his divine will and Providence.

17 For the time is come that judgment muſt

17. & 18. In fine, the time is now come, when even the *Chriſtian*

A. D. 66.

must begin at the house of God, and if it first begin at us, what shall the end be of them that obey not the gospel of God?

18 And if the righteous scarcely be saved, where shall the ungodly and the sinner appear?

stian church itself is to undergo the sharp discipline of present trials and afflictions. And, if the *believing* part of the *Jewish* nation be, by Divine Wisdom, permitted to suffer such things, how dreadful must be the judgment upon the *infidel* and *obstinate* part of that people? And, if their destruction will be so general and terrible, that the very *Christian* members are likely to escape it only by a special act of mercy and providence; what must be the condition of those, upon whose heads these judgments are intended *principally* to fall?

19 Wherefore, let them that suffer according to the will of God, commit the keeping of their souls to him in well doing as unto a faithful Creator.

19. Wherefore, as you Christians are sure of the divine protection, bear your present persecutions with an easy and cheerful mind. Keep steady to your duty, and commit your lives into *his* hands, who is your faithful Creator, and cannot fail to be your merciful deliverer, and eternal preserver.

CHAP. V.

The Elder and Superior Officers of the Church exhorted to a diligent, cheerful, disinterested, and humble Management in the governing the Christian Church. The Younger and Inferior Officers charged to obey their Superiors; and to the Exercise of Humanity, and all kind Offices to each other. All Christians encouraged to patient Submission and Resignation, under their present Sufferings; to a vigilant Sobriety against the prevalent Temptations of the Devil, and his wicked Instruments. The Apostle's Prayer for them. The Salutations and Conclusion.

1 THE elders which are among you I exhort, who am also

1. HAVING thus given you these general directions, I now particularly exhort the *clergy* of

so an elder, and a witness of the sufferings of Christ, and also a partaker of the glory that shall be revealed.

of your churches to a special care of their duty. Let all the elder || and superior church-officers, then, take this advice, as coming from one that is himself one of the chief of their sacred order, an *apostle* that saw * the sufferings of Christ, and is ready to bear witness to the truth of them, by suffering for his religion; and is under a sure expectation of sharing in the future glory promised to his true disciples.

|| πρεσβυτεροί.

* μάρτυς.

2 Feed the flock of God which is among you, taking the oversight thereof, not by constraint, but willingly: not for filthy lucre, but of a ready mind.

3 Neither as being lords over God's heritage: but being ensamples to the flock.

2. & 3. Let them govern their churches with great diligence, both in doctrine and example; with the utmost cheerfulness and freedom from all sinister and secular designs. Neither exercising any imperious behaviour ‡ toward their people, nor disposing of the public ‡ revenues committed to their care, in an arbitrary or humoursome manner: But acting like faithful stewards over God's people, and looking on the charitable *collections* of the church as dedicated to *his* service.

‡ κυριεύοντες τῶν κλήρων.

4 And when the chief Shepherd shall appear, ye shall receive a crown of glory that fadeth not away.

4. And, by so doing, they shall receive the crown of eternal reward, at the great appearance of Christ to judgment, who is the Lord and Head over the whole church.

5 Likewise ye younger, submit yourselves unto the elder; yea, all of you be subject one to another, and be clothed with humility, for God resisteth the proud and giveth grace to the humble.

5. In like manner, let all the *inferior* clergy pay a just respect and submission to those of the *superior* orders. And, in fine, be all, of every degree whatever, ready to do all kind and good offices to each other; making that great virtue of *humility* their chief and most valuable ornament: Remembering those words of Solomon, Prov. iii. 34. "Surely he scorneth the scorners, but his favour is with the lowly."

A. D. 66. 6 Humble yourselves therefore under the mighty hand of God, that he may exalt you in due time;

7 Casting all your care upon him, for he careth for you.

6. & 7. And let both *clergy* and *people* commit themselves to the divine care and providence, with all pious and humble resignation, under their present sufferings; depending upon God for a seasonable deliverance, and a glorious reward.

8 Be sober, be vigilant; because your adversary the devil as a roaring lion, walketh about, seeking whom he may devour.

8. Let your care and circumspection be particular, at this time, when the rage of the *devil* and his wicked instruments your *persecutors*, is so violent to draw you into *apostacy* from the Christian faith.

9 Whom resist, stedfast in the faith, knowing that the same afflictions are accomplished in your brethren that are in the world.

9. Your courage and resolution, therefore, ought to be proportionable to your danger. And it will add something to it, to consider, that your *Christian* brethren in other parts of the world, are now labouring under the same persecutions.

10 But the God of all grace, who hath called us unto his eternal glory by Christ Jesus, after that ye have suffered a while, make you perfect, stablish, strengthen, settle *you*.

11 To him *be* glory and dominion for ever and ever. Amen.

10. & 11. And may God, the Author of all divine favours and blessings, who has given us a sure prospect of eternal glory and happiness, by the *Christian* religion, shorten your present sufferings, and enable you to improve them into a complete resignation to his divine will and providence; whereby you cannot fail of the final rewards proposed to you. To him be ascribed all glory and dominion for ever and ever. Amen.

12 By Silvanus a faithful brother unto you (as I suppose) I have written briefly, exhorting and testifying, that this is the true grace of God wherein ye stand.

12. This epistle, intended, in the shortest compass I could, to comfort and confirm you in the true faith, I now send by Silvanus (or Silas) of whose integrity I presume you all have a great opinion.

13 The

13. All

A. D. 66.

13 The *church that is* at Babylon elected together with *you*, saluteth you, and *so doth* Marcas my son.

13. All your fellow Christians here at * Rome, send their hearty love to your churches. And particularly (John) Mark, who has served and assisted me with the most filial respect. See Phil. ii. 22.

14 Greet ye one another with a kiss of charity. Peace *be* with you all that are in Christ Jesus. Amen

14. Salute each other with your usual kiss of charity for my sake. All blessing and happiness attend every Christian in your respective countries. *Amen.*

---

* [Babylon.] So it is most generally thought Rome, is here and in Rev. xvii. and xviii. figuratively called, from its heathen *idolatry* and *superstition*, as some think, but much more probably as it was foreseen to be the head and mistress of vicious corruptions in the *Christian* church. The learned Bp. Pearson understands by Babylon, in this place, the Egyptian Babylon. Op. Post. de Success. Rom. Episcop. cap. 8.

A PARAPHRASE ON THE SECOND EPISTLE GENERAL OF *St.* PETER.

Note, This epiſtle being written in the latter end of the ſame *year*, to the ſame *people*, and upon the ſame *occaſion* with the foregoing; the reader is referred to the *Preface* thereunto prefixed.

CHAP. I.

The Title and Salutation. The great Bleſſings of the Chriſtian Religion. Chriſtians exhorted to the reſolute practice of ſuch Virtues as are ſuitable to ſuch bleſſings. The neceſſity and glorious Effects of thoſe Chriſtian Virtues. The deſign of this Epiſtle, *much the ſame with that of the* Former. *St. Peter foretels his own approaching Martyrdom. Reminds them of the Truth and Certainty of their Chriſtian Religion, from the Teſtimonies of a Divine Voice from* Heaven, *and the Completion of Scripture Prophecies.*

Written A. D. 66.

1 SImon Peter a ſervant and an apoſtle of Jeſus Chriſt, to them

1. SImon Peter a ſervant and apoſtle of Jeſus Chriſt, ſendeth this epiſtle to the Chriſtian churches

A. D. 66.

them that have obtained like precious faith with us, through the righteousness of God, and our Saviour Jesus Christ:

churches of Pontus, Galatia, Capadocia, the Lesser Asia, and Bithynia, to all, whether *Jewish* || or *Gentile* converts, that place their hopes of pardon and salvation in the *Christian religion*, as I myself do.

|| See Pref. to 1 Epist. § 4. Chap. i. 1.

2 Grace and peace be multiplied unto you, through the knowledge of God, and of Jesus our Lord.

3 According as his divine power hath given unto us all things that *pertain* unto life and godliness, through the knowledge of him that hath called us to glory * and virtue;

2. & 3. Wishing you all that happiness and blessing which is the fruit of truly knowing God to be our supreme *Father*, and Jesus Christ to be our *Lord* and *Saviour*. By whose glorious power * and authority we are now called into the privileges and profession of a holy religion, that will qualify us for eternal life.

4 Whereby are given unto us exceeding great and precious promises; that by these you might be partakers of the divine nature, having escaped the corruption that is in the world through lust.

4. A religion, whereby you are reformed from the vices and corruptions of the rest of mankind; have enjoyed the promises made to the Christian church, of being inspired with the *Holy* ‡ *Ghost here*, and wrought into such a resemblance and imitation of God, as cannot fail to render you, for ever, happy in him *hereafter*.

‡ θείας φύσεως κοινωνοί.

5 And besides this, giving all diligence, add to your faith, virtue; and to virtue, knowledge;

6 And to knowledge, temperance; and to temperance, patience;

5. 6. & 7. Wherefore, † seeing the blessings of your religion, are such, make it your utmost endeavour to perform the reasonable and necessary conditions of *finally* enjoying them, viz. courage in *profession*, and sincerity in *practice*.

† καὶ αὐτὸ τοῦτο.

Let

---

* Ver. 3. [Called us to glory and virtue; Διὰ δόξης καὶ ἀρετῆς —By his glory and power; or, by his glorious power;] the same with θεία δύναμις in the former part of the verse. So the Alexand. and other MSS. ἰδίᾳ δόξῃ; and the *Vulg. Propriâ sua Gloriâ & Virtute.*

A. D. 66. patience; and to patience, godliness;
7 And to godliness, brotherly kindness; and to brotherly kindness, charity.

Let that courage be supported by a careful study and knowledge of its true *principles;* those principles backed and secured by a strict abstinence from all sensual and unlawful *pleasures;* and exert themselves in rendering you patient under afflictions, constant in the true worship of God, and loving and charitable in your thoughts and behaviour to all your Christian *brethren.*

8 For if these things be in you, and abound, they make *you, that you shall* neither *be* barren nor unfruitful in the knowledge of our Lord Jesus Christ.

8. These are the true characters of a good Christian; and the only things that will improve you in your holy profession.

9 But he that lacketh these things, is blind, and cannot see far off, and hath forgotten that he was purged from his old sins.

9. And the Christian that neglects these virtues, has lost all true notions of his religion, and forgotten the very end and design of his *baptism.*

10 Wherefore the rather, brethren, give diligence to make your calling and election sure: for if ye do these things, ye shall never fall:
11 For so an entrance shall be ministred unto you abundantly into the everlasting kingdom of our Lord and Saviour Jesus Christ.

10. & 11. Make the diligent practice of these duties, therefore, the only certain condition of the *gospel* blessings. And then, as you have done your part, you may be perfectly assured of the complete fruition of Christ's future and eternal kingdom.

12 Wherefore I will not be negligent to put you always in remembrance of these things, though ye know them, and be established in the present truth.
13 Yea, I think it meet so long as I am in this tabernacle, to stir

12. & 13. Wherefore though you cannot but, in general, know this to be the great concern of your Christianity, yet, in this present state of trials and temptations, I could not but think it proper, once and again, to remind you of a thing of such infinite importance: Especially considering, I have but a short while

ſtir you up, by putting *you* in remembrance:

while to be your *living* remembrancer.

A. D. 66.

14 Knowing that ſhortly I muſt put off *this* my tabernacle, even as our Lord Jeſus Chriſt hath ſhowed me.

14. For I expect, very ſoon to die a *martyr* for the religion of Chriſt, and, by the ſame kind ‖ of death that he *himſelf* was pleaſed to foretel me I ſhould. (See John xxi. 20.)

‖ *Viz.* Crucifixion.

15 Moreover, I will endeavour that you may be able after my deceaſe, to have theſe things always in remembrance.

15. And therefore, I leave you theſe my *epiſtles*, to revive your courage, and preſerve you in conſtancy to the true faith, after I am gone.

16 For we have not followed cunningly deviſed fables, when we made known unto you the power and coming of our Lord Jeſus Chriſt, but were eye-witneſſes of his majeſty.

16. And you ought to look upon the teſtimonies of the truth of your profeſſion (and particularly of this great article of Chriſt's *future coming*) given you by *me*, and the reſt of the *apoſtles*, not like the uncertain *traditions* and *forgeries* of the *Jewiſh* doctors; but as truths confirmed by unſuſpected eye-witneſſes of the life, miracles, death and reſurrection of Jeſus Chriſt; all which are demonſtrations of that great article of his *future* appearance, to be the Great Judge of all the world.

17 For he received from God the Father, honour and glory, when there came ſuch a voice to him from the excellent Glory, This is my beloved Son, in whom I am well pleaſed.

18 And this voice which came from heaven, we heard when we were with him in the holy mount.

17. & 18. I myſelf was one of them, who at his glorious transfiguration, upon the mount, ſaw thoſe diſplays of the Divine Majeſty, and heard the voice from heaven declaring him to be the *Son of* God, the true Meſſiah and Saviour of mankind. (See Matt. xvii. 1. and Mark ix. 2, 3, &c. Luke ix. 28, &c.)

A. D. 66.

19 We have alfo * a more fure Word of prophecy; whereunto ye do well that ye take heed, † as unto a light that fhineth in a dark place, until the day dawn, and the day-ftar arife in your hearts:

19. Now, all thefe kind of evidences muft render our religion of ftill more unconteftable authority, as they are *facts* that are the completion of ancient *prophecies*; an argument the moft obftinate *Jews* can never withftand. But whatever *their* perverfenefs be, reft *you* fatisfied in fuch convincing proofs. Read, and compare thofe *prophecies* with the tranfactions of Chrift, remembering the predictions Chrift made concerning himfelf; and you will find the authority of the *one* to be as clear from the *other*, as light † itfelf; and, by ftill future concurring circumftances, and the bleffings of Chrift upon your honeft endeavours, you will be more and more enlightened and confirmed in the truth and excellency of religion ‡.

20 Knowing this firft, that no prophecy of the fcripture is of any private interpretation §.

21 For

20. & 21. Thefe predictions rightly compared and underftood, cannot but, at the fame time fatisfy *you*, and confound your *adverfaries*; efpecially thofe of the *Jewifh* part; for

---

* Ver 19. [A more fure word.]—Not more fure than the *facts* fpoken of in the 17th and 18th verfes; but more fure than the *cunningly devifed fables* in the 16th verfe.

† [As unto a light fhining in a dark place;] *i. e.* Though the *prophecies* feem *dark* and obfcure, yet by applying them to Chrift they will become *clear* and plain. See and compare 2 Cor. iii. 14, 15, 16, 17, 18. Or perhaps, the *dark place* may be the fame with *darknefs*, John i. 5. [The light fhineth in darknefs, and the darknefs comprehended it not. See Dr. Clarke's paraph. on that paffage.

‡ [The day:] So the gofpel religion is called, Rom. xiii. 12, 16. [The-day ftar:] So Chrift is called the *day fpring*, Luke i. 78. [The morning ftar,] Rev. ii. 28.

§ Ver. 20. [Of any private interpretation.] Note, ἰδίας ἐπιλύσεως, may be very properly rendered thus; *None of the prophetic predictions of the Old Teftament* (or at leaft not the generality of them] *were of fo exprefs, clear, and plain a nature, as to be their own interpreters:* It is Chrift and his *gofpel* that perfectly

21 For the prophecy came not in old time by the will of man: but holy men of God ſpake *as they* were moved by the Holy Ghoſt.

for *they* as well as *we*, do all allow those prophecies concerning the *Meſſiah*, not to be *human* inventions, or the ſuggeſtions † of *private* fancy, but the clear predictions of men inſpired with the Holy Ghoſt. And conſequently, it is impoſſible but the *Chriſtian* religion, which is the completion of thoſe *prohecies*, muſt have the ſame characters of divine truth with the *prophecies* themſelves.

A. D. 66.

† ἰδίας ἐπιλύσεως. & θελήματι ἀνθρώπου.

---

perfectly opens and explains them. And then the following words, " For prophecy came not by the will of man," may have this ſenſe, viz. " For thoſe prophets, though truly inſpired of God, yet could not prophecy concerning theſe matters, when, or as much, and many things, as themſelves pleaſed, or their then preſent hearers might deſire; but were confined to the dictates of the Holy Ghoſt. Now all the obſcurities and defects of their doctrines are fully cleared up, and ſupplied by the life, and tranſactions of that Chriſt of whom they propheſied." Thus the ſenſe of theſe three verſes is moſt ingeniouſly and judiciouſly connected by Sam. Werenſels. Diſcertat. Theolog. Diſſert. 10. Edit. Baſil. 1709.

CHAP.

CHAP. II.

Warning against False and Heretical Teachers in the Christian Church. A black Account of their Principles and Practices. Their severe Judgment and Condemnation. Their Characters exactly and principally agree to the Zealots among the Jewish Converts, among whom Nicholas of Antioch, mentioned Acts vi. 5. *was the Broacher of a lewd Heresy; and whose Followers are mentioned by St. John,* Revel. ii. 6. *and are thought by the Ancient Commentators to be here particularly referred to.*

A. D. 66.

1 BUT there were false prophets also among the people, even as there shall be false teachers among you, who privily shall bring in damnable heresies †, even denying the Lord that bought them, and bring upon themselves swift destruction.

1. THUS, I say, the * prophecies of the Old Testament prove the truth of our religion. But, as in those former ages of the *Jewish* church, there were some *false* as well as *true* prophets: So, you know, Christ and his *apostles* have foretold, there would be the same mixture in the *Christian* church: Which predictions of theirs are now verified in those raging *zealots* of the *Judaizing* faction: ‡ A set of men, that are broaching the most pernicious doctrines, by practising upon which, while they boast themselves *as the peculiar* || *and purchased people of God*, they really renounce him that is indeed their *Lord* || and *Redeemer*; and shall, in due time, feel the fatal effects of such obstinate malice and ingratitude.

* Chap. i. 19, 20, 21.

‡ Compare St. Jude's epistle.

|| See Deut. xxxii. 6. 1 Cor. vi. 20.

2. These

† Ver. 1. [Even denying the Lord that bought them.] Note, They who take this to be meant of Jesus Christ are much mistaken. It was God the Father, the Lord of the whole world, the God of Jews and Christians, of whom it is said—" Is he not thy Father who hath bought thee?" Deut. xxxii. 6.

A. D. 66.

2 And many ſhall follow their pernicious ways, by reaſon of whom the way of truth ſhall be evil ſpoken of.

2. Theſe people, by their violent zeal, and plauſible pretences, are like to ſeduce many converts to their party, to the great ſcandal of the *Chriſtian* name.

3 And through covetouſneſs ſhall they with feigned words make merchandiſe of you, whoſe judgment now of a long time lingereth not, and their damnation ſlumbereth not.

3. They inſinuate themſelves into your affections, and ſtrive to gain proſelytes for temporal ends, ‡ and the gratification of their own impure paſſions. But that divine judgment long ſince pronounced || againſt the authors of ſuch wickedneſs, is drawing on, and will ſoon overtake them.

‡ ἐν πλεονεξίᾳ.

|| ἔκπαλαι. See Jude 4.

4 For if God ſpared not the angels that ſinned, but caſt them down to hell, *and* delivered them into chains of darkneſs, to be reſerved unto judgment:

4. For, however they may at preſent prevail, and whatever their malicious endeavours againſt you be, reſt yourſelves ſatisfied, from all the courſe of the divine diſpenſations, that *they* are ſure of their puniſhment, and *you* of a gracious and timely deliverance. Remember, the apoſtate *angels* themſelves reigned but a little while in their pride, were expelled the regions of heavenly light, thruſt down into this dark * and lower world, and are here confined, like priſoners, in chains, until the final day of judgment upon them and all wicked men.

5 And ſpared not the old world, but ſaved Noah the eighth *perſon*, a preacher of righteouſneſs, bringing in the flood upon the world of the ungodly:

6 And turning the cities of Sodom and Gomorrha into aſhes, con-

5. & 6. You may conclude the certainty of your reſcue from theſe impious perſecutors, from the inſtance of Noah, that preached repentance to the antediluvian world, and was one of the † eight that were ſaved in the *ark*. And *theſe* may as aſſuredly gather *their* approaching vengeance, from the deſtruction of that wicked generation,

† ὄγδοον. Gen. vi. 9. 1 Pet. iii. 20.

* Ταρταρώσας. See Epheſ. ii. 2. and Dr. Whitby on this place.

A. D. 66. condemned them with an overthrow, making them an ensample unto those that after should live ungodly:

tion, by the flood, and from the dreadful examples of Sodom and Gomorrha.

7 And delivered just Lot, vexed with the filthy conversation of the wicked:

8 (For that righteous man dwelling among them, in seeing and hearing, vexed his righteous soul from day to day with *their* unlawful deeds.)

7. & 8. Remember, how special a deliverance that good man Lot had, from the ruins of those lewd people, after all the many vexations he was forced to endure at the sight of such profligate and numerous examples.

9 The Lord knoweth how to deliver the godly out of temptations; and to reserve the unjust unto the day of judgment to be punished:

9. From all which instances, good Christians ought to assure themselves of a proportionable share of Divine care and providence, for their deliverance from present afflictions, and of a future vengeance upon their cruel persecutors.

10 But chiefly them that walk after the flesh, in the lusts of uncleanness, and despise government. Presumptuous *are they*, self-willed; they are not afraid * to speak evil of dignities:

10. And, if ever Divine justice were due to any crimes, it must fall with terrible weight upon the abominable lusts, the unmasterly pride, and incurable prejudices of the *false teachers* of those times; several of which are arrived to that presumption, as to vilify their superiors, not only upon *earth*, but in * *heaven* too.

11 Whereas angels, which are greater in power and might, bring not railing accusation against them before the Lord.

11. How contrary was the behaviour of those much superior beings, the good *angels*, toward these wicked *spirits* which they had engaged and overcome! Even Michael the *archangel*, returned *Satan* none of his railing accusations, but only said, *The Lord rebuke thee.* See Jude, ver. 9.

12. But

* [To speak evil of dignities,] may refer either to their vilifying their *civil* governors, or to the base and wicked notions which the *ancients* tell us these *heretics* vented about the *angels* and heavenly *spirits*. See Jude, ver. 8.

A. D. 66.

12 But these are natural brute beasts, * made to be taken and destroyed, speak evil of the things that they understand not, *and* shall utterly perish in their own corruption.

12. But these proud *mortals*, more like beasts of prey * than men, being prone to mischief and ripe for destruction, revile and blaspheme every thing, without reason or distinction; and shall accordingly feel the natural and woful effects of so wilful a degeneracy.

13 *And* shall receive the reward of unrighteousness, *as* they that count it pleasure to riot in the day-time: spots *they are* and blemishes sporting themselves with their own deceivings, while they feast with you:

14 Having eyes full of adultery, and that cannot cease from sin, beguiling unstable souls: an heart they have exercised with covetous practices: cursed children.

13. & 14. So habituated are they to all sensuality, fraud, covetousness and hypocrisy, that when at some times they appear fair and religious, to betray men to a good opinion of their principles; at other times they commit their lewdness in open day-light: they make a jest of the worst impieties; attend upon your *sacraments* || and *love-feasts*, only for some riotous and lustful gratification. In fine, are a perfect scandal to religion, and shall at last receive the vengeance due to those that are accursed and utterly forsaken of God.

|| 1 Cor. xi. 20, 21. and Jude 12.

15 Which have forsaken the right way, and are gone astray, following the way of Balaam *the son* of Bosor, who loved the wages of unrighteousness.

16 But was rebuked for his iniquity: the dumb ass speaking with man's voice, for-

15. & 16. And well may God be supposed to abandon such wretches to themselves, who have renounced all principles of sober reason and true religion, and instead of deserving the name of Christians, may be called the followers of Balaam; while for their secular advantages, they corrupt and delude *Christian* people, as he did the Israelites † against the plain dictates

* [Made to be taken and destroyed.] Or thus, γεγεννημένα εἰς ἅλωσιν, ϗ φθορὰν; [made for rapine and destruction.] I express both senses, but our translation is the most agreeable.

† See Numb. xxxvi. 16. and Joseph. Antiq. Lib. IV. chap. vi.

A. D. 66. bade the madneſs of the prophet.

dictates of his own conſcience, for the ſake of *preferment*. Nor does the miraculous reproof, by the mouth of a dumb aſs, upon the firſt attempt || of that infatuated man, move *theſe* his *followers* to the leaſt remorſe of conſideration.

|| Numb. xxii.

17 Theſe are wells without water, clouds that are carried with a tempeſt, to whom the midſt of darkneſs is reſerved for ever.

17. What ſhall I ſay more of them, or how ſhall I deſcribe them? So empty are they of all good, that I might compare them to ſprings quite dried up. So pernicious are their principles, that like *clouds* void of all refreſhing moiſture, but full of noxious vapours, they blaſt and deſtroy all before them. Surely the moſt exquiſite of future puniſhments muſt be the portion of ſuch people!

18 For when they ſpeak great ſwelling *words* of vanity, they allure through the luſts of the fleſh, through much wantonneſs, thoſe that were clean eſcaped from them who live in error.

18. Yet, as worthleſs as they are, their pretences to religion run high, to the utmoſt degree of pride and vanity. The ſecret deſign of all which is, the better to miſlead others into their filthy and impure practices.

19 While they promiſe them liberty, they themſelves are the ſervants of corruption: for of whom a man is overcome, of the ſame is he brought in bondage.

19. They promiſe their *votaries* the liberties and privileges of God's *church* and people, while *themſelves* are enſlaved to luſt and debauchery. And no man is ſo perfect a *ſlave* as he that is governed by his luſts, and ridden by his paſſions.

20 For if after they have eſcaped the pollutions of the world, through the knowledge of the Lord and Saviour Jeſus Chriſt, they are again entangled therein, *and* overcome, the latter end is worſe with them than the beginning.

20. And verily, their caſe, as *apoſtates* from the clear light of the *goſpel*, is much worſe than if they had never been converted at all to it.

21 For it had been better for them not to have known the way

21. For the ingratitude of an apoſtate Chriſtian, in ſinning againſt ſuch plain and happy methods of ſalvation,

way of righteousness, than after they have known it, to turn from the holy commandment delivered unto them.

salvation, must needs render him more incurable and justly condemnable, than any *heathen* that was never brought to such a conviction. A. D. 66.

22 But it is happened unto them according to the true proverb: The dog is turned to his own vomit again, and the sow that was washed to her wallowing in the mire.

22. And thus the wilful indulgence of their brutish passions has reduced these men to the worst instances of habitual brutality; to return to the vilest of their former vices, as the *dog* does to his vomit, or the *sow* to the mire.

CHAP. III.

He repeats the Design of his Epistle, viz. To arm them against the false and Heretical Teachers, *by reminding them of what the ancient* Prophets, *Christ and his* Apostles *have foretold of them. These* Teachers *insult the orthodox Christians, upon the long Delay of Christ's Judgment threatened to the Adversaries of his Religion. An Answer to their Objection The Certainty of this Judgment, both upon the* Jewish *Nation in particular, and upon the whole wicked* World *in general. The Earth shall be destroyed by* Fire *at the last Judgment, as it was once by* Water. *An Inference from hence, for the Patience and Purity of a Christian Life.*

1 THIS second epistle (beloved) I now write unto you, in both which I stir up your pure minds by way of remembrance:

2 That ye may be mindful of the words which

1. & 2. WELL then, the prevalency of these lewd and heretical * *teachers* being now such, it was a chief part of my design, in this *second* epistle, to arm you against them, by reminding you of what the ancient *prophets*, Christ and his *apostles* have foretold

* Chap. ii.

A. D. 66. which were spoken before by the holy prophets, and of the commandment of us the apostles of the Lord and Saviour.

foretold concerning them, and the judgments that are to overtake them.

3 Knowing this first that there shall come in the last days scoffers, walking after their own lusts,

3. That, being thus specially warned beforehand, you may be the less surprised, and influenced by this wicked and profane set of men, that infest the Christian church.

4 And saying †, Where is the promise of his coming: for since the fathers fell asleep, all things continue as they were from the beginning of the creation.

4. According to those *predictions*, you have now an instance of their daring impiety in deriding the *Christian* doctrine of *Christ's solemn appearance to judge and punish the obstinate adversaries of his true religion.* You tell us, *say they*, of wonderful blessings upon good, and dreadful punishments upon wicked men, at this *great* day: And this notion you support by *prophecies* and *predictions*. But we have not seen an article of it fulfilled. The *patriarchs* and *prophets*, to whom ye pretend these promises, and by whom these threats were pronounced, are all dead and gone; and the world is just as it was from the beginning.

5 For this they willingly are ignorant of, that by the word of God the heavens were of old, and the earth standing out of the water, and in the water.

6 Whereby the world that then was, being overflowed with water, perished.

5. & 6. Unthoughtful wretches! Have they, or can they forget all the *facts*, and wink thus hard at all the former *demonstrations* of divine justice and providence over mankind! Can they be ignorant, that the very God who created the *earth*, consisting of sea and land, destroyed it once by its own waters, for a punishment to its wicked inhabitants?

7 But the heavens and the earth which are now, by the same word

7. And, had they but any regard to the plain pr.dictions of Christ, and the doctrine of his *apostles*, they must

† See Dr. Mill. Prolegom. § 126, 127, 128.

word are kept in store, reserved unto fire, against the day of judgment and perdition of ungodly men.

must know too, that as the *antediluvian* world perished by the *flood*, so shall the *present* world we inhabit be destroyed by a conflagration of *fire*; and all wicked and irreclaimable men be left to perish in its flames * at the great day of universal judgment.

A. D. 66.

*See 1 Thes. iv. 16. 2 Pet. ii. 4. Matth. xxv. 41—46.

8 But (beloved) be not ignorant of this one thing, that one day is with the Lord as a thousand years, and a thousand years as one day.

8. But, for a further answer to their impious objection; when God has expressly promised a *future* blessing, or threatened a *future* judgment, but not stated to us the precise *time* of its accomplishment; it is the lowest degree of ignorance in us to account him slow and tardy in the performance of his word, or to suspect he will never perform it at all, because it is not done so *soon* as we may wish or expect: For this is to measure the *divine* mind by our *own* infirm conceptions and imagination. A *thousand years* seem a long and tedious time to *us*, that seldom out-live a *hundred*: And whatever *we* propose to do must be done speedily, or else opportunity may be lost, and time will fail us. But with the *Eternal Being* it is quite otherwise. He can lose no time, nor want opportunity. Whatever he promiseth or threateneth he can as certainly and effectually perform a thousand years hence, as to-day or to-morrow: And a thousand years are infinitely less to him, than a day is to us.

9 The Lord is not slack concerning his promise (as some men count slackness), but is long-suffering to us ward, not willing that any should perish, but that all should come to repentance.

9. Beside, in the present case of divine *promises* and *judgments*, it is the effect of perfect wisdom and mercy, for God to defer the execution, in order to exercise and improve the faith and patience of *good* men; and to afford to all that are *obstinate* and incredulous, the utmost opportunity of seeing their errors and reforming their practices; it being the gracious intent of Heaven to do the utmost that justice and goodness will permit, for the salvation of all his rational creatures.

A. D. 66. 10 But the day of the Lord will come as a thief in the night, in the which the heavens ſhall paſs away with a great noiſe, and the elements ſhall melt with fervent heat: the earth alſo, and the works that are therein, ſhall be burnt up.

10. But how long ſoever God may think fit to defer his deliverances of *good* and his vengeance upon *ſinful* men; yet the great day of *recompence*, we ſpeak of, will aſſuredly come, according to all the predictions concerning it. And, whether you conſider it in relation to the deſtruction of the *Jewiſh* nation in particular (which is but a ſhort figure of the *grand judgment*, and now ſoon to be fulfilled, by the Roman armies), yet even *that* will be a time of unexpected and terrible calamity, to the ſinful part of that people; and may well be figuratively expreſſed by *the convulſions of heaven and earth, and all nature**. But infinitely more dreadful will the day of *univerſal doom*, when, in a *literal* ſenſe, both air and earth, ſea and land, with all the appurtenances of this our habitable world, ſhall, with the moſt aſtoniſhing circumſtances, be deſtroyed by the *conflagration**.

11 Seeing then that all theſe things ſhall be diſſolved, what manner of perſons ought ye to be in all holy converſation and godlineſs,

12 Looking for, and haſting unto the coming of the day of God, wherein the heavens being on fire, ſhall be diſſolved, and the element ſhall melt with fervent heat!

11. & 12. The certainty of which things ought to make the *Jewiſh* Chriſtians particularly careful to avoid all the impure luſts and vices of their nation, thereby to eſcape the common ruin now coming upon it; and, in like manner, all *Chriſtians* in general, to ſtrive after the utmoſt purity of life and converſation, as the condition of their deliverance, at the great diſſolution of the *whole world*; and to be every way prepared for this *day of God*, that will be ſo tremenduous in all its circumſtances. (See ver. 10.)

13. For

* For the double conſtruction of this and the three following verſes, let the reader compare Matth. xxiv. 29, 30—42. Chap. xxv. 1—11—14, &c. Mark xiii. 24, 25, 26, 27. with Dr. Clarke's Paraph. and 1 Theſſ. v. 2, 3, 4.

13 Neverthelefs we, according to his promife, look for new heavens and * a new earth, wherein dwelleth righteoufnefs.

13. For, to all true and fincere Chriftians, these fearful revolutions will be only introductions to a *new*, and more *happy* ftate *, according to the *prophetic* expreffions. *Thus the deftruction of the* Jewifh *ftate, and ceremonial religion, will be followed by the eftablifhment* ||, *and freer propagation of the* Chriftian *faith. And, at the diffolution of the* whole *wicked world, we fhall be tranflated into* another, *where we fhall live in the complete exercife of all true virtue, and in the enjoyment of perfect happinefs.*

A. D. 66.

|| Ifa. lxv. 16, 17, 18. & lxvi. 22.

14 Wherefore (beloved) feeing that ye look for fuch things, be diligent that ye may be found of him in peace, without fpot, and blamelefs.

14. Let thefe confiderations, then, fpirit you forward to that innocence and fteady piety, which will render you acceptable to Chrift, and fure of his glorious rewards.

15 And account that the long-fuffering of our Lord is falvation, even as our beloved brother Paul alfo, according to the wifdom given unto him, hath written unto you †.

16 As alfo in all his epiftles, fpeaking in them of thefe things, in which are fome things hard to be underftood, which they that are unlearned and unftable wreft, as

15. & 16. And, to conclude, look upon this merciful delay of the divine judgments upon your wicked perfecutors, with a different eye, from what thofe irrational people view it withal. Confider it, as an inftance of Divine compaffion, in giving further time and fpace for repentance, to that obftinate *nation*. Agreeably to my brother Paul's difcourfe in Rom. xxiv. Rom. xi. and in other paffages of his *epiftles*, where he fpeaks of the *rejection of Jewifh people, the coming of Chrift*, and the *day of the Lord, &c.* which,

1 Theff. iv. & v. Philip. iv. 5. —iii 11. 20. Rom. ii. 4.

* [A new heaven and a new earth.] See note on ver. 10. See my Paraph. on Revelation chap. xxi. with the note thereon, ver. 5.

† Ver. 15. [Hath written unto you,] viz. To you Jews; Hebrews, in his epiftle to the Hebrews, chap. ii. 28.—x. 23—35. 37. See Dr. Mill's Prolegom. § 85, 86, &c.

A. D. 66.

|| δυσνοητὰ See Heb. v. 11.

as they do alſo the other ſcriptures, unto their own deſtruction.

which, ‡ though they be plain enough to be underſtood ||, by ſuch as will attend to the predictions of the *prophets*, or the warnings of Chriſt and his *apoſtles*; yet, by men prejudiced and prepoſſeſſed with notions of *temporal* greatneſs, and accuſtomed to vicious principles, are miſunderſtood and perverted, to wrong and deſtructive meanings.

17. Ye therefore, beloved, ſeeing ye know *theſe things* before, beware leſt ye alſo being led away with the error of the wicked, fall from your own ſtedfaſtneſs.

17. But you, dear brethren, having better apprehenſions, ought to be watchful, never to be led away by their pernicious doctrines, nor by any hardſhips whatever, diſcouraged from your profeſſion.

18 But grow in grace, and in the knowledge of our Lord and Saviour Jeſus Chriſt: to him be glory both now and for ever. Amen.

18. On the contrary, endeavour continually to improve in the true faith and practice of the religion of your Lord and Saviour Jeſus Chriſt; to whom be aſcribed all honour and glory, now and for ever. Amen.

---

‡ Ἐν οἷς, in which diſcourſes: Or rather, as ſome MSS. read it ἐν αἷς, in which epiſtles.

A PARA-

A

PARAPHRASE

ON THE

FIRST EPISTLE GENERAL

OF

St. JOHN.

THE PREFACE.

THERE being no reaſonable diſpute againſt St. John's being the *author* of theſe epiſtles, it will be needful only to obſerve ſomething concerning the people to *whom*, the time *when*, and the occaſion upon *which* they were written.

§ 1. St. John being one of thoſe apoſtles, whoſe main buſineſs was to convert the Jews *, as that of Paul and Barnabas was to preach to the Gentiles and Jews together, in foreign parts; and, it being agreed on by antiquity, that he exerciſed his miniſtry in the parts of Aſia the Greater, after he had left Judea; and in thoſe of the Leſſer Aſia, after the death of St. Peter and St. Paul; theſe circumſtances, with the ſtrain of theſe writings themſelves, render it ſufficiently clear that this *firſt epiſtle* was directed to the *Jewiſh Chriſtians* (not *excluding* the *Gentile* ones) of thoſe provinces in *general;* as the *two latter* were, the one to the *elect lady*, the o-

To whom.

* Gal. ii. 9.

ther

ther to Gaius in *particular*. Though, from what *place* they were dated, must be confessed a secret, from the perfect silence of all ancient writings concerning it.

The time. § 2. His mentioning the *last hour*; i. e. *Christianity* abolishing the *Jewish* dispensation, along with the *Antichrists* and false prophets that our Saviour foretold would be the forerunners of the destruction of that nation, seems most strongly to intimate (if not absolutely concludes) the *time* of this *first epistle* to have been before the destruction of Jerusalem; and is, therefore, I think, with the most probability, placed by Dr. Whitby in, or about the year 67 or 68.

The occasion. § 3. The incurable obstinacy, wickedness and rage of the infidel Jews, which we have observed, in the *prefaces* to several of the foregoing *epistles*, to have been growing up to a desperate height, and wherewith the *Jewish Christians* were, in several respects, too much tainted, was now so far advanced in its wretched effects, as to shoot out into several pernicious *heresies* in the Christian church: Simon Magus, the head of these *heretics*, was followed by the lewd train of the *Nicholaitans*, *Corinthians*, *Ebionites*, *Menandrians*, *Gnostics*, &c. most of them probably of *Jewish* extraction, and all possessed with the wicked notions of their *zealots*. The vile maxims wherewith they had infected the Christian church, as we learn from the earliest antiquity, were such as these*.

(A) 1. That mere *external* profession, and the privileges of being the *true church*, would justify and save men, whatever

---

* I will here refer the reader to such few passages of the ancient Christian writers, relating to the opinions and practices of these *heretics*, as appear plainly to be the true key to St. John's *epistles*.

(*A*) Thus Irenæus. Lib. I. chap. 20. "Simon Magus "taught, That they who hoped in him needed not take any "further care; but might live as they pleased—Accordingly the priests of their mysteries live uncleanly." And Lib. I. 24. "The *Carpocratians* lead a life of luxury—And "say, that actions are good or bad only in the opinions of "men." Again, Lib. I 27. "As for the *Nicholaitans*— "They live disorderly; as teaching that fornication, &c.

whatever their life and *practice* were. Againſt this the apoſtle urges, 1 Epiſt. i. 1—5. to the end. Chap. ii. 1—8—15, 16, 17. Chap. iii. 3—12. Chap. v. 2, 3, 4.

2. That thoſe privileges would warrant the moſt virulent and uncharitable behaviour toward all that differed from them. Againſt this St. John warns them in this 1 Epiſt. chap. ii. 9—11. Chap. iii. 10. to the end. Chap. iv. 7, 8—11, 12—20, 21. (*B*)

3. That the man Jeſus was not Chriſt, was not *the Son of God*, and that Chriſt did not *really* and *actually* live and ſuffer in our fleſh, but in appearance only. This is confuted, 1 Epiſt. i. 1—5. Chap. ii. 23—27. Chap. iii. 1—7—14. 15, 16. Chap. v. 1—5. 16—20. Chap. iv. 1, 2, 3. (*C*)

4. That, to avoid *perſecution*, it was lawful for *Chriſtians* to diſſemble their faith, to deny Chriſt, and to join in *idolatrous* worſhip: Againſt which are warnings of Chap. v. 16—21. (*D*)

Antichriſt, who.

§ 4. Againſt theſe pernicious principles, then prevailing, were the ſeveral parts of theſe *epiſtles* levelled, and from

---

" are indifferent things. Wherefore the text ſays—The " deeds *of the* Nicholaitans, *which I hate;* Rev. ii. 6.

(*B*) Iren. Lib. I. 34. " Others of the Gnoſticks ſay, " that Cain—with Eſau, Corah, and the Sodomites were al- " lied to them." Ignat. Epiſt. ad Philad. " Avoid the " impure *Nicholaitans*, thoſe lovers of pleaſure, thoſe calum- " niators." And Tertullian de Preſcript. Hær. § 47. *They magnify Cain* [*the murderer.*]

(*C*) Thus Iren. Lib. I. chap. 25. Corinthus taught, That Chriſt [the *Word*] deſcended upon Jeſus [the *Man*] at his *baptiſm;* but afterwards flew away from Jeſus; and Jeſus ſuffered again, but Chriſt was impaſſible: But, ſays he, Lib. III. chap. 18. " St. John knew but *one* and the *ſame* " *Word of God*, namely, he that was the *only begotten*, who " was *incarnate*, even Jeſus Chriſt our Lord." See him at large in Lib. I. 4. iii. x. xi. xii. xvii. & xviii. chapters, and Lib. IV. 4—16. and elſewhere. So Origen. " Hic Chriſtus " natus eſt, et paſſus eſt in *veritate*, et non per *imaginem;* " vere mortuus eſt, *vere* enim a morte reſurrexit," Proleg. in περὶ ἀρχ.

(*D*) Iren. Lib. I. 27. " As for the *Nicholaitans*, they " live diſorderly; as teaching that fornication, and eating " what is offered to idols, are indifferent things."

from the observation whereof the *phrases* made use of, in them, are to receive their due light. The authors of these wretched errors St. John brands with the name of *Antichrists*, (chap. ii. 18.) The characters given of *Antichrist* in this epistle, is that of *denying the Father with the Son, or that Jesus was the true Christ* (chap. ii. 22. and iv. 3.) Which being compared with the virulent and persecuting spirit spoken of, and referred to in the several passages of the 2, 3, and 4 chapters, show the people he speaks of, to be the same with St. Paul's *man of sin*, and *wicked one*, 2 Thess. ii. Moreover, there being a plain distinction between St. John's ὁ ἀντιχριστος (chap. ii. 22. and iv. 3.) *great* or *special Antichrist*, and the *many Antichrists* even *then* come, chap. ii. 18. seems to make it very clear that what these two *apostles* spoke of the Jews and *heretical Christians* of their *own* times, they in a much higher, and more *eminent* sense intended to mean of those *Christian* corrupters of the true faith in *after* ages, who, by the exorbitant use of *temporal* and *persecuting* power, would arbitrarily impose such doctrines and practices upon mankind, as contradicted the plain rules and designs of *Christianity*, and destroyed its credit, i. e. *in effect*, denied its *truth* and authority. See Sir Isaac Newton's Observat. on the Apoc. chap. 2. p. 256—and in many other places of that incomparable book.

Wherefore, that dispute, whether the church of Rome be *Antichrist*, or no, is reduced to a small compass. That she is not the *Jewish* or *heretical Antichrist*, whom St. John affirms to have been *already come* in *his* time, is easily granted. But whether, for almost a thousand years last past, the *inspirations* she has falsely pretended to, the *miracles* she has forged, the monstrous *articles* she has coined, and the *brethren* she has *hated* and persecuted, be not so many, as to make her the *great Christian antichrist*, and the *man of sin*, will be no longer a doubt with impartial readers of St. Paul and St. John, than until there arise *another* community that can excel *her* in *error*, *superstition* and *cruelty*. See and compare *preface* to the Thessalonians, § 4. and see my Paraph. on the Revelations.

CHAP.

CHAP. I.

The Clear and Evident Testimonies of the Life and Actions of Christ, the Ground of our Christian *Hope. Moral Virtue the only Condition of future Happiness, and the chief Mark of a true* Christian. *Pardon and Salvation by Christ to be, not by mere External Profession of his Religion, but by Confession of Sins, and Reformation of Life, as the Fruit of Faith.*

1 THAT which was from the beginning, which we have heard, which we have seen with our eyes, which we have looked upon, and our hands have handled of the word of life:

1. MY design in this epistle, dear brethren, is to preserve you from those false and dangerous notions, spread among you by the *Jewish* zealots, and such *heretical teachers* in the Christian church, as are corrupted by *their* principles, relating to the doctrines of the *gospel*, and the conditions of our enjoying the final blessings promised in it. And particularly to warn you against that notion of theirs, "That Jesus was not that Christ, or *Word*, "or *Son of God*, who was with the *Father* before the "world was made; and was incarnate and suffered for "us here upon earth:" Which I shall do, by laying them before you, as I received them, by undoubted evidences from Christ * himself.

Written A. D. 67.

* ἀπ' ἀρχῆς

2 (For the life was manifested, and we have seen it, and bear witness, and show unto you that eternal life which was with the Father, and was manifested unto us.)

3 That which we have seen and heard, declare we unto you, that ye also may have fellowship with us; and

2. & 3. And first, as to the reality and certainty of the *life, actions*, and *death* of Christ (whom the infidel Jews deny to have been sent into the world as the true *Messiah*, and these *heretics* pretend to have lived and died in *appearance* only), let me remind you, that these *facts* were the very things determined by God the *Father* concerning Christ, foretold all along by the *prophets*, and now

A. D. 67.

and truly our fellowship *is* with the Father, and with his Son Jesus Christ.

now *actually* fulfilled, before the face of the whole *Jewish* nation, and of us the *apostles* in particular, with the utmost evidences that a distinct knowledge, and all the demonstrations of our senses can give a thing*. These we deliver to you as articles, the belief whereof is the fundamental condition of your sharing with us in the happy privileges of being the *church* and children of God the *Father*, through *Christ the Son*; and of enjoying the future and eternal felicity promised in the *gospel*.

*See John i. 10—14.

4 And these things write we unto you, that your joy may be full.

4. My aim therefore is, that by giving you a repeated assurance, and full satisfaction in these important truths, you may, with perfect cheerfulness, and undaunted vigour, persevere in the profession of them, against all the malice and insinuations of these corrupt *teachers*.

5 This then is the message which we have heard of him, and declare unto you that God is light, and in him is no darkness at all.

6 If we say that we have fellowship with him, and walk in darkness, we lie, and do not the truth:

5. & 6. Now, as to the *doctrines* of the Christian religion, the main purpose, and sum total of them is this, *viz.* That as God is a being absolutely holy and perfect in goodness, the only original of truth and righteousness, without the least possible mixture of moral impurity; the absolute condition of mens enjoying his favour, or of expecting happiness from him, is the imitation of these his moral perfections. And consequently, for any people to profess themselves members of his *church*, while they indulge themselves in such instances of lewdness and immorality (as do the false *teachers* ‖ of these times) is to act in direct contradiction both to his divine nature and revelation.

‖ See the Pref. § 3.

7 But if we walk in the light, as he is in the light, we have fellowship one with another, and the blood of Jesus Christ his Son cleanseth us from all sin.

7. That, therefore, the favour of God, and the privilege of being members of his true *church*, by the full pardon of our past sins, procured for us by the death and sufferings of his Son Jesus Christ, runs upon this same condition, of endeavouring,

vouring, as much as in us lies, to conform our tempers A. D. 67.
and practice to this divine pattern and example.

8 If we say that we have no sin, we deceive ourselves, and the truth is not in us.
9 If we confess our sins, he is faithful and just to forgive us our sins, and to cleanse us from all unrighteousness.
10 If we say that we have not sinned, we make him a liar, and his word is not in us.

8. 9. & 10. So that, for any *Christian* to embrace that notion of the *Jewish* zealots and *heretics*, *That mere external profession, and barely joining one's self to the true religion, renders a man pure* and acceptable to God, whatever *his dispositions and practices be*, and that there is really such as *sin* and *guilt* in the world, at least, none amongst their party; is to put the most fatal delusion upon himself, by giving God the lie, and contradicting the nature of the *gospel* religion; which supposes men to be *sinners*, and is principally designed to bring them to the humble confession and sincere reformation of every wicked practice; and so to depend upon the divine promise for perfect pardon and salvation.

CHAP. II.

The same Argument continued to verse 8. *The Virulent and Uncharitable Temper of the* Jewish Zealots *and* Heretical *Christians Condemned. Christian Love and Charity called a* New *Commandment, and why. This Virtue an Essential Property of a true Christian. A Warning against the prevalent Love of* Temporal *Greatness and Pleasures. The* Jewish *Dispensation is at an end. and the* Christian *Religion succeeds in its Place.* Antichrist *was foretold to come among* Christians. *The* Jewish Zealots, *and* Heretical *Christians in* St. John's *Time are, in some sense, called* Antichrists. *The first Original of them. Cautions against their Errors.*

1 MY little children, these things write I unto you,

1. & 2. MY purpose then is to arm you against the vicious principles ‡ of these men. Indulge-

‡ Chap. i. 5, 6—10.

A. D. 67. you, that ye ſin not.
And if any man ſin,
we have an advocate
with the Father, Je-
ſus Chriſt the righte-
ous:
2 And he is the
propitiation for our
ſins: and not for
ours only, but alſo for
the ſins of the whole
world.

Indulge yourſelves in no inſtance of groſs and habitual ſin: And you may, then, whether *Jewiſh* or *Gentile* Chriſtians, depend, that both your paſt tranſgreſſions, and all the future failings of your lives, committed by human frailty, ignorance, or ſurpriſe, ſhall, upon your true repentance, be fully pardoned, by the interceſſion of Jeſus Chriſt, our great *Advocate* with *God the Father*: The merits of whoſe *ſufferings*, and power of whoſe *interceſſion*, is not confined to the believers of the *Jewiſh* nation (as their *zealots* vainly imagine), but extends itſelf to *all* ſincere Chriſtians, of what denomination ſoever.

3 And hereby we
do know that we
know him, if we keep
his commandments.
4 He that ſaith, I
know him, and keep-
eth not his command-
ments, is a liar, and
the truth is not in
him.
5 But whoſo keep-
eth his word, in him
verily is the love of
God perfected: here-
by know we that we
are in him.
6 He that ſaith he abideth in him, ought himſelf alſo ſo
to walk, even as he walked.

3. 4. 5. & 6. Look, therefore, upon a careful obedience to the *moral* commands of the goſpel, as the beſt and ſureſt character of a true *Chriſtian**. To imitate the life, and follow the example of Chriſt, was the grand deſign of our call to his religion. This is truly to love God, and to be beloved of him. To pretend to be his *people*, and yet live contrary to the *moral* and plaineſt perfections of his *nature*, is to pretend to perfect contradictions.

7. In

* The common reader may obſerve here, once for all, that theſe phraſes, "To know God, to be in him, to love God, to be in Chriſt, to abide in him, to know the truth, *to be* born of God, or Chriſt, &c." are ſo many expreſſions to ſignify mens being true *Chriſtians*.

A. D. 67.

7 Brethren, I write * no new commandment unto you, but an old commandment which ye had from the beginning: the old commandment is the word which ye have heard from the beginning.

7. In thus preſſing you to the obſervance of this great point, in * *general*, I propoſe nothing *new* to you, nothing but what you muſt needs know to be the main purpoſe of your *Chriſtianity*. Nothing but what Chriſt our Maſter has taught us, in his own expreſs words, John xiv. 21, 23.—xv. 10. And my buſineſs *now* is, only to remind you of, and ſecure you in it, againſt the ſuggeſtions of your falſe *teachers*.

8 Again, a new commandment I write unto you, which thing ‡ is true in him and in you: becauſe the darkneſs is paſt, and the true light now ſhineth.

8. Only let me remind you, that *our* duty of *love* and *charity* to our fellow Chriſtians, hath ſomething both in the *degree* of it, and the *obligation* to it, *peculiar* to the *Chriſtian* religion. Chriſtians are to love each other, not after the ordinary manner of other people, but with an affection proportionable to *that* wherewith Chriſt || *hath loved us*.|| ‡ Now there was never any love like *his*: And conſequently the *goſpel* religion has advanced and improved *this* duty, and obliged us Chriſtians to a degree that may be called *new*, and by an argument that is *proper* to *us*.

|| See and compare John xiii. 15—34, 35.

9 He that ſaith he is in the light, and hateth his brother, is in darkneſs, even until now.

9. 10. & 11. Wherefore, it is an effect of the moſt malicious prejudice and ſtupid ignorance of plain truth, for any man to profeſs himſelf a true diſciple of Chriſt, while he

* Ver. 7. [No new commandment.] Which being underſtood to refer to the foregoing diſcourſe, makes the cleareſt ſenſe and connection. Or elſe thus; The duty of *love* was not *new* to ſuch as knew it to be enjoined by Chriſt himſelf; but only as Chriſtianity has raiſed that duty *higher* than any *other* religion.

‡ [Which thing (i. e. the newneſs of the commandment) is true in him and in you.] In *him*, as having ſet us a *peculiar* example: And in us Chriſtians, as having from that example a peculiar *obligation* to it.

A. D. 67.

* See the Pref. § 3.

10 He that loveth his brother abideth in the light, and there is none occaſion of ſtumbling in him.

11 But he that hateth his brother, is in darkneſs, and walketh in darkneſs, and knoweth not whither he goeth, becauſe that darkneſs hath blinded his eyes.

he harbours revengeful thoughts, * and uncharitable principles toward other *men*. On the contrary, a kind behaviour, and tender diſpoſition toward all our *brethren*, is one of the beſt inſtances of *Chriſtian* perfection, and ſecures us from all the ſcandal and miſchievous effects of a cenſorious and perſecuting temper.

12 I write unto you, little children, becauſe your ſins are forgiven you for his names ſake.

13 I write unto you, fathers, becauſe ye have known him that is from the beginning. I write unto you, young men, becauſe ye have overcome the wicked one. I write unto you, little children, becauſe ye have known the Father.

14 I have written unto you, fathers, becauſe ye have known him *that is* from the beginning. I have written unto you, young men, becauſe ye are ſtrong, and the word of God abideth in yon, and ye have overcome the wicked one.

12. 13. & 14. The cautions I here give you, ought to be equally regarded by all *degrees* of Chriſtian profeſſors. The *new converts* and *younger* Chriſtians are to conſider themſelves as newly put into a ſtate of ſalvation, the pardon of ſin, and the favour of God, through Jeſus Chriſt; and endeavour to confirm themſelves in it, by the careful practice of true Chriſtian virtue. Such as are come to more *maturity* in their *profeſſion*, and are in the ſtrength and vigour of their *age*, have a great advantage, and ought to employ the utmoſt of that vigour in reſiſting the utmoſt temptations of the devil, and perfecting their conqueſt over him, and all his wicked inſtruments. And the *aged* Chriſtians, cannot but have ſo clear a knowledge of God, and the revelation of his will by Jeſus Chriſt, during the long ſeaſon from their firſt converſion, that it would be utterly inexcuſable for *them* to be wanting in theſe *eſſential* duties, or be drawn from them by the falſe *teachers*.

15. & 16. To

15 Love not the world, neither the things that are in the world. If any man love the world, the love of the Father is not in him.

16 For all that is in the world, the lust of the flesh, the lust of the eyes, and the pride of life, is not of the Father, but is of the world.

15. & 16. To proceed then: Endeavour to wean your affections from all immoderate desires of the pleasures, riches, dignities and preferments of this world. Show no sinful compliance to attain them; love them not in any higher degree, than to be ready to part with any of them, for the sake of Christ and his religion. For all such immoderate affections of temporal things, are utterly inconsistent with the love of God and true religion.

17 And the world passeth away, and the lust thereof: but he that doth the will of God, abideth for ever.

17. And, it should serve to cure you of all such love for the greatest pleasures of this kind, to consider how fading, unsatisfactory and short they are. Whereas the habitual practice of *Christian virtue* is, what will for ever continue with, and be a blessing and an ornament to you.

18 Little children, it is the last time, and as ye have heard that Antichrist shall come, even now are there many Antichrists, whereby we know that it is the last time.

18. My dear Christians, the *Jewish* dispensation is now past, and the *Christian* religion succeeds in its place; the religion that is to take place in the *last age*, or *latter days* of the world, as the ancient *prophets* foretold: and as our Saviour himself, and we his apostles have foretold you of *great corruptions* * that would be brought into the Christian church, by men of *temporal*, and secular designs; so what you see of it fulfilled *already*, in the practices of the *Jewish zealots* and *heretical teachers* crept into the church, is sufficient to convince you of the truth of these prophecies, to confirm you in your *Christianity*, and secure you from their dangerous infection.

* See the *Pref.* § 4. and the *Pref.* to 1 Thess. § 4. with 2 Thess. chap. ii.

A. D. 67.

19 They went out from us, but they were not of us: for if they had been of us, they would no doubt have continued with us: but *they went out* *, that they might be made manifest, that, they were not all of us.

|| See Acts xv. 1, 24. Gal. ii. 4. 2 Cor. xi. 13.

19. The first broachers of these lewd errors, pretended to come with a commission from the college of *apostles* at Jerusalem ||, to preach up the necessity of *circumcision* and the *ceremonial law* to Christian *believers*. And Simon Magus himself pretended to be a *Christian*, and was baptized (Acts viii. 13.). Had these men been indeed true *Christians*, they could never have been so audacious, as to have forged a commission from *us*, but would have continued to preach the same doctrine with us. In like manner, had Simon and his followers been sincere, they would still have followed the *apostles* of Christ: and therefore, by presuming in so foul a manner, to do quite contrary, it is but too plain they were never *true believers* at all *.

20 But ye have an unction from the holy One, and ye know all things.

‡ χρίσμα.

20. But however specious their pretences may now be, I hope *you* are so fully instructed in the great truths, so sensible of the noble ‡ privileges of your religion, and so confirmed in it by the gifts and endowments of the Holy Ghost, as not to be in much danger of being perverted by them.

21 I have not written unto you, because ye know not the truth: but because ye know it, and that no lie is of the truth.

21. And therefore I *now* represent the case to you, to let you see how great a sin it would be in *you*, ever to hearken to people so full of impudence and falsehood.

22 Who is a liar, but he that denieth that Jesus is the Christ? he is Antichrist

§ See v. 18. and the Pref. § 4.

22. & 23. It is true indeed, the corruption of the *Christian* faith is not yet come to its height: the *great Antichrist* § is not yet come: but

---

* [That they might be made manifest; ἵνα φανερωθῶσιν. So that they appear.]

† [Not all of us; ὅτι οὐκ εἰσὶ πάντες; That none of them were of us.] So οὐκ ἂν πᾶσα σάρξ, is, No flesh, Matth. xxiv. 22. Mark xiii. 20.

A. D. 67.

christ that denieth the Father and the Son.

23 Whosoever denieth the Son, the same hath not the Father: *but he that acknowledgeth the Son, hath the Father also.*

but nothing can be more like him, nor more truly deserve to be branded with his titles and characters, than these turbulent *zealots* of the *Jewish* faction, some of which, against all the divine evidences given them, flatly deny Christ to be the true *Messiah;* and the rest maintain and impose such principles as utterly destroy the design of his religion: for they affirm, that Jesus, who suffered upon the cross, was a mere *man*, not Christ the *Word* and *Son of God;* which is as much in effect to deny Christ *himself*, and consequently God the *Father* that sent him. (See the Pref. § 3.)

24 Let that therefore abide in you, which ye have heard from the beginning: if that which ye have heard from the beginning shall remain in you, ye also shall continue in the Son, and in the Father.

24. & 25. Wherefore endeavour to secure your interest in God through Christ, by adhering firmly to the doctrines of *Christianity*, as at first taught to us by Christ himself, and by us to *you*. Remember the great *gospel* promise of eternal life and happiness is to be enjoyed only upon *this* condition.

25 And this is the promise that he hath promised us, even eternal life.

26 These things have I written unto you, concerning them that seduce you.

27 But the * anointing which ye have received of him, abideth in you, and ye need not that any man teach you: But, as the same anointing teacheth you of all things, and is truth, and is no lie, and even as it hath taught you, ye shall abide in him.

26. & 27. I remind you of these things (as I said, ver. 20. and 21.) to arm you the more strongly against the errors spread amongst you; by assuring myself the deep sense you have of the great truths and noble * blessings of your profession, will effectually prevent you from being imposed upon by such palpable deceits.

* Ver. 27. [The anointing.] See verse 20.

A. D. 67.

† Ver. 24.

28 And now, little children, abide in him, that when he ſhall appear, we may have confidence and not be aſhamed before him at his coming.

28. And therefore again † I entreat you, dear diſciples, not to forfeit the glories you are to partake of, at the great day of Chriſt's judgment, by ſuffering yourſelves to be miſled into any ſinful courſes.

29 If ye know that he is righteous, ye know that every one that doth righteouſneſs is born of him.

29. For, as ſurely as perfect holineſs and purity is the nature of God, ſo certain is it that they, and none but they, who by mortifying their corrupt paſſions, ſtrive to imitate him, in the practice of true virtue, ſhall be accounted his true ſervants, and eternally rewarded as ſuch.

CHAP. III.

The great Privilege of Chriſtianity. *Conformity to the* Moral *Perfections of the Divine Nature, is our Duty here, and will be our Happineſs hereafter. Moral Obedience is therefore the moſt eſſential Mark of a true* Chriſtian. Immorality *denotes a* wicked *Man be his Profeſſion what it will.* Charity *is one of the ſpecial Inſtances of* Chriſtian *Morality. An obedient* Chriſtian *has the undoubted Teſtimony of his own Conſcience, confirmed by the Gifts of the* Holy Spirit, *that he is acceptable to God as a true Diſciple of* Jeſus Chriſt.

‡ Chap. ii. 27, 28, 29.

1 BEhold, what manner of love the Father hath beſtowed upon us, that we ſhould be called the ſons of God! therefore the world knoweth us not, becauſe it knew him not.

1. I Have been ‡ exhorting you to ſecure to yourſelves the privileges of your *Chriſtianity*, by the careful practice of its commands. A thing you cannot fail to do, would you ſeriouſly conſider how noble and valuable a bleſſing it is to be made the children of God, members of his church, and imitators of his divine excellencies. No wonder, therefore, the

generality

generality of mankind ſhould have ſo deſpicable a notion A. D. 67.
of us Chriſtians, while they have ſo little apprehenſions of the nature and will of that God, whoſe ſervants we are.

2 Beloved, now are we the ſons of God, and it doth not yet appear what we ſhall be: but we know, that when he ſhall appear, we ſhall be like him: for we ſhall ſee him as he is.

2. Meanwhile, let *us* duly eſteem the happineſs propoſed to us. And, though the *future* perfection of it be ſuch as ſurpaſſes the reach of human conception, yet thus much in general, is plain and ſatisfactory to us, that by arriving to a clearer knowledge of his divine nature, we ſhall be exalted to that delightful reſemblance of him, wherein our perfection and happineſs chiefly conſiſts.

3 And every man that hath this hope in him purifieth himſelf, even as he is pure.

3. And, if this be our expected enjoyment, all that hope for it, muſt begin *now*, to lay a foundation for it, by ſtriving, as far as human infirmity will permit, to imitate God, by the practice of *Chriſtian* virtue in this life.

4 Whoſoever committeth ſin, tranſgreſſeth alſo the law: for ſin is the tranſgreſſion of the law.

5 And ye know that he was manifeſted to take away our ſins, and in him is no ſin.

4. & 5. Wherefore it is moſt evident, that the wilful and habitual practice of thoſe vices now ſo much encouraged by the *heretical teachers*, is perfectly deſtructive of the end of our *Chriſtianity*. He that deliberately breaks the divine *law*, defeats the very means and methods of reſembling the divine nature. And to indulge any known and groſs ſin, is to act againſt the very purpoſe of Chriſt's coming into the world, which was nothing elſe but to free us of the guilt, habit and power of ſin.

6 Whoſoever abideth in him, ſinneth not: whoſoever ſinneth, hath not ſeen him, neither known him.

6. 7. & 8. And be not impoſed upon by the loudeſt boaſts, and moſt ſpecious pretences, of theſe wicked men. The pretences they make to higher and deeper *knowledge* of God than all others. A good Chriſtian

7 Little

and

A. D. 67.

7 Little children, let no man deceive you: he that doth righteousness, *is* righteous, even as he is righteous.

8 He that committeth sin, is of the devil: for the devil sinneth from the beginning: for this purpose the Son of God was manifested, that he might destroy the works of the devil.

and a lewd *liver*, are direct contradictions. And, as *purity* of life is the mark of God's children, so does a *vicious* course demonstrate a man to be a servant of the *devil*, the first author of all wickedness; and is a manifest abetting of his impious power and contrivance, which Christ, the Son of God, came into the world on purpose to countermine and destroy.

9 Whosoever is born of God, doth not commit sin: for his seed remaineth in him, and he cannot sin, because he is born of God.

10 In this the children of God are manifest, and the children of the devil: whosoever doth not righteousness, is not of God, neither he that loveth not his brother.

9. & 10. In fine, while a man preserves his *Christian* principle, and answers the character of a true member of God's church, he can never be guilty of *deliberate* and *habitual* vice. Make it therefore a sure *test* to whom a man belongs, in whose service he is listed, and from whom he must expect his wages; whether of God, or the *devil*, by the good or wicked practices of his *life*, by his behaviour towards God, and towards his brethren.

11 For this is the message that ye heard from the beginning, that we should love one another.

|| See chap. ii. 8, &c.

11. His *brethren*, I say, for the doctrine of Christ || and all his *apostles*, do most plainly show Christian *charity* to be the *peculiar* virtue of *our* religion.

12 Not as Cain, *who* was of that wicked one, and slew his brother: and wherefore slew he him? because his own works were evil, and his brothers righteous.

13 Marvel

12. & 13. You know what it was that provoked that wicked creature Cain to murder his own brother, viz. the antipathy of a *vicious* to a *religious* temper. So it is with you *now*, the generality of the corrupted world hate you upon the *same* principle,

13 Marvel not, my brethren, if the world hate you.

ciple, and becauſe the purity of your lives are a ſtanding reproach upon their impieties, and you ought the leſs to be ſurpriſed at it.

14 We know that we have paſſed from death unto life, becauſe we love the brethren: he that loveth not his brother abideth in death.

15 Whoſoever hateth his brother, is a murderer, and ye know that no murderer hath eternal life abiding in him.

14. & 15. Bear it therefore patiently, ſince the charitable diſpoſition that poſſeſſes you, is ſo ſure a mark of your being true diſciples of Chriſt, and entitled to the future happineſs promiſed in his *goſpel*. As, on the contrary, the ſpiteful and malicious temper of thoſe *zealots*, demonſtrates them to be in an unregenerate ſtate; nay, in the eye of God (who judges by the inward principle of the *heart*, and not by the outward *actions* only) to be no leſs than *murderers*, and conſequently void of all true hopes of eternal ſalvation.

16 Hereby perceive we the love of God *, becauſe he laid down his life for us: and we ought to lay down our lives for the brethren.

16. When you conſider that amazing inſtance of divine love, in the death of * Chriſt, for the redemption of mankind, you cannot think it too much, that, in imitation of ſo wondrous an example, *Chriſtians* ſhould be obliged, not only to bear and forbear, but to be ready to offer their own *lives*, whenever the religion of Chriſt, the good of his church, and the welfare of their Chriſtian *brethren*, calls them to it.

17 But whoſo hath this worlds good, and ſeeth his brother have need, and ſhutteth up his

17. How infinitely ſhort of *this* love, then, nay, how contrary to *this* divine pattern are thoſe men, who, while they have power and ability

* Ver. 16. [Hereby perceive we the love (of God.) Note, The words (*of God*) are not in the Greek: the text is ἐν τούτῳ ἐγνώκαμεν τὴν ἀγάπην—Hereby we have experienced love, i. e. the greateſt love becauſe he, i. e. Chriſt, laid down his life for us.]

A. D. 67. his bowels of compassion from him, how dwelleth the love of God in him?

ability to do good, remain unmoved at the wants of their fellow *Christians?*

18 My little children, let us not love in word, neither in tongue, but in deed, and in truth.

18. Remember, dear brethren, the charity of a *Christian* disciple is not to express itself in fair pretences and kind speeches, but in *actions* of bounty and liberality.

19 And hereby we know that we are of the truth, and shall assure our hearts before him.

20 For if our heart condemn us, God is greater than our heart, and knoweth all things.

21 Beloved, if our heart condemn us not, *then* have we confidence towards God.

19. 20. & 21. This will show us to be *Christians* indeed, and while the impartial testimony, and inward sense of our own consciences, assures us of the sincere performance of our duty; we may safely conclude, that God, the searcher of hearts, and standard of all truth, will approve of, and reward us. And, on the contrary, whoever, by the clear conviction of his own mind, knows and feels himself to be a hypocritical transgressor of his *moral* duty, must be assured, that God, who knows him better than he does himself, cannot fail to be his more severe judge and revenger.

22 And whatsoever we ask, we receive of him, because we keep his commandments, and do those things that are pleasing in his sight.

22. This sincerity will warrant our perfect dependance upon God, and the sense of having done our duty, to the best of our power, fully secures us, that all our Christian *prayers* shall be answered in the most seasonable time, and in the best manner.

23 And this is his commandment, that we should believe on the name of his Son Jesus Christ, and love one another, as he gave us commandment.

24 And

23. & 24, For, in short, true faith in the doctrine of Christ, and true charity to *mankind*, especially to our *Christian* brethren, is the sum total of our duty. And *you*, that have already duly performed it, have a sufficient pledge and *earnest* of your acceptance with

with God, as true disciples of Christ, by the gifts and graces of his *Holy Spirit* conferred upon you. A. D. 67.

24 And he that keepeth his commandments, dwelleth in him, and he in him: and hereby we know that he abideth in us, by the Spirit which he hath given us.

CHAP. IV.

A Caution against false Prophets *and Pretenders to* Inspiration. *The Rule whereby to judge of them. The Exhortation to Love and Charity, renewed, as the proper Badge and Token of a true* Christian.

1 BEloved, believe not every spirit, but try the spirits whether they are of God; because many false prophets are gone out into the world.

1. THE time being now come, wherein the *Jews* expect the appearance of their *Messiah*, according to the scripture *prophecies*; there are so many *impostors*, that set themselves up for Christs, and so many pretenders to inspiration and miracles, among the *heretical teachers* of these times, all striving to gain belief, by diabolical delusions and forgeries; that it highly concerns you to look well, and examine them thoroughly to prevent your being imposed upon.

2 Hereby know ye the Spirit of God: Every spirit that confesseth that Jesus Christ is come in the flesh, is of God.

3 And every spirit that confesseth * not that Jesus Christ is come

2. & 3. Now, you have a safe *rule*, whereby to judge of all pretences to *prophecy*, *miracles* or *inspiration* of any kind. Your *Christian* religion, both as to the life, doctrine and death, &c. of Christ, being, in so ample and unexceptionable a manner, confirmed by God; you ought to conclude, that whatever

* Ver. 3. [Confesseth not that Jesus Christ is come in the flesh.] He points at Cerinthus. See the Pref. § 3.

A. D. 67.

come in the fleſh, is not of God: and this is that *ſpirit* of Antichriſt, whereof you have heard that it ſhould come, and even now already is it in the world.

whatever *Jewiſh* or *heretical* pretender ſets up againſt the great truth *of the incarnation of Jeſus Chriſt*, denying him to be the true * *Meſſiah*, or ſaying that our Jeſus is not the real and very Chriſt, the *Word*, and *Son of God;* let him pretend to what *gifts* and *miracles* he will, to confirm it by; is an *impoſtor*, acting by *diabolical* deluſions and conjurations; and one of thoſe very Antichriſts and falſe *prophets*, the forerunners of the great Antichriſt foretold by Chriſt and the *apoſtles*. On the contrary, whatever Chriſtian works any *miracles* in confirmation of the true articles of our *faith*, ſo inconteſtibly eſtabliſhed *beforehand*, muſt be thought to perform them by the *Spirit of God;* it being impoſſible to conceive the devil would lend *his* power, toward the ſupporting a religion ſo oppoſite and deſtructive to his *own* kingdom; or, that Chriſt ſhould give the power of *his Spirit* to ſuch as embrace not his true *faith*†.

† See and compare 1 Cor. xii. 3.

4 Ye are of God, little children, and have overcome them: becauſe greater is he that is in you, than he that is in the world.

4. Thus, the powers of the Holy Ghoſt diſplayed by Chriſt, conferred on us his *apoſtles*, and reſiding *yet* upon many members of your ſeveral churches, give teſtimony to *your* religion, far ſuperior to what theſe worldly minded *impoſtors* can pretend to, in favour of their falſe doctrines.

5 They are of the world; therefore ſpeak they of the world, and the world heareth them.

6 We are of God: he that knoweth God, heareth us; he that is not of God, heareth

5. & 6. You cannot but perceive too, an eſſential mark of diſtinction between *theſe*, and a truly *Chriſtian* prophet. The *one* have no other views but of *temporal* power, greatneſs and dominion; no other notions of Chriſt but that of a temporal *monarch*, to raiſe and aggrandize the *Jewiſh* nation, by the

* [That Jeſus Chriſt is come in the fleſh.] Or thus, Ἰησοῦν Χριστὸν ἐν σαρκὶ ἐληλυθότα, [That Jeſus is the Chriſt come in the fleſh.] Dr. Mill ſays many copies read it ὁ λύει τὸν Ἰησοῦν, [which diſſolveth Jeſus.] Of which ſee the notes on § 3. of the Pref. to this epiſtle.

A. D. 67.

eth not us. Hereby know we the Spirit of truth, and the ſpirit of error.

the ſpoil and deſtruction of the reſt of *mankind*. Whereas, a true *Chriſtian* is acted by the hope of *ſpiritual* good, and the love of true *virtue*; and muſt be be approved of, by all that have a juſt reliſh of God, and true goodneſs; as on the contrary, it is no wonder to ſee the falſe *teachers* of theſe times followed and thronged by the majority, that are of the ſame temper with themſelves*.

* See and compare John vi. 45. & viii. 47.

7 Beloved, let us love one another: for love is of God; and every one that loveth is born of God, and knoweth God.
8 He that loveth not, knoweth not God; for God is love.

7. & 8. As, therefore, *we* juſtly pretend to be the true children of God, let it be our ſpecial care to give a proof of it, by the imitation of his peculiar attribute of *love* and *mercy*, ſo abundantly diſplayed to all mankind, and to us *Chriſtians* in particular; without which, we fail of the chiefeſt inſtance of reſembling *him*, and moſt plainly ſhow we are none of his.

9 In this was manifeſted the love of God towards us, becauſe that God ſent his only begotten Son into the world, that we might live through him.
10 Herein is love, not that we loved God but that he loved us, and ſent his Son *to be* the propitiation for our ſins.

9. & 10. That *act* of Divine Love in procuring the pardon and ſalvation of a ſinful world, by ſending the very *Son* of God to become *man* for our ſakes, has this conſideration, to magnify it beyond all compariſon, that it began, on God's part, was voluntary and free, without the leaſt merit or obligation on *our* part to incline him to it.

11 Beloved, if God ſo loved us, we ought alſo to love one another.

11. And ſurely ſuch an unparalelled inſtance of *heavenly* compaſſion to *ſinful creatures*, ought to make *us* expreſs the tendereſt regard to the welfare of all thoſe, whom God was pleaſed to ſet ſo high a value on; and to demonſtrate the ſenſe we have of it, by ſhowing *mercy*, even to ſuch as leaſt deſerve it at our hands.

12. & 13. It

A. D. 67.

12 No man hath seen God at any time. If we love one another, God dwelleth in us, and his love is perfected in us.

13 Hereby know we that we dwell in him, and he in us, because he hath given us of his Spirit.

12. & 13. It is not enough to say, you love God, in return for his love to you, unless you give evidence of it by your charity to your fellow *Christians*. God himself is not the object of your *senses*, and can affect your thoughts no way, but by laborious and raised meditations; whereas, your fellow *Christians*, *their* wants and miseries strike your very *senses*, and move you, by the strongest and most immediate impressions. So that, if you do not perform the *easier*, it is not to be imagined you should discharge the more *difficult* part of this duty: The *one*, therefore, is the proper test of the *other*. We show whose children we truly are, by the likeness of our dispositions; and God, accordingly, confirms us for his own, by the gifts and graces of his Holy Spirit bestowed upon us.

14 And we have seen, and do testify, that the Father sent the Son *to be* the Saviour of the world.

15 Whosoever shall confess that Jesus is the Son of God, God dwelleth in him, and he in God.

14. & 15. And by the extraordinary and miraculous powers of this Holy Spirit are we qualified to demonstrate, and have, beyond all exception, evidenced the truth of those *facts*, whereof we *apostles* were eye-witnesses, viz. *That Jesus is the true Messiah, the very Son of God*, the *Word*, the *Christ*, who was with the *Father; and actually sent into the world, for the redemption of mankind by his death and sufferings*. An *article* most essentially necessary to be embraced by every *Christian;* and whoever denies it, deserves not that character, nor is entitled to any privileges of God's true *church* *.

* See chap. i. 1, 2, 3. and here ver. 2, 3.

16 And we have known and believed the love that God hath to us. God is love; and he that dwelleth in love, dwelleth in God, and God in him.

17 Herein

16. & 17. By firmly adhering to this *fundamental* truth of his religion, and by the practice of that love and *charity*, so especially enjoined in it, and which is the principal instance of our conformity to his excellencies, and of our return of gratitude to him; in short,

17. Herein is our love made perfect, that we may have boldneſs in the day of judgment: becauſe as he is, ſo are we in this world.

ſhort, by loving our *brethren*, as God loved *us*, and being ready to ſuffer for *their* ſakes, as Chriſt ſuffered for *us all*; we prove ourſelves his true *diſciples*, in full and perfect communion with him, and may *aſſuredly* expect the glorious reward he has promiſed, at the great day of final *judgment*. A. D. 67.

18 There is * no fear in love; but perfect love caſteth out fear: becauſe fear hath torment: he that feareth, is not made perfect in love.

18. Nay, we not only then ſafely *may*, but *ought* to depend upon this * reward, with the utmoſt aſſurance, joy, and ſatisfaction; for, to be diffident, fearful, and diſtracted about the certainty of our future happineſs, is a ſign, either that a man has not a due and grateful apprehenſion of the mercy, truth, and love of God, through Chriſt, to us; or, that he is not truly conſcious of his having ſincerely performed the duties of his profeſſion.

19 We love him, becauſe he firſt loved us.

19. Infinite reaſon have we to love, truſt, and depend upon *him*, that has given ſuch an inſtance of love to us and all mankind.

20 If a man ſay, I love God, and hateth his brother, he is a liar; for he that loveth not his brother whom he hath ſeen, how can he love God whom he hath not ſeen?

21 And

20. & 21. Only remember again, that we muſt teſtify our regards to God, by charity and compaſſion to our *brethren*. Not only the expreſs command of Chriſt, but the very reaſon of the *thing* requires it. For, as I ſaid (ver. 12.), if we love not them, whoſe perſons and wants ſtrike

* [No fear in love.] *Fear* here ſeems, in the moſt natural conſtruction, to ſtand oppoſed to *boldneſs* in the foregoing verſe.

A. D. 67. 21 And this commandment have we from him, that he who loveth God, love his brother also.

stike and affect our very *senses*, we can hardly be supposed to be carried with much affection to *him*, with whom we cannot converse, but at a distance, who is neither the object of our *senses*, nor within the compass of our *charity*.

CHAP. V.

The Argument of Chap. iv. 1, 2, 3, *&c. resumed, viz. The Certainty of Jesus being the Messiah and Saviour of Mankind, and that the Truth and Sincerity of Man's Profession is to be judged of by their belief of it, and the good effect it has upon their Tempers and Practices. The Divine Evidences of this Great Article. The Witnesses in Heaven, and on Earth. The Unexceptionableness of this Argument, especially to the* Jews. *The belief of it, the indispensable Condition of future Happiness, and of the acceptance of our Christian Prayers. The Sin unto* Death, *What? Directions what to do in that Case. True Christian Principles sufficient to keep any Man from such Sin. Christianity the true Religion, and utterly inconsistent with all acts of* Heathen Idolatry.

† Chap. iv. 1, &c.

1 WHosoever believeth that Jesus is the Christ, is born of God, and every one that loveth him that begat, loveth him also that is begotten of him.

1. I Observed to you † before, that the truth of Christ's *Messiahship* was the rule whereby you are to judge of mens pretences in religious matters. Keep then to that *rule*, and be assured, that to deny Jesus to be the real Christ, the *Son* of God, and *Saviour* of mankind, is in effect to deny God the *Father*, that sent him into the world for that purpose. And, on the contrary, sincerely to embrace the *one*, is to embrace the *other*.

2. & 3. And

A. D. 67.

2 By this we know that we love the children of God, when we love God and keep his commandments *.

3 For this is the love of God, that we keep his commandments: and his commandments are not grievous.

2. & 3. And withal, you must never forget, that charity to our *brethren* is one principal * test of our being true disciples of Christ; as it is a chief instance of our practical obedience to his commands, *without* which, all external profession of religion is insignificant, and mere pretence; but *with* it, Christianity will prove the most pleasant and profitable profession.

4 For whatsoever is born of God overcometh the world: and this is the victory that overcometh the world, *even* our faith.

5 Who is he that overcometh the world, but he that believeth that Jesus is the Son of God?

4. & 5. The *Christian* will, then, find his faith in Jesus as the true *Messiah*, the *Son of God*, to answer its true and intended effects, *viz.* to set him above the vanities and unlawful pleasures of this world, make him despise its granduer, conquer all its temptations by filling him with assurance of a better state: A perfection too high for any but true *Christians* to arrive to.

6 This is he that came by water and blood, *even* Jesus Christ; not by water only, but by water and blood: and it is the Spirit that beareth witness, because the Spirit is truth.

6. Nor are the effects and influences of this great || truth more excellent and noble, than is the ground and foundation of it strong and certain. The testimonies †† given him at his *baptism*, when God, by a voice from heaven, declared him *to be his beloved Son, the Saviour of mankind:* The miracles at his crucifixion ‡, when at the shedding of his innocent blood, we saw both water and blood come out of his side; the *sun* was darkened, the *earth* trembled, and the

|| Ver. 1.

†† *The water.*

‡ *The blood.*

* Ver. 2. *By this we know that we love the children of God, when we love God.*———Note: The *context* and the apostle's *argument* plainly show, that these words are transposed: The reading should be, *By this we know that we love God —When we love the children of God.* And I have paraphrased them accordingly.

A. D. 67. the vail of the *temple* was rent. The signs ‖ and wonders done by *him* and by *others* in his *name*, are all, I say, testimonies of the authority of his *person* and *mission*, most unexceptionable, as being evidences of that *Holy Spirit* that cannot deceive us.

‖ *The Spirit.*

7 For there are three that bear record in heaven, the Father, the Word, and the Holy Ghost: and these three are one.

8 And there are three that bear witness in earth, the spirit, and the water, and the blood: and these three agree in one.

7. & 8. In all controversies about human affairs, the positive testimonies of two or three credible witnesses is thought sufficient to determine the truth in any *court*: and the Jews allowed it by their own *law* to be so. So that the evidence of Jesus *being the true Messiah*, and the very Christ, the *Word* and *Son of* God, who died upon the cross, is, according to their *own* notions, established beyond all contradiction. For, as in heaven there are three divine persons, the *Father*, the *Son*, and the *Holy Spirit*: so do the three forementioned * *testimonies* given of Chist, while he was upon *earth*, concur in the full demonstration of this great truth: These powers and miracles of the *Holy Ghost* incontestably showing the *Father* to have *sent* him, and the *Son* to have actually *come* into the world, for the salvation of mankind.

9 If we receive the witness of men, the witness of God is greater: * for this is the witness of God, which he hath testified of his Son.

9. Now, if two or three credible (though yet fallible) *men* are to be depended upon, when concurring and clear in their evidence; how much more ought we to rely upon the testimony * of the infallible *God*?

10 He that believeth on the Son of God, hath the witness in

10. All sincere believers cannot but reflect on the insufficiency of this testimony, with the utmost comfort

* *For this is the witness of God*——ὅτι ἄυτη ἐςὶν ἡ μαρτυρία τῦ Θεῦ. For *such*, or of *this kind*, is the witness of God, *viz.* A *threefold* testimony.

in himself: he that believeth not God, hath made him a liar, because he believeth not the record that God gave of his Son.

comfort * and satisfaction: Finding themselves continually confirmed in it, by the gifts and graces of that very *Spirit*, that, in so ample a manner, at first gave it. Whereas such *Jews* or *heretics* as deny it, do no less than give God the lie.

A. D. 67.

* μαρτυρίαν ἐν ἑαυτῷ.

11 And this is the record, that God hath given to us eternal life: and this life is in his Son.

12 He that hath the Son, hath life; *and* he that hath not the Son of God, hath not life.

11. & 12. So then, the sum of our *Christianity* is this: *That God has promised to, and provided eternal happiness for good men, and that the indispensible condition of enjoying it, is a sincere belief in Christ incarnate, and in his religion, by all to whom it and its evidences are fairly proposed.*

13 These things have I written unto you that believe on the name of the Son of God; that ye may know that ye have eternal life, and that ye may believe on the name of the Son of God.

14 And this is the confidence that we have in him, that if we ask any thing according to his will, he heareth us.

15 And if we know that he hear us, whatsoever we ask, we know that we have the petitions that we desired of him.

13. 14. & 15. And accordingly, my design in this *epistle* was, to satisfy all such true believers of the safety of their future condition; and to encourage them to a firm perseverance in this principle, upon a full assurance that God will deny them nothing that is truly needful for them; but will, in due time and manner, answer all their Christian prayers.

16 If any man see his brother sin a sin *which is* not unto death, he shall ask, and he shall give him life for them that sin not unto death. There is a sin unto death: I do not say that he shall pray for it.

16. Before I conclude, I must advise you in *one* particular more, relating to such offenders amongst you as are struck with any *extraordinary* sickness † as a divine punishment for any notorious sins. Now, where the offence is not of the most *wilful* and *obstinate* kind, where,

† See and compare Gal. vi. 1. 1 Cor. xi. 13. Jam. v. 14, 15.

A. D. 67. where, by the circumstances, you gather, that the punishment inflicted was not sent for his *destruction*, but only to *awaken* the person to a sense of his *miscarriage*, and you find him inclined to repentance; in such a case, let the Christian *ministers* attend upon him, interceding with God for him by earnest prayer, which, upon his repentance, shall avail for the pardon of his sin *, and for restoring him to health again. But if you know the person so afflicted to be struck from *heaven*, for a *malicious*, *habitual*, and *incurable* degree of scandalous *vice* and *immorality*, or for wilful *apostacy* from the *Christian* religion; in *that* case, you have no obligation to throw away your *prayers* upon him ‖ but may justly leave such a man to the justice of God, as one that has defeated all methods of repentance and salvation †.

‖ See Heb. vi. 4. 5, 6. and x. 26, 27.

17 All unrighteousness is sin: and there is a sin not unto death.

17. It is true, every wilful offence against either God or our neighbour, is a breach of the *divine law*, and, in strict justice, deserves *death*. But as you know there were degrees of offences under the *Mosaical* law §, some whereof were, while

§ Numb. xxxv. 30, 31. Deut. xvii. 2, 3, 4, 5. and xiii. 5, 9, 10, 11.

* *He* (i. e. God) *shall give him life*. Or, *life shall be given him*, i. e. to the sinner. The same *Hebraism* with that of Matth. i. 23. *They shall call his name Jesus*, i. e. his name shall be *called*.

† Ver. 16. *I do not say that he shall pray for it*, i. e. That you are either not *at all* to pray for such a person, or if you *do*, it cannot be with that degree of *faith*, and assurance of *success* as in other cases. See and compare Jam. v. 14, 15, 16, 17, 18. Moreover, it is possible, these *first Christians* might not have any certain and absolute *signs* whereby to distinguish the *sin unto death* from *other* sins that were *pardonable*; or the distempers that were *curable*, from such as were *incurable*, by their *prayers*. And then the design of St. John in these words, *I do not say that he shall pray for it*, is to satisfy them, That, though every instance of their prayers were not equally effectual toward the recovery of sinners, yet the promise in verse 14, 15. was still good; none being exempted from it. that he had not *so sinned* as to be doomed by divine justice to present *death* for it. Of which they might be satisfied by the *effect* of their prayers.

while others were not, puniſhed with immediate *death*, A. D. 67.
but admitted of an atonement by *ſacrifice*; ſo in theſe cafes, under the *goſpel* diſpenſation, as long as there are remains of true principles and diſpoſitions, and any hopes of true repentance, there is hope of recovery, and a promiſe of pardon.

18 We know that whoſoever is born of God ſinneth not; but he that is begotten of God, keepeth himſelf, and that wicked one toucheth him not.

18. In the mean time, no ſincere and true *Chriſtian* is, without his own great default, in much danger of falling into ſuch a deſperate *degree* of ſin, or of wilful *apoſtacy* from the ſervice of Chriſt to that of Satan.

19 *And* we know that we are of God, and the whole world lieth in wickedneſs.

20 And we know that the Son of God is come, and hath given us an underſtanding that we may know him that is true: and we are in him that is true, *even* in his Son Jeſus Chriſt. This is the true God, and eternal life.

19. & 20. For to conclude: While the reſt of the obſtinate and unrepenting world continue enſlaved to ignorance, idolatry, ſin and Satan, we *Chriſtians* are fully and happily aſſured, that we are members of the *church* of the *true* God, by ſincerely believing in Jeſus Chriſt *his Son*, who came into the world to teach us the way of true religion, and, being made *man*, ſuffered and died, in order to our eternal life and happineſs.

21 Little children, keep yourſelves from idols. Amen.

21. Which, ſince he has ſo fully done, it would be utterly inexcuſable in any *Chriſtian*, by any temptation or example whatever, to be drawn into any act of *heatheniſh* and idolatrous * *worſhip*, by forſaking ſo pure and holy a profeſſion. And may God preſerve you ever from it! *Amen*.

* See the Pref. § 4.

 A PARA-

A
PARAPHRASE
ON THE
SECOND EPISTLE
OF
St. JOHN.

THE PREFACE AND CONTENTS.

To whom? § 1. BY *the* Elect Lady, *to whom this Epistle is directed, we may understand, either some particular* Person *of honourable Descent, a Friend, and (perhaps)* Disciple of *St.* John; *or else some Christian* Church; *the Word* Elect *being so frequently used of the* Jewish *Church in the* Old, *of* Christian *Churches in the* New *Testament; and that of* Children, *to signify the* Members *of those Collective* Bodies. *The Salutation at the Close, from the* Children of the Elect Sister, *ver.* 13. *seem, indeed, to bid most fairly for this* latter *Acceptation, as signifying a* Sister-Church; *as do also his speaking in the* plural *Number*, ver. 12. *And, whereas the Church of* Jerusalem *was the Great* Original *from whence all they of the* Circumcision *at first received the* Christian *Doctrine*, She, *of all others, lays the best Claim to this Title of* (κυρία) *the* Mistress *or* Mother-*Church; though other Learned Men think it probable to be meant of some* Asian *Church, and most likely that of* Philadelphia. *I will only add, That St.* John, *in styling this* Christian Church *a* Lady, *follows the Language of the Old Scriptures. Thus* Babylon *called herself* The Lady of Kingdoms,

doms, *Isai.* xlvii. 5, 7. *And the* Antichristian Babylon *is represented as saying in her Heart,* I sit as a Queen, *Revel.* xviii. 7. *What these* arrogantly *and* falsely *applied to themselves, the* Apostle *here* truly *applies to the* Christian *Believers.*

§ 2. *The Strain of this* Epistle, *both in its* Argument, *and the very* Expressions, *is so clearly the same, in the main, with that of the foregoing, that I refer the Reader to the* Preface *thereto prefixed, for the proper Key to them.* The design.

§ 3. *The* Shortness *of this Letter, though to so* principal *a Church, is sufficiently accounted for, from* ver. 12. *viz. that the* Apostle *very soon expected to* visit *that Church, and give full Instructions as ot the matters here so briefly handled.* Why so short.

1 THE elder unto the elect lady, and her children, whom I love in the truth; and not I only, but also all they that have known the truth;

2 For the truths sake which dwelleth in us, and shall be with us for ever:

3 Grace be with you, mercy *and* peace from God the Father, and from the Lord Jesus Christ, the Son of the Father, † in truth and love.

1. & 2. *JOHN*, the now aged * *apostle* of Christ, sendeth this epistle to the church of || Jerusalem, to the clergy and people thereof, whom I, and all good Christians, cannot but most sincerely esteem and love, for their constancy and perseverance in those *gospel* doctrines that will prove of eternal and happy § advantage to us.

Written A. D. 67.

|| See the Pref. § 1.

§ See 1 Pet. i. 23, 25.

3. Wishing you all divine favours and blessings from God the Father, and from Jesus Christ his only *Son*, our Saviour and Governor; to preserve you in true faith towards God, and true love towards your Christian *brethren* †.

 4. It

* *The elder:* πρεσβύτερος, *Presbyter*, here, and in 1 Pet. v. 1. may be a name of honour and *dignity;* or, as in Phil. ix. it signifies, *aged;* and so it fitly expresseth both the *apostolical office*, and his long *continuance* in it, he being now at least *seventy* years of age.

† Ver. 3. *In truth and love:* These words may be connected, either with those immediately foregoing. *The Son of the Father, in truth and love;* i. e. the Author of the *true Christian religion*, so full of *love* to mankind; or else with, *Grace, mercy and peace be with you*, as in the paraphrase: Which I choose as most agreeable to the verse following.

A. D. 67.

4 I rejoiced greatly that I found of thy children walking in truth, as we have received a commandment from the Father.

4. It is a mighty comfort to me to hear of ſuch a number of your church, that firmly and uncorruptedly adhere to the *Chriſtian* religion, as delivered by Chriſt and his apoſtles, from God the *Father*.

5 And now, I beſeech thee, lady, not as though I wrote a new * commandment unto thee, but that which we had from the beginning, that we love one another.

5. Let me now only *remind* you, that true *Chriſtianity* muſt be joined to true *faith*, in order to make a true *Chriſtian*. And thoſe of your church, where Chriſt himſelf immediately delivered his doctrines, * cannot but know it to be one of his *ſpecial* commands.

6 And this is love; that we walk after his commandments. This is the commandment, that as ye have heard from the beginning, ye ſhould walk in it.

6. For there is no way of expreſſing our true love and regard to † God, but by the entertainment and belief of his *revelation*, as he has plainly delivered it to us, and by obſervance of its *moral* precepts, whereof this of *love* and *charity* is one of the moſt principal.

7 For many deceivers are entered into the world, who confeſs not that Jeſus Chriſt is come in the fleſh. This is a deceiver and an Antichriſt.

8 Look to yourſelves, that we loſe not thoſe things which we have wrought, but receive a full reward.

‡ See 1 John iv. 2, 3. the Note there.

7. & 8. I am thus particular in my cautions in this matter, to prevent you from being miſled in your principles, and ſo deprived of your future and glorious ſtate of happineſs, by the deceitful endeavours of a ſet of men, *viz.* the Jewiſh *zealots*, that would perſuade the world *that* Jeſus *is not the true* ‡ *Meſſiah;* and thoſe *heretical* Chriſtians that uphold he did not live, and preach, and die in *reality*, but in *appearance;* that he was not himſelf the real *Word* who was *with* God his *Father*, the *Son* of God made *man*, but a mere *man*, diſtinct in reality

* See 1 John ii. 7, 8.

† Ἡ ἀγαπη, viz. τȣ Θεȣ, as in 1 John v. 3.—iv. 21.

reality from that *Word* or *Son* of the *Father*. These are the very false *prophets* and *Antichrists*, foretold by our *Saviour* himself *. Beware therefore, and avoid them. A. D. 67.

* 1 John ii. 18, 19—26. iv. 1, 2, 3.

9 Whosoever transgresseth, and abideth not in the doctrine of Christ, hath not God: he that abideth in the doctrine of Christ, he hath both the Father and the Son.

9. Your *Christian* religion, and the plain facts and doctrines of it, are so fully and unexceptionably demonstrated, that you must make *them* the *rule* whereby to judge of all pretenders in religious matters †. You know your own principles are true; and therefore all that contradict them must be false, as plainly giving God himself the lie.

† See 1 John v. 1—12.

10 If there come any unto you, and bring not this doctrine, receive him not into your house, neither bid him God speed.

11 For he that biddeth him God speed, is partaker of his evil deeds.

10. & 11. If you find any of these *teachers*, therefore, that are thus unsound in their doctrines, and loose in their morals; have nothing to do with them, and give them no entertainment, for fear the countenance you afford them should bring you into a share of their guilt and punishment.

12 Having many things to write unto you, I would not *write* with paper and ink; but I trust to come unto you, and speak face to face, that our joy may be full.

12. I give you now only these *brief* cautions, in hopes very soon to *visit* your church, and furnish you with more full directions, to your complete comfort and satisfaction in your true *Christian* principles, against the designs of these *deceivers*.

13 The children of * thy elect sister greet thee. Amen.

13. The Christian *church* I am now * with, give hearty love and good wishes to you. God preserve you. *Amen*.

A PARA-

* *Thy elect sister.* What *church* it was, from whence St. John wrote this, is no way certainly to be known: Dr. Lightfoot thinks it to be Ephesus; which, as it was the metropolis of Asia, might indeed properly be called *sister* to the great church of Jerusalem.

PARAPHRASE

ON THE

THIRD EPISTLE

OF

St. J O H N.

The Preface and Contents.

Caius, who? § 1. GAIUS *is here generally taken for the ſame Chriſtian of* Corinth, *whom St.* Paul *calls* His Hoſt, *Rom.* xvi. 23. *A Perſon very much noted for the Hoſpitable and Liberal Entertainment he gave to St.* Paul *and* Barnabas, *who took no* Maintenance *of the* Gentile *Churches they preached to, particularly that of* Corinth, *(ſee* 1 Cor. ix.) *as neither did* Timothy, Titus, *or others ſent by St.* Paul *thither. To this St.* John *refers here,* ver. 5, 6, 7, 8. *It ſhould ſeem, from* ver. 9, 10. *that the Apoſtle intended a longer Epiſtle, and to have directed it to the whole Church of* Corinth; *but fearing the Effects of his Letter might be defeated by* Diotrephes, *and his Prevailing Party, he laid aſide that Deſign, upon a Proſpect of doing more Good by viſiting the* Corinthians *in Perſon,* ver. 13, 14.

§ 2. *Mean-*

§ 2. *Meanwhile, he ſends this* Brief *Exhortation to* Gaius, *commending him for his Hoſpitality to the Teachers ſent to his Church, exhorting him to continue it; and aſſuring him, that his Adverſary* Diotrephes (*who ſeems to have been one of the* Jewiſh *zealots, or* Heretical *Teachers, ſpoken of in his* Firſt *Epiſtle*) *ſhould ſoon feel the Weight of his* Apoſtolical *Power.* The ſubject.

§ 3. *If theſe* Second *and* Third *Epiſtles be ſtyled* General, *it cannot be upon the ſame Account with that of the* Firſt, *and thoſe of St.* James *and St.* Peter, [*thoſe being directed to* Several *Churches; while the One of* Theſe *were Written either to a ſingle* Family, *or* Church, *the other to a ſingle* Perſon]; *but from that* General *and* Catholic *Reception they found from the Chriſtian Churches.* If general?

1 THE elder unto the well-beloved Gaius, whom I love in the truth.

2 Behold, I wiſh above all things that thou mayeſt proſper, and be in health, even as thy ſoul proſpereth.

1. & 2. JOHN, the now aged * apoſtle, ſendeth this epiſtle to Gaius of Corinth, my dear *Chriſtian* brother: Moſt heartily wiſhing him to flouriſh in health and *temporal* proſperity, as he does in true *Chriſtian* piety.

Written A. D. 67.

* See 2 Epiſt. ver. 1.

3 For I rejoiced greatly when the brethren came and teſtified of the truth that is in thee, even as thou walkeſt in the truth.

4 I have no greater joy than to hear that my children walk in truth.

3. & 4. Nothing on this ſide heaven, is matter of ſuch comfort to me, as to hear of the ſincerity and conſtancy of *Chriſtian* people. I love them *all*, without diſtinction, as my ſpiritual *children.* And this made me ſo highly rejoice at the account I have received, how good and generous a Chriſtian *you* are in particular.

5 Beloved, thou doeſt faithfully whatſoever thou doeſt to the brethren, and to ſtrangers;

6 Which have born witneſs of that charity before the church: whom if thou bring forward

5. & 6. I now ſend you this ſhort *letter*, to expreſs the juſt ſenſe I have of your liberal hoſpitality toward all your fellow Chriſtians, eſpecially to ſuch as are ſent by the *apoſtles*, to teach and inſtruct your church; and to encourage your perſeverance in ſo good a principle, by

A. D. 67. forward on their journey, after a godly sort, thou shalt do well:

by acquainting you how great a character you bear in the Christian church upon this account.

7 Because that for his names sake they went forth, taking nothing of the Gentiles.

8 We therefore ought to receive such, that we might be fellow-helpers to the truth.

7. & 8. For, indeed, our Christian bounty can never be better spent than upon such men, whose zeal for the honour and religion of Christ is so true and generous, that to prevent prejudices, and take off the objections of some of our adversaries, they preach the gospel to several Gentile churches, ‡ without any contributions from them, and earn their living by their own *labours*. By assisting such preachers, you yourself become an instrument of promoting the *gospel*, as indeed, it is every *Christian's* duty to be as far as he is able.

‡ Acts xv. 26. 1 Cor. ix. 18. See Pref. § 1.

9 I wrote * unto the church: but Diotrephes, who loveth to have the pre-eminence among them, receiveth us not.

9. I was * once minded to have writ at large, ‖ to your whole *church*, to encourage all its members to pay a due respect to their orthodox ministers, and to avoid the false and wicked † doctrines of *heretical* teachers; but Diotrephes, who is one of them, and his party, I find are so prevalent, that I considered, a *letter* was not likely to have much effect, and so resolved upon another § method;

‖ Ver. 13.

† Ver. 11.

§ Ver. 14.

10 Wherefore if I come, I will remember his deeds which he doeth, prating against us with malicious words: and not content therewith; neither doth he himself receive the brethren, and forbiddeth them

10. *Viz.* To come and visit your church in *person*, and take due cognizance of that malicious and busy man, that presumes to reproach *me*, and the rest of the *apostles*, for not imposing *circumcision* upon the Gentile Christians; that deniesall entertainment to the *ministers* sent by us, to your church, and

* *I wrote*; ἐγεάψα, *I had* written, or *would have* written. So the Vulg. and Syr. very rightly, according to the common latitude of *tense* in the Eastern tongues. See 1 Cor. xv. 32.

them that would, and calleth *them* out of the church.

and even persecutes and excommunicates such Christians as adhere to them. A. D. 67.

11 Beloved, follow not that which is evil, but that which is good. He that doeth good, is of God; but he that doeth evil, hath not seen God.

11. Meantime, I earnestly entreat you all to avoid the wicked principles and practices of such men. Make it your *rule*, that *moral* obedience is the essential mark of a true *Christian*; and the loudest pretences will never make a *wicked* man a true member of God's *church* *.

* 1 John iii. 6—10.

12 Demetrius hath good report of all men, and of the truth itself: yea, and we *also* bear record, and ye know that our record is true.

12. Demetrius has the general character of a sincere Christian: Make *him* your example; for I can recommend him, by all the rules of our Christianity, as worthy of that character: And you know, you may depend upon what I say.

13 I had many things to write, but I will not with ink and pen write unto thee:

14 But I trust I shall shortly see thee, and we shall speak face to face. Peace *be* to thee. Our friends salute thee. Greet the friends by name.

13. & 14. I must wave further particulars, till I see you, which I hope will be soon. All happiness attend you the mean while. Our Christian friends here send hearty love to you: Give mine and theirs, as particularly as you can, to all in your parts.

A PARA-

A

PARAPHRASE

ON THE

EPISTLE GENERAL

OF

St. *J U D E.*

THE PREFACE.

To whom, and on what occasion.

§ 1. THE whole Argument of this Epistle has an exact Agreement, and several of its Expressions are so perfectly the same with the *Second* of *St.* Peter, that the most judicious Writers make it a strong Conclusion, it must have been Written about the same *Time*, and levelled at the Lewd Principles of the same *Jewish* Zealots, and *Herctical* Teachers. For the Particulars whereof the Reader is referred to the *Preface* of 1 Peter, § 4. and to *Preface* 1 John, § 3.

Why general?

§ 2. As his Brother James directed *His* Epistle to the Churches of the *Jewish Dispersion*, so *St.* Jude's seems plainly to have been sent to the Christians of the whole *Circumcision*, both Foreign and Domestic; and therefore it bears the Title of a *General Epistle:* Though I make no question but it had a *Peculiar* Respect to *Such* amongst whom he had exercised his *Ministry*.

The

The Salutation and Deſign of the Epiſtle; viz. To arm them againſt the Errors and Vices of Falſe and Heretical Teachers. The Certainty of their ſevere Puniſhment, inferred from the Inſtances of the Rebellious Iſraelites, *the Fallen Angels,* Sodom *and* Gomorrah. *Very Black Deſcriptions of theſe Heretics. The Traditional Hiſtory of* Michael, *and Prophecy of* Enoch *referred to. Chriſtians not to be ſurpriſed at theſe Heretics, becauſe foretold by the Prophets, and by* Chriſt *Himſelf. He Exhorts them to Steadineſs in the True Faith. Prays for them, and concludes.*

1 JUDE the ſervant of Jeſus Chriſt, and brother of James, to them that are ſanctified by God the Father, and preſerved in Jeſus Chriſt, and called.

2 Mercy unto you, and peace, and love be multiplied.

1. & 2. *JUDE* (called in the *goſpels* Thaddeus, and Lebbeus, to diſtinguiſh him from Judas Iſcariot) the brother of James, biſhop of Jeruſalem, an *apoſtle* of Jeſus Chriſt, ſendeth this epiſtle to the Jewiſh *Chriſtians*, to all that in theſe corrupted, perſecuting, and apoſtatizing times, remain firm and ſteady to their profeſſion: Wiſhing you the utmoſt degree of Divine favour and happineſs.

Written A. D. 67.

3 Beloved, when I gave all diligence to write unto you of the common ſalvation; it was needful for me to write unto you, and exhort you, that ye ſhould earneſtly contend for the faith which was once * delivered unto the ſaints.

3. In writing to you, dear brethren, upon the great ſubject of our *Chriſtianity*, the chief and moſt neceſſary argument I can chooſe to inſiſt upon, is, that of *courage* and *conſtancy* to the plain and original doctrines of it *.

6 4. One

* Ver. 3. *The faith once delivered:* ἅπαξ παραδοθείσῃ; *Delivered once for all;* i. e. So as to need no *further* confirmation beſide the evidences given of it by Chriſt and his *apoſtles;* and ſo as to admit of no *alterations* or *additions.* See the Note on Heb. ix. 26.

A. D. 67.

3 For there are certain men crept in unawares, who were before * of old ordained to this condemnation, ungodly men, turning the grace of our God into lasciviousness, and denying the only Lord God, and our Lord Jesus Christ.

4. One would think, indeed, this were a needless topic to men really professing themselves disciples of Christ: But, that lewd and wicked *set of men*, whose vices and punishment were * foretold by the *prophets* and by Christ himself, some of them denying Christ to ‡ be the true *Messiah* at all, others || affirming he lived, and preached, and died in *appearance* only, and not in *reality;* and all of them, by promoting some vicious practice or other, have so insinuated themselves into, and corrupted the Christian church, that we are forced to run back to the defence of its *first* and plainest principles.

‡ The Jewish zealots.
|| Heretics. See Pref. 1 John

5 I will therefore put you in remembrance, though ye once knew this, how that the Lord having saved the people out of the land of Egypt, afterward destroyed them that believed not.

5. Wherefore, to prevent you from being drawn into that desperate principle of theirs, *viz. That the external profession of religion, and the privilege of being members of the true church*, is enough to save a man, whatever his practice be; and, at the same time, to satisfy you, how certain the punishment of such wretches will be; let me remind you of the former dealings of God in the like cases. The Israelites you know were the *chosen people*, and *church* of God: yet how were *they*, that had the favour of a miraculous deliverance from Egyptian bondage, destroyed for their disobedience, and never saw the promised land!

6. And

---

* *Of old fore-ordained to this condemnation:* προγεγραμμένοι εἰς τῦτο το κρίμα; *Men of whom it was before-written that they would deserve this condemnation.* 2 Pet. ii. 3.

Ibid. *Denying the only* Lord God; i. e. denying *him*, in effect, by denying Christ *his Son*, or by corrupting the true religion, as to defeat all the main designs of it. See 1 John ii. 22, 23.

6 And the angels which kept not their first estate, but left their own habitation, he hath reserved in everlasting chains under darkness unto the judgment of the great day.

6. Nay, to go higher, the very *angels* themselves, that acted unworthy of the blissful station and † dignity God has placed them in, were thrust down from those bright regions of light and happiness, and are here kept in this dark and lower ‖ world, as prisoners reserved in chains, against the great day of judgment upon them, and all wicked men.

A. D. 67.

† ἀρχὴν.

‖ 2 Pet ii. 4.

7 Even as Sodom and Gomorrah, and the cities about them, in like manner giving themselves over to fornication, and going after strange flesh, are set forth for an example, suffering the vengeance of eternal fire.

7. What was the total and irreparable destruction of those lewd and beastly cities of Sodom and Gomorrah, but an emblem of that more dreadful and *eternal* punishment that will be the final portion of the debauched ‡ *heretics* of these times?

‡ See 2 Pet. ii. 6.

8 Likewise also these filthy dreamers defile the flesh, despise dominion, and speak evil of dignities.

8. Who not only equal, but even exceed the Sodomites in their impieties; indulging themselves not only in the same excess of *carnal* gratifications, but in the most vain and extravagant fancies, and imaginations of the *mind* too. They are not only lawless, ungovernable and arrogant against all *temporal* authority, but have notions that are disgraceful to, and reflecting upon, the dignity of *heavenly* * and superior beings.

* See 2 Pet. ii. the Note there.

9 Yet Michael the archangel, when contending with the devil, he disputed about the body of Moses, durst † not bring against him any railing accusation, but said, The Lord rebuke thee.

9. & 10. You cannot but stand amazed at their insolence, when you compare it with the *traditional* account you Jews have had about the strife between Michael and Samael ‖‖ the devil, called the *Angel of Death*, concerning the body of Moses. Your *traditions* tell you, the *archangel* returned the

‖‖ See Lightfoot.

† Ver. 9. *Durst not bring*, &c. ὐκ ἐτόλμησε; he did not think it *fit* or *meet*: So that *Greek* word is often used to signify.

A. D. 67.

10 But theſe ſpeak evil || of thoſe things which they know not: but what they know naturally, as brute beaſts; in thoſe things they corrupt themſelves.

|| See 2 Pet. ii. 11, 12.

devil none of his railing accuſations, but only ſaid, *The Lord rebuke thee* *. While *theſe* impudent creatures, like ſavage beaſts, fly at and vilify every thing, of what rank and quality ſoever, without reaſon or diſtinction.

11 Wo unto them, for they have gone in the way of Cain, and ran greedily after the error of Balaam for a reward, and periſhed in the gainſaying of Core.

11. Wo unto them! for if Cain's murdering his *brother* was ſo dreadful a crime, what muſt it be in *them* to perſecute ſuch *numbers* of their innocent *brethren!* if Balaam was ſo wicked in ſeducing the Iſraelites to idolatry, what muſt be *their* guilt, who, againſt the more clear light of the *goſpel*, ſeduce *Chriſtian* people into lewdneſs, darkneſs and deſtruction! And, if the earth was made to ſwallow up Corah and his company, for pretending to rival and affront Moſes, what muſt be the end of them that reſiſt the authority of Chriſt, and, by forgeries and deluſions, ſet up againſt his inſpired *apoſtles!*

12 Theſe are ſports in your ‡ feaſts of charity, when they feaſt with you, feeding themſelves without fear: clouds they are without water, carried about of winds; trees whoſe fruit withereth, without fruit, twice dead, plucked up by the roots;

13 Raging

† σπιλάδες, Rocks. See 2 Pet. ii. 13—17.

12. & 13. It is impoſſible to deſcribe them by any compariſons that are black enough to reach them. When they are invited, to gratify their appetites, it is indifferent to them, whether it be to an *idol-feaſt*, or a *feaſt* ‡ *of charity*, among the true worſhippers of *God*. They bring nothing but ſcandal and † danger to all they communicate with. The lewdneſs and

* There is another interpretation of this verſe, which makes it refer to *Zech.* iii. 2. For his view and choice whereof I refer the more curious reader to Mr. *Le Clerk*, *Not. on Hammond. N. T.*

‡ *Feaſts of charity*. It is not clear whether theſe were meant of *ſacramental* feaſts among *Chriſtians*, or *Jewiſh* feaſts, uſual in the evening of their *Sabbaths*, called κοινωνίαι, and ξενοδοχίαι. I have therefore ſo expreſſed it as to include both.

A: D 67.

13 Raging waves of the sea, foaming out their own shame; * wandering stars, to whom is reserved the blackness of darkness for ever.

and slanders of their conversation are as blasting as a *tempest*, and a virtuous word or action is no more to be expected from them, than fruit is from a tree that is perfectly withered and stubbed up. They vent their shameful and malicious calumnies as plentifully as the sea throws out its foam in stormy weather; and while they set up for *teachers* and *doctors*, *guides* and * *lights* to other men, they are no better than those irregular *meteors* that deceive and mislead the mariner in a dark night: And accordingly, eternal darkness and the utmost degree of misery will be their final portion.

14 And Enoch also, the seventh from Adam, prophesied of these, saying, Behold, the Lord cometh with ten thousands of his saints,

15 To execute judgment upon all, and to convince all that are ungodly among them, of all their ungodly deeds which they have ungodly committed, and of all their hard *speeches*, which ungodly sinners have spoken against him.

14. & 15. That *traditional* prophesy the Jews have of Enoch, concerning the destruction of the old world, may as fitly be applied to these men; for as their impiety and injustice, both in words and actions, do not only equal, but even surpass *theirs*, the divine judgments upon them will certainly be still more solemn, dreadful and exemplary.

16 These are murmurers, complainers, walking after their own lusts, and their mouth speaketh great swelling *words*, having mens persons in admiration because of advantage.

16. For nothing can exceed the pride, lust and vanity of this set of people, that yet have the face, many of them, to call themselves the people and *church* of *God*; while, to gratify their worldly and sensual principles, they will caress, flatter, and join in with the worst of *men*.

17 But, Dd2 17. & 18.

* *Wandering stars.* The Jewish doctors were styled, *Lights* and *Stars*.

A. D. 67.

17 But, beloved, remember ye the words which were spoken before of the apostles of our Lord Jesus Christ:

‖ 2 Pet. iii. 2, 3.

18 *How* that they told you there should be mockers in the last time, who should walk after their own ungodly lusts.

17. & 18. But, dear brethren, you ought not to be surprised and disheartened to find the *Christian* church pestered with such a vicious crew, when you consider that Christ and his *apostles* plainly ‖ foretold us it would be so.

19 These be they who separate themselves, sensual, having not the Spirit.

19. And you see it now come to pass, in these leaders of faction and divisions in the church, who are destitute of those gifts and graces of the *Holy Spirit*, that true *Christians* are endowed with.

20 But ye, beloved, building up yourselves on your most holy faith, praying in the Holy Ghost,

21 Keep yourselves in the love of God, looking for the mercy of our Lord Jesus Christ unto eternal life.

20. & 21. Instead, therefore, of being discouraged, be careful to strive against them, by constant improvement in all the duties of your profession, by the exercise of devout Christian *prayer*, wherein you are assisted by the inspirations of the *Holy Ghost*; and support yourselves under all present calamities, by the joyful and sure prospect you have of eternal life and happiness through Jesus Christ.

22 And of some have compassion, making a difference:

23 And others save with fear, pulling them out of the fire *: hating even the garment spotted by the flesh.

22. & 23. Show your utmost * aversion then, against the practisers of such wickedness, by condemning them, and renouncing all conversation with them. Only be careful to make a prudent difference in your behaviour, in proportion to the guilt of mens miscarriages. Such as deceive others through perfect *malice* and *design*, are utterly to be avoided: But such as are led away through *ignorance* and *simplicity*, are to be treated with

* *Hating even the garment:* An allusion to the strictness of the Jewish law against *touching unclean things.*

with pity, tenderneſs and good humour, in hopes to be recovered from ſo wretched and hazardous a condition. A thing you ought moſt earneſtly to endeavour for. A. D. 67.

24 Now unto him that is able to keep you from falling, and to preſent you faultleſs before the preſence of his glory with exceeding joy,

25 To the only wiſe God our Saviour, be glory and majeſty, dominion and power, now and ever. Amen.

24. & 25. Now to the infinitely wiſe and powerful, God, the Creator and Saviour of mankind, who is both able and graciouſly ready ſo to aſſiſt your honeſt endeavours, as to keep you ſteady to your profeſſion, under all difficulties and temptations, and, by innocency of life, to render you worthy the enjoyment of his glorious and bleſſed preſence: To him be aſcribed all glory and majeſty, dominion and power, both now and ever. *Amen.*

FINIS.

A

GENERAL AND COMPLETE

INDEX

TO ALL THE

PRINCIPAL MATTERS, WORDS AND PHRASES

IN THE

NEW TESTAMENT,

EXCEPTING THE *REVELATIONS*.

A

Adria,

INDEX.

BABY.

B

C

DAMNED,

D

E

Flesh,

G

2. Grace, *i. e.* the gospel religion, John i. 17. Acts xiii. 43. xv. 11. xviii. 27. Rom. iv. 2. vi. 14, 15. xi. 5, 6. Gal. i. 6. ii. 21. v. 4. Eph. i. 6. ii. 5. 8. 2 Thess. i. 12. ii. 16. Heb. xii. 15, 28. xiii. 9. 1 Pet. v. 12. 2 Pet. iii. 18. Jude iv. 1 Cor. i. 4.
3. Grace, *i. e.* the happy success of the gospel, Acts ix. 23. 1 Cor. i. 4.
4. Grace taken adjectively, by a Hebraism, signifies as much as Gracious, Acts xiv. 3. xx. 24, 32.
5. Grace, *i. e.* the apostolical office, and the endowments of the Spirit that qualified the apostles to discharge it, Rom. xii. 3. xv. 15. 1 Cor. iii. 10. Gal. ii. 9. Eph. iii. 2, 7, 8. iv. 7. 1 Pet. iv. 10, 11.
6. Grace, *i. e.* Charity, a charitable collection, 2 Cor. viii. 1, 6, 19. ix. 14.
7. Grace seems to signify the honour of suffering for Christianity, Phil. i. 7.
8. Grace, *i. e.* Edification, profit, Eph. iv. 29.
9. Grace, *i. e.* our final reward, 1 Pet. ii. 10. 13.

—Spirit of grace, Heb. x. 29. Let us have grace, Heb. xii. 28.
—Throne of grace, Heb. iv. 16. Grace for grace, John i. 16.
—Singing with grace, Col. iii. 16.
—Your speech be with grace, Col. iv. 6.
—Heart established with grace, Heb. xiii. 9.

Grafted in, Rom. xi. 17, 19.
Greeks, Grecians, *i. e.* Gentiles proselyted to the Jewish religion, Acts vi. 1. ix. 28. xi. 20. xiv. 1. xvii. 4. xix. 20. and elsewhere.
——Greeks, *i. e.* Gentiles, Acts xvi. 1. xvii. 12. xviii. 17. xix. 17. xx. 21. Rom. x. 12. Gal. iii. 28. Col. iii. 11. 1 Cor. i. 22, 23. and elsewhere.
Grieve a brother, Rom. xiv. 15.
——Grieved, the sense of it, 2 Cor. ii. 4, 5.
——Grieve the Holy Spirit, Eph. iv. 30.
Groanings, that cannot be uttered, Rom. viii. 26.
———— We groan, Rom. viii. 22, 23. 1 Cor. v. 2, 4.

H

HAGAR, Gal. iv. 21, &c.
Hair, long hair, 1 Cor. xi. 14, 15.
Habitation of God, Eph. vi. 22.
Hanged himself, the sense of it, Matth. xxvii. 5. Acts i. 18.
Hard to be understood, the sense of it, 2 Pet. iii. 16.
Hand of God. Luke i. 66. Acts xi. 21. and elsewhere.
——Right hand of God, Acts ii. 25, 33, 34. v. 31. vii. 55, 56. Eph. i 20. Coloss. iii. 1. Heb. i. 3, 13. viii. 1. x. 12. xii. 2. 1 Pet. iii. 22.
——At hand, the Lord is at hand, Phil. iv. 5.

K

L

Rom. xiv. 17. 1 Pet. i. 15, 16. 1 John ii. 3, 4, 5, 6. v. 2, 6. 3 John 4. James i. 27. ii. 22. See *Ceremonies*.
Mortification recommended, Col. iii. 5. 2 Cor. ix. 27.
Moses, his faith and virtue, Heb. iii. 2, 5. xi. 24.
Mothers, elder women as mothers, 1 Tim. v. 2.
Mother of us all, Gal. iv. 26.
———Mother, sister, and brother, Matth. xii. 48, 49, 50. Mark iii. 33, &c.
Must, must be, a limited sense of it, 1 Cor. xi. 19.
Mystery, signifies any thing not expected or known before, but now revealed, Rom. xi. 25. xvi. 25. 1 Cor. ii. 7. xiii. 2. xiv. 2. xv. 51. Ephes. i. 9, 10. iii. 3, 4, 9. vi. 19. Col. i. 26, 27. ii. 2. iv. 3.
Mysteries of the kingdom of God, mystery of godliness signify the gospel doctrine and religion in general, Matth. xiii. 11. Mark iv. 11. Luke viii. 10. 1 Tim. iii. 9, 16. 1 Cor. xiv. 5.
Mystery, signifies a comparison or analogy, Eph. v. 32. Rev. i. 20. and xvii. 7.
———Of iniquity, 2 Theff. ii. 7.

N

NAME, of God, of Christ, signify,
1. God, or Christ himself, Acts iii. 16. xv. 4. Heb. xiii. 15. James ii. 7. 1 Pet. iv. 14. Rom. ix. 17.
2. The authority, power, and religion of Christ, Acts xvii 10, 12. 1 Cor. i. 10. Acts iii. 6. xxvi. 9. 1 Pet. iv. 14. Mark xvi. 17. and elsewhere.
—To do a thing, to do all in the name of Christ, Col. iii. 17. 1 Cor. v. 4.
—To call on the name of Christ, of God, is,
1. To profess his true religion, Acts ii. 28. ix. 14. xxii. 16. xv. 17. Rom. x. 11, 12, 13, 14. 1 Cor. i. 2. 2 Tim. ii. 19, 22. James ii. 7.
2. Invoking and praying to him, Acts vii. 59.
—Or through his intercession, Heb. xiii. 15.
3. Invoking him for miraculous cures, Acts xix. 13. iii. 6.
—Names written in heaven, Heb. xii. 23. Phil. iv. 3.
—Words and names, Acts xviii. 15.
—Signifies things or persons, Acts i. 15. Acts iv. 12. Ephes. i. 21. Phil. ii. 9.
Nation, why St. Paul accuseth not his nation, Acts xxviii. 19.
Nature, the sense of it, 1 Cor. xi. 14. Heb. ii. 16. 1 Pet. i. 4.
Nazarene, Nazarite.
—Jesus called a Nazarene, Matth. ii. 23.
—Christians called Nazarenes, Acts xxiv. 5.
Nigh, the word is nigh thee, Rom. x. 8.

Report,

S

2. Being

INDEX.

Sorrow,

T

V

WAGES,

W

F I N I S.

www.ingramcontent.com/pod-product-compliance
Lightning Source LLC
Chambersburg PA
CBHW020857130726
47900CB00014B/906

* 9 7 8 3 3 3 7 2 8 3 1 9 3 *